IMAGE COMICS

DYNAMO5

POST-NUCLEAR FAMILY

CREATED BY

JAY FAERBER &
MAHMUD A. ASRAR

STRANGERS BOUND BY FATE AND A FATHER THEY NEVER KNEW

DYNAMO 5

SCATTERBRAIN

SLINGSHOT

SCRAP

VISIONARY

MYRIAD

MADDIE WARNER

JAY FAERBER
STORY

MAHMUD A. ASRAR
ART

RON RILEY
COLORS

CHARLES PRITCHETT
LETTERS

WWW.DYNAMO5.COM

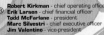

IMAGE COMICS, INC.

Robert Kirkman - chief operating officer
Erik Larsen - chief financial officer
Todd McFarlane - president
Marc Silvestri - chief executive officer
Jim Valentino - vice-president

eric stephenson - publisher
Joe Keatinge - pr & marketing coordinator
Branwyn Bigglestone - accounts manager
Tyler Shainline - administrative assistant
Traci Hui - traffic manager
Allen Hui - production manager
Drew Gill - production artist
Jonathan Chan - production artist
Monica Howard - production artist
www.imagecomics.com

ISBN: 978-1-58240-859-0

DYNAMO 5, VOL.1: POST-NUCLEAR FAMILY. Second Printing. Published by Image Comics, Inc., Office of publication: 2134 Allston Way, 2nd Floor, Berkeley, California 94704. Copyright © 2009 Jay Faerber and Mahmud A. Asrar. All rights reserved. Originally published in single magazine format as DYNAMO 5 #1-7. DYNAMO 5™ (including all prominent characters featured herein), its logo and all character likenesses are trademarks of Jay Faerber and Mahmud A. Asrar, unless otherwise noted. Guest characters are trademark and copyright their respective owners. All rights reserved. Image Comics® is a trademark of Image Comics, Inc. All rights reserved. No part of this publication may be reproduced or transmitted, in any form or by any means (except for short excerpts for review purposes) without the express written permission of Image Comics, Inc. All names, characters, events and locales in this publication are entirely fictional. Any resemblance to actual persons (living or dead), events or places, without satiric intent, is coincidental. PRINTED IN SOUTH KOREA.

International Rights Representative: Christine Jensen (christine@gfloystudio.com)

INTRODUCTION

One of the many cool things about working in comics is that you get to meet all kinds of cool folks who also make comics. They'll call you or email you out of the blue or you'll meet them at a con or whatever, it happens, you get to meet people you respect and admire all the time. It's a whole lot of fun.

You get to chat with folks about stuff and bounce ideas off of each other and generally just shoot the breeze about nonsense. It's a whole lot of fun and over the years I've had the privilege to get to know a lot of cool people along the way.

Jay Faerber is one of those dudes.

Jay's a cool guy, he's very kind and down to Earth, but even so there's a problem that sometimes pops up. You see, when you make friends with a comic guy, from time to time they start new comics and y'know, since they're your friends you feel obligated to read them. I mean, people share issues early and ask for opinions and what not, it's really done all the time. That part, is really no problem.

The problem is when you don't like their book. I mean, not everyone's separate projects are created equal. Lord knows I've had some stinkers along the way, I don't expect everyone to like everything I've ever done... not even my friends. But still, you do feel obligated to read them... and it's no fun to read a comic you don't enjoy.

So when Jay came up with Dynamo 5, I heard about it. He told me the premise — and I thought it was great. When Mahmud turned in his character sketches I looked them over and they were quite awesome. I was really looking forward to reading the book... and then the time came.

There's nothing worse than reading a friend's book for the first time, especially if you've liked everything you've seen so far. I mean, you like the ideas and you like the creators but sometimes the execution just doesn't fall in line with all the cool stuff around it. It's unfortunate, it's uncomfortable... it's awkward. You don't really know what to say to the person.

On the flipside — there's nothing cooler than reading a friend's book, knowing the concept is cool, knowing the creators are cool — and then having the book be an absolute slam dunk. That is very much the case (thank god) with Dynamo 5. It's a great book. I enjoy it from top to bottom. The characters are great — the premise is solid, the art is fantastic... it really is just a great book.

I'd go as far as to say it's the best work to date of everyone involved... and I LOVE Noble Causes.

Mahmud is a great find and he really shines on this book. He brings so much life to the characters and the action stuff is clear and fast paced — he's an excellent superhero artist working on an excellent superhero book — and for my money, you couldn't ask for anything more.

Ron Riley and I go way back, I've worked with him on a number of projects and hope to one day get to have his hues strewn over more pages I've written — but in the mean time he's doing a fantastic job on this book (and Jay's other book Noble Causes — you really should give it a look too if you haven't already). His color choices, his lighting effects — all superb work. Look at his night scenes — they're excellent.

And then there's Jay, cuddly, lovable, talented Jay Faerber, writing his little heart out on this book, providing twists and turns and a kind of super-hero book that has become his own distinct brand.

But I don't need to tell you, you're one of the lucky ones, you're reading this because you've already bought the book — and maybe you're reading this before diving into a fine collection of Dynamo 5's first issues. Maybe you're wondering what lies ahead for you as you continue to turn these pages.

Well, I'm here to say — don't worry my friend, this book is awesome!

Robert Kirkman
Backwoods, Kentucky 2007

CHAPTER ONE

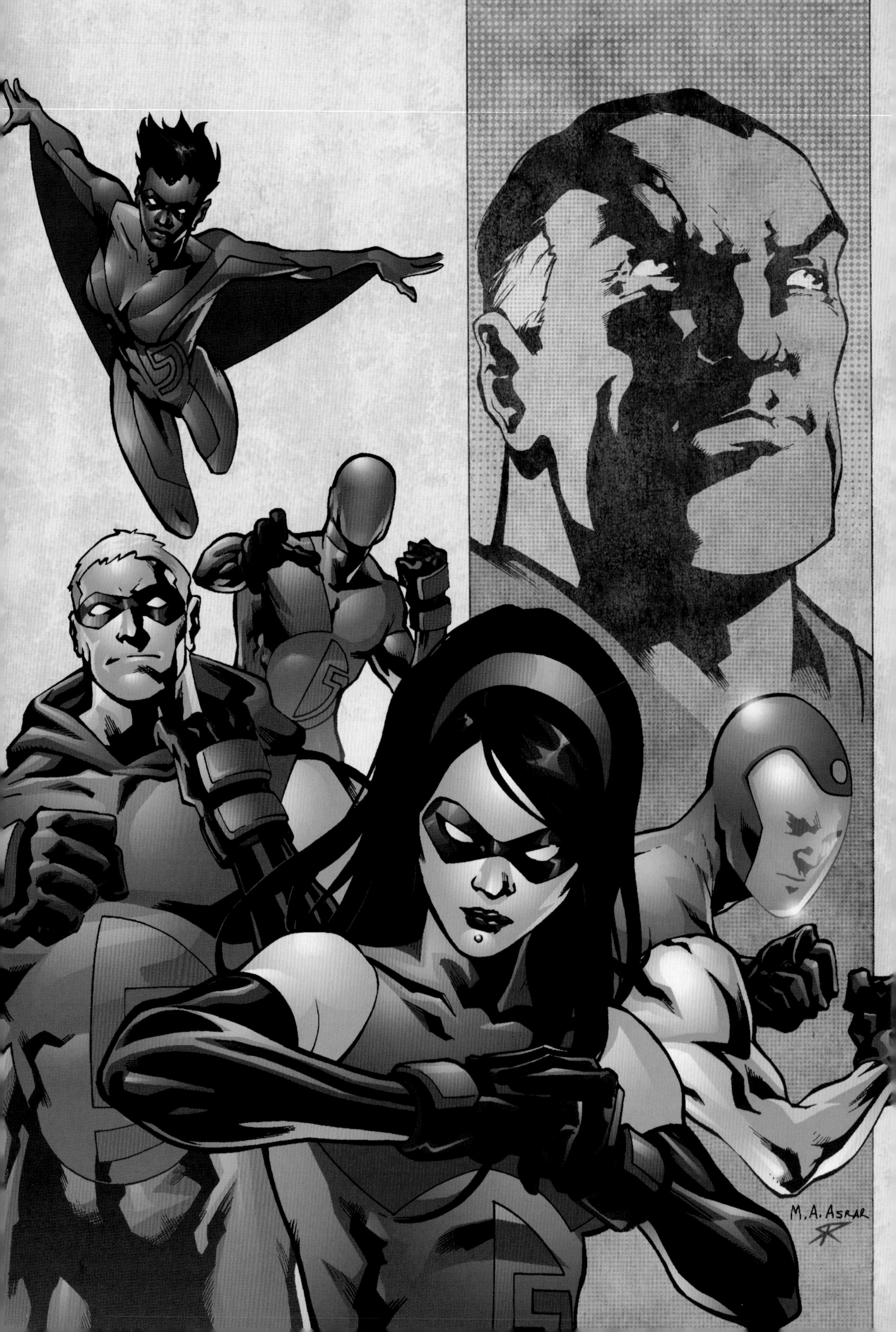
M.A. ASRAR

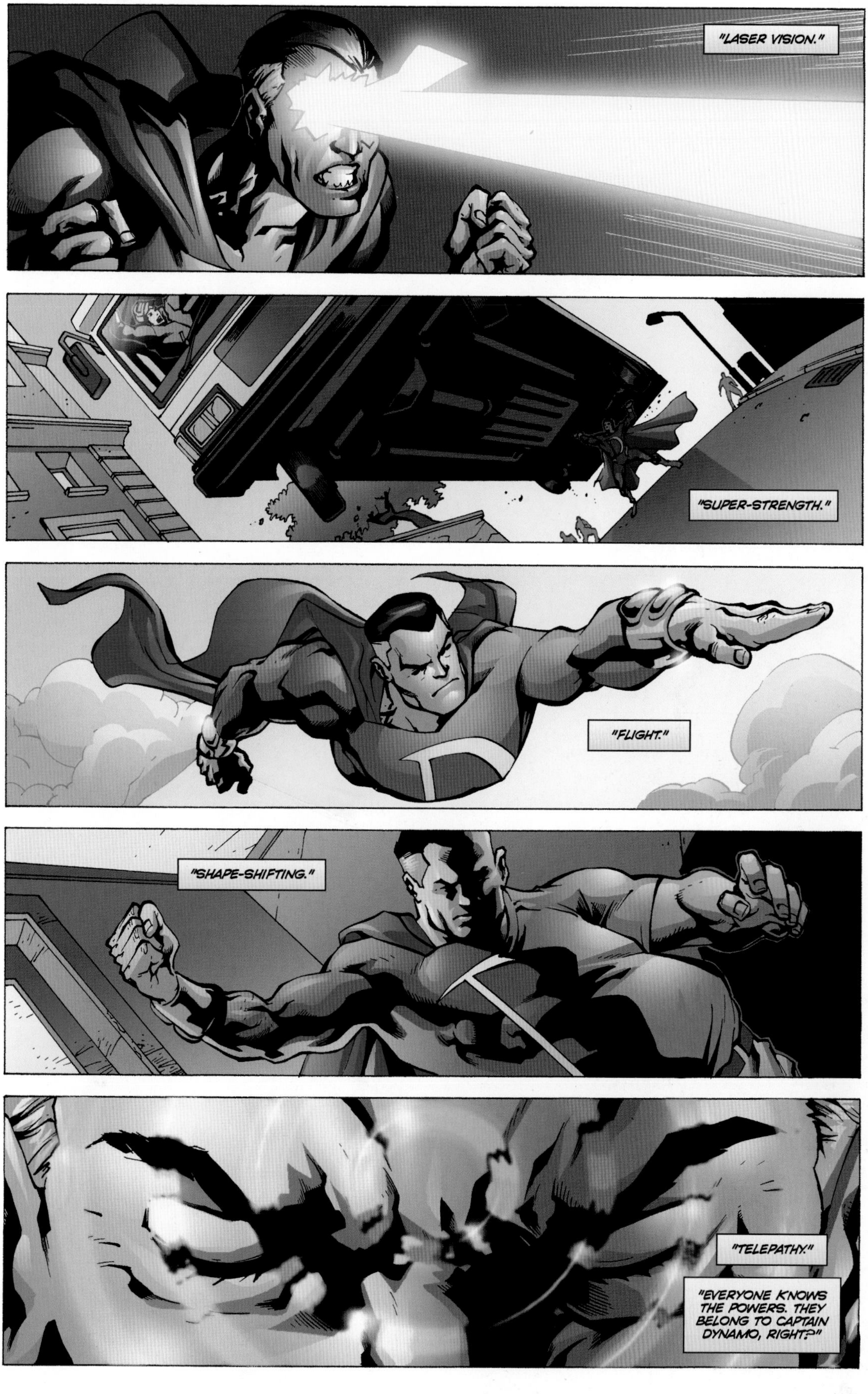
"LASER VISION."
"SUPER-STRENGTH."
"FLIGHT."
"SHAPE-SHIFTING."
"TELEPATHY."
"EVERYONE KNOWS THE POWERS. THEY BELONG TO CAPTAIN DYNAMO, RIGHT?"

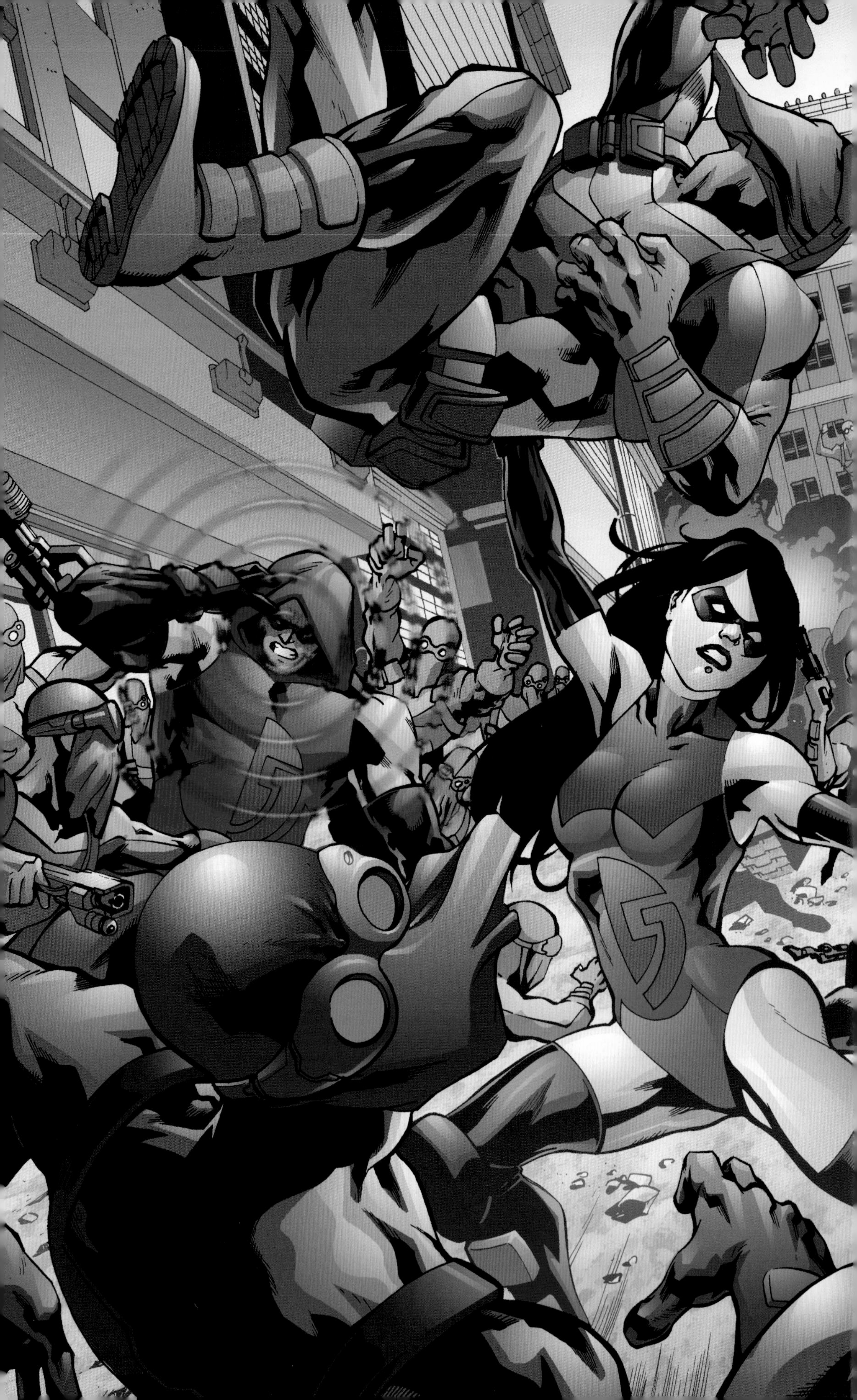

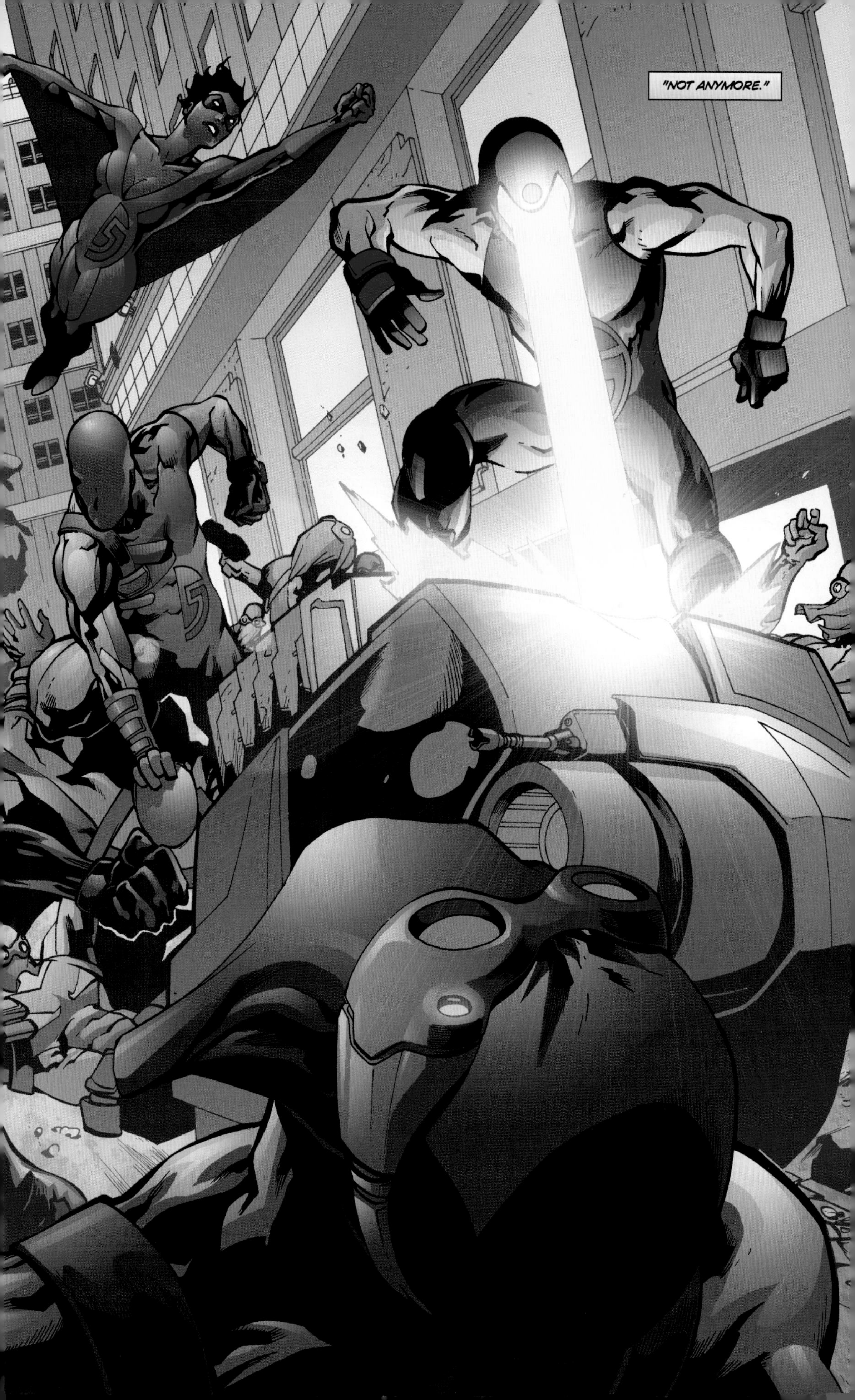
"NOT ANYMORE."

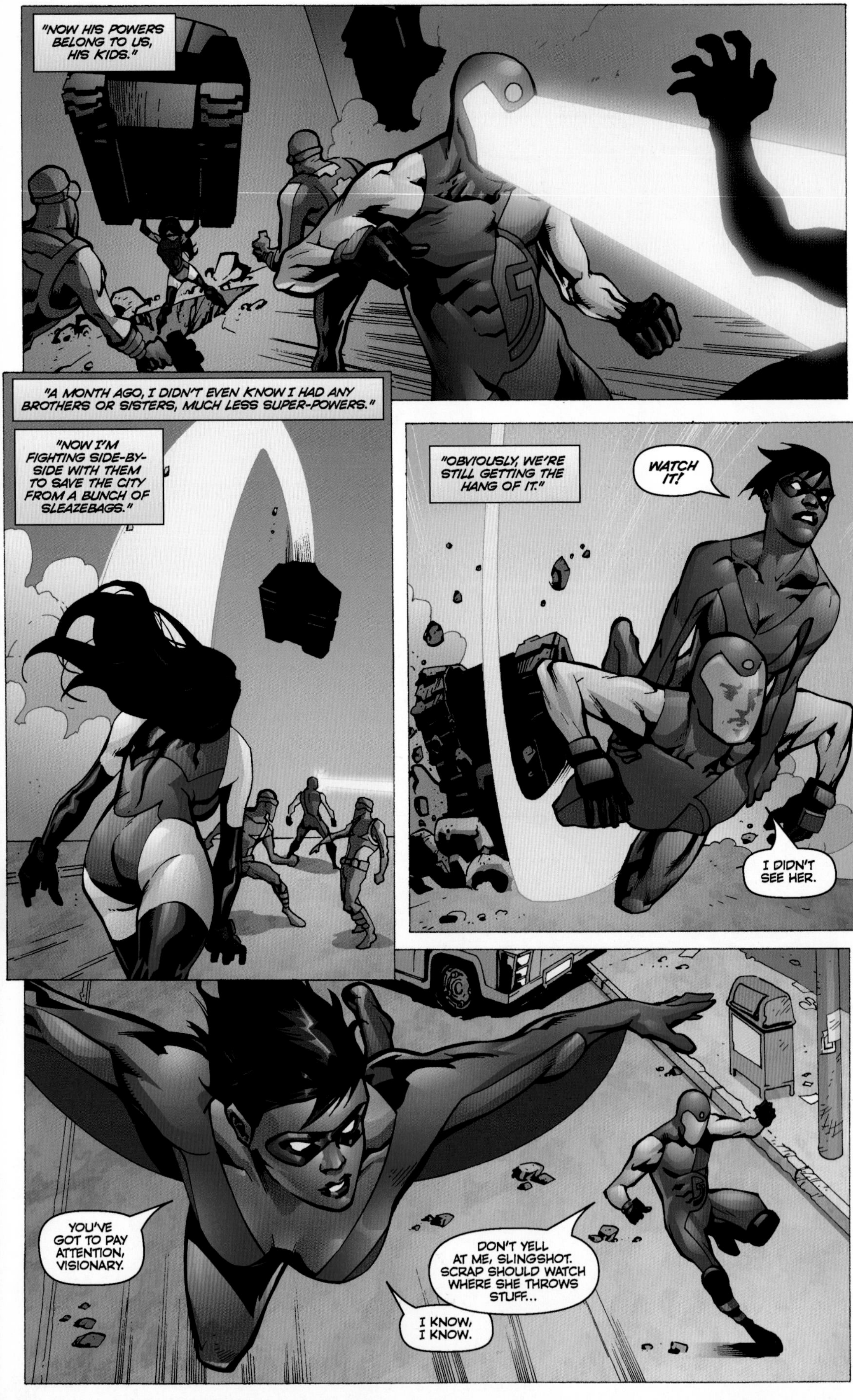
"NOW HIS POWERS BELONG TO US, HIS KIDS."
"A MONTH AGO, I DIDN'T EVEN KNOW I HAD ANY BROTHERS OR SISTERS, MUCH LESS SUPER-POWERS."
"NOW I'M FIGHTING SIDE-BY-SIDE WITH THEM TO SAVE THE CITY FROM A BUNCH OF SLEAZEBAGS."
"OBVIOUSLY, WE'RE STILL GETTING THE HANG OF IT."
WATCH IT!
I DIDN'T SEE HER.
YOU'VE GOT TO PAY ATTENTION, VISIONARY.
DON'T YELL AT ME, SLINGSHOT. SCRAP SHOULD WATCH WHERE SHE THROWS STUFF...
I KNOW, I KNOW.

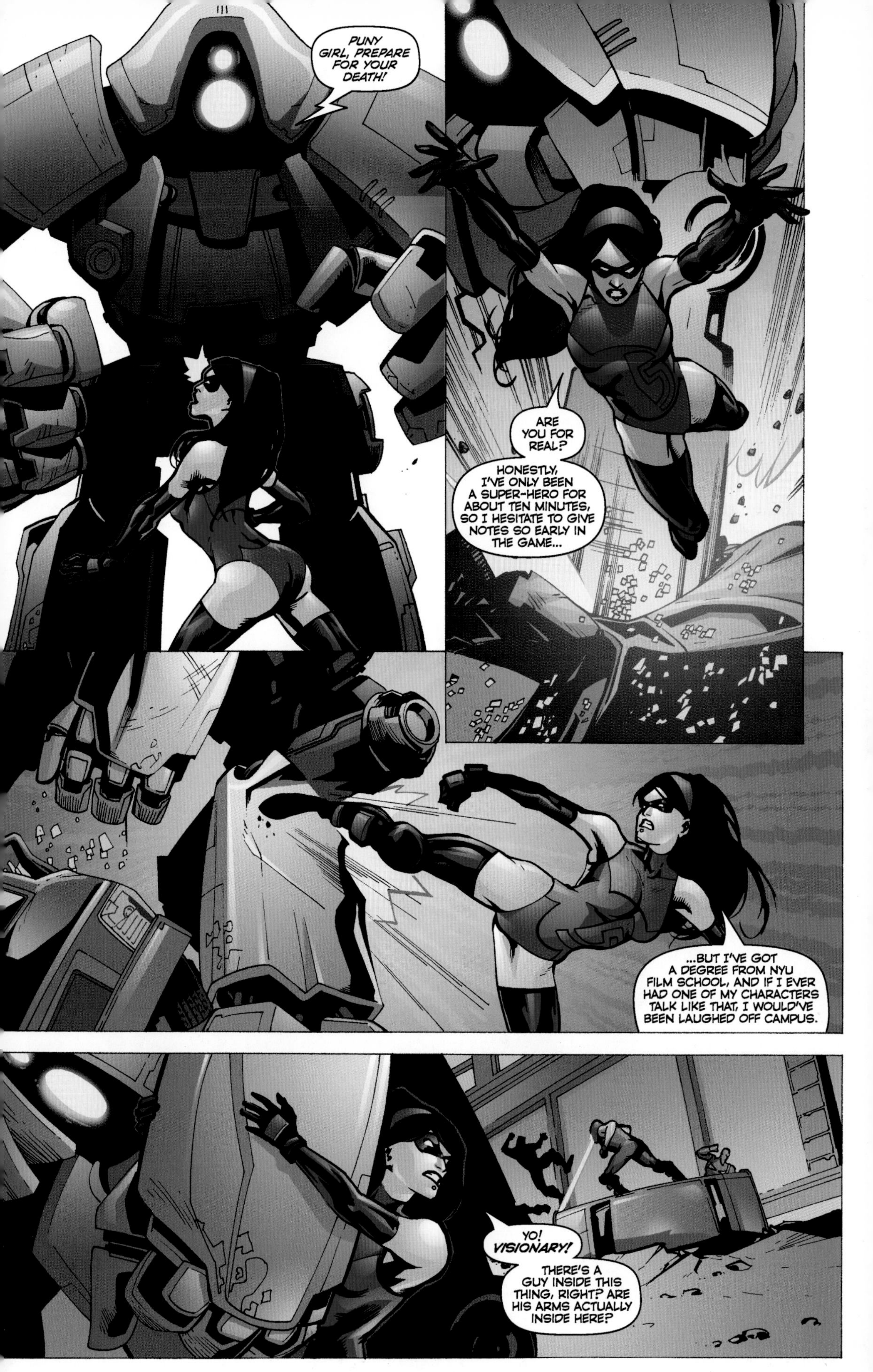
PUNY GIRL, PREPARE FOR YOUR DEATH!
ARE YOU FOR REAL?
HONESTLY, I'VE ONLY BEEN A SUPER-HERO FOR ABOUT TEN MINUTES, SO I HESITATE TO GIVE NOTES SO EARLY IN THE GAME...
...BUT I'VE GOT A DEGREE FROM NYU FILM SCHOOL, AND IF I EVER HAD ONE OF MY CHARACTERS TALK LIKE THAT, I WOULD'VE BEEN LAUGHED OFF CAMPUS.
YO! VISIONARY!
THERE'S A GUY INSIDE THIS THING, RIGHT? ARE HIS ARMS ACTUALLY INSIDE HERE?

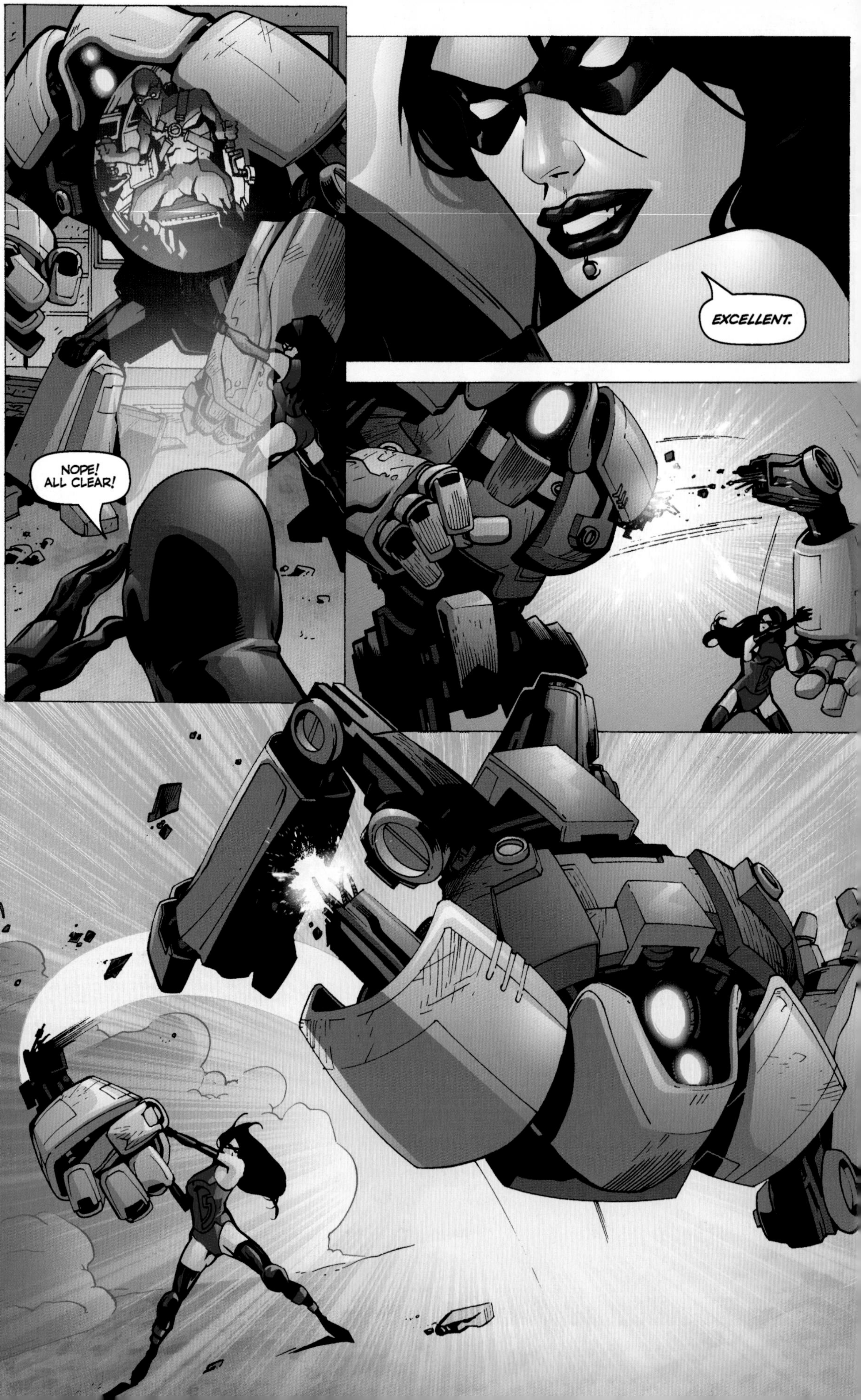
NOPE! ALL CLEAR!
EXCELLENT.

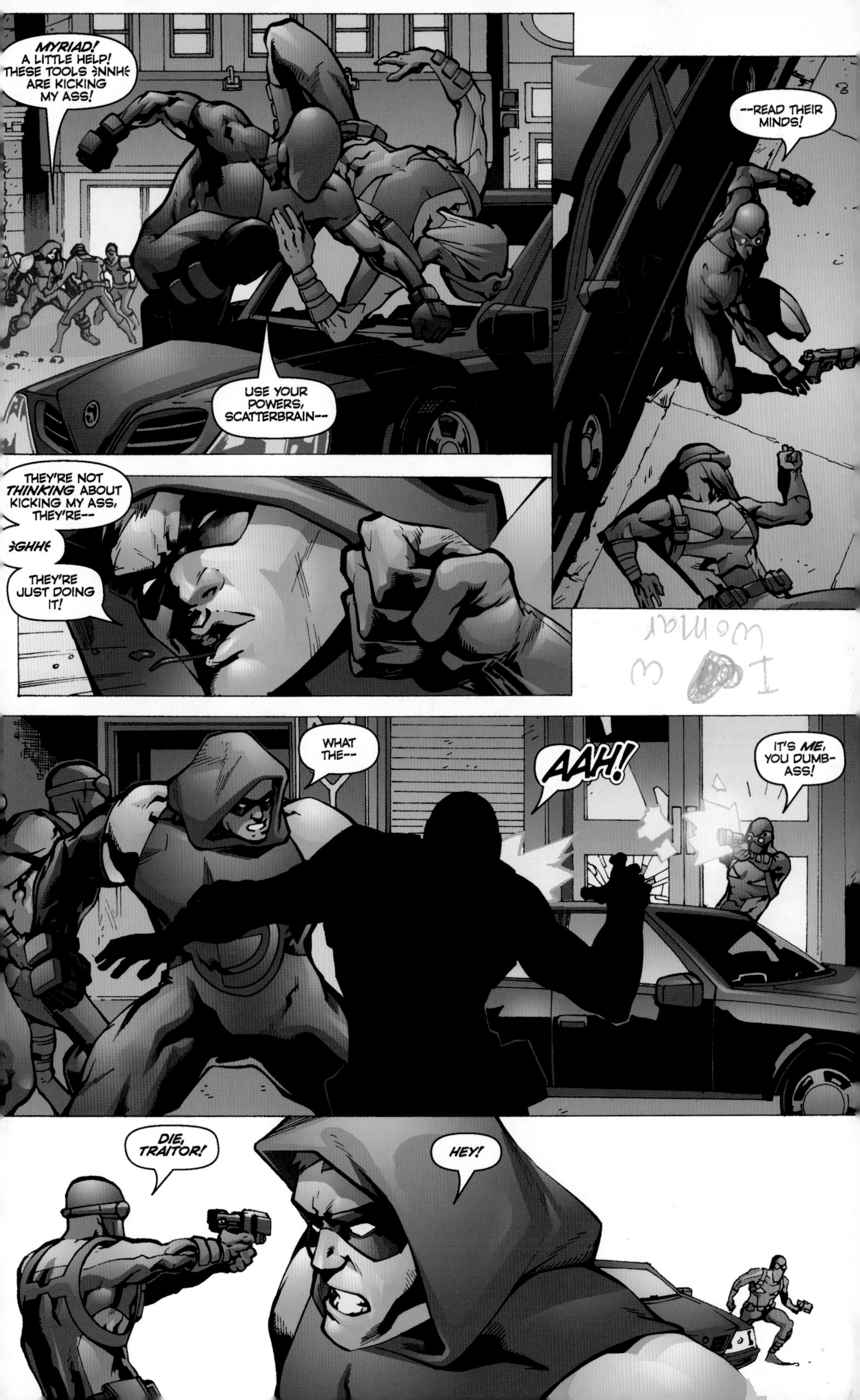
MYRIAD! A LITTLE HELP! THESE TOOLS ≶NNH≷ ARE KICKING MY ASS!
USE YOUR POWERS, SCATTERBRAIN--
--READ THEIR MINDS!
THEY'RE NOT THINKING ABOUT KICKING MY ASS, THEY'RE--
≶GHH≷
THEY'RE JUST DOING IT!
WHAT THE--
AAH!
IT'S ME, YOU DUMB-ASS!
DIE, TRAITOR!
HEY!

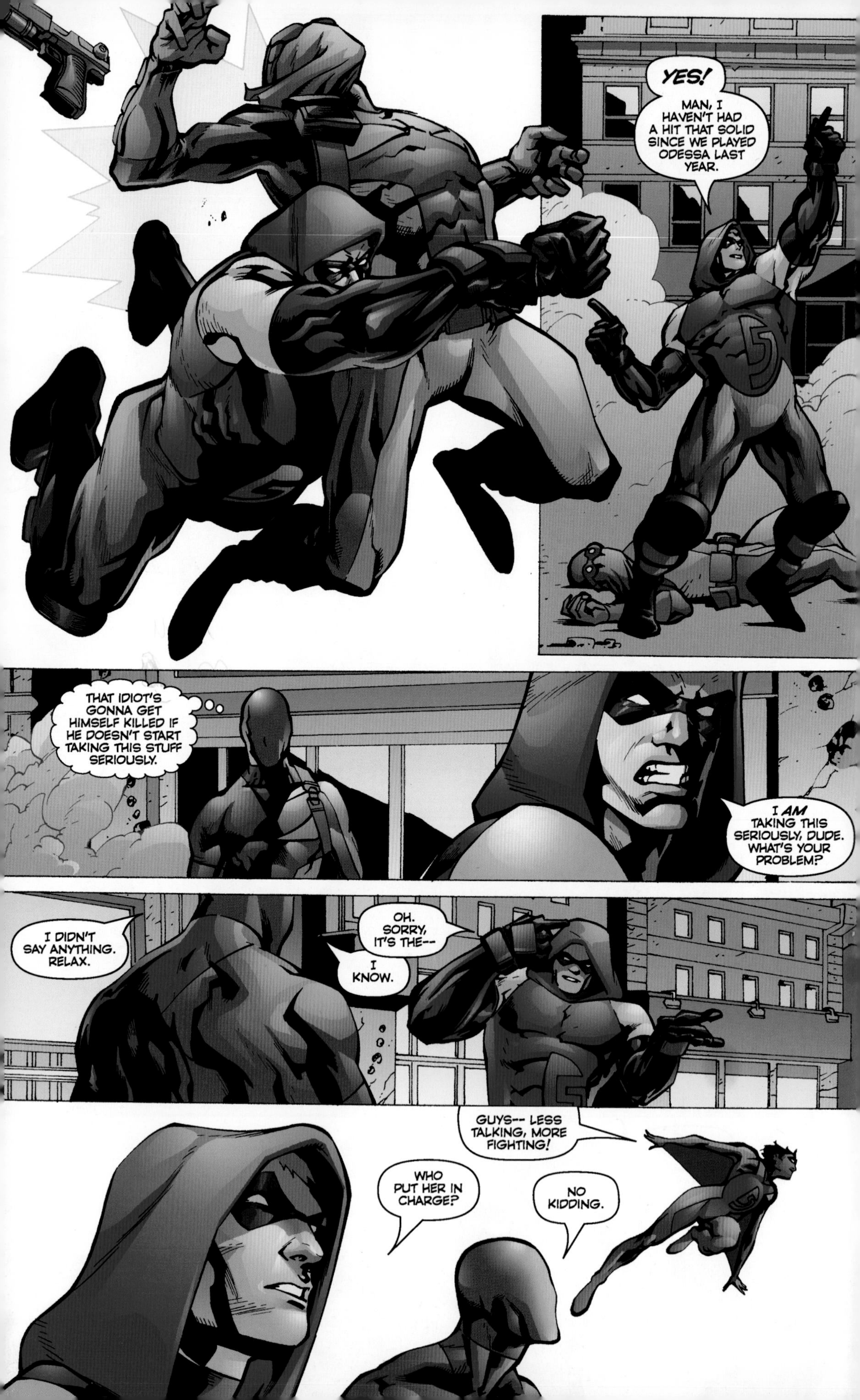
YES!
MAN, I HAVEN'T HAD A HIT THAT SOLID SINCE WE PLAYED ODESSA LAST YEAR.
THAT IDIOT'S GONNA GET HIMSELF KILLED IF HE DOESN'T START TAKING THIS STUFF SERIOUSLY.
I AM TAKING THIS SERIOUSLY, DUDE. WHAT'S YOUR PROBLEM?
I DIDN'T SAY ANYTHING. RELAX.
OH. SORRY, IT'S THE--
I KNOW.
GUYS-- LESS TALKING, MORE FIGHTING!
WHO PUT HER IN CHARGE?
NO KIDDING.

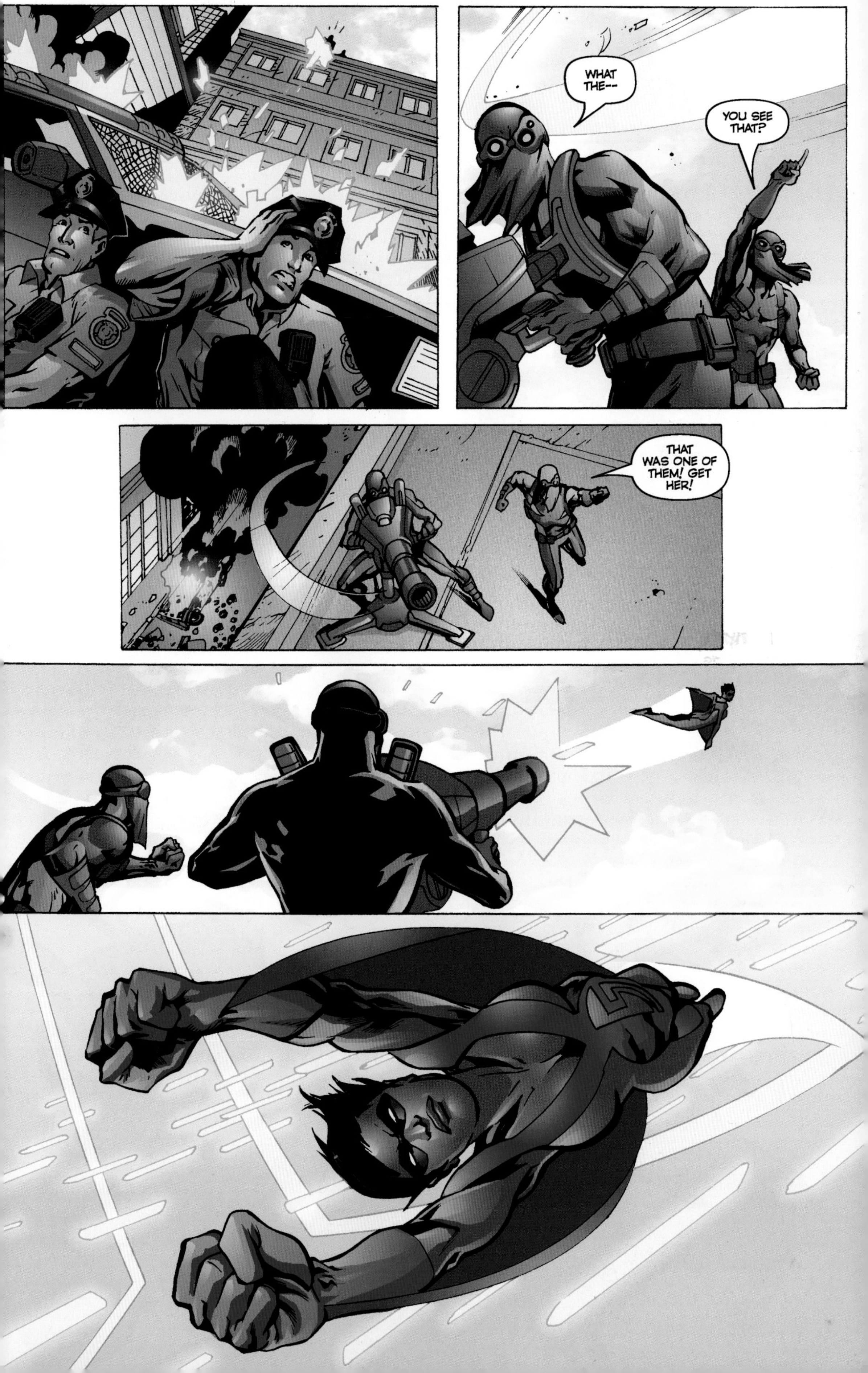
WHAT THE--
YOU SEE THAT?
THAT WAS ONE OF THEM! GET HER!

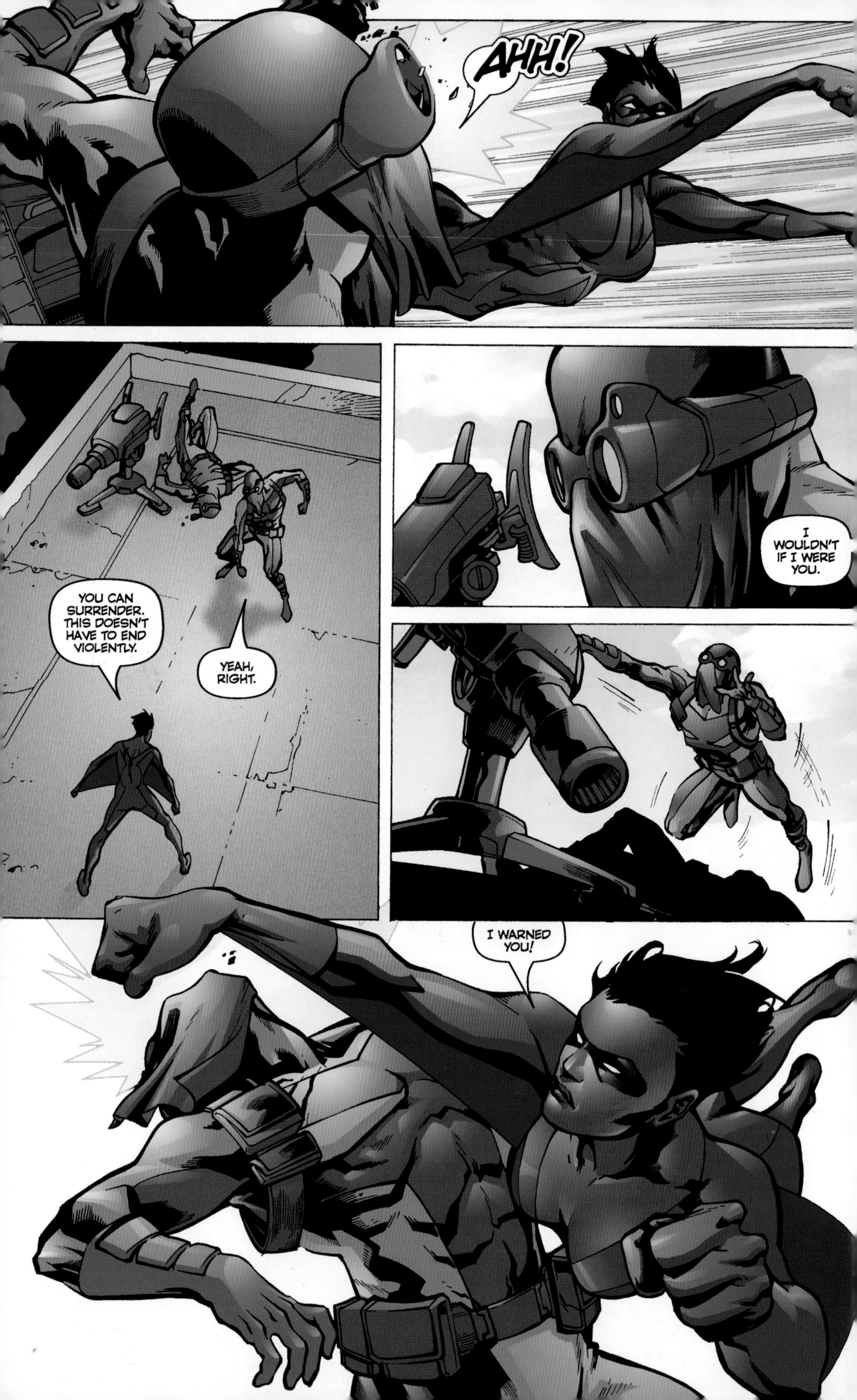
AHH!
YOU CAN SURRENDER. THIS DOESN'T HAVE TO END VIOLENTLY.
YEAH, RIGHT.
I WOULDN'T IF I WERE YOU.
I WARNED YOU!

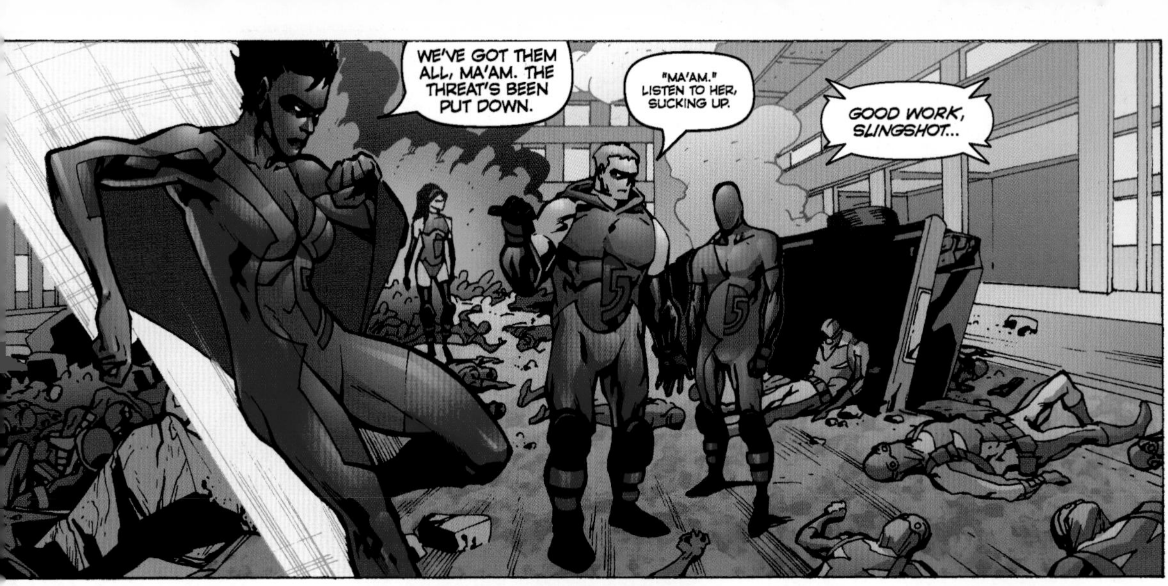
WE'VE GOT THEM ALL, MA'AM. THE THREAT'S BEEN PUT DOWN.
"MA'AM." LISTEN TO HER, SUCKING UP.
GOOD WORK, SLINGSHOT...

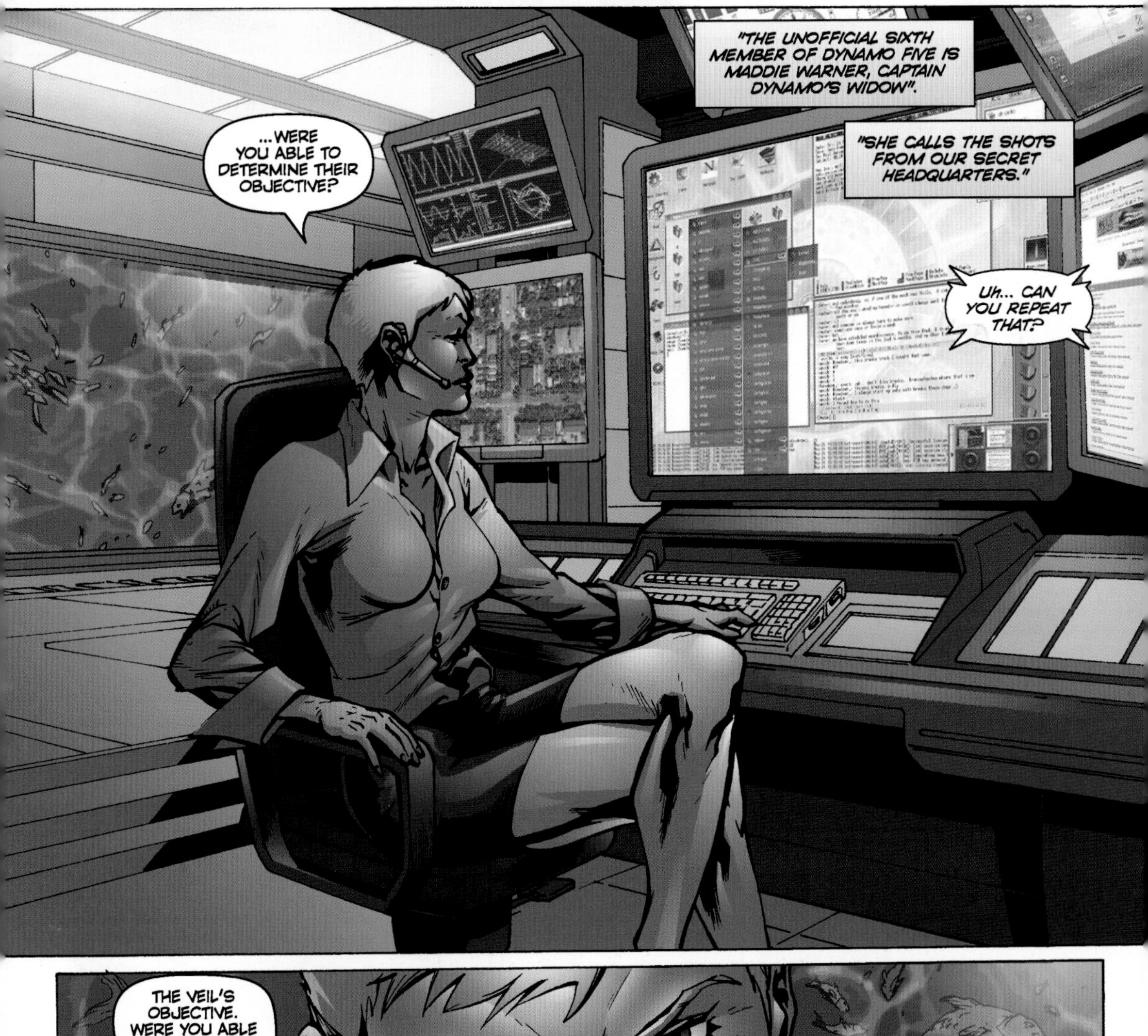
"THE UNOFFICIAL SIXTH MEMBER OF DYNAMO FIVE IS MADDIE WARNER, CAPTAIN DYNAMO'S WIDOW".
...WERE YOU ABLE TO DETERMINE THEIR OBJECTIVE?
"SHE CALLS THE SHOTS FROM OUR SECRET HEADQUARTERS."
Uh... CAN YOU REPEAT THAT?

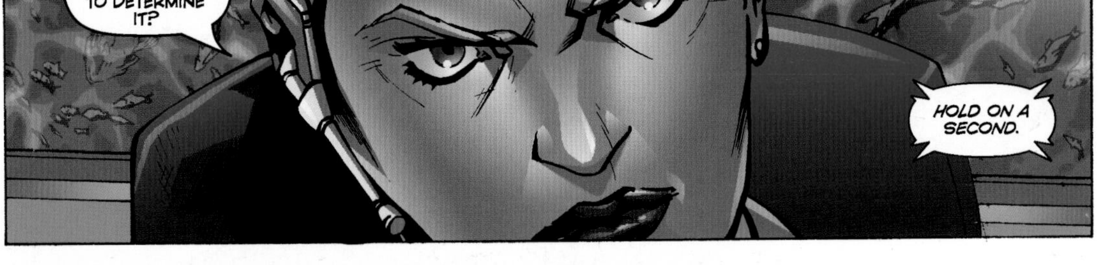
THE VEIL'S OBJECTIVE. WERE YOU ABLE TO DETERMINE IT?
HOLD ON A SECOND.

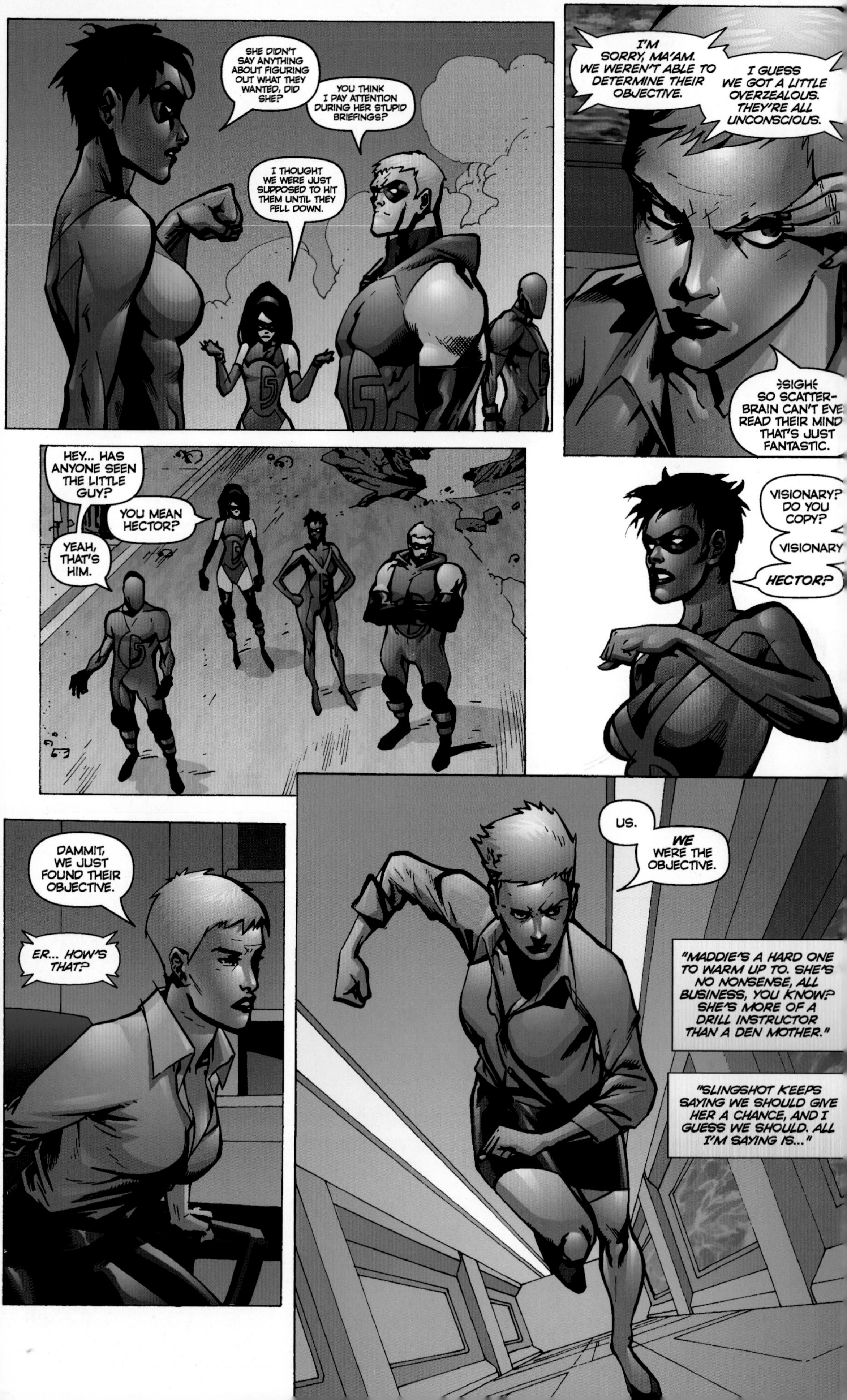

SHE DIDN'T SAY ANYTHING ABOUT FIGURING OUT WHAT THEY WANTED, DID SHE?
YOU THINK I PAY ATTENTION DURING HER STUPID BRIEFINGS?
I THOUGHT WE WERE JUST SUPPOSED TO HIT THEM UNTIL THEY FELL DOWN.
I'M SORRY, MA'AM. WE WEREN'T ABLE TO DETERMINE THEIR OBJECTIVE.
I GUESS WE GOT A LITTLE OVERZEALOUS. THEY'RE ALL UNCONSCIOUS.
SIGH SO SCATTER-BRAIN CAN'T EVE READ THEIR MIND THAT'S JUST FANTASTIC.
HEY... HAS ANYONE SEEN THE LITTLE GUY?
YOU MEAN HECTOR?
YEAH, THAT'S HIM.
VISIONARY? DO YOU COPY?
VISIONARY
HECTOR?
DAMMIT, WE JUST FOUND THEIR OBJECTIVE.
ER... HOW'S THAT?
US.
WE WERE THE OBJECTIVE.
"MADDIE'S A HARD ONE TO WARM UP TO. SHE'S NO NONSENSE, ALL BUSINESS, YOU KNOW? SHE'S MORE OF A DRILL INSTRUCTOR THAN A DEN MOTHER."
"SLINGSHOT KEEPS SAYING WE SHOULD GIVE HER A CHANCE, AND I GUESS WE SHOULD. ALL I'M SAYING IS..."

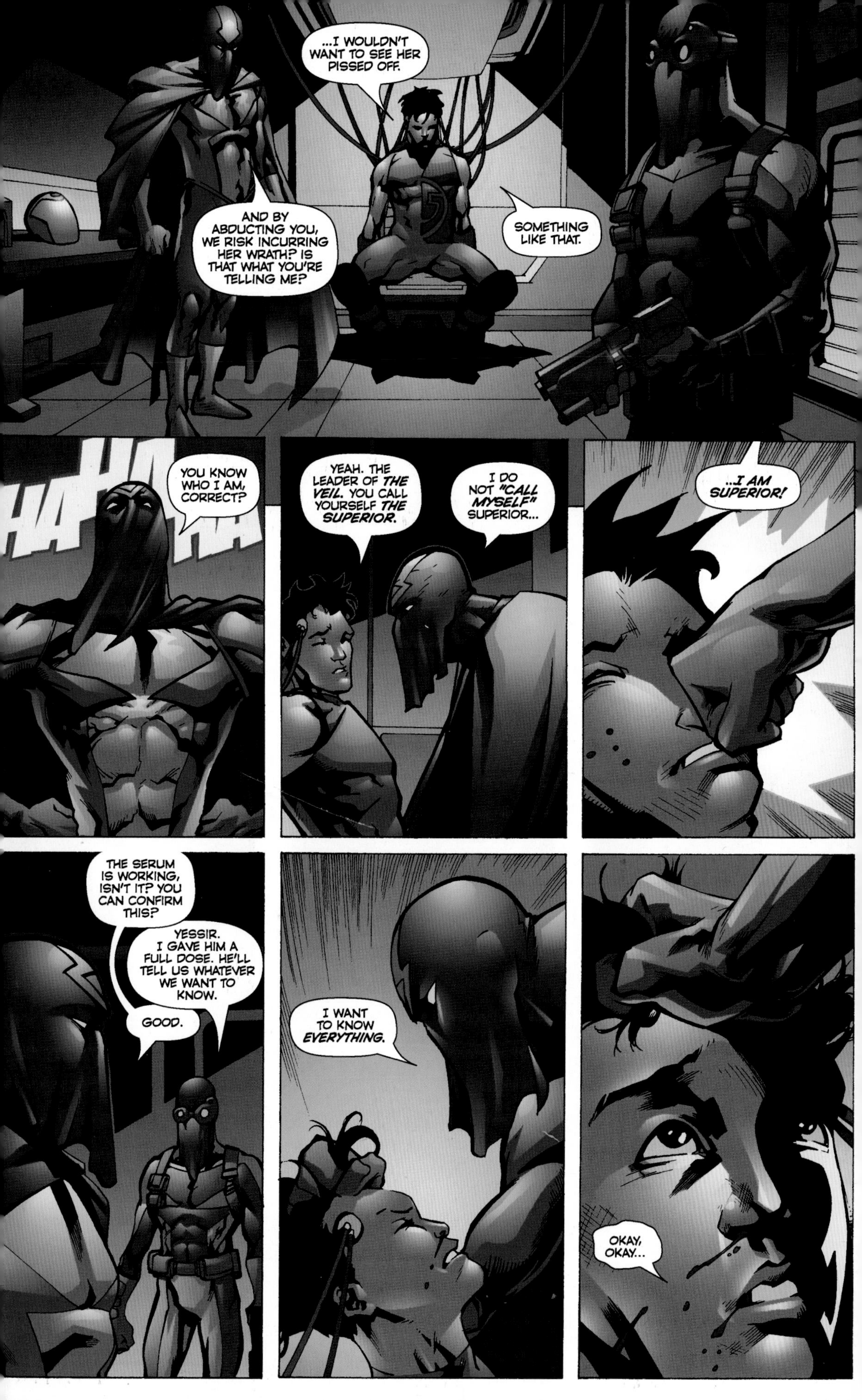
...I WOULDN'T WANT TO SEE HER PISSED OFF.
AND BY ABDUCTING YOU, WE RISK INCURRING HER WRATH? IS THAT WHAT YOU'RE TELLING ME?
SOMETHING LIKE THAT.
HAHAHA
YOU KNOW WHO I AM, CORRECT?
YEAH. THE LEADER OF THE VEIL. YOU CALL YOURSELF THE SUPERIOR.
I DO NOT "CALL MYSELF" SUPERIOR...
...I AM SUPERIOR!
THE SERUM IS WORKING, ISN'T IT? YOU CAN CONFIRM THIS?
YESSIR. I GAVE HIM A FULL DOSE. HE'LL TELL US WHATEVER WE WANT TO KNOW.
GOOD.
I WANT TO KNOW EVERYTHING.
OKAY, OKAY...

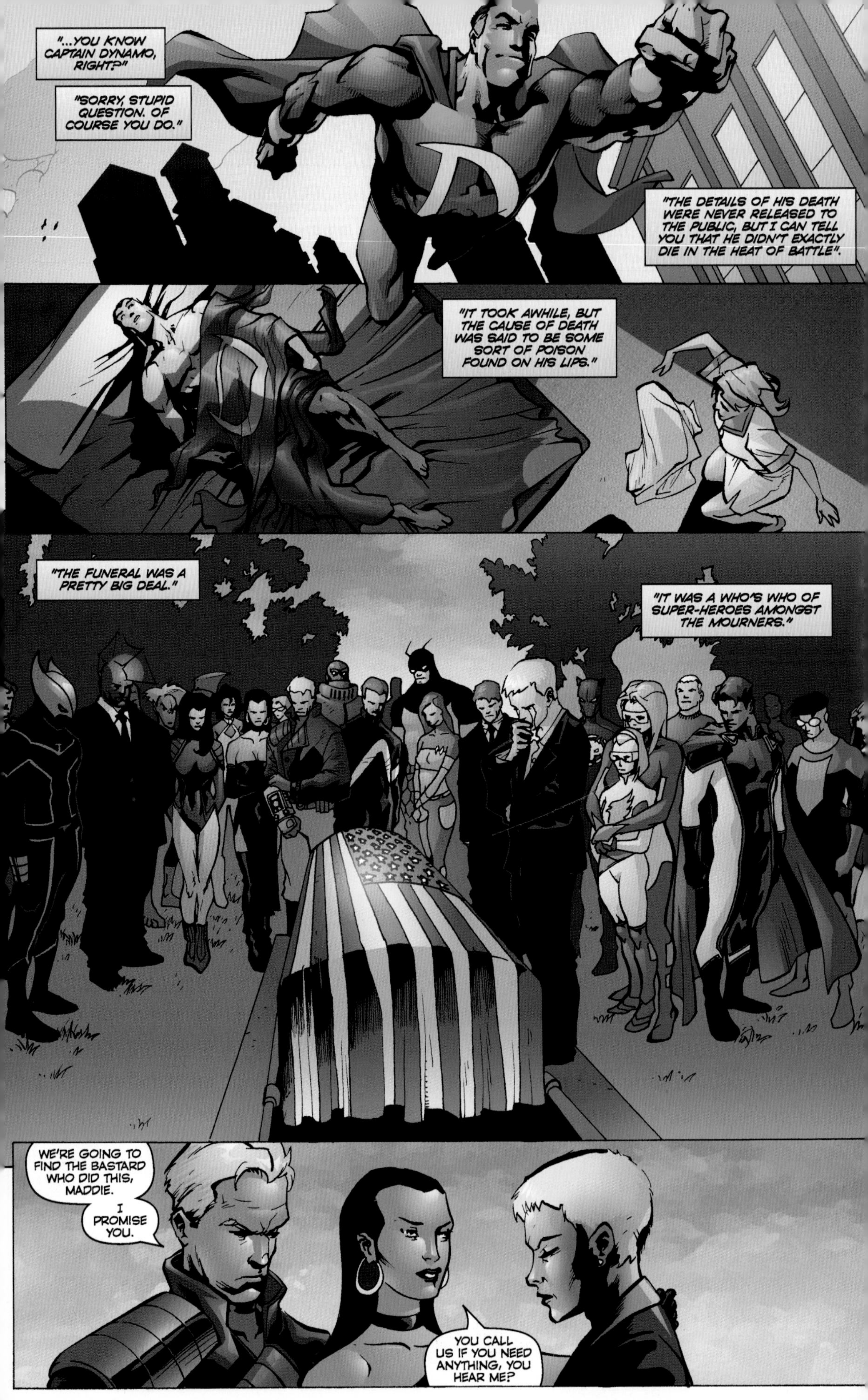
"...YOU KNOW CAPTAIN DYNAMO, RIGHT?"
"SORRY, STUPID QUESTION. OF COURSE YOU DO."
"THE DETAILS OF HIS DEATH WERE NEVER RELEASED TO THE PUBLIC, BUT I CAN TELL YOU THAT HE DIDN'T EXACTLY DIE IN THE HEAT OF BATTLE".
"IT TOOK AWHILE, BUT THE CAUSE OF DEATH WAS SAID TO BE SOME SORT OF POISON FOUND ON HIS LIPS."
"THE FUNERAL WAS A PRETTY BIG DEAL."
"IT WAS A WHO'S WHO OF SUPER-HEROES AMONGST THE MOURNERS."
WE'RE GOING TO FIND THE BASTARD WHO DID THIS, MADDIE.
I PROMISE YOU.
YOU CALL US IF YOU NEED ANYTHING, YOU HEAR ME?

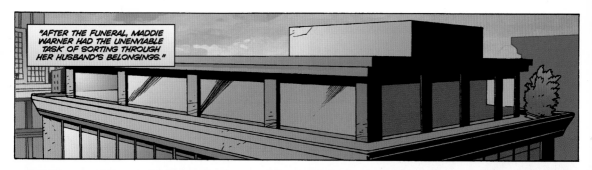

"AFTER THE FUNERAL, MADDIE WARNER HAD THE UNENVIABLE TASK OF SORTING THROUGH HER HUSBAND'S BELONGINGS."

"AND I'M NOT JUST TALKING ABOUT HIS PERSONAL BELONGINGS, EITHER."

"MADDIE HAD TO SORT THROUGH ALL THE OTHER STUFF HER HUSBAND LEFT BEHIND."

"STUFF LIKE..."

"...HIS SECRET HEADQUARTERS BENEATH AN INDUSTRIAL PIER AND EVERYTHING HE KEPT THERE."

"THAT'S WHEN SHE FOUND IT."

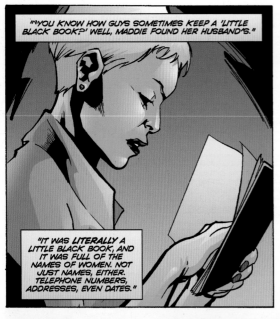

"'YOU KNOW HOW GUYS SOMETIMES KEEP A 'LITTLE BLACK BOOK?' WELL, MADDIE FOUND HER HUSBAND'S."

"IT WAS *LITERALLY A LITTLE BLACK BOOK,* AND IT WAS FULL OF THE NAMES OF WOMEN. NOT JUST NAMES, EITHER. TELEPHONE NUMBERS, ADDRESSES, EVEN DATES."

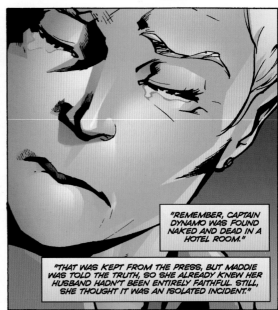

"REMEMBER, CAPTAIN DYNAMO WAS FOUND NAKED AND DEAD IN A HOTEL ROOM."

"THAT WAS KEPT FROM THE PRESS, BUT MADDIE WAS TOLD THE TRUTH, SO SHE ALREADY KNEW HER HUSBAND HADN'T BEEN ENTIRELY FAITHFUL. STILL, SHE THOUGHT IT WAS AN ISOLATED INCIDENT."

"HELL, DEEP DOWN SHE'D BEEN TELLING HERSELF MAYBE HIS BODY WAS LEFT THAT WAY BY ONE OF HIS ENEMIES, TO EMBARRASS HIM. YOU KNOW, ADD INSULT TO INJURY."

"SHE HELD ONTO THE IDEA THAT MAYBE HE REALLY *WAS* KILLED IN ACTION."

"BUT THIS... THIS WAS TOO MUCH. HER HUSBAND HADN'T JUST CHEATED ON HER ONCE OR TWICE. IT WAS AN ONGOING THING, WITH DOZENS OF WOMEN."

"IF SHE WAS LOOKING FOR SOMETHING TO KEEP HER MIND OFF OF HER GRIEF (AND OUTRAGE), SHE DIDN'T HAVE TO LOOK FAR."

"IN THE DAYS FOLLOWING CAPTAIN DYNAMO'S DEATH, HIS MANY ENEMIES REALIZED SOMETHING--"

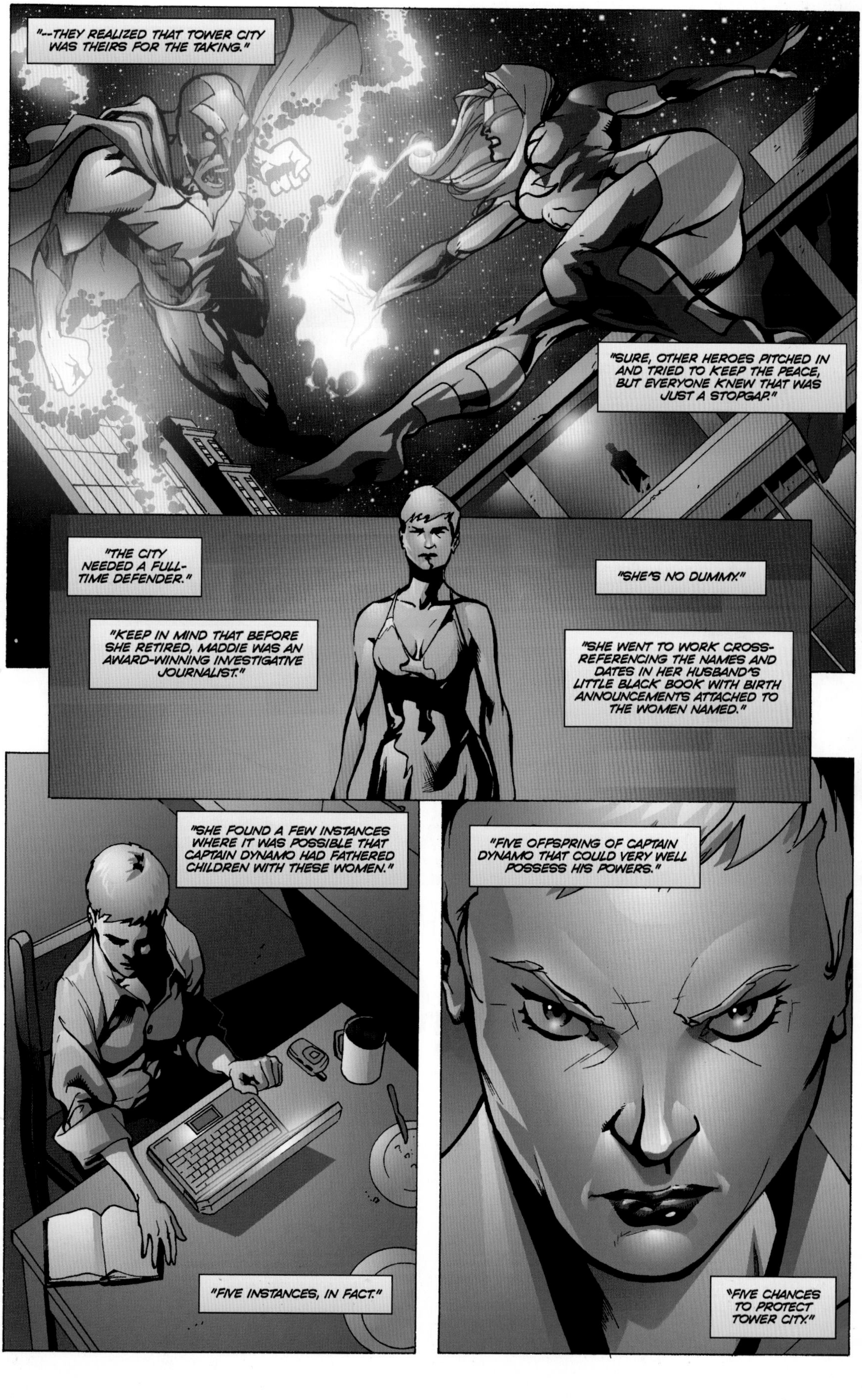
"--THEY REALIZED THAT TOWER CITY WAS THEIRS FOR THE TAKING."
"SURE, OTHER HEROES PITCHED IN AND TRIED TO KEEP THE PEACE, BUT EVERYONE KNEW THAT WAS JUST A STOPGAP."
"THE CITY NEEDED A FULL-TIME DEFENDER."
"KEEP IN MIND THAT BEFORE SHE RETIRED, MADDIE WAS AN AWARD-WINNING INVESTIGATIVE JOURNALIST."
"SHE'S NO DUMMY."
"SHE WENT TO WORK CROSS-REFERENCING THE NAMES AND DATES IN HER HUSBAND'S LITTLE BLACK BOOK WITH BIRTH ANNOUNCEMENTS ATTACHED TO THE WOMEN NAMED."
"SHE FOUND A FEW INSTANCES WHERE IT WAS POSSIBLE THAT CAPTAIN DYNAMO HAD FATHERED CHILDREN WITH THESE WOMEN."
"FIVE INSTANCES, IN FACT."
"FIVE OFFSPRING OF CAPTAIN DYNAMO THAT COULD VERY WELL POSSESS HIS POWERS."
"FIVE CHANCES TO PROTECT TOWER CITY."

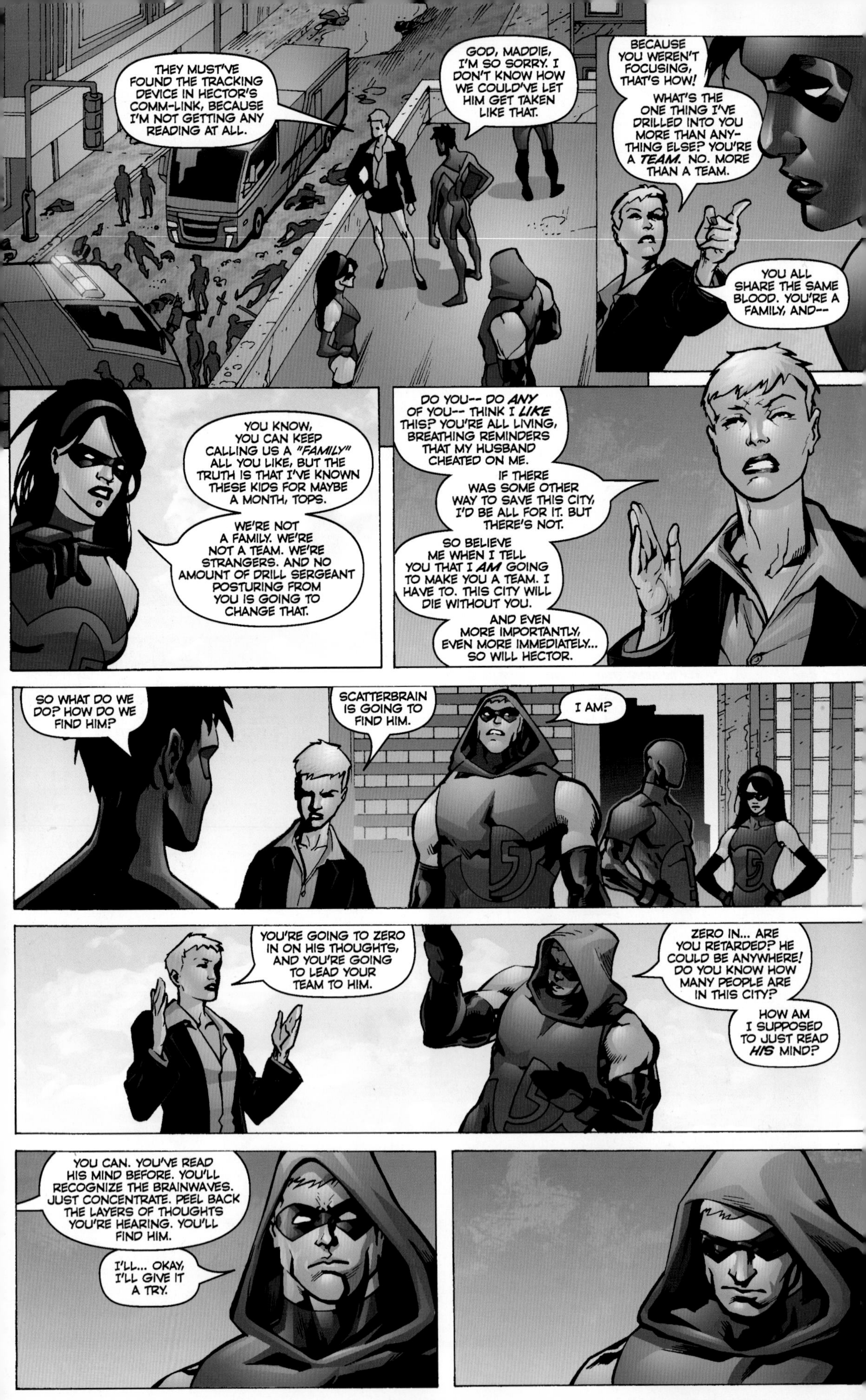
THEY MUST'VE FOUND THE TRACKING DEVICE IN HECTOR'S COMM-LINK, BECAUSE I'M NOT GETTING ANY READING AT ALL.
GOD, MADDIE, I'M SO SORRY. I DON'T KNOW HOW WE COULD'VE LET HIM GET TAKEN LIKE THAT.
BECAUSE YOU WEREN'T FOCUSING, THAT'S HOW!
WHAT'S THE ONE THING I'VE DRILLED INTO YOU MORE THAN ANY-THING ELSE? YOU'RE A *TEAM*. NO. MORE THAN A TEAM.
YOU ALL SHARE THE SAME BLOOD. YOU'RE A FAMILY, AND--
YOU KNOW, YOU CAN KEEP CALLING US A *"FAMILY"* ALL YOU LIKE, BUT THE TRUTH IS THAT I'VE KNOWN THESE KIDS FOR MAYBE A MONTH, TOPS.
WE'RE NOT A FAMILY. WE'RE NOT A TEAM. WE'RE STRANGERS. AND NO AMOUNT OF DRILL SERGEANT POSTURING FROM YOU IS GOING TO CHANGE THAT.
DO YOU-- DO *ANY* OF YOU-- THINK I *LIKE* THIS? YOU'RE ALL LIVING, BREATHING REMINDERS THAT MY HUSBAND CHEATED ON ME.
IF THERE WAS SOME OTHER WAY TO SAVE THIS CITY, I'D BE ALL FOR IT. BUT THERE'S NOT.
SO BELIEVE ME WHEN I TELL YOU THAT I *AM* GOING TO MAKE YOU A TEAM. I HAVE TO. THIS CITY WILL DIE WITHOUT YOU.
AND EVEN MORE IMPORTANTLY, EVEN MORE IMMEDIATELY... SO WILL HECTOR.
SO WHAT DO WE DO? HOW DO WE FIND HIM?
SCATTERBRAIN IS GOING TO FIND HIM.
I AM?
YOU'RE GOING TO ZERO IN ON HIS THOUGHTS, AND YOU'RE GOING TO LEAD YOUR TEAM TO HIM.
ZERO IN... ARE YOU RETARDED? HE COULD BE ANYWHERE! DO YOU KNOW HOW MANY PEOPLE ARE IN THIS CITY?
HOW AM I SUPPOSED TO JUST READ *HIS* MIND?
YOU CAN. YOU'VE READ HIS MIND BEFORE. YOU'LL RECOGNIZE THE BRAINWAVES. JUST CONCENTRATE. PEEL BACK THE LAYERS OF THOUGHTS YOU'RE HEARING. YOU'LL FIND HIM.
I'LL... OKAY, I'LL GIVE IT A TRY.

"MADDIE'S FIRST STOP WAS DOMINIC DA VINCI HIGH SCHOOL IN VANCOUVER, BRITISH COLUMBIA."

"HECTOR CHANG WAS JUST A NORMAL KID. SOME MIGHT SAY GEEKY, BUT IF ANYONE EVER TOOK THE TIME TO LOOK, THEY'D SEE HE WAS REALLY A GOOD-LOOKING GUY."

"PROBLEM WAS, NO ONE TOOK THE TIME TO EVEN NOTICE HECTOR."

"WELL, ALMOST NO ONE."

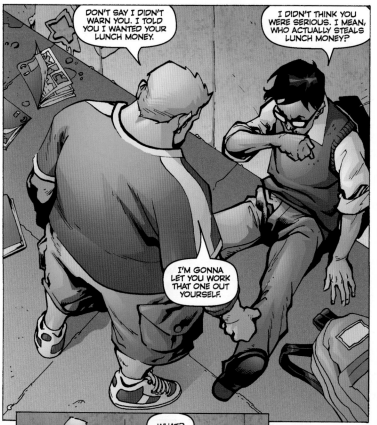

DON'T SAY I DIDN'T WARN YOU. I TOLD YOU I WANTED YOUR LUNCH MONEY.

I DIDN'T THINK YOU WERE SERIOUS. I MEAN, WHO ACTUALLY STEALS LUNCH MONEY?

I'M GONNA LET YOU WORK THAT ONE OUT YOURSELF.

I'LL BE BACK TOMORROW.

TAKE YOUR TIME, YOU FAT PIG.

I DON'T THINK HE HEARD YOU.

WHAT?

NOTHING. YOU'RE HECTOR CHANG, RIGHT?

YEAH... WHY?

"MADDIE WARNER SAID SHE WAS GOING TO CHANGE HECTOR'S LIFE. HE'D HEARD THAT SORT OF CRAP BEFORE FROM GUIDANCE COUNSELORS, SO HE WASN'T EXACTLY HOLDING HIS BREATH."

"BUT NOTHING COULD'VE PREPARED HIM FOR HER STORY."

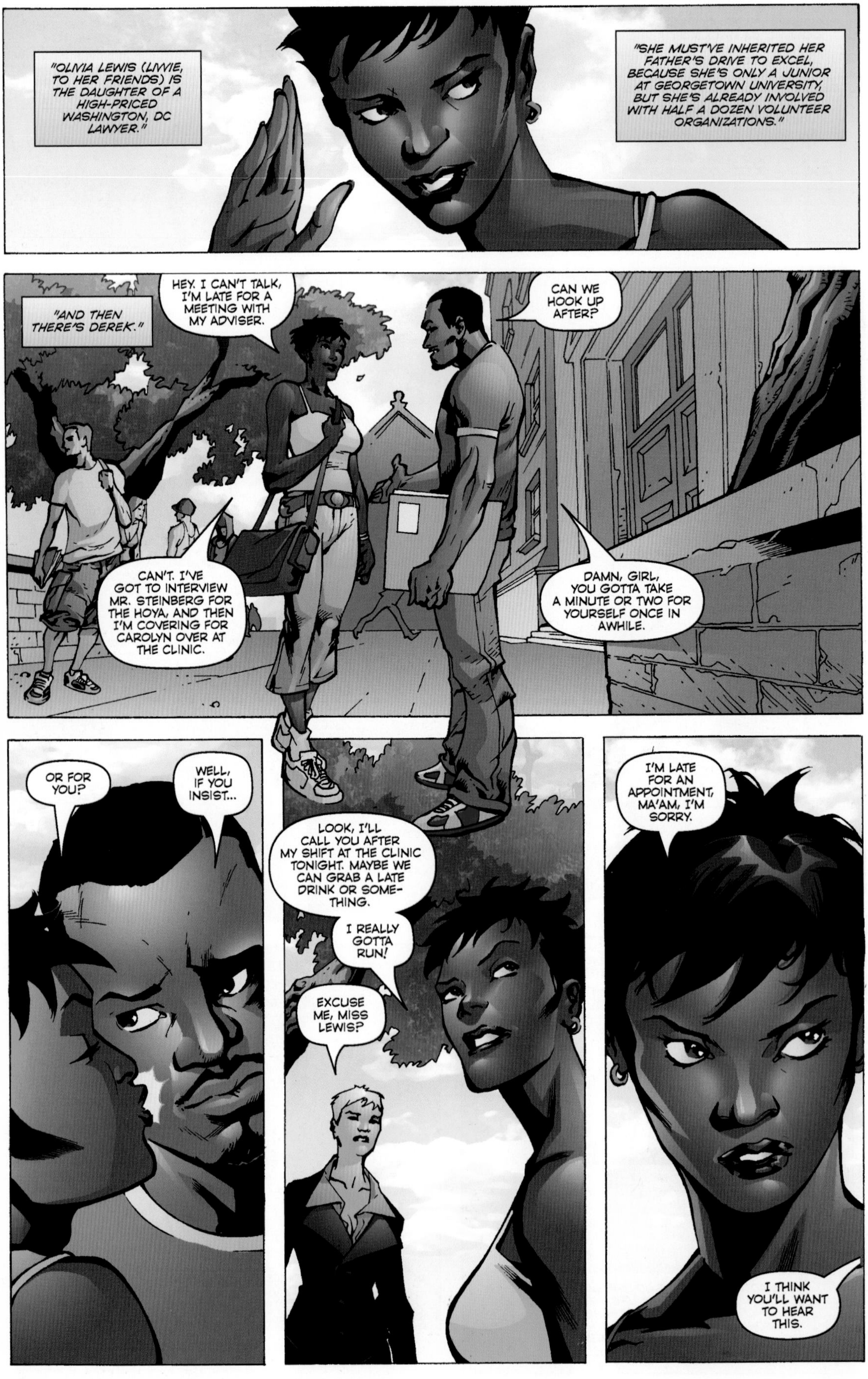
"OLIVIA LEWIS (LIVVIE, TO HER FRIENDS) IS THE DAUGHTER OF A HIGH-PRICED WASHINGTON, DC LAWYER."
"SHE MUST'VE INHERITED HER FATHER'S DRIVE TO EXCEL, BECAUSE SHE'S ONLY A JUNIOR AT GEORGETOWN UNIVERSITY, BUT SHE'S ALREADY INVOLVED WITH HALF A DOZEN VOLUNTEER ORGANIZATIONS."
"AND THEN THERE'S DEREK."
HEY. I CAN'T TALK, I'M LATE FOR A MEETING WITH MY ADVISER.
CAN WE HOOK UP AFTER?
CAN'T. I'VE GOT TO INTERVIEW MR. STEINBERG FOR THE HOYA, AND THEN I'M COVERING FOR CAROLYN OVER AT THE CLINIC.
DAMN, GIRL, YOU GOTTA TAKE A MINUTE OR TWO FOR YOURSELF ONCE IN AWHILE.
OR FOR YOU?
WELL, IF YOU INSIST...
LOOK, I'LL CALL YOU AFTER MY SHIFT AT THE CLINIC TONIGHT. MAYBE WE CAN GRAB A LATE DRINK OR SOME-THING.
I REALLY GOTTA RUN!
EXCUSE ME, MISS LEWIS?
I'M LATE FOR AN APPOINTMENT, MA'AM, I'M SORRY.
I THINK YOU'LL WANT TO HEAR THIS.

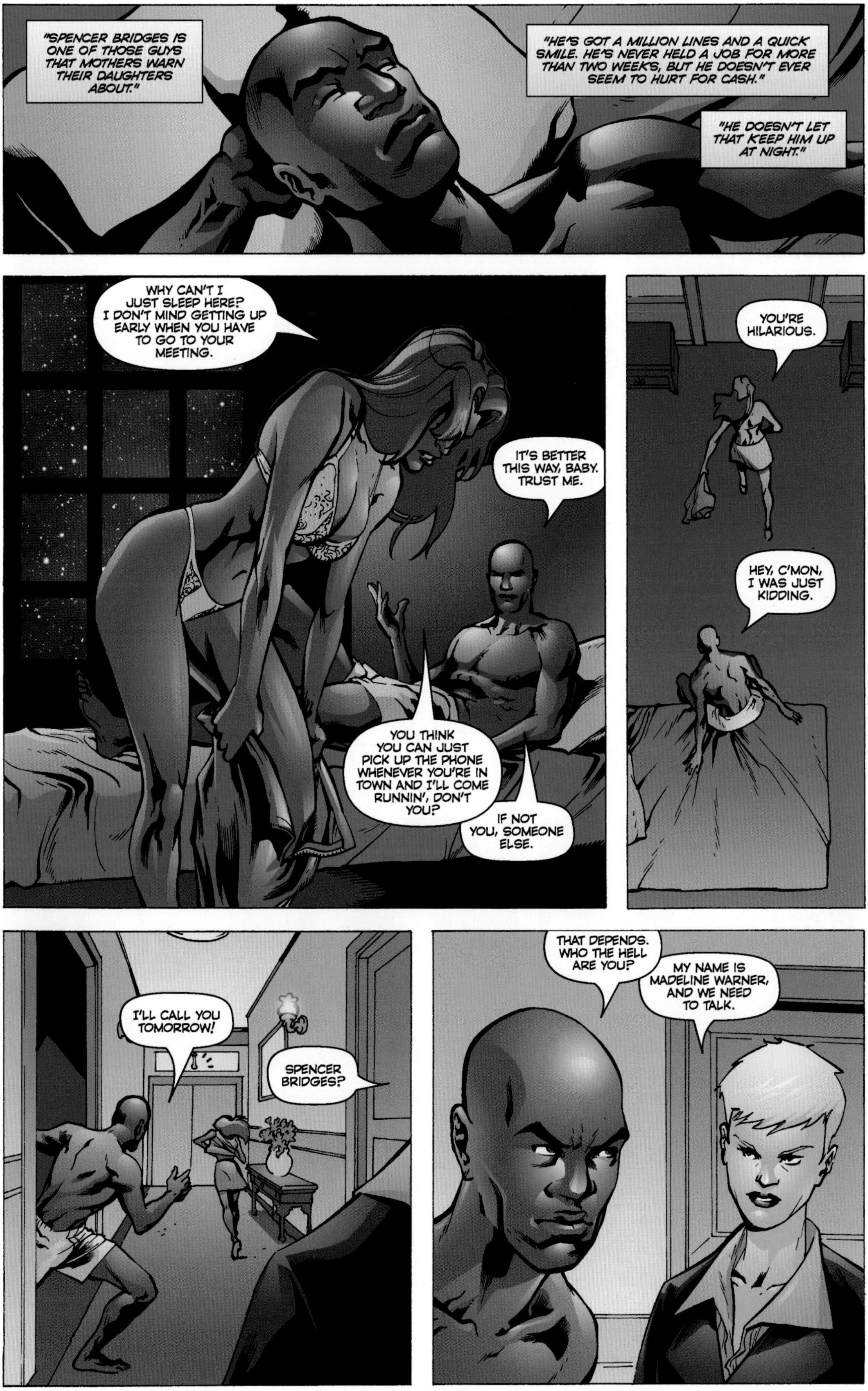

"SPENCER BRIDGES IS ONE OF THOSE GUYS THAT MOTHERS WARN THEIR DAUGHTERS ABOUT."
"HE'S GOT A MILLION LINES AND A QUICK SMILE. HE'S NEVER HELD A JOB FOR MORE THAN TWO WEEKS, BUT HE DOESN'T EVER SEEM TO HURT FOR CASH."
"HE DOESN'T LET THAT KEEP HIM UP AT NIGHT."
WHY CAN'T I JUST SLEEP HERE? I DON'T MIND GETTING UP EARLY WHEN YOU HAVE TO GO TO YOUR MEETING.
IT'S BETTER THIS WAY, BABY. TRUST ME.
YOU THINK YOU CAN JUST PICK UP THE PHONE WHENEVER YOU'RE IN TOWN AND I'LL COME RUNNIN', DON'T YOU?
IF NOT YOU, SOMEONE ELSE.
YOU'RE HILARIOUS.
HEY, C'MON, I WAS JUST KIDDING.
I'LL CALL YOU TOMORROW!
SPENCER BRIDGES?
THAT DEPENDS. WHO THE HELL ARE YOU?
MY NAME IS MADELINE WARNER, AND WE NEED TO TALK.

"BRIDGET FLYNN ALWAYS TOLD PEOPLE SHE WANTED TO WORK IN HOLLYWOOD."

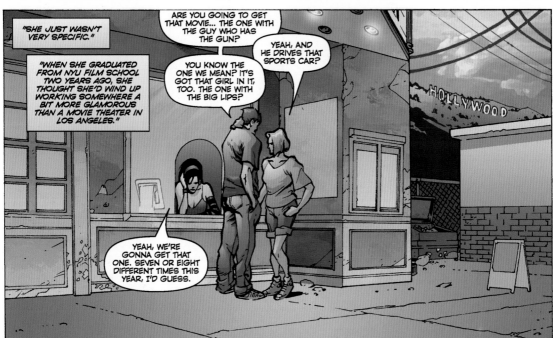

"SHE JUST WASN'T VERY SPECIFIC."

"WHEN SHE GRADUATED FROM NYU FILM SCHOOL TWO YEARS AGO, SHE THOUGHT SHE'D WIND UP WORKING SOMEWHERE A BIT MORE GLAMOROUS THAN A MOVIE THEATER IN LOS ANGELES."

ARE YOU GOING TO GET THAT MOVIE... THE ONE WITH THE GUY WHO HAS THE GUN?

YEAH, AND HE DRIVES THAT SPORTS CAR?

YOU KNOW THE ONE WE MEAN? IT'S GOT THAT GIRL IN IT, TOO. THE ONE WITH THE BIG LIPS?

YEAH, WE'RE GONNA GET THAT ONE. SEVEN OR EIGHT DIFFERENT TIMES THIS YEAR, I'D GUESS.

HEY, BRIDGET. DINO JUST CALLED IN SICK. YOU DIDN'T HAVE ANY PLANS TONIGHT, DID YOU?

LIKE ANYTHING COULD COMPARE TO THIS.

SO... YOU'LL STAY?

≥SIGH≤ YES.

BRIDGET FLYNN?

YEAH?

WHAT TIME DOES YOUR SHIFT END?

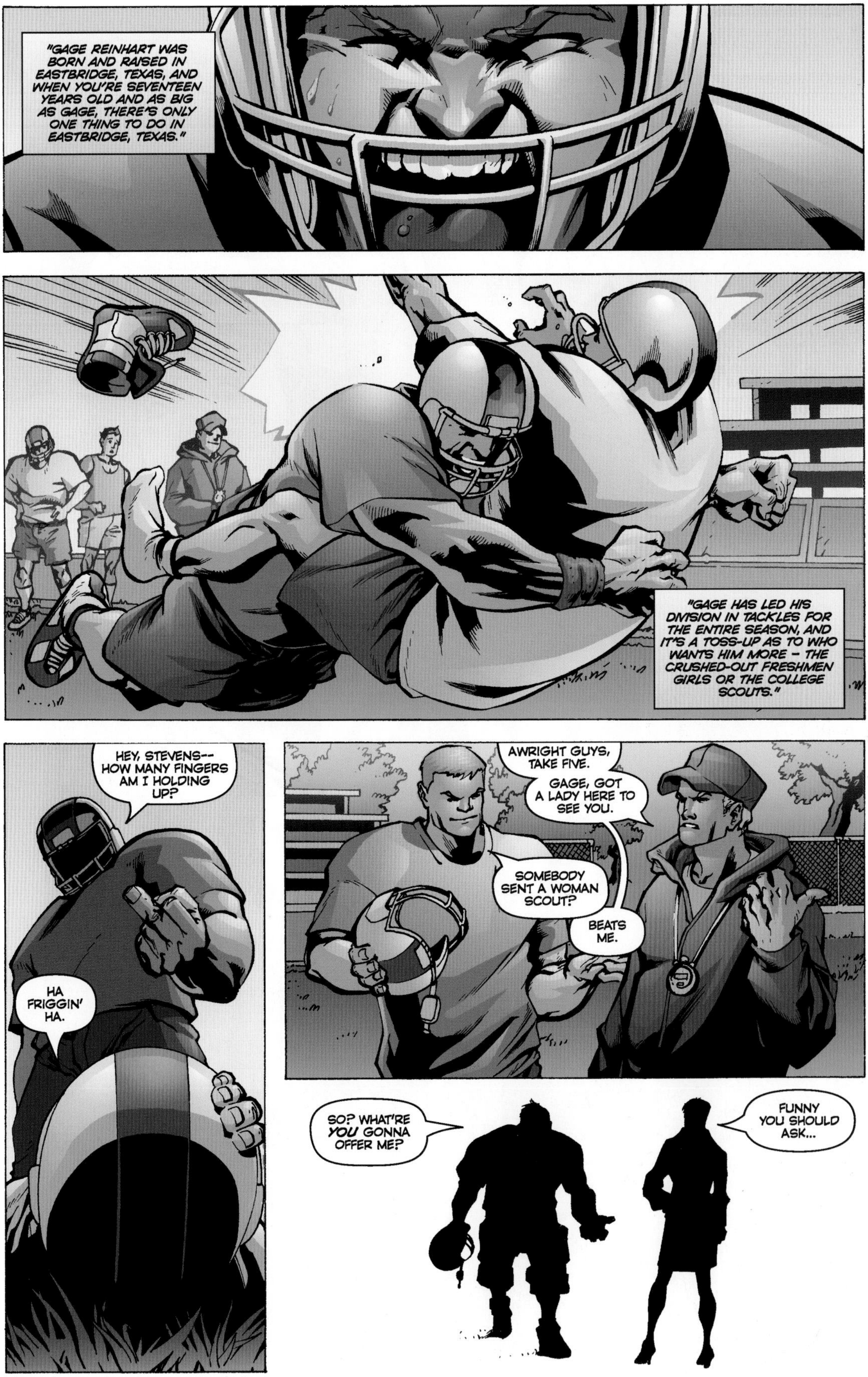
"GAGE REINHART WAS BORN AND RAISED IN EASTBRIDGE, TEXAS, AND WHEN YOU'RE SEVENTEEN YEARS OLD AND AS BIG AS GAGE, THERE'S ONLY ONE THING TO DO IN EASTBRIDGE, TEXAS."
"GAGE HAS LED HIS DIVISION IN TACKLES FOR THE ENTIRE SEASON, AND IT'S A TOSS-UP AS TO WHO WANTS HIM MORE – THE CRUSHED-OUT FRESHMEN GIRLS OR THE COLLEGE SCOUTS."
HEY, STEVENS-- HOW MANY FINGERS AM I HOLDING UP?
HA FRIGGIN' HA.
AWRIGHT GUYS, TAKE FIVE.
GAGE, GOT A LADY HERE TO SEE YOU.
SOMEBODY SENT A WOMAN SCOUT?
BEATS ME.
SO? WHAT'RE YOU GONNA OFFER ME?
FUNNY YOU SHOULD ASK...

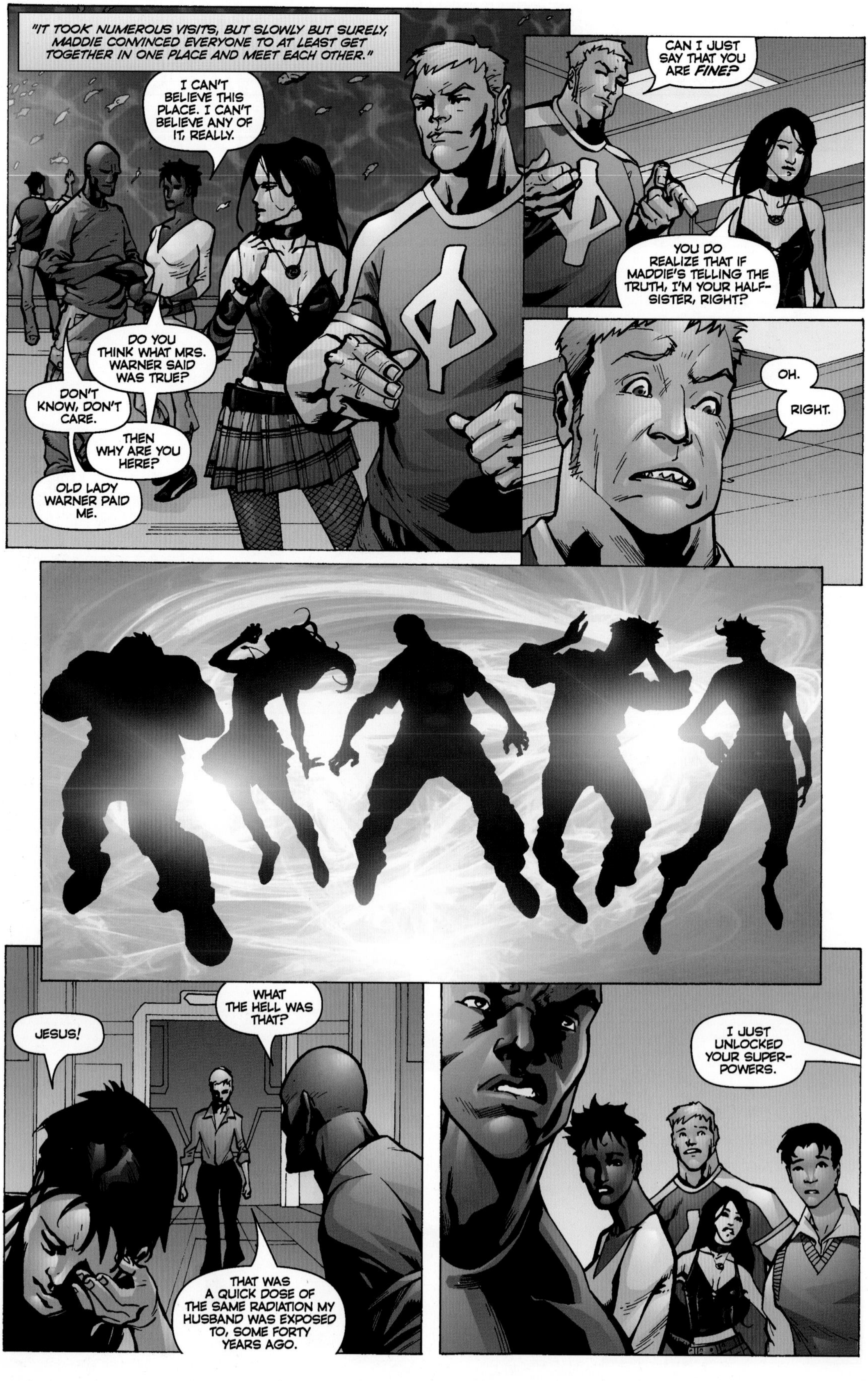
"IT TOOK NUMEROUS VISITS, BUT SLOWLY BUT SURELY, MADDIE CONVINCED EVERYONE TO AT LEAST GET TOGETHER IN ONE PLACE AND MEET EACH OTHER."
I CAN'T BELIEVE THIS PLACE. I CAN'T BELIEVE ANY OF IT, REALLY.
DO YOU THINK WHAT MRS. WARNER SAID WAS TRUE?
DON'T KNOW, DON'T CARE.
THEN WHY ARE YOU HERE?
OLD LADY WARNER PAID ME.
CAN I JUST SAY THAT YOU ARE FINE?
YOU DO REALIZE THAT IF MADDIE'S TELLING THE TRUTH, I'M YOUR HALF-SISTER, RIGHT?
OH.
RIGHT.
JESUS!
WHAT THE HELL WAS THAT?
THAT WAS A QUICK DOSE OF THE SAME RADIATION MY HUSBAND WAS EXPOSED TO, SOME FORTY YEARS AGO.
I JUST UNLOCKED YOUR SUPER-POWERS.

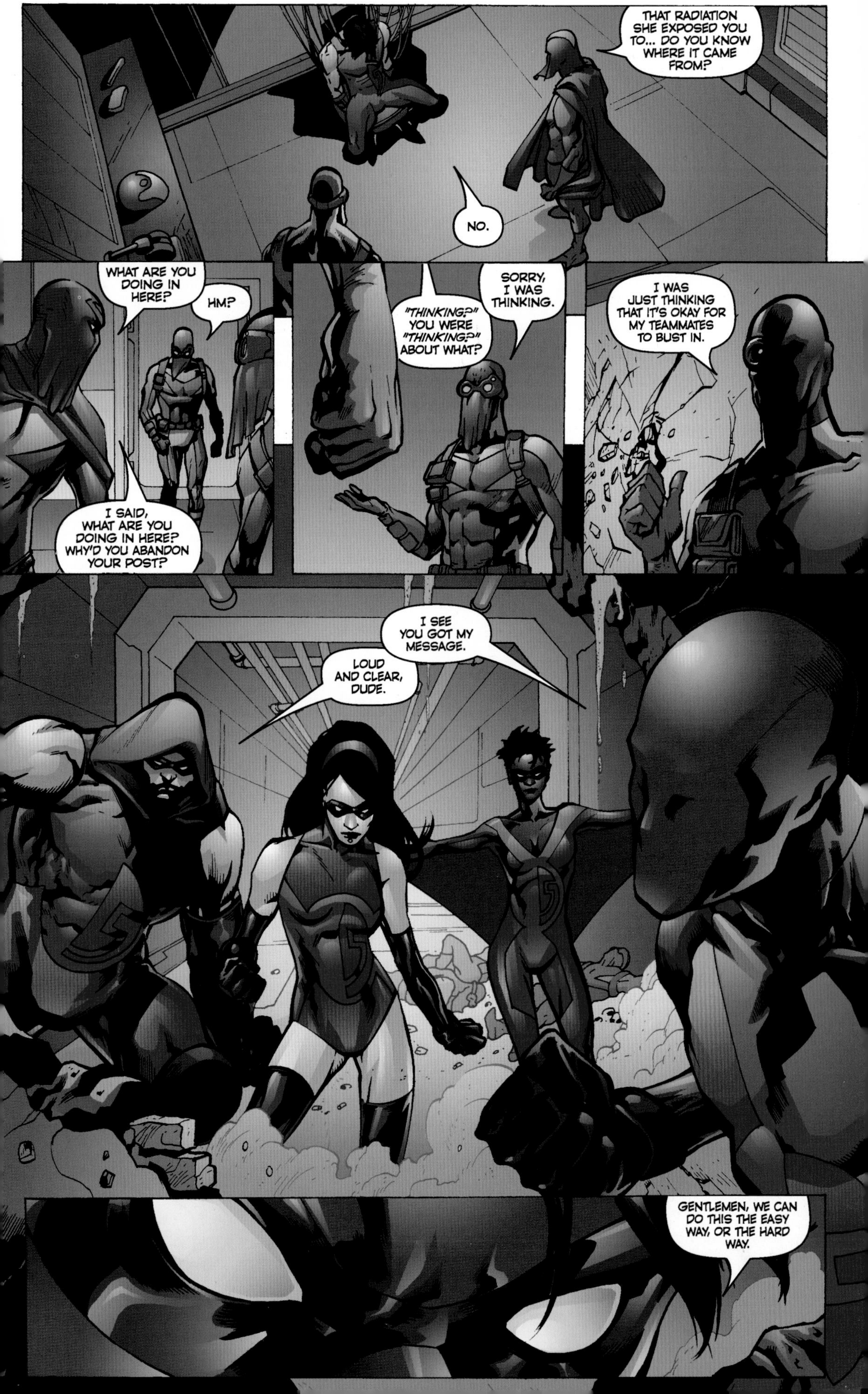
THAT RADIATION SHE EXPOSED YOU TO... DO YOU KNOW WHERE IT CAME FROM?
NO.
WHAT ARE YOU DOING IN HERE?
HM?
I SAID, WHAT ARE YOU DOING IN HERE? WHY'D YOU ABANDON YOUR POST?
SORRY, I WAS THINKING.
"THINKING?" YOU WERE "THINKING?" ABOUT WHAT?
I WAS JUST THINKING THAT IT'S OKAY FOR MY TEAMMATES TO BUST IN.
I SEE YOU GOT MY MESSAGE.
LOUD AND CLEAR, DUDE.
GENTLEMEN, WE CAN DO THIS THE EASY WAY, OR THE HARD WAY.

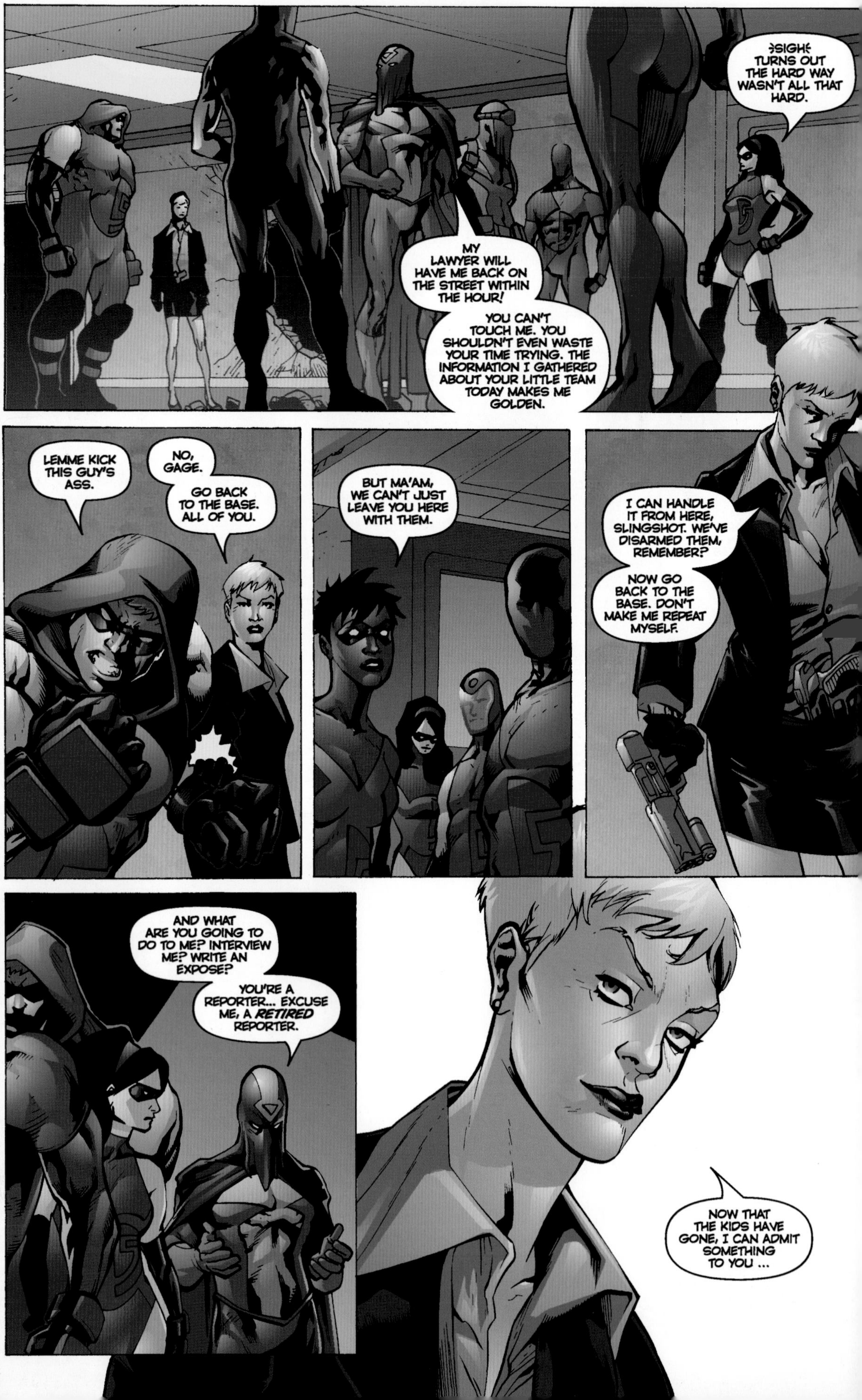

⸗SIGH⸗ TURNS OUT THE HARD WAY WASN'T ALL THAT HARD.
MY LAWYER WILL HAVE ME BACK ON THE STREET WITHIN THE HOUR!
YOU CAN'T TOUCH ME. YOU SHOULDN'T EVEN WASTE YOUR TIME TRYING. THE INFORMATION I GATHERED ABOUT YOUR LITTLE TEAM TODAY MAKES ME GOLDEN.
LEMME KICK THIS GUY'S ASS.
NO, GAGE.
GO BACK TO THE BASE. ALL OF YOU.
BUT MA'AM, WE CAN'T JUST LEAVE YOU HERE WITH THEM.
I CAN HANDLE IT FROM HERE, SLINGSHOT. WE'VE DISARMED THEM, REMEMBER?
NOW GO BACK TO THE BASE. DON'T MAKE ME REPEAT MYSELF.
AND WHAT ARE YOU GOING TO DO TO ME? INTERVIEW ME? WRITE AN EXPOSE?
YOU'RE A REPORTER... EXCUSE ME, A *RETIRED* REPORTER.
NOW THAT THE KIDS HAVE GONE, I CAN ADMIT SOMETHING TO YOU ...

I LIED.

SURE, I WAS A REPORTER. BUT THAT WAS JUST MY COVER. I WAS ACTUALLY AN AGENT WITH F.L.A.G.

NOT EVEN THE KIDS KNOW THAT.

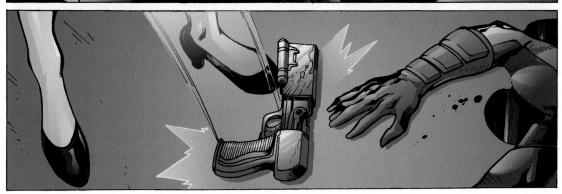

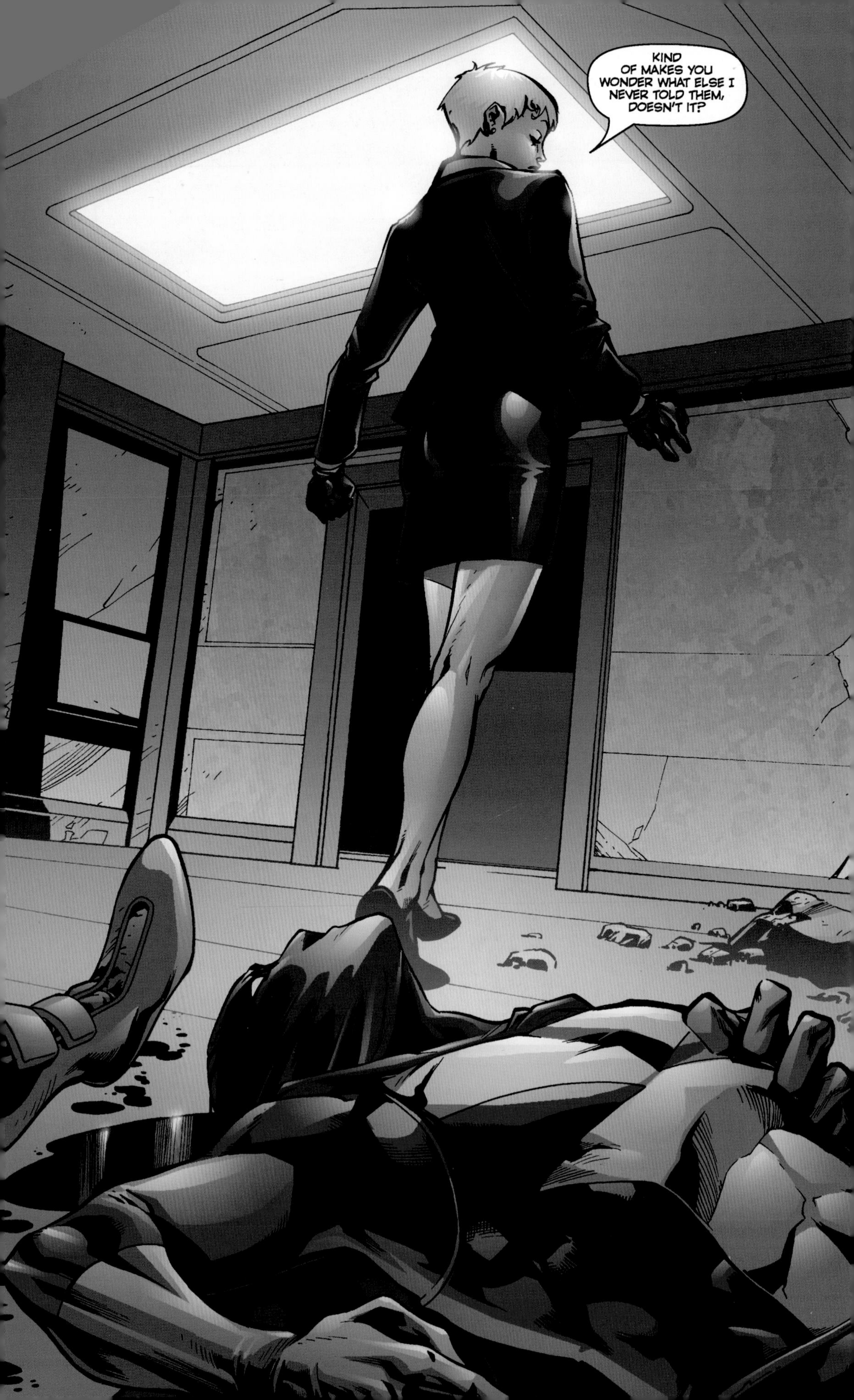
KIND OF MAKES YOU WONDER WHAT ELSE I NEVER TOLD THEM, DOESN'T IT?

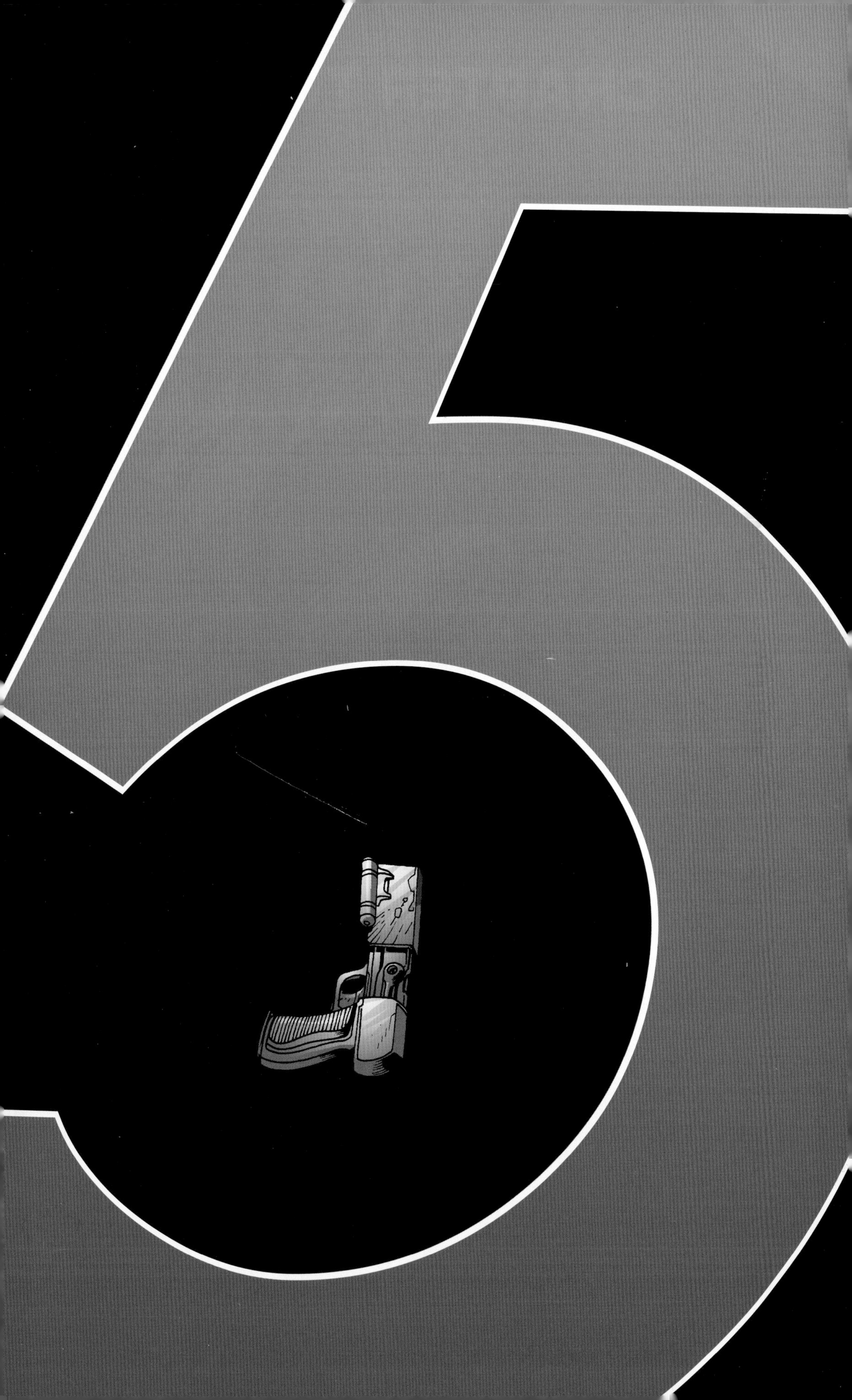
5

CHAPTER TWO

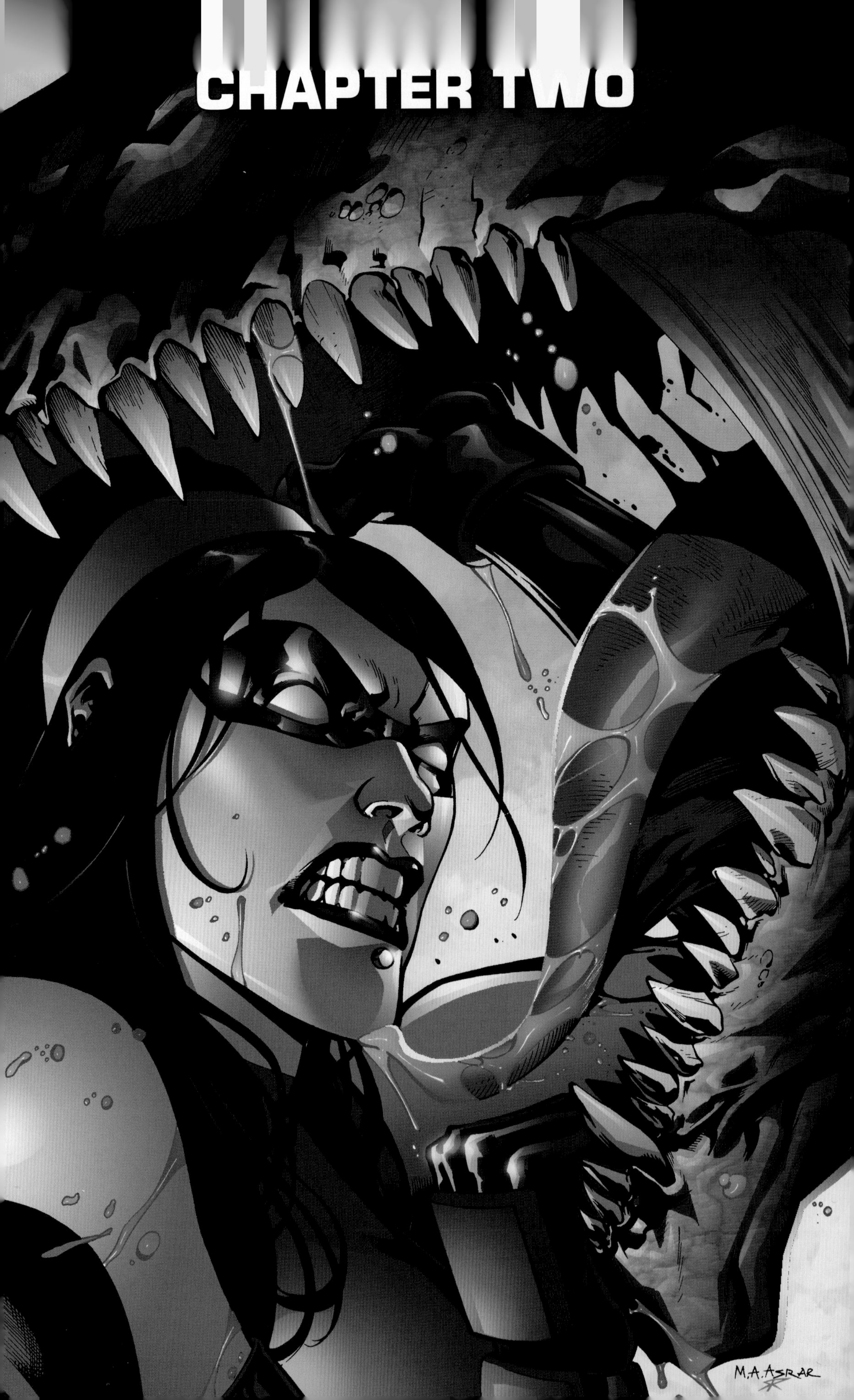
M.A.ASRAR

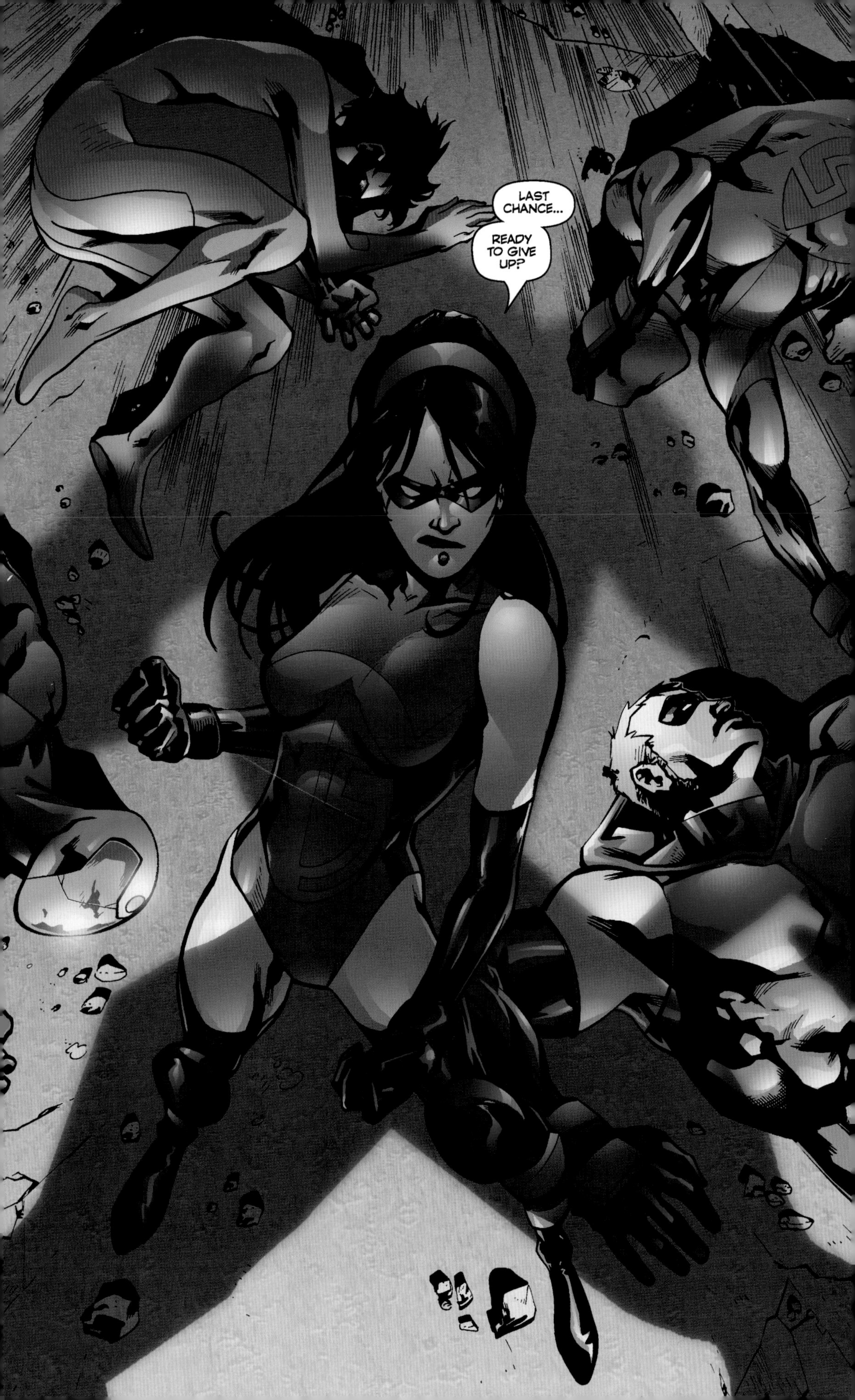
LAST CHANCE...
READY TO GIVE UP?

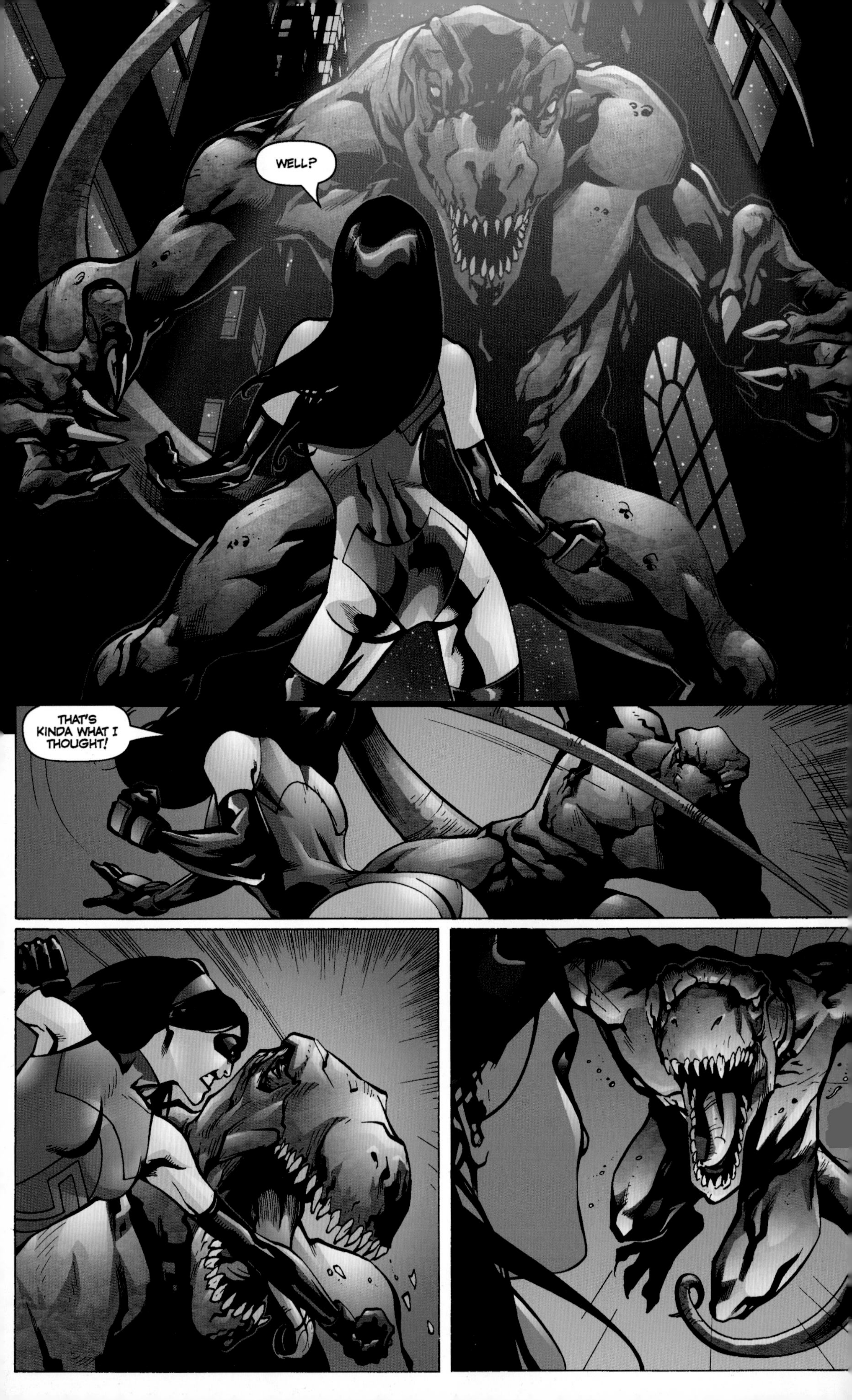
WELL?
THAT'S KINDA WHAT I THOUGHT!

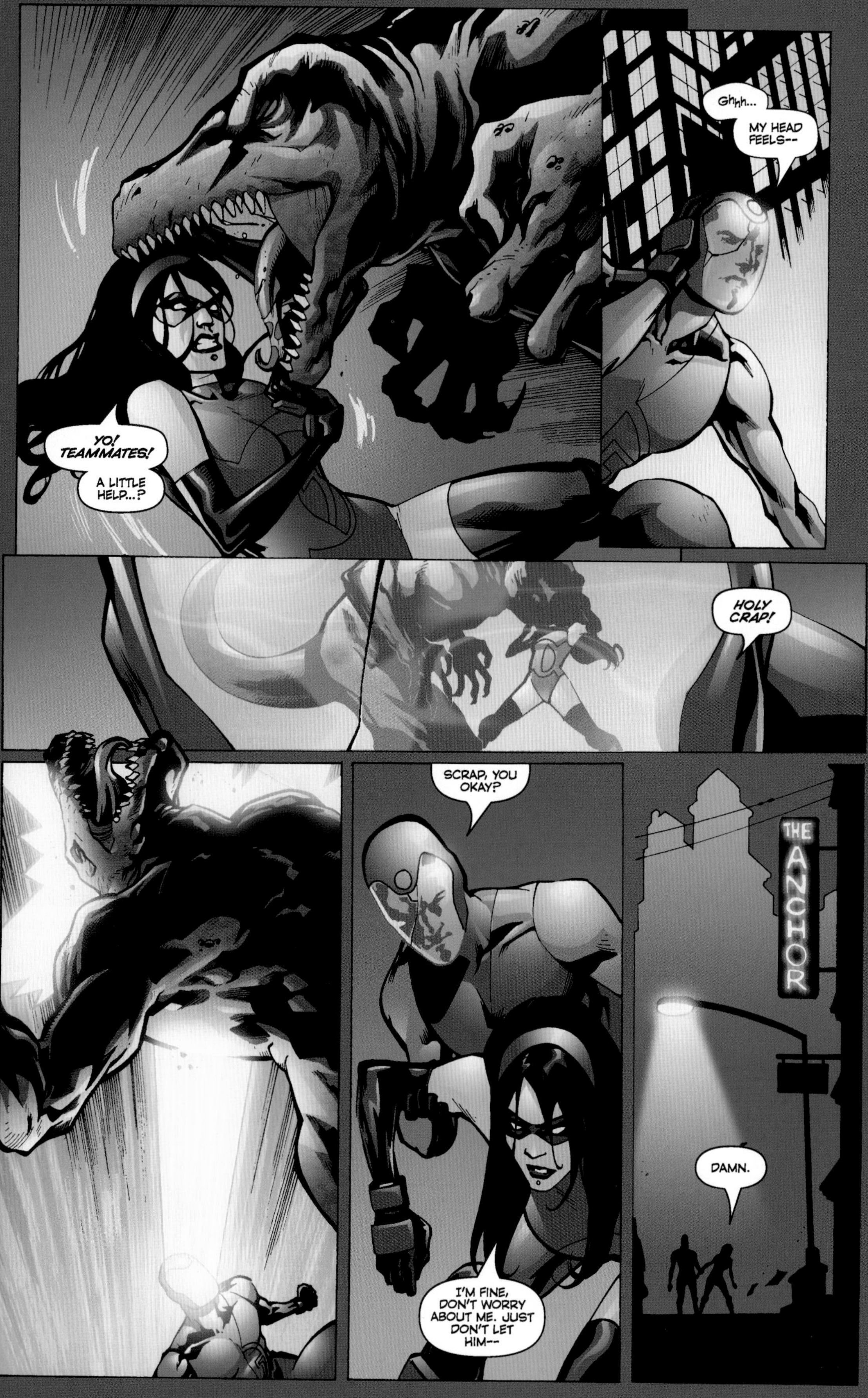
YO! TEAMMATES!
A LITTLE HELP...?
Ghhh...
MY HEAD FEELS--
HOLY CRAP!
SCRAP, YOU OKAY?
I'M FINE, DON'T WORRY ABOUT ME. JUST DON'T LET HIM--
THE ANCHOR
DAMN.

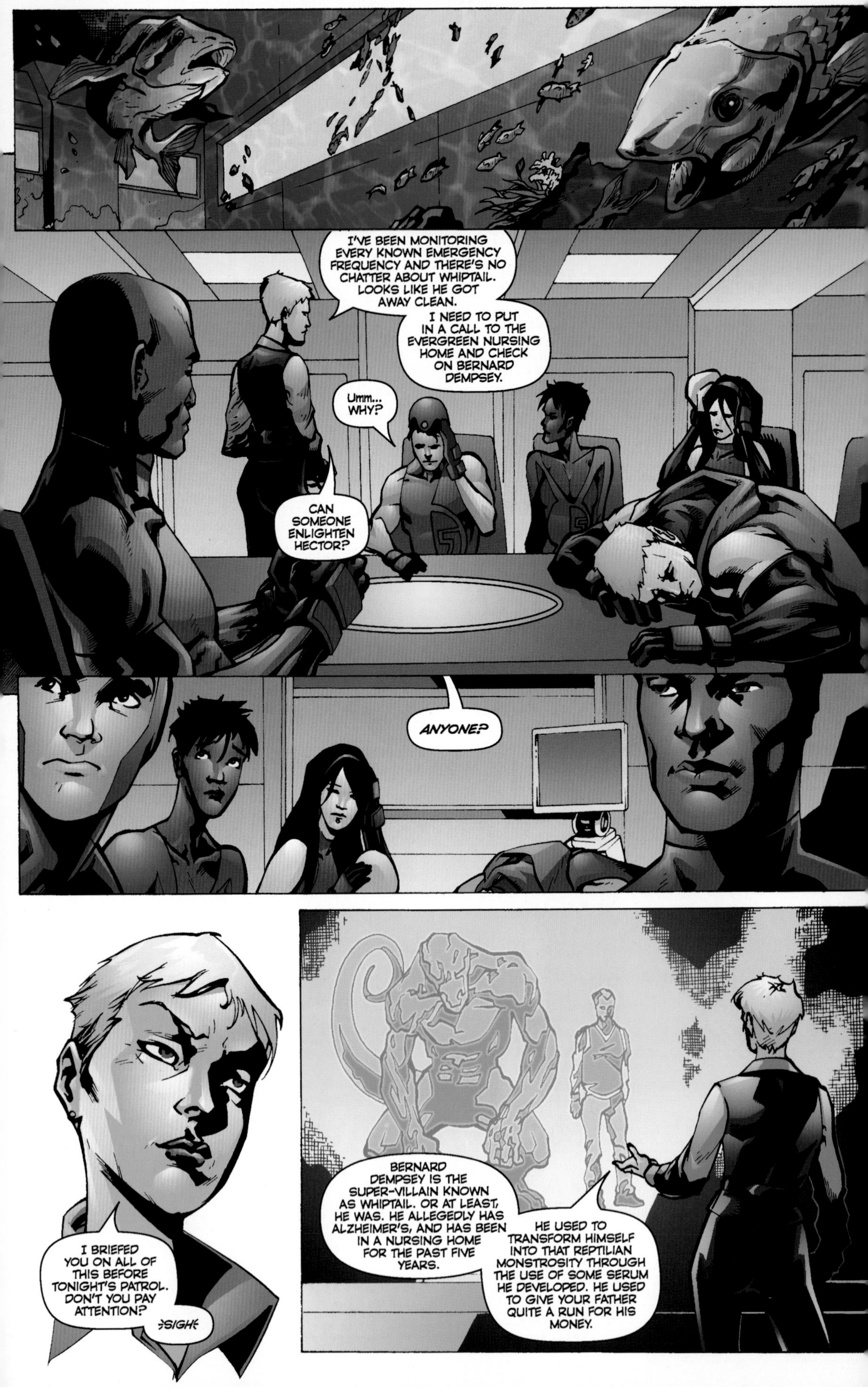
I'VE BEEN MONITORING EVERY KNOWN EMERGENCY FREQUENCY AND THERE'S NO CHATTER ABOUT WHIPTAIL. LOOKS LIKE HE GOT AWAY CLEAN.
I NEED TO PUT IN A CALL TO THE EVERGREEN NURSING HOME AND CHECK ON BERNARD DEMPSEY.
Umm... WHY?
CAN SOMEONE ENLIGHTEN HECTOR?
ANYONE?
I BRIEFED YOU ON ALL OF THIS BEFORE TONIGHT'S PATROL. DON'T YOU PAY ATTENTION?
SIGH
BERNARD DEMPSEY IS THE SUPER-VILLAIN KNOWN AS WHIPTAIL. OR AT LEAST, HE WAS. HE ALLEGEDLY HAS ALZHEIMER'S, AND HAS BEEN IN A NURSING HOME FOR THE PAST FIVE YEARS.
HE USED TO TRANSFORM HIMSELF INTO THAT REPTILIAN MONSTROSITY THROUGH THE USE OF SOME SERUM HE DEVELOPED. HE USED TO GIVE YOUR FATHER QUITE A RUN FOR HIS MONEY.

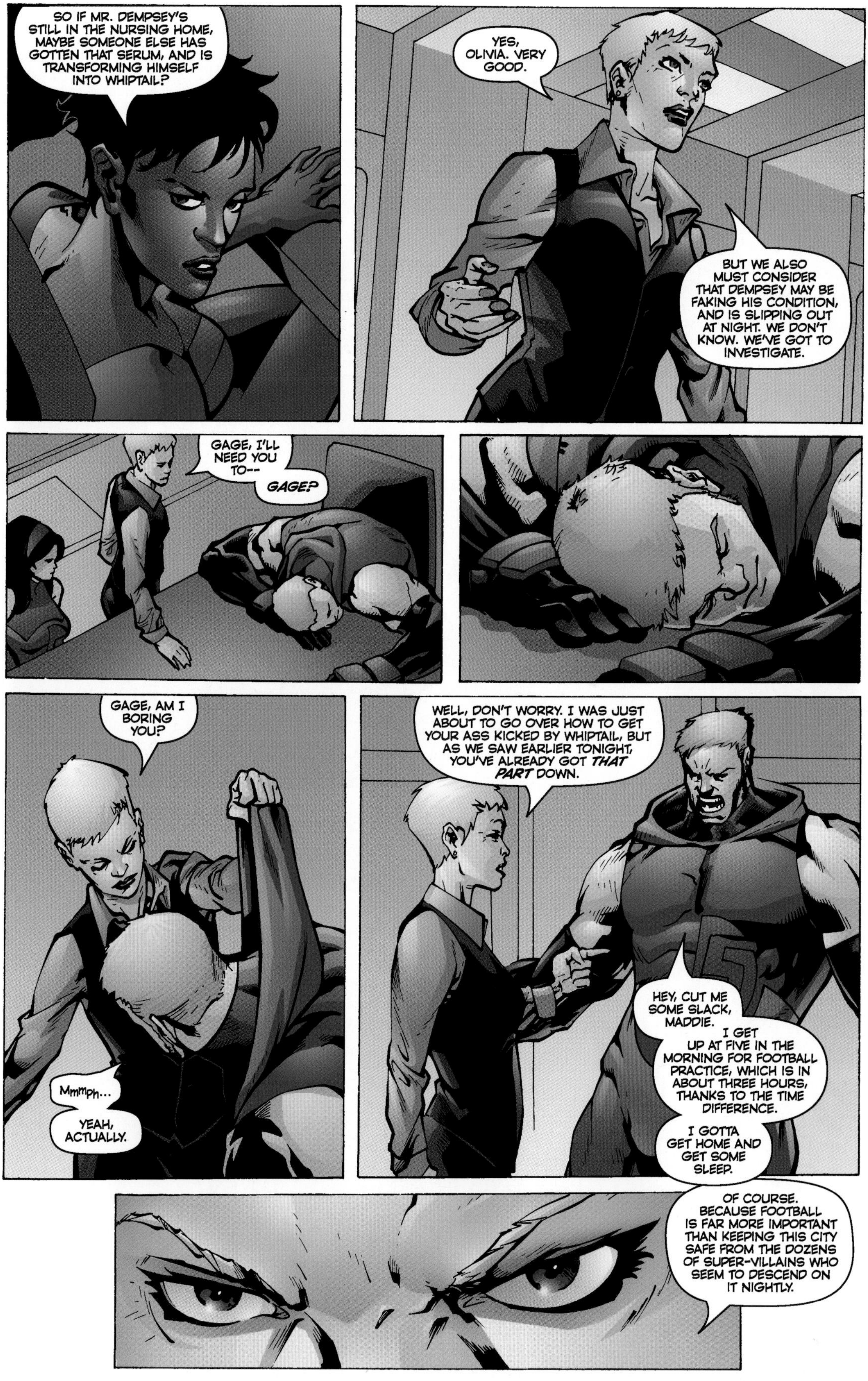

SO IF MR. DEMPSEY'S STILL IN THE NURSING HOME, MAYBE SOMEONE ELSE HAS GOTTEN THAT SERUM, AND IS TRANSFORMING HIMSELF INTO WHIPTAIL?
YES, OLIVIA. VERY GOOD.
BUT WE ALSO MUST CONSIDER THAT DEMPSEY MAY BE FAKING HIS CONDITION, AND IS SLIPPING OUT AT NIGHT. WE DON'T KNOW. WE'VE GOT TO INVESTIGATE.
GAGE, I'LL NEED YOU TO-- GAGE?
GAGE, AM I BORING YOU?
Mmmph...
YEAH, ACTUALLY.
WELL, DON'T WORRY. I WAS JUST ABOUT TO GO OVER HOW TO GET YOUR ASS KICKED BY WHIPTAIL, BUT AS WE SAW EARLIER TONIGHT, YOU'VE ALREADY GOT THAT PART DOWN.
HEY, CUT ME SOME SLACK, MADDIE.
I GET UP AT FIVE IN THE MORNING FOR FOOTBALL PRACTICE, WHICH IS IN ABOUT THREE HOURS, THANKS TO THE TIME DIFFERENCE.
I GOTTA GET HOME AND GET SOME SLEEP.
OF COURSE. BECAUSE FOOTBALL IS FAR MORE IMPORTANT THAN KEEPING THIS CITY SAFE FROM THE DOZENS OF SUPER-VILLAINS WHO SEEM TO DESCEND ON IT NIGHTLY.

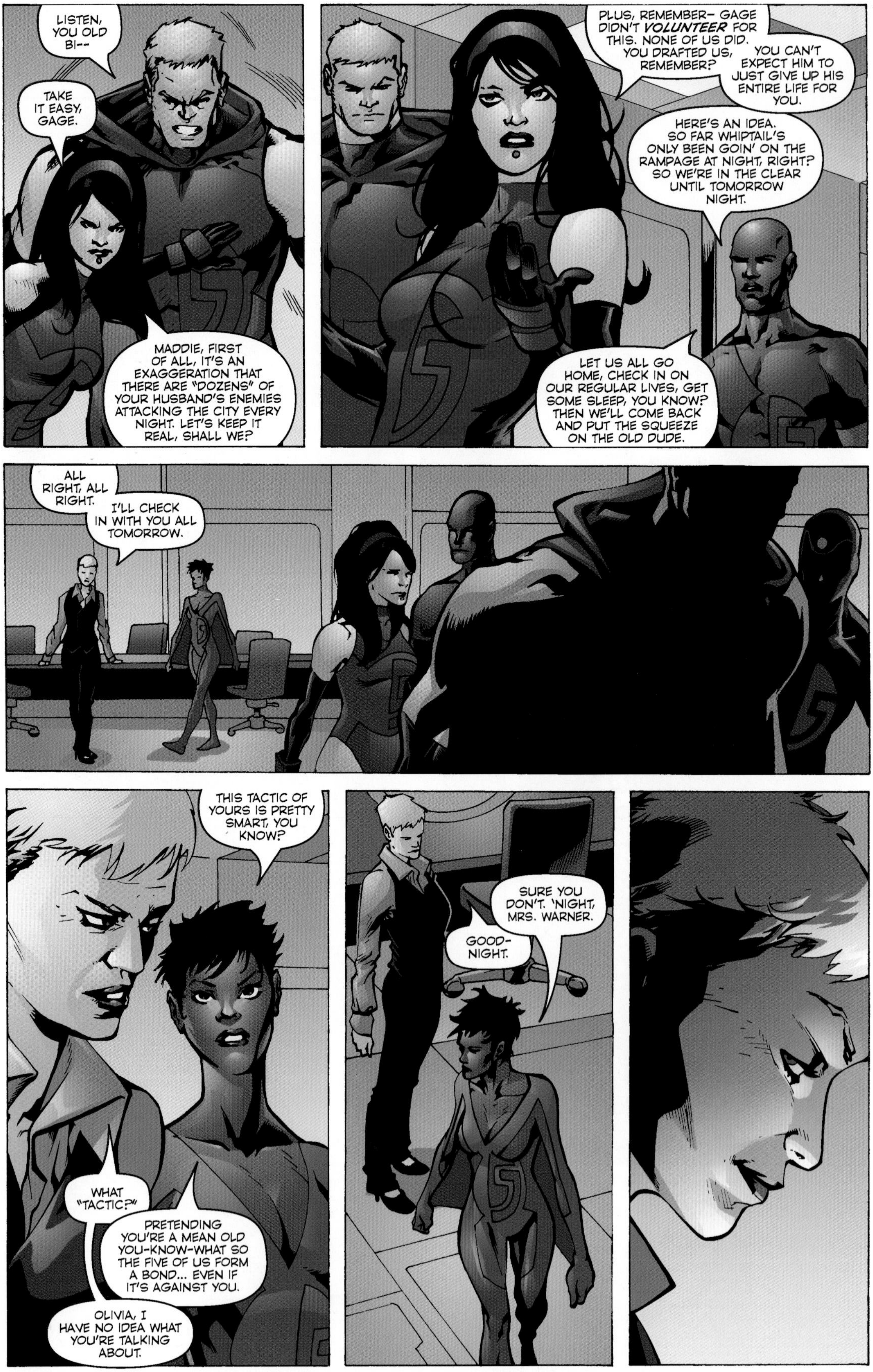

LISTEN, YOU OLD BI--
TAKE IT EASY, GAGE.
MADDIE, FIRST OF ALL, IT'S AN EXAGGERATION THAT THERE ARE "DOZENS" OF YOUR HUSBAND'S ENEMIES ATTACKING THE CITY EVERY NIGHT. LET'S KEEP IT REAL, SHALL WE?
PLUS, REMEMBER-- GAGE DIDN'T VOLUNTEER FOR THIS. NONE OF US DID. YOU DRAFTED US, REMEMBER?
YOU CAN'T EXPECT HIM TO JUST GIVE UP HIS ENTIRE LIFE FOR YOU.
HERE'S AN IDEA. SO FAR WHIPTAIL'S ONLY BEEN GOIN' ON THE RAMPAGE AT NIGHT, RIGHT? SO WE'RE IN THE CLEAR UNTIL TOMORROW NIGHT.
LET US ALL GO HOME, CHECK IN ON OUR REGULAR LIVES, GET SOME SLEEP, YOU KNOW? THEN WE'LL COME BACK AND PUT THE SQUEEZE ON THE OLD DUDE.
ALL RIGHT, ALL RIGHT.
I'LL CHECK IN WITH YOU ALL TOMORROW.
THIS TACTIC OF YOURS IS PRETTY SMART, YOU KNOW?
WHAT "TACTIC?"
PRETENDING YOU'RE A MEAN OLD YOU-KNOW-WHAT SO THE FIVE OF US FORM A BOND... EVEN IF IT'S AGAINST YOU.
OLIVIA, I HAVE NO IDEA WHAT YOU'RE TALKING ABOUT.
SURE YOU DON'T. 'NIGHT, MRS. WARNER.
GOOD-NIGHT.

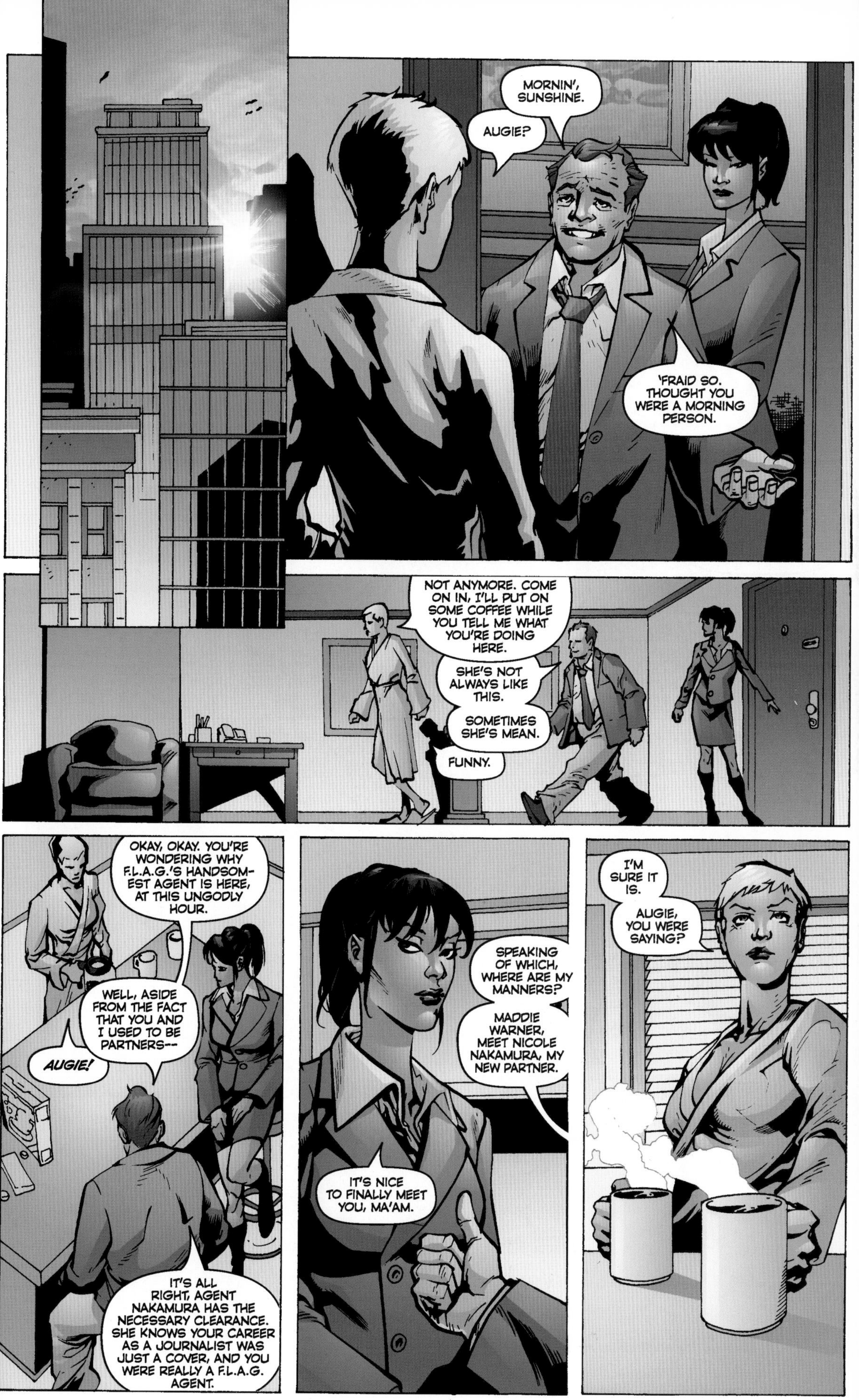
AUGIE?
MORNIN', SUNSHINE.
'FRAID SO. THOUGHT YOU WERE A MORNING PERSON.
NOT ANYMORE. COME ON IN, I'LL PUT ON SOME COFFEE WHILE YOU TELL ME WHAT YOU'RE DOING HERE.
SHE'S NOT ALWAYS LIKE THIS.
SOMETIMES SHE'S MEAN.
FUNNY.
OKAY, OKAY. YOU'RE WONDERING WHY F.L.A.G.'S HANDSOMEST AGENT IS HERE, AT THIS UNGODLY HOUR.
WELL, ASIDE FROM THE FACT THAT YOU AND I USED TO BE PARTNERS--
AUGIE!
IT'S ALL RIGHT, AGENT NAKAMURA HAS THE NECESSARY CLEARANCE. SHE KNOWS YOUR CAREER AS A JOURNALIST WAS JUST A COVER, AND YOU WERE REALLY A F.L.A.G. AGENT.
SPEAKING OF WHICH, WHERE ARE MY MANNERS?
MADDIE WARNER, MEET NICOLE NAKAMURA, MY NEW PARTNER.
IT'S NICE TO FINALLY MEET YOU, MA'AM.
I'M SURE IT IS.
AUGIE, YOU WERE SAYING?

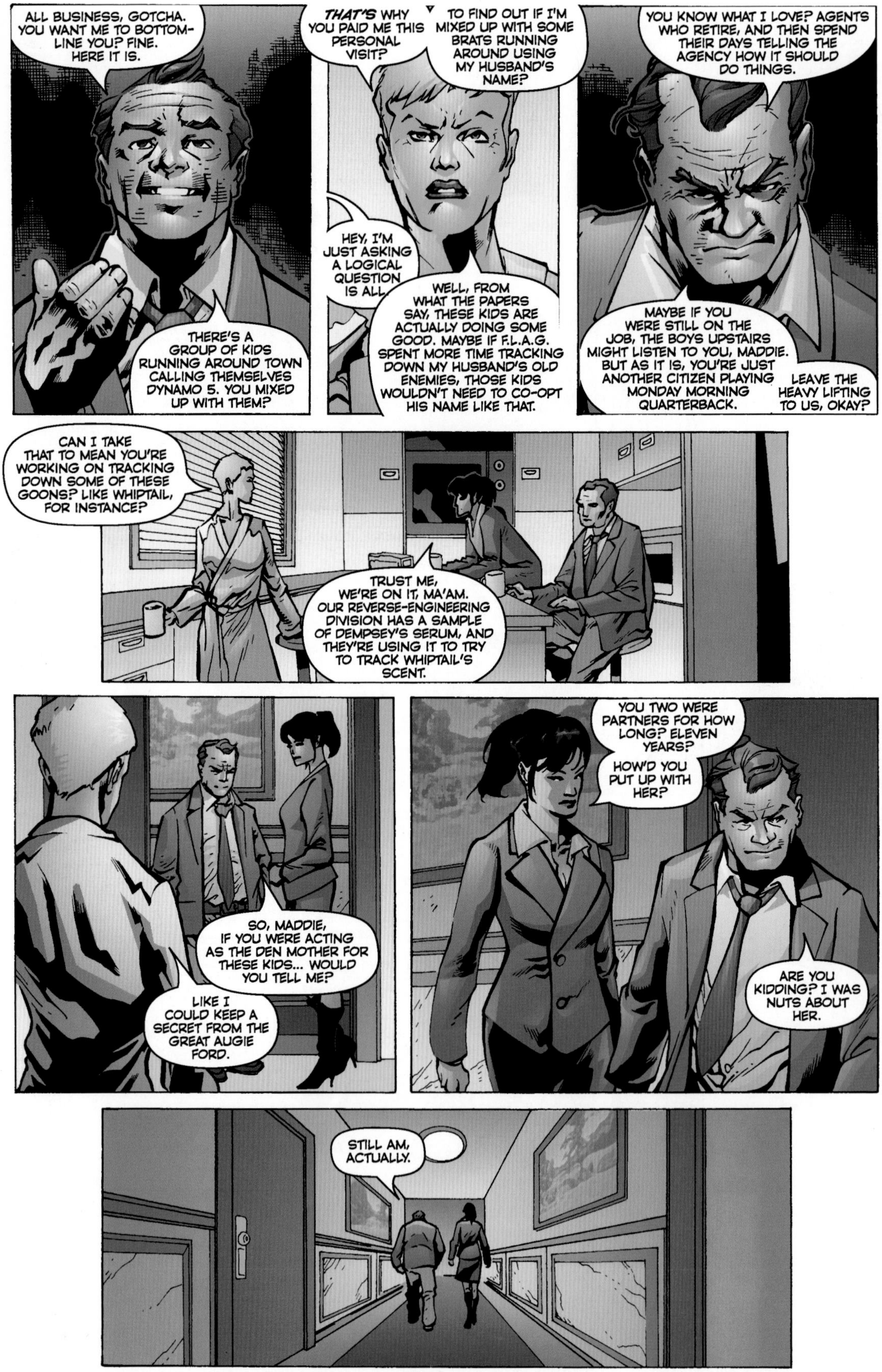
ALL BUSINESS, GOTCHA. YOU WANT ME TO BOTTOM-LINE YOU? FINE. HERE IT IS.
THERE'S A GROUP OF KIDS RUNNING AROUND TOWN CALLING THEMSELVES DYNAMO 5. YOU MIXED UP WITH THEM?
THAT'S WHY YOU PAID ME THIS PERSONAL VISIT?
TO FIND OUT IF I'M MIXED UP WITH SOME BRATS RUNNING AROUND USING MY HUSBAND'S NAME?
HEY, I'M JUST ASKING A LOGICAL QUESTION IS ALL.
WELL, FROM WHAT THE PAPERS SAY, THESE KIDS ARE ACTUALLY DOING SOME GOOD. MAYBE IF F.L.A.G. SPENT MORE TIME TRACKING DOWN MY HUSBAND'S OLD ENEMIES, THOSE KIDS WOULDN'T NEED TO CO-OPT HIS NAME LIKE THAT.
YOU KNOW WHAT I LOVE? AGENTS WHO RETIRE, AND THEN SPEND THEIR DAYS TELLING THE AGENCY HOW IT SHOULD DO THINGS.
MAYBE IF YOU WERE STILL ON THE JOB, THE BOYS UPSTAIRS MIGHT LISTEN TO YOU, MADDIE. BUT AS IT IS, YOU'RE JUST ANOTHER CITIZEN PLAYING MONDAY MORNING QUARTERBACK.
LEAVE THE HEAVY LIFTING TO US, OKAY?
CAN I TAKE THAT TO MEAN YOU'RE WORKING ON TRACKING DOWN SOME OF THESE GOONS? LIKE WHIPTAIL, FOR INSTANCE?
TRUST ME, WE'RE ON IT, MA'AM. OUR REVERSE-ENGINEERING DIVISION HAS A SAMPLE OF DEMPSEY'S SERUM, AND THEY'RE USING IT TO TRY TO TRACK WHIPTAIL'S SCENT.
SO, MADDIE, IF YOU WERE ACTING AS THE DEN MOTHER FOR THESE KIDS... WOULD YOU TELL ME?
LIKE I COULD KEEP A SECRET FROM THE GREAT AUGIE FORD.
YOU TWO WERE PARTNERS FOR HOW LONG? ELEVEN YEARS?
HOW'D YOU PUT UP WITH HER?
ARE YOU KIDDING? I WAS NUTS ABOUT HER.
STILL AM, ACTUALLY.

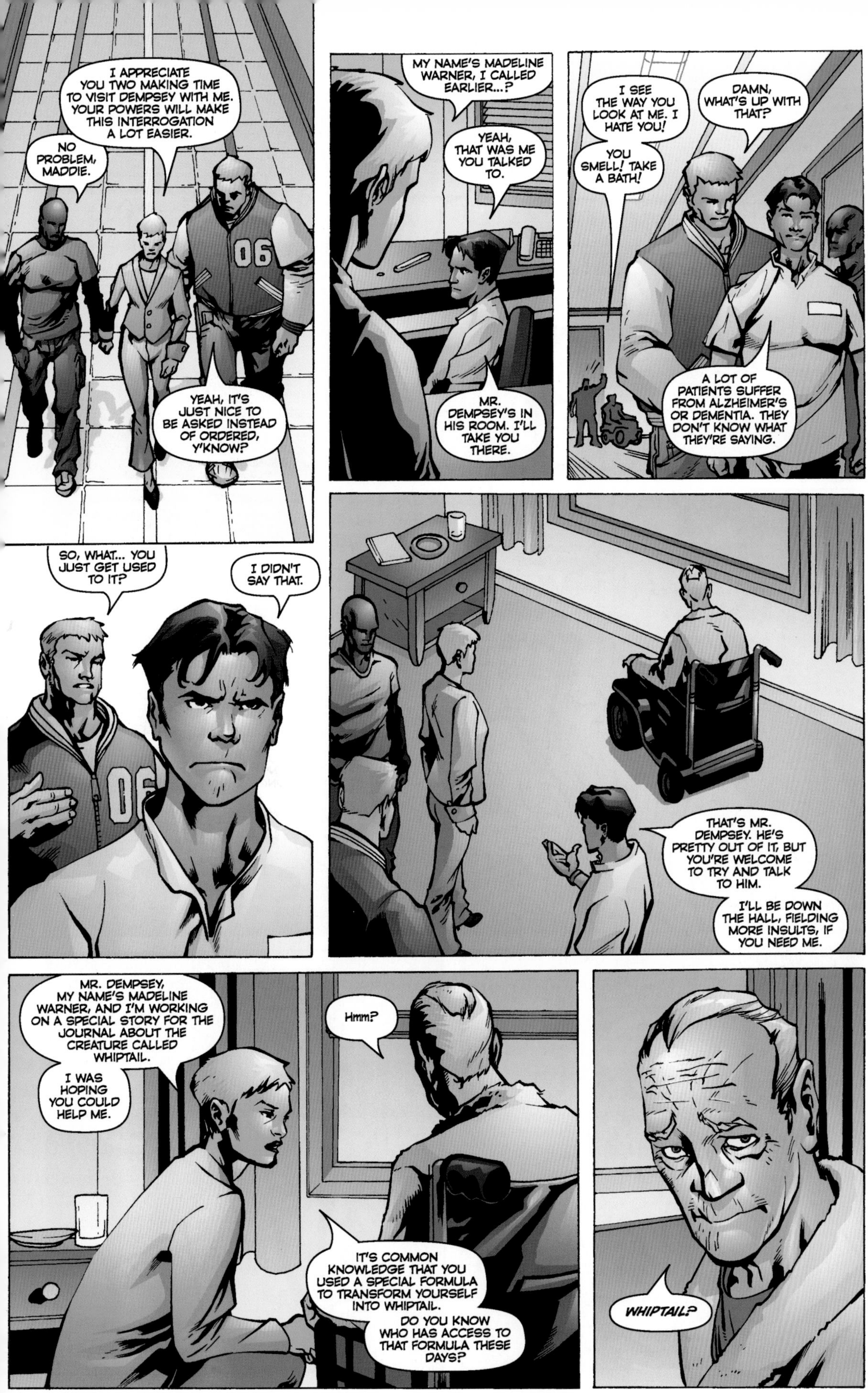
I APPRECIATE YOU TWO MAKING TIME TO VISIT DEMPSEY WITH ME. YOUR POWERS WILL MAKE THIS INTERROGATION A LOT EASIER.
NO PROBLEM, MADDIE.
YEAH, IT'S JUST NICE TO BE ASKED INSTEAD OF ORDERED, Y'KNOW?
MY NAME'S MADELINE WARNER, I CALLED EARLIER...?
YEAH, THAT WAS ME YOU TALKED TO.
MR. DEMPSEY'S IN HIS ROOM. I'LL TAKE YOU THERE.
I SEE THE WAY YOU LOOK AT ME. I HATE YOU!
YOU SMELL! TAKE A BATH!
DAMN, WHAT'S UP WITH THAT?
A LOT OF PATIENTS SUFFER FROM ALZHEIMER'S OR DEMENTIA. THEY DON'T KNOW WHAT THEY'RE SAYING.
SO, WHAT... YOU JUST GET USED TO IT?
I DIDN'T SAY THAT.
THAT'S MR. DEMPSEY. HE'S PRETTY OUT OF IT, BUT YOU'RE WELCOME TO TRY AND TALK TO HIM.
I'LL BE DOWN THE HALL, FIELDING MORE INSULTS, IF YOU NEED ME.
MR. DEMPSEY, MY NAME'S MADELINE WARNER, AND I'M WORKING ON A SPECIAL STORY FOR THE JOURNAL ABOUT THE CREATURE CALLED WHIPTAIL.
I WAS HOPING YOU COULD HELP ME.
Hmm?
IT'S COMMON KNOWLEDGE THAT YOU USED A SPECIAL FORMULA TO TRANSFORM YOURSELF INTO WHIPTAIL.
DO YOU KNOW WHO HAS ACCESS TO THAT FORMULA THESE DAYS?
WHIPTAIL?

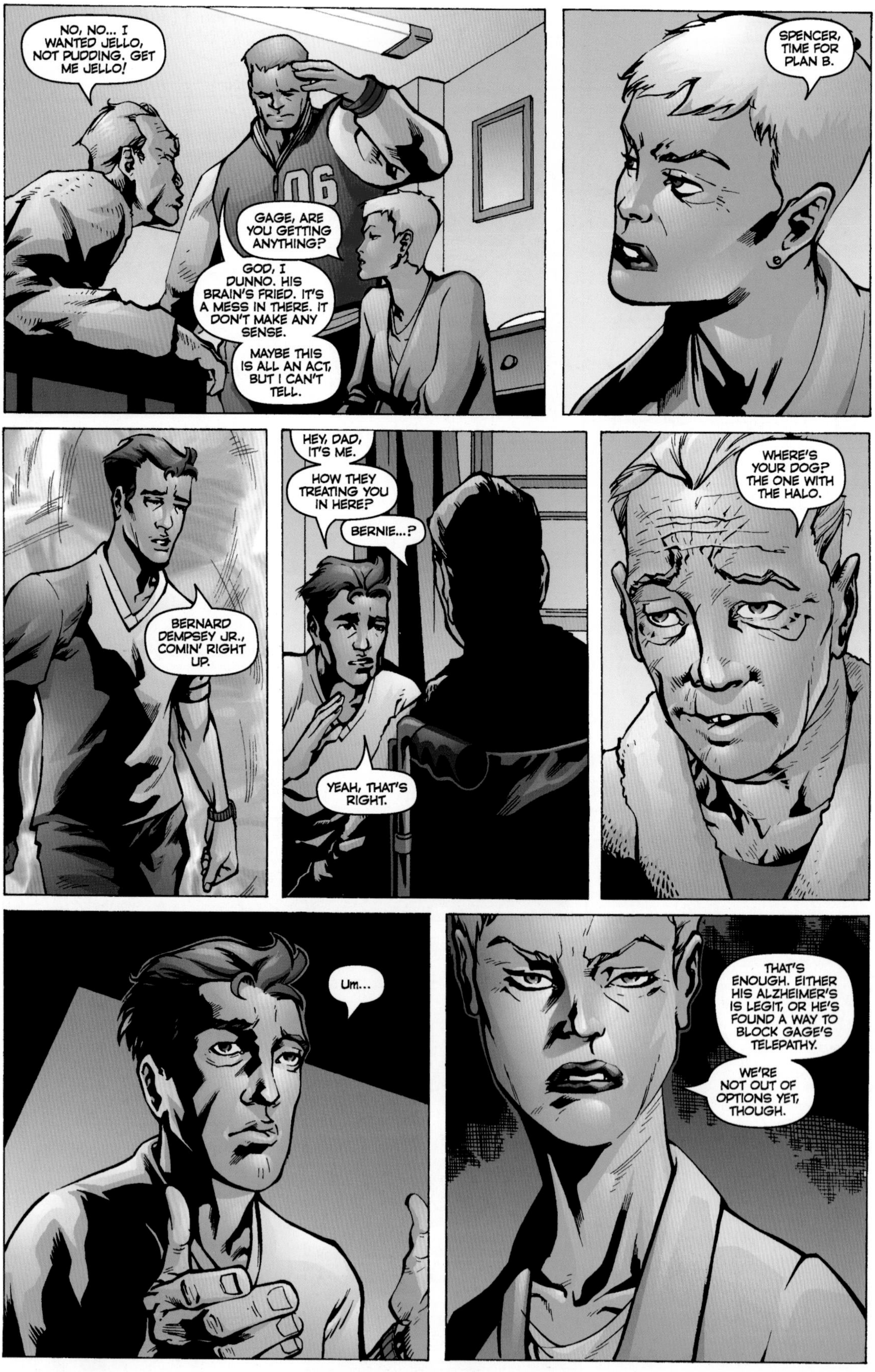
NO, NO... I WANTED JELLO, NOT PUDDING. GET ME JELLO!
GAGE, ARE YOU GETTING ANYTHING?
GOD, I DUNNO. HIS BRAIN'S FRIED. IT'S A MESS IN THERE. IT DON'T MAKE ANY SENSE.
MAYBE THIS IS ALL AN ACT, BUT I CAN'T TELL.
SPENCER, TIME FOR PLAN B.
BERNARD DEMPSEY JR., COMIN' RIGHT UP.
HEY, DAD, IT'S ME.
HOW THEY TREATING YOU IN HERE?
BERNIE...?
YEAH, THAT'S RIGHT.
WHERE'S YOUR DOG? THE ONE WITH THE HALO.
Um...
THAT'S ENOUGH. EITHER HIS ALZHEIMER'S IS LEGIT, OR HE'S FOUND A WAY TO BLOCK GAGE'S TELEPATHY.
WE'RE NOT OUT OF OPTIONS YET, THOUGH.

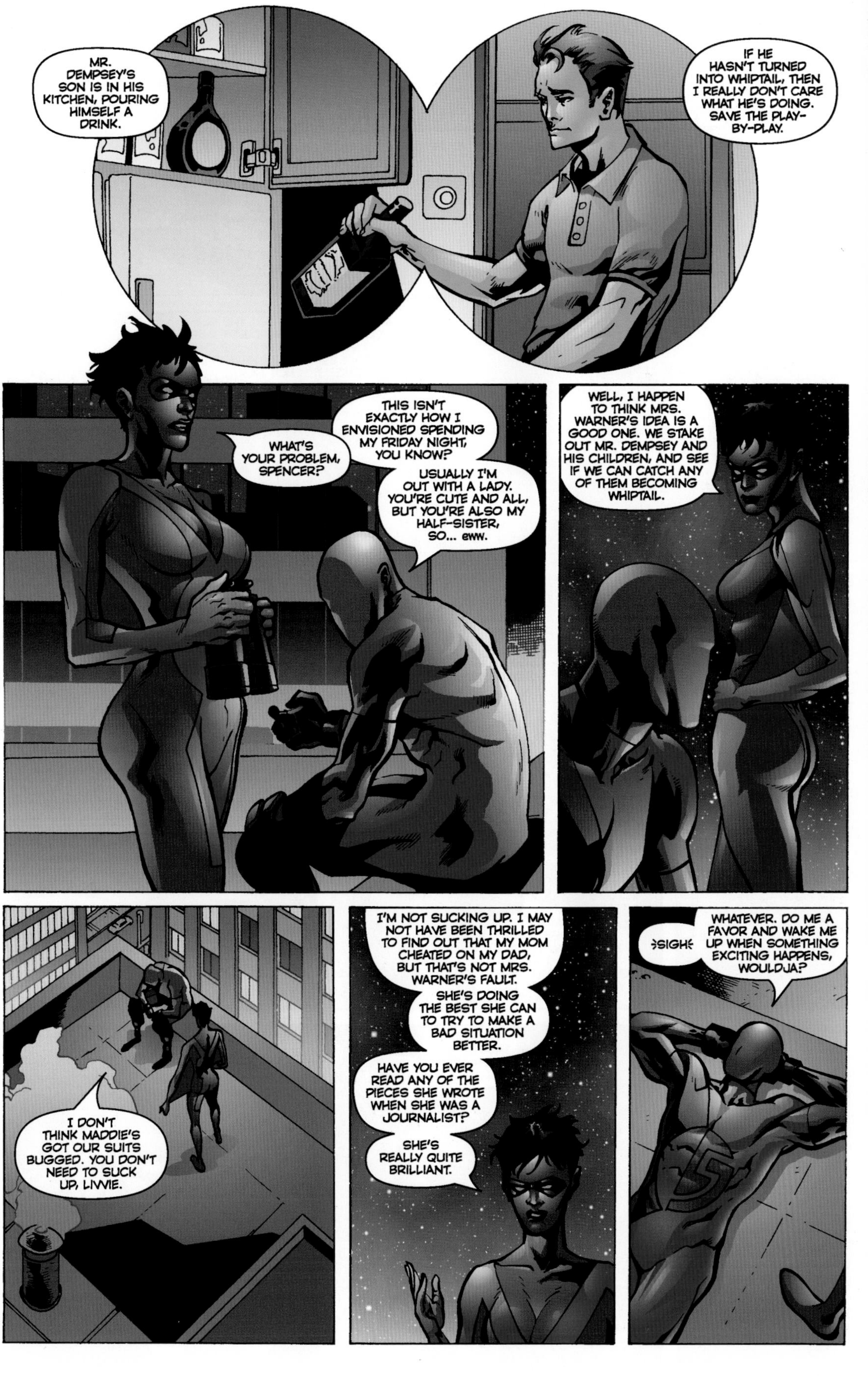
MR. DEMPSEY'S SON IS IN HIS KITCHEN, POURING HIMSELF A DRINK.
IF HE HASN'T TURNED INTO WHIPTAIL, THEN I REALLY DON'T CARE WHAT HE'S DOING. SAVE THE PLAY-BY-PLAY.
WHAT'S YOUR PROBLEM, SPENCER?
THIS ISN'T EXACTLY HOW I ENVISIONED SPENDING MY FRIDAY NIGHT, YOU KNOW?
USUALLY I'M OUT WITH A LADY. YOU'RE CUTE AND ALL, BUT YOU'RE ALSO MY HALF-SISTER, SO... eww.
WELL, I HAPPEN TO THINK MRS. WARNER'S IDEA IS A GOOD ONE. WE STAKE OUT MR. DEMPSEY AND HIS CHILDREN, AND SEE IF WE CAN CATCH ANY OF THEM BECOMING WHIPTAIL.
I DON'T THINK MADDIE'S GOT OUR SUITS BUGGED. YOU DON'T NEED TO SUCK UP, LIVVIE.
I'M NOT SUCKING UP. I MAY NOT HAVE BEEN THRILLED TO FIND OUT THAT MY MOM CHEATED ON MY DAD, BUT THAT'S NOT MRS. WARNER'S FAULT.
SHE'S DOING THE BEST SHE CAN TO TRY TO MAKE A BAD SITUATION BETTER.
HAVE YOU EVER READ ANY OF THE PIECES SHE WROTE WHEN SHE WAS A JOURNALIST?
SHE'S REALLY QUITE BRILLIANT.
SIGH
WHATEVER. DO ME A FAVOR AND WAKE ME UP WHEN SOMETHING EXCITING HAPPENS, WOULDJA?

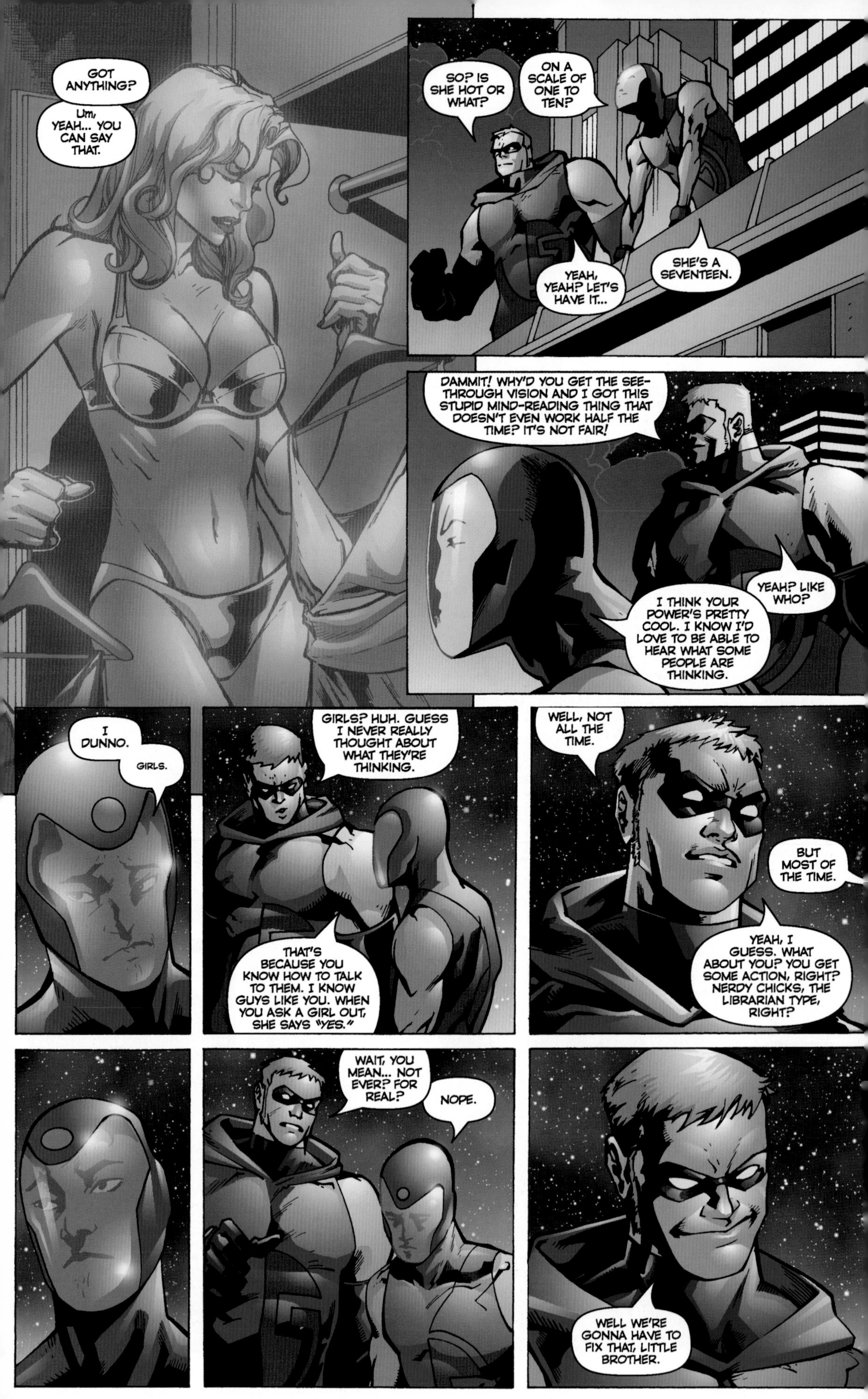
GOT ANYTHING?
Um, YEAH... YOU CAN SAY THAT.
SO? IS SHE HOT OR WHAT?
ON A SCALE OF ONE TO TEN?
YEAH, YEAH? LET'S HAVE IT...
SHE'S A SEVENTEEN.
DAMMIT! WHY'D YOU GET THE SEE-THROUGH VISION AND I GOT THIS STUPID MIND-READING THING THAT DOESN'T EVEN WORK HALF THE TIME? IT'S NOT FAIR!
I THINK YOUR POWER'S PRETTY COOL. I KNOW I'D LOVE TO BE ABLE TO HEAR WHAT SOME PEOPLE ARE THINKING.
YEAH? LIKE WHO?
I DUNNO.
GIRLS.
GIRLS? HUH. GUESS I NEVER REALLY THOUGHT ABOUT WHAT THEY'RE THINKING.
THAT'S BECAUSE YOU KNOW HOW TO TALK TO THEM. I KNOW GUYS LIKE YOU. WHEN YOU ASK A GIRL OUT, SHE SAYS "YES."
WELL, NOT ALL THE TIME.
BUT MOST OF THE TIME.
YEAH, I GUESS. WHAT ABOUT YOU? YOU GET SOME ACTION, RIGHT? NERDY CHICKS, THE LIBRARIAN TYPE, RIGHT?
WAIT, YOU MEAN... NOT EVER? FOR REAL?
NOPE.
WELL WE'RE GONNA HAVE TO FIX THAT, LITTLE BROTHER.

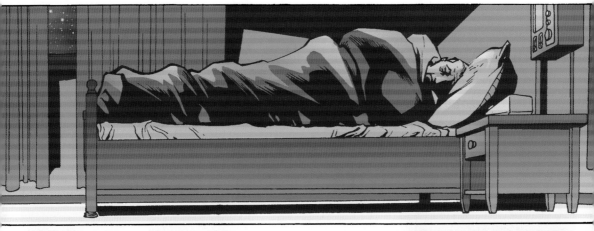

I'M STARTING TO THINK HE ISN'T OUR GUY.

NICE WORK SLIPPING IN THAT CAMERA WHEN YOU WERE IN HIS ROOM TODAY.

THANK YOU, BRIDGET.

NOT A PROBLEM. I GOT SOMEONE TO COVER MY SHIFT AT THE THEATER.

AND YES, IT LOOKS LIKE DEMPSEY WASN'T FAKING HIS ALZHEIMER'S. BUT WE COULDN'T TAKE ANY CHANCES, SO I APPRECIATE YOU JOINING ME.

I'VE BEEN MEANING TO ASK YOU ABOUT THAT. I SAW YOUR TRANSCRIPTS AND I READ ONE OF THE SPEC SCRIPTS YOU WROTE IN FILM SCHOOL. YOU'RE QUITE TALENTED.

SO WHY ARE YOU WORKING AT A MOVIE THEATER?

THANKS, BUT... I DON'T KNOW... I DON'T WANT ANY SPECIAL TREATMENT.

I DUNNO. IT'S TOUGH OUT THERE. I THOUGHT I COULD GET BY ON TALENT ALONE, BUT IT REALLY IS ABOUT WHO YOU KNOW.

I'M NO GOOD AT THAT SCHMOOZING BULLSHIT.

I'M FRIENDLY WITH ONE OF THE ENTERTAINMENT REPORTERS FROM THE PAPER, AND HE KNOWS DAMNED NEAR EVERYONE.

I COULD INTRODUCE YOU. MAYBE HE COULD OPEN A FEW DOORS FOR YOU.

YOU JUST SAID IT'S ALL ABOUT WHO YOU KNOW. ALL I'M DOING IS TRYING TO EXPAND THE LIST OF PEOPLE YOU KNOW.

OR WOULD YOU RATHER REMAIN IN THE SAFETY OF YOUR CRAPPY JOB, BITCHING ABOUT HOW YOU CAN'T GET A BREAK, RATHER THAN TAKING THE BREAK I'M OFFERING AND RISKING FAILURE?

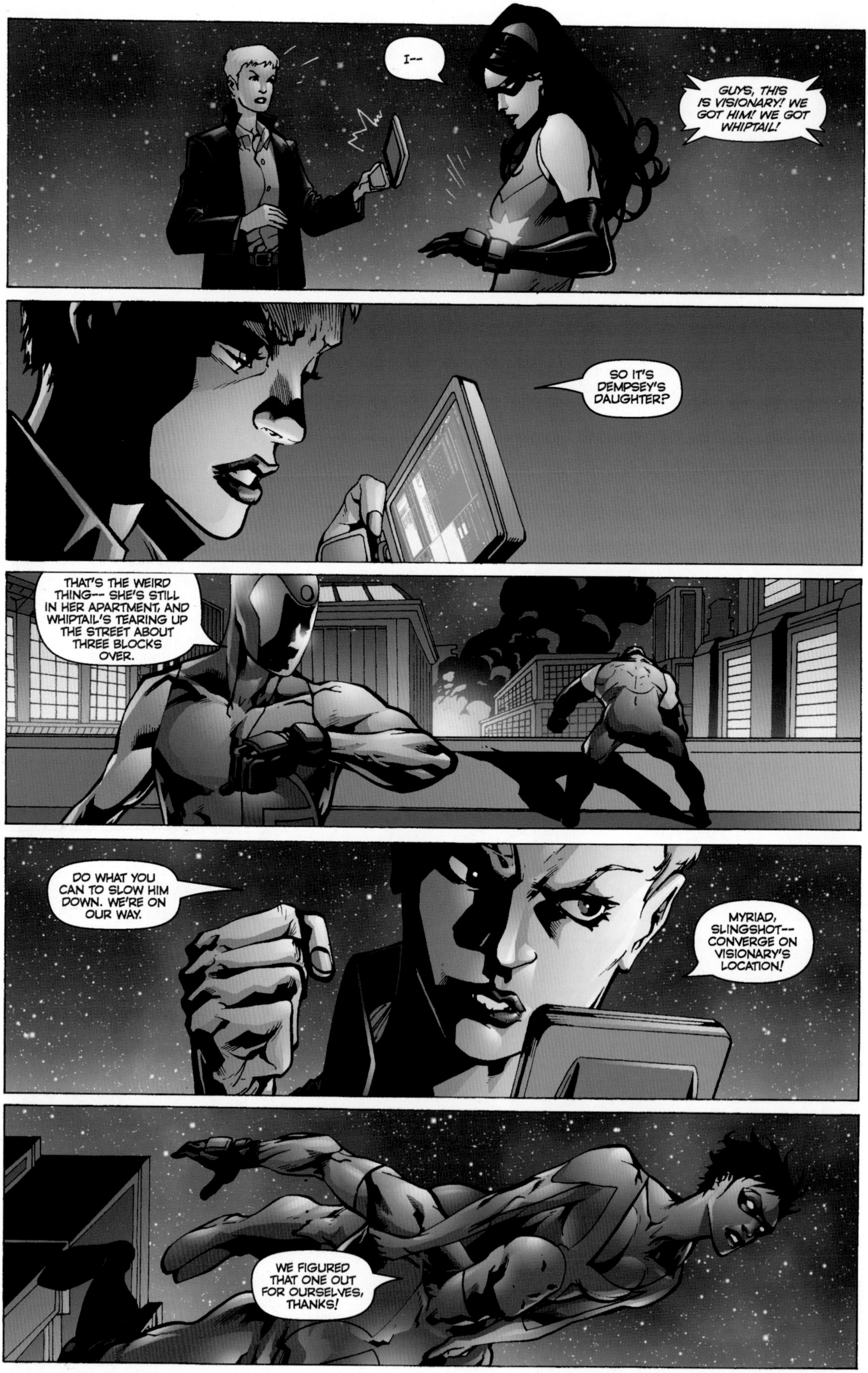
I--
GUYS, THIS IS VISIONARY! WE GOT HIM! WE GOT WHIPTAIL!
SO IT'S DEMPSEY'S DAUGHTER?
THAT'S THE WEIRD THING-- SHE'S STILL IN HER APARTMENT, AND WHIPTAIL'S TEARING UP THE STREET ABOUT THREE BLOCKS OVER.
DO WHAT YOU CAN TO SLOW HIM DOWN. WE'RE ON OUR WAY.
MYRIAD, SLINGSHOT-- CONVERGE ON VISIONARY'S LOCATION!
WE FIGURED THAT ONE OUT FOR OURSELVES, THANKS!

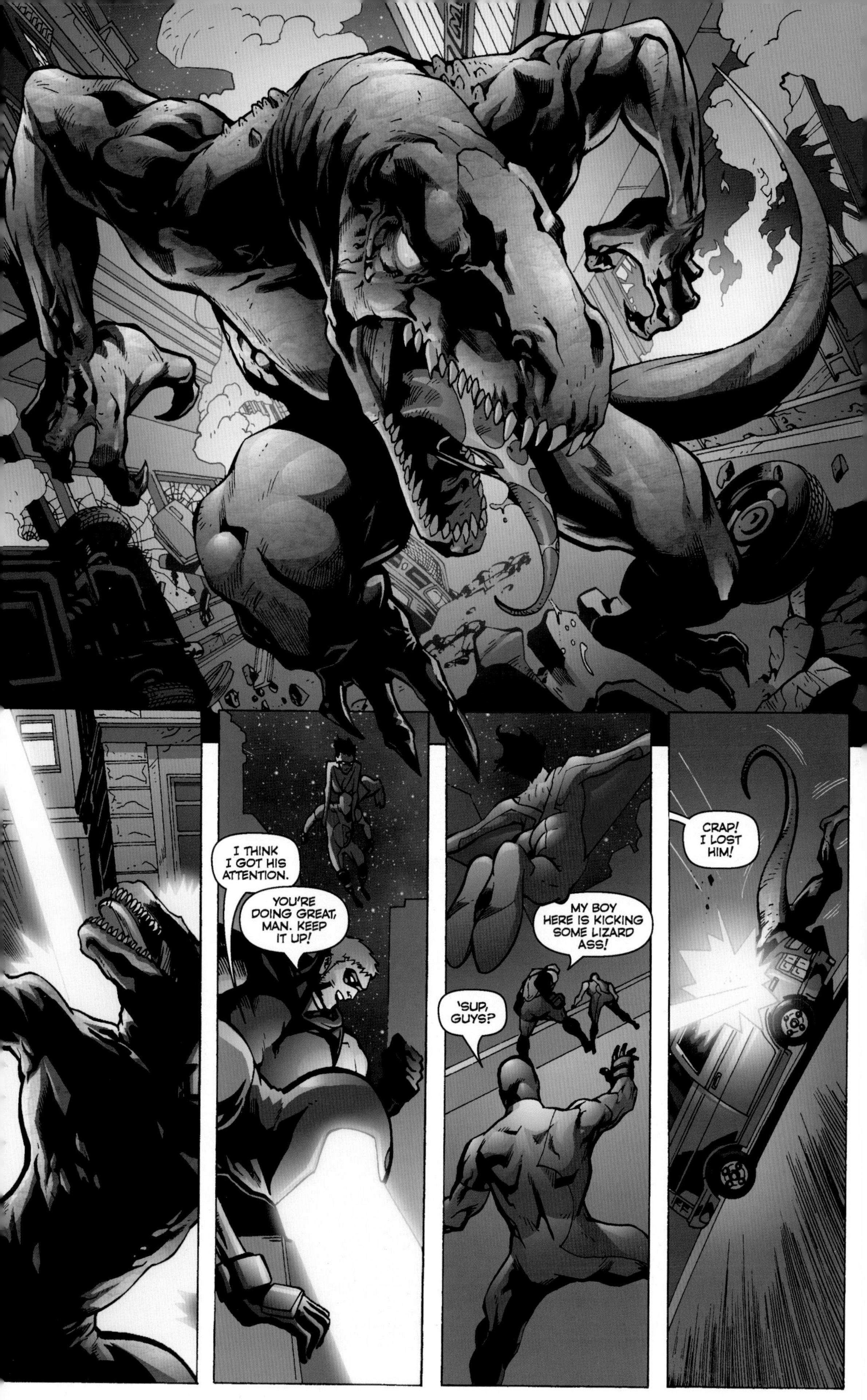
I THINK I GOT HIS ATTENTION.
YOU'RE DOING GREAT, MAN. KEEP IT UP!
MY BOY HERE IS KICKING SOME LIZARD ASS!
'SUP, GUYS?
CRAP! I LOST HIM!

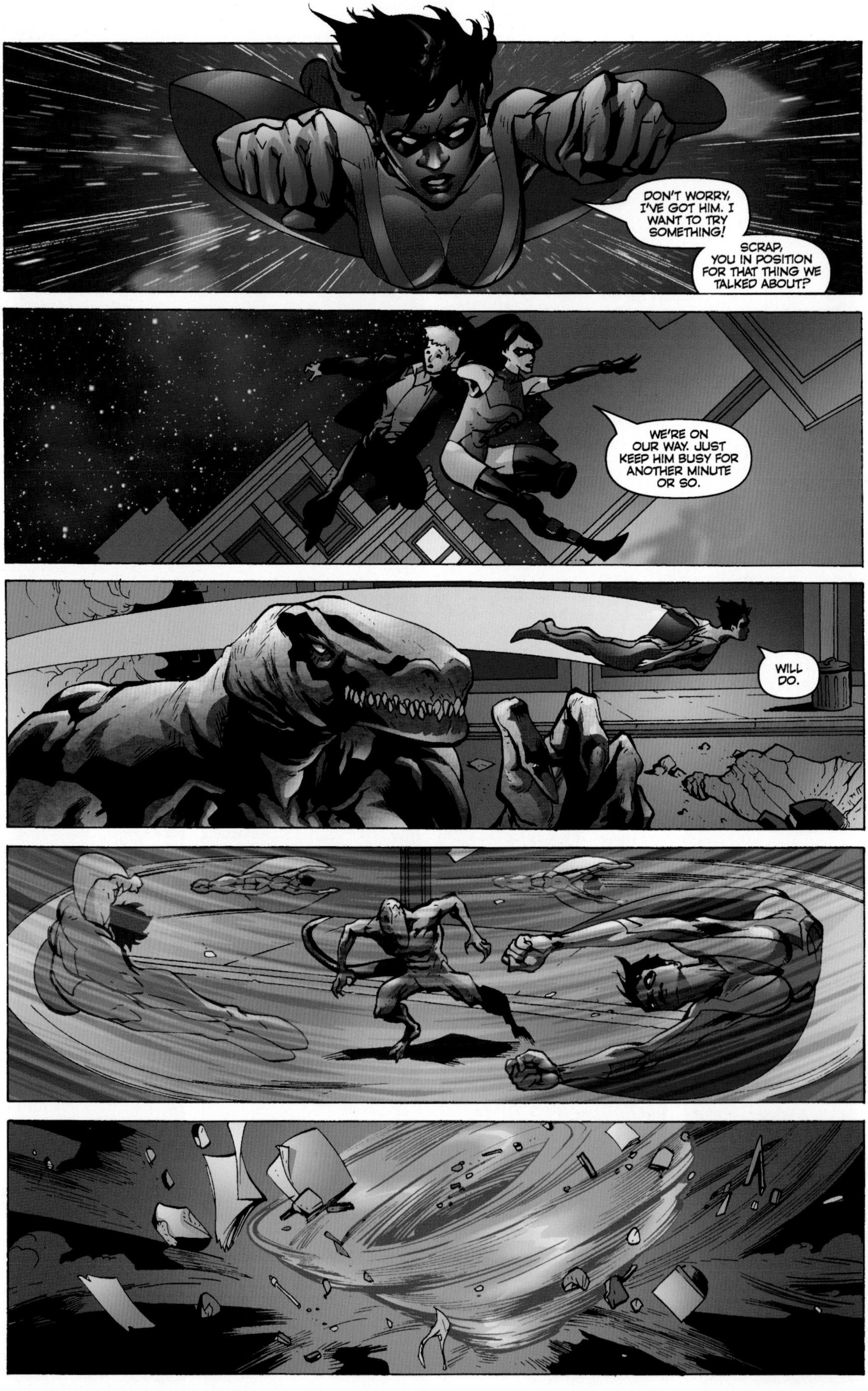
DON'T WORRY, I'VE GOT HIM. I WANT TO TRY SOMETHING!
SCRAP, YOU IN POSITION FOR THAT THING WE TALKED ABOUT?
WE'RE ON OUR WAY. JUST KEEP HIM BUSY FOR ANOTHER MINUTE OR SO.
WILL DO.

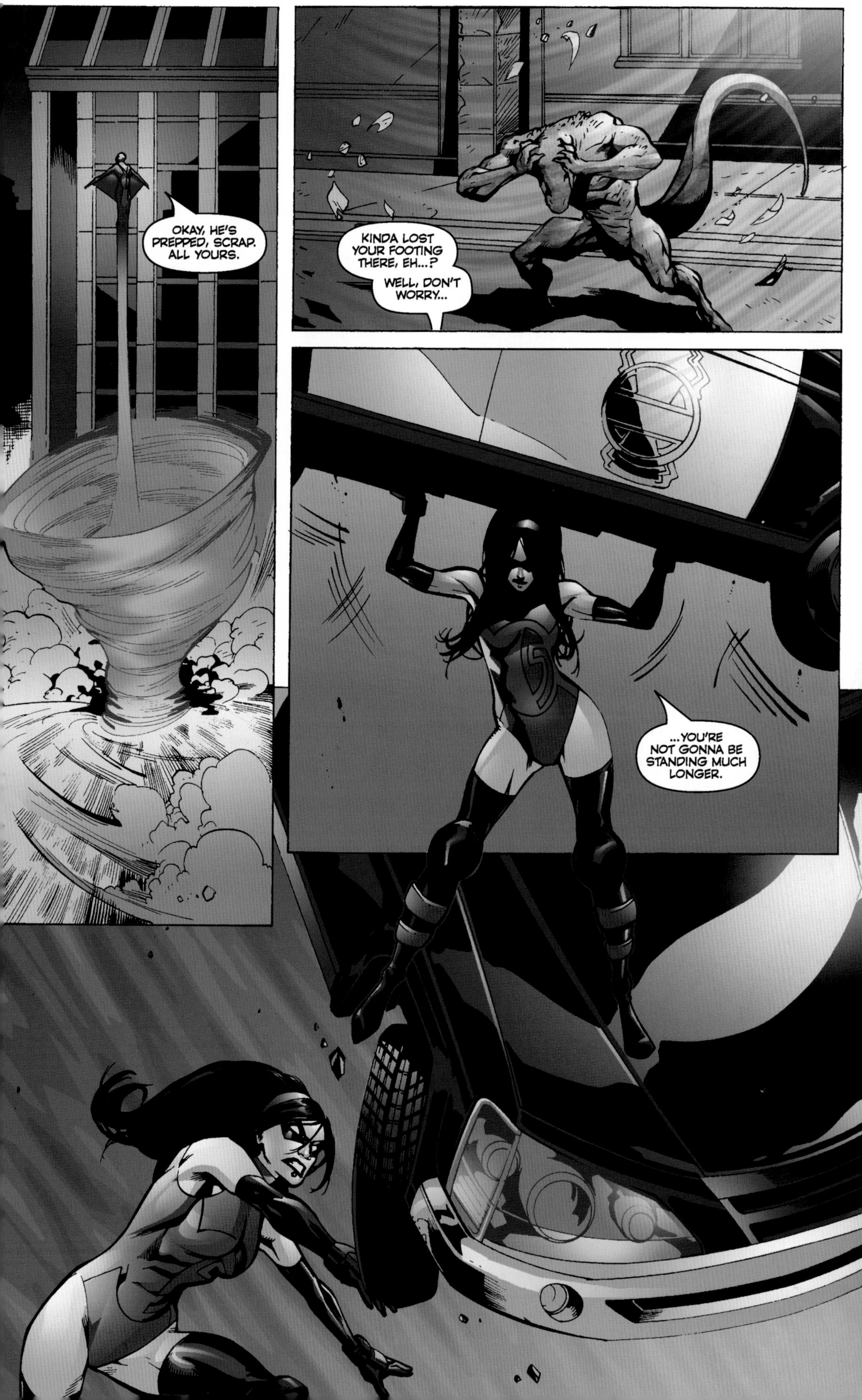

OKAY, HE'S PREPPED, SCRAP. ALL YOURS.
KINDA LOST YOUR FOOTING THERE, EH...?
WELL, DON'T WORRY...
...YOU'RE NOT GONNA BE STANDING MUCH LONGER.

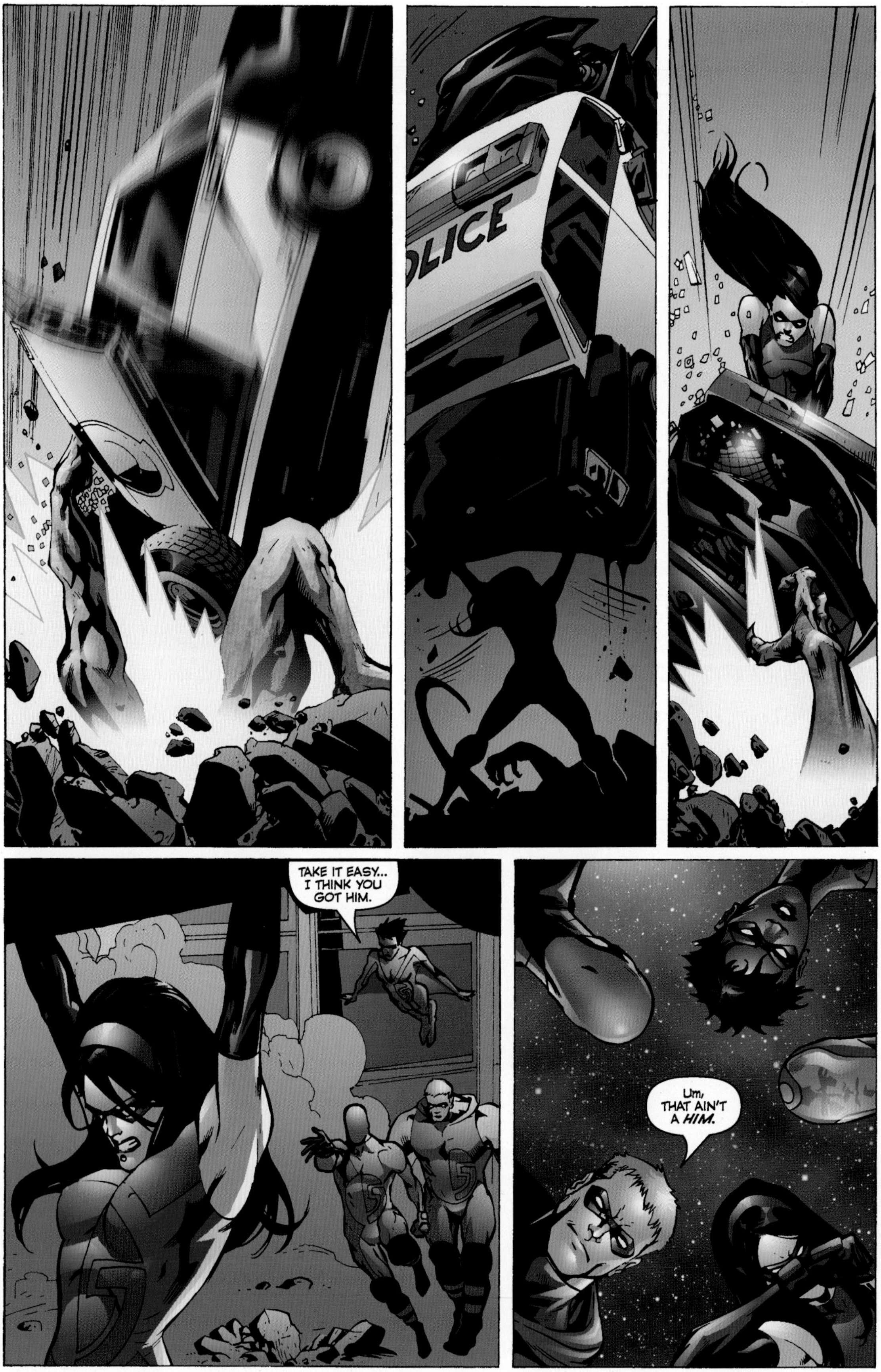
POLICE
TAKE IT EASY... I THINK YOU GOT HIM.
Um, THAT AIN'T A *HIM*.

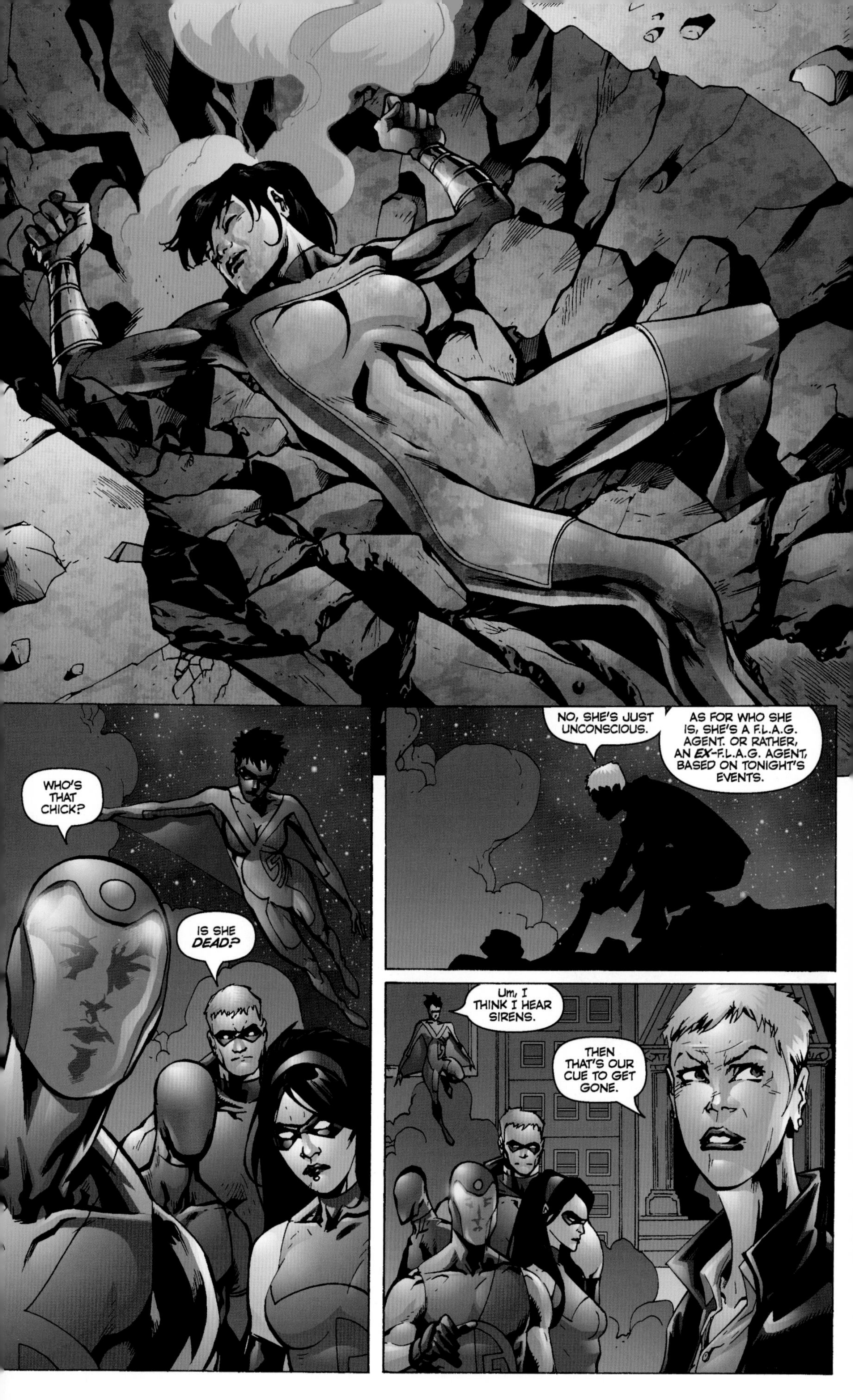
WHO'S THAT CHICK?
IS SHE DEAD?
NO, SHE'S JUST UNCONSCIOUS.
AS FOR WHO SHE IS, SHE'S A F.L.A.G. AGENT. OR RATHER, AN EX-F.L.A.G. AGENT, BASED ON TONIGHT'S EVENTS.
Um, I THINK I HEAR SIRENS.
THEN THAT'S OUR CUE TO GET GONE.

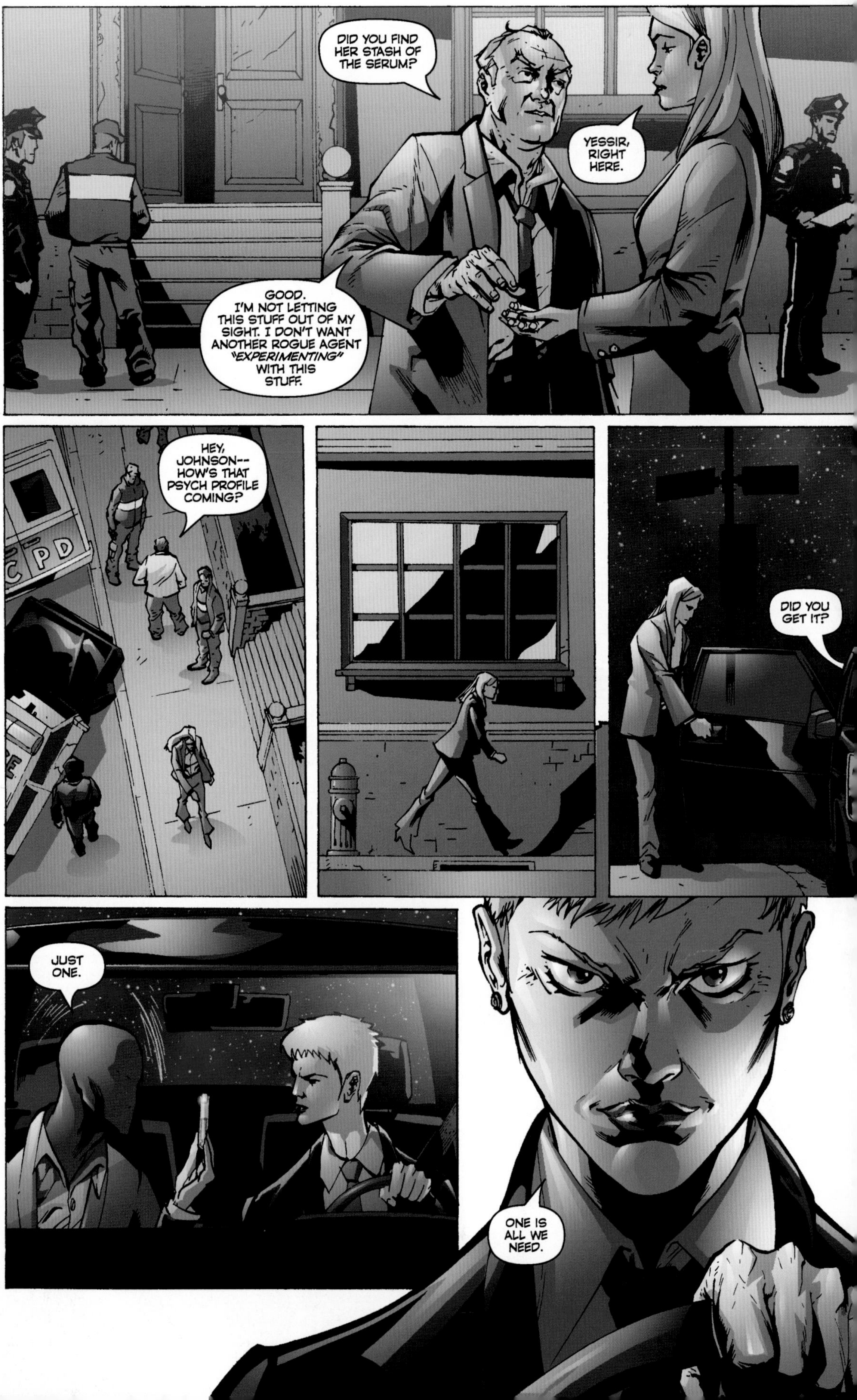
DID YOU FIND HER STASH OF THE SERUM?
YESSIR, RIGHT HERE.
GOOD. I'M NOT LETTING THIS STUFF OUT OF MY SIGHT. I DON'T WANT ANOTHER ROGUE AGENT "EXPERIMENTING" WITH THIS STUFF.
HEY, JOHNSON-- HOW'S THAT PSYCH PROFILE COMING?
CPD
DID YOU GET IT?
JUST ONE.
ONE IS ALL WE NEED.

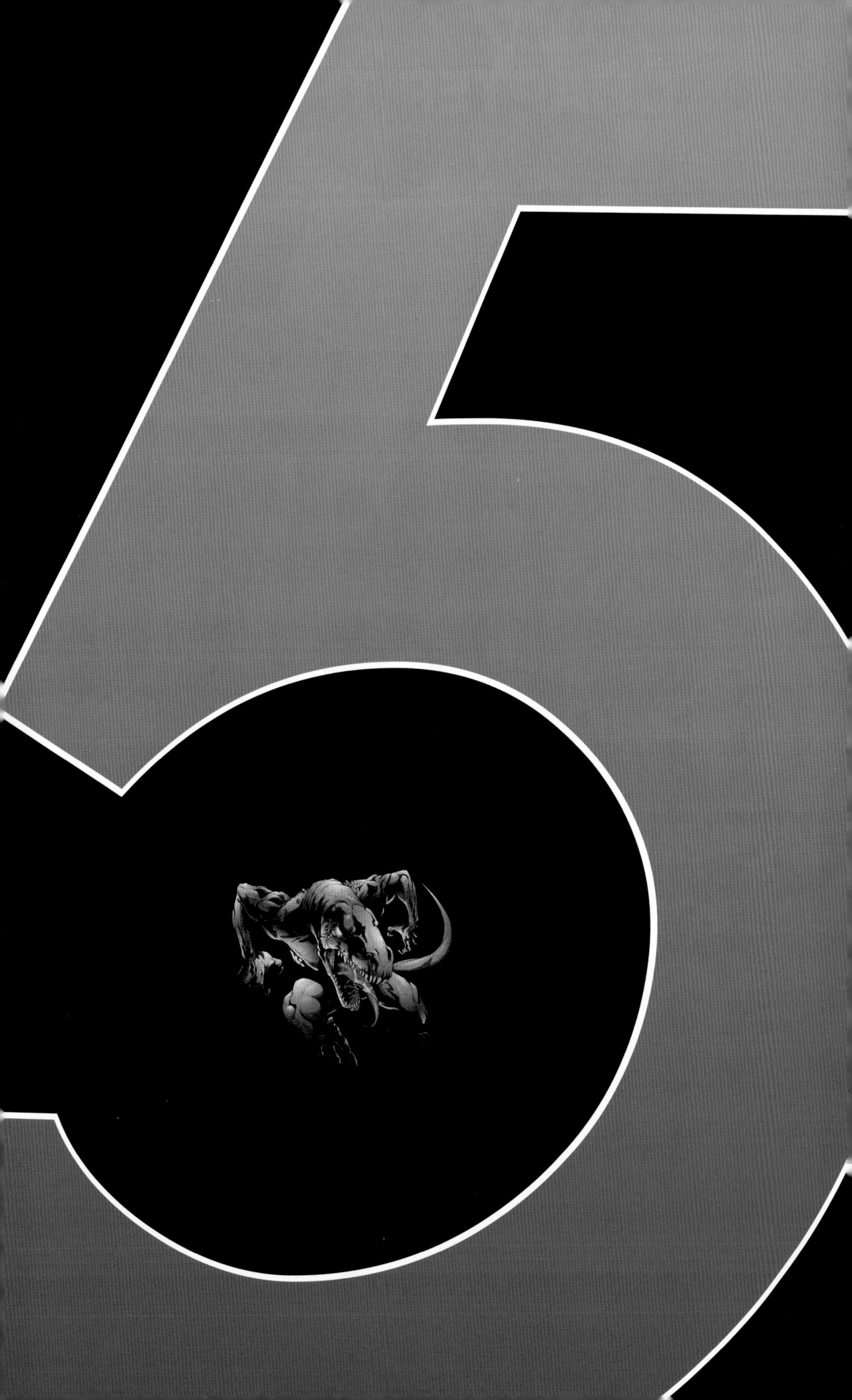
5

CHAPTER THREE

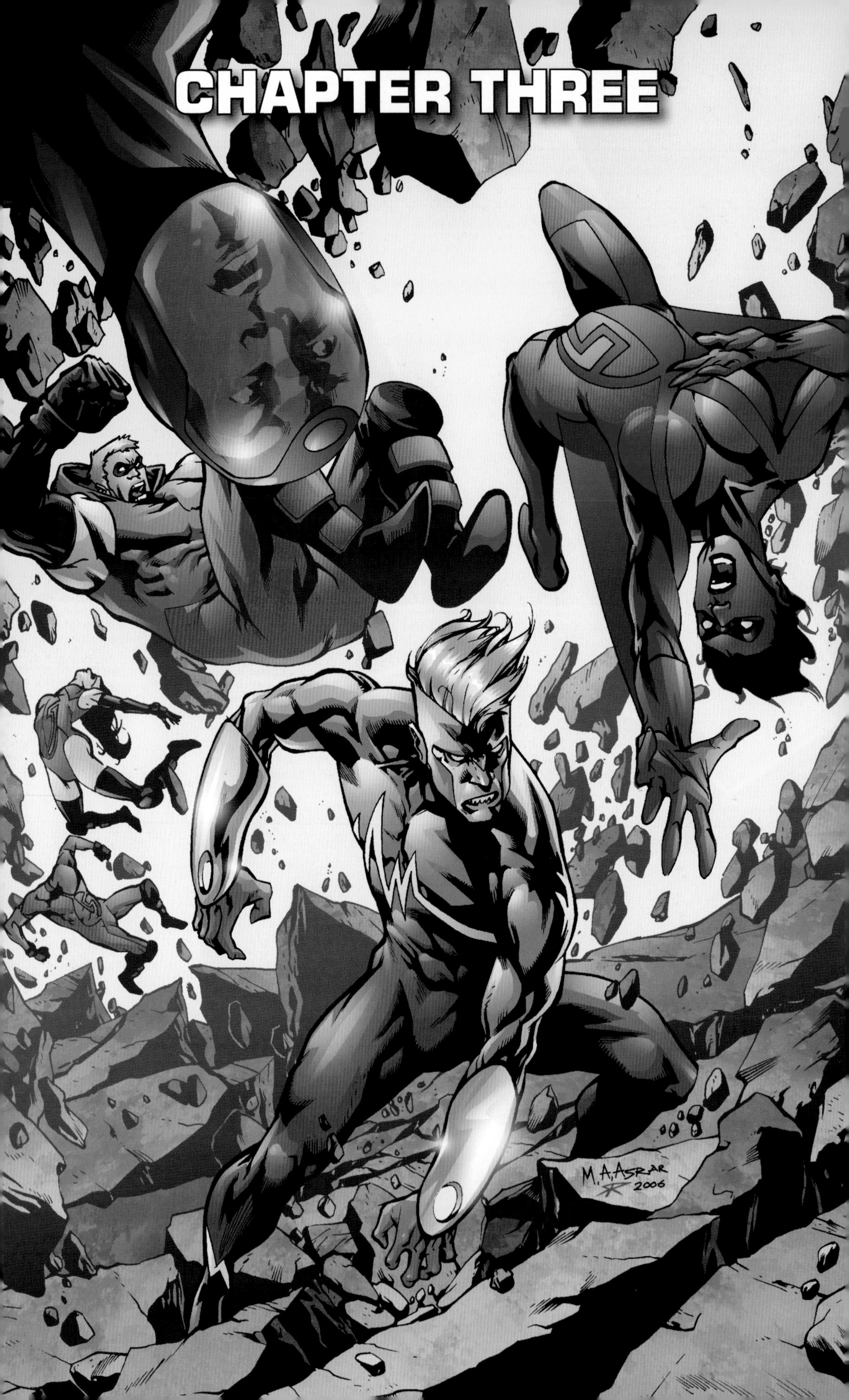
M.A.ASRAR
2006

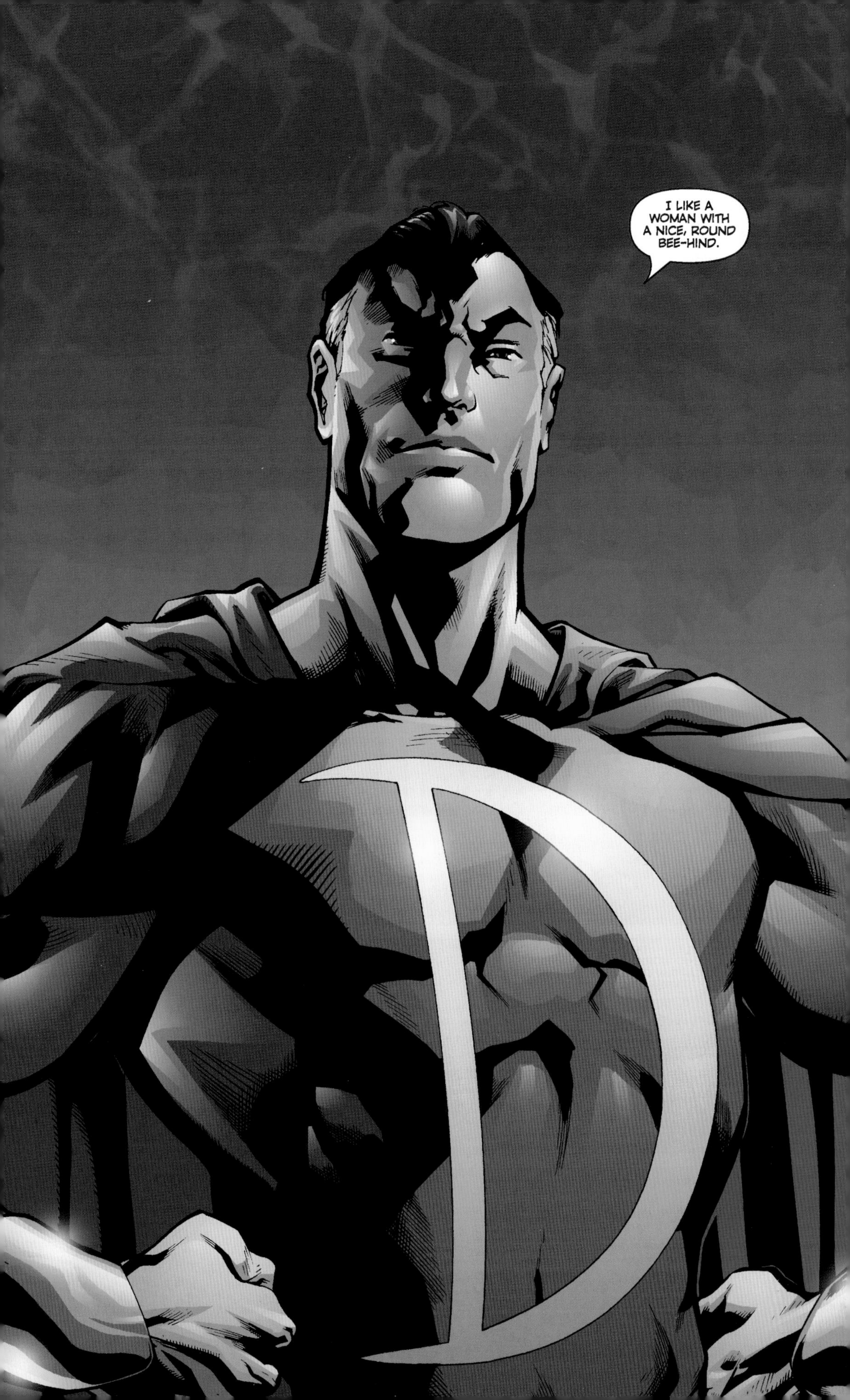
I LIKE A WOMAN WITH A NICE, ROUND BEE-HIND.

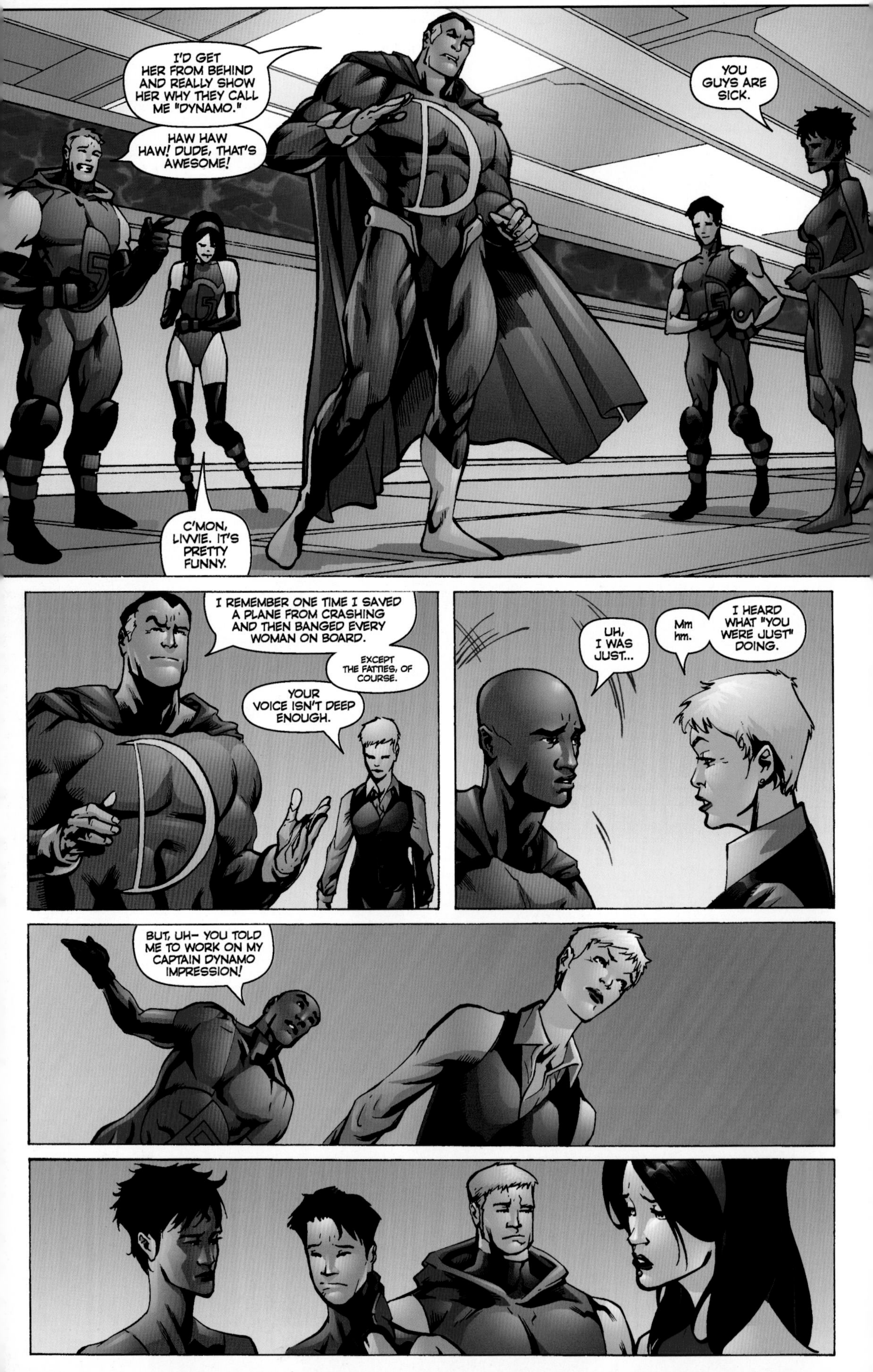
I'D GET HER FROM BEHIND AND REALLY SHOW HER WHY THEY CALL ME "DYNAMO."
HAW HAW HAW! DUDE, THAT'S AWESOME!
YOU GUYS ARE SICK.
C'MON, LIVVIE. IT'S PRETTY FUNNY.
I REMEMBER ONE TIME I SAVED A PLANE FROM CRASHING AND THEN BANGED EVERY WOMAN ON BOARD.
EXCEPT THE FATTIES, OF COURSE.
YOUR VOICE ISN'T DEEP ENOUGH.
UH, I WAS JUST...
Mm hm.
I HEARD WHAT "YOU WERE JUST" DOING.
BUT, UH- YOU TOLD ME TO WORK ON MY CAPTAIN DYNAMO IMPRESSION!

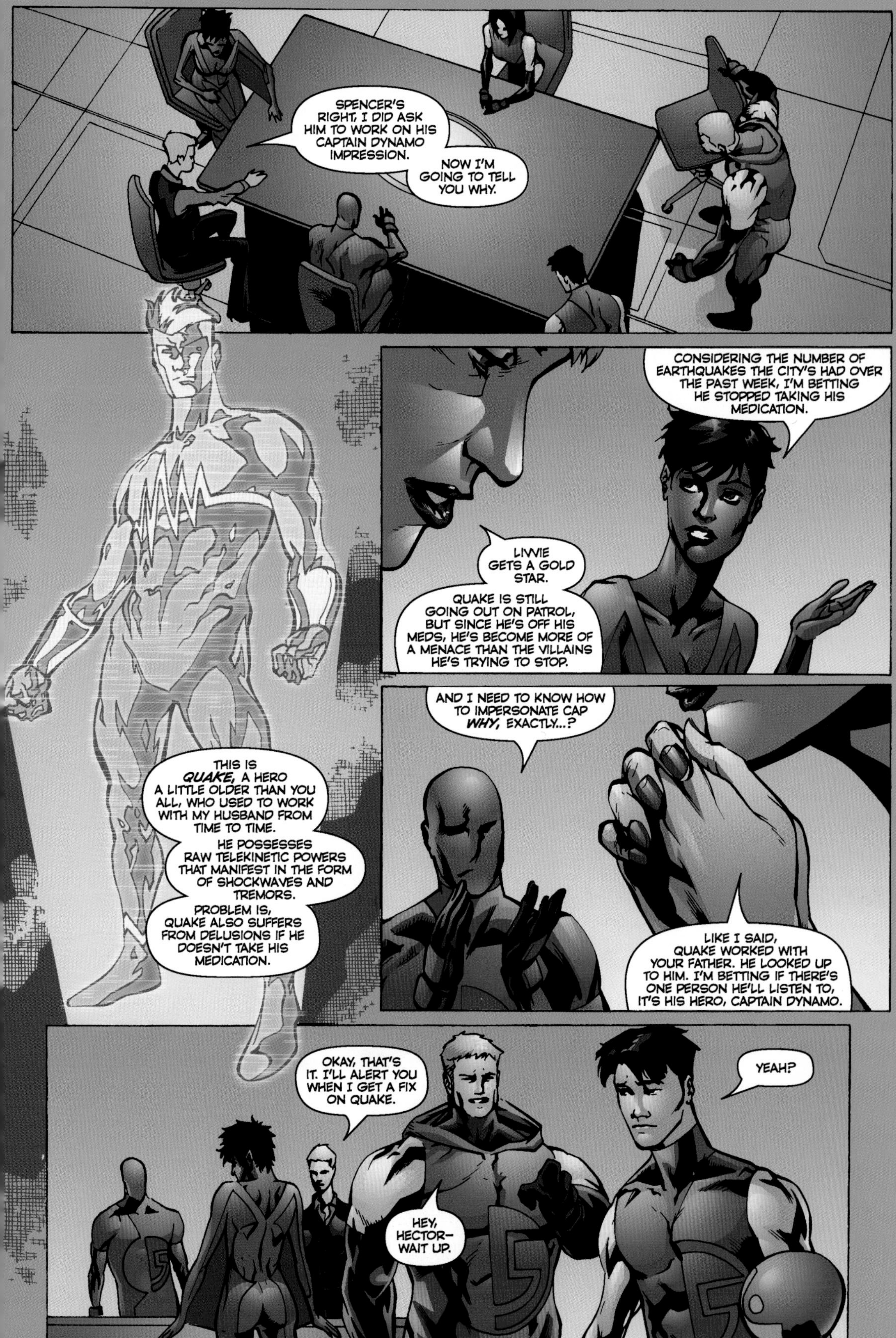
SPENCER'S RIGHT, I DID ASK HIM TO WORK ON HIS CAPTAIN DYNAMO IMPRESSION.
NOW I'M GOING TO TELL YOU WHY.
THIS IS *QUAKE,* A HERO A LITTLE OLDER THAN YOU ALL, WHO USED TO WORK WITH MY HUSBAND FROM TIME TO TIME.
HE POSSESSES RAW TELEKINETIC POWERS THAT MANIFEST IN THE FORM OF SHOCKWAVES AND TREMORS.
PROBLEM IS, QUAKE ALSO SUFFERS FROM DELUSIONS IF HE DOESN'T TAKE HIS MEDICATION.
CONSIDERING THE NUMBER OF EARTHQUAKES THE CITY'S HAD OVER THE PAST WEEK, I'M BETTING HE STOPPED TAKING HIS MEDICATION.
LIVVIE GETS A GOLD STAR.
QUAKE IS STILL GOING OUT ON PATROL, BUT SINCE HE'S OFF HIS MEDS, HE'S BECOME MORE OF A MENACE THAN THE VILLAINS HE'S TRYING TO STOP.
AND I NEED TO KNOW HOW TO IMPERSONATE CAP *WHY,* EXACTLY...?
LIKE I SAID, QUAKE WORKED WITH YOUR FATHER. HE LOOKED UP TO HIM. I'M BETTING IF THERE'S ONE PERSON HE'LL LISTEN TO, IT'S HIS HERO, CAPTAIN DYNAMO.
OKAY, THAT'S IT. I'LL ALERT YOU WHEN I GET A FIX ON QUAKE.
HEY, HECTOR-WAIT UP.
YEAH?

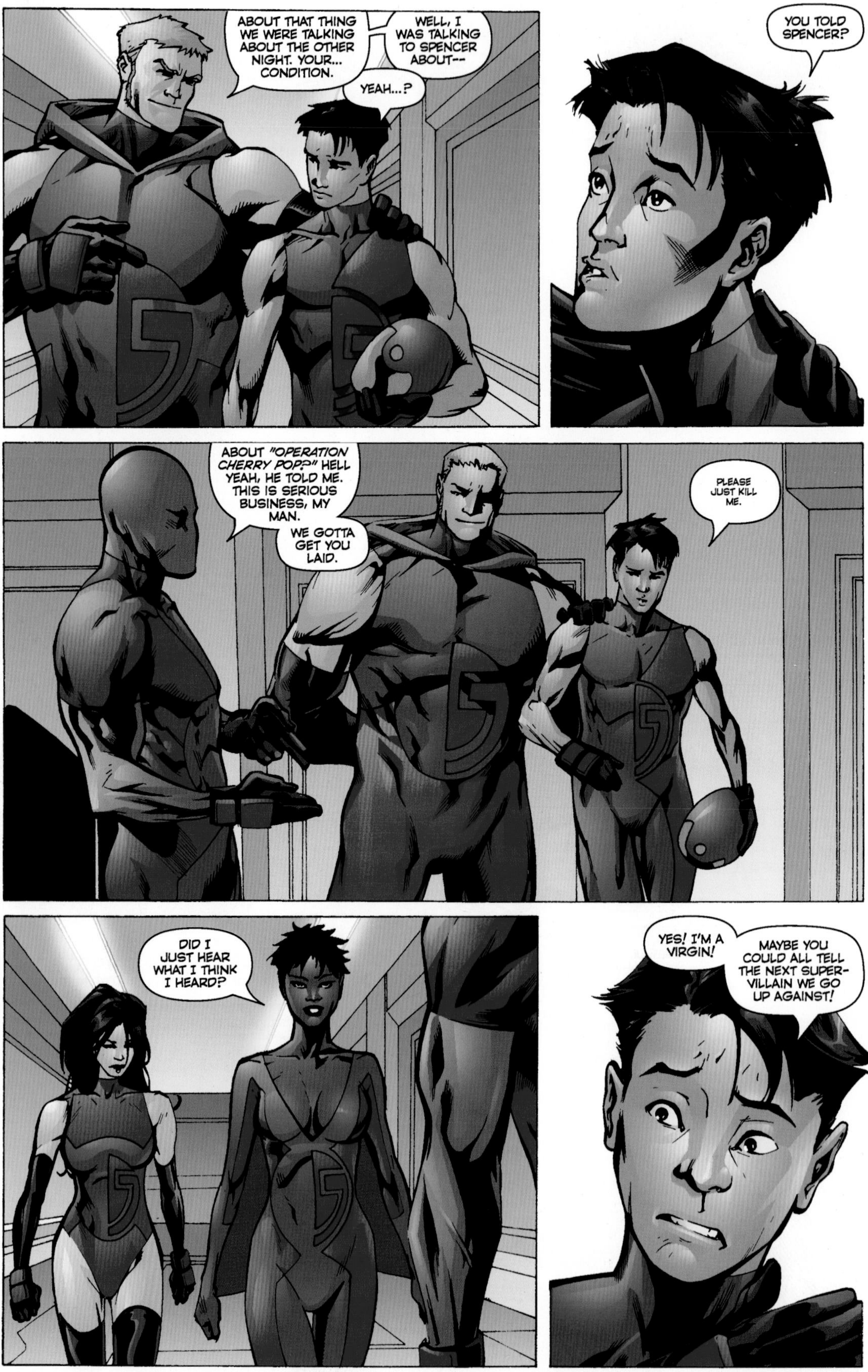
ABOUT THAT THING WE WERE TALKING ABOUT THE OTHER NIGHT. YOUR... CONDITION.
YEAH...?
WELL, I WAS TALKING TO SPENCER ABOUT--
YOU TOLD SPENCER?
ABOUT "OPERATION CHERRY POP?" HELL YEAH, HE TOLD ME. THIS IS SERIOUS BUSINESS, MY MAN.
WE GOTTA GET YOU LAID.
PLEASE JUST KILL ME.
DID I JUST HEAR WHAT I THINK I HEARD?
YES! I'M A VIRGIN!
MAYBE YOU COULD ALL TELL THE NEXT SUPER-VILLAIN WE GO UP AGAINST!

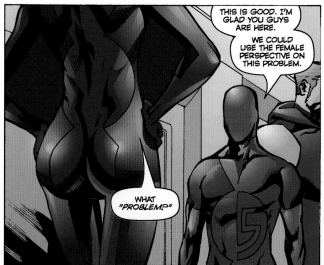

THIS IS GOOD. I'M GLAD YOU GUYS ARE HERE.

WE COULD USE THE FEMALE PERSPECTIVE ON THIS PROBLEM.

WHAT *"PROBLEM?"*

YOU HEARD THE V-WORD, RIGHT?

YES, BUT I DON'T SEE IT AS A PROBLEM.

RIIIGHT.

WHY AM I NOT SURPRISED?

DON'T LISTEN TO THESE TWO, HEC. IT'LL HAPPEN WHEN IT HAPPENS.

RIGHT NOW, THERE ARE FAR MORE IMPORTANT THINGS FOR YOU TO BE WORRIED ABOUT THAN GETTING LAID.

I KNOW, IT'S JUST--

DUDE, JUST WATCH AND LEARN...

HELLOOOO, LADIES.

I MISS BEING AN ONLY CHILD.

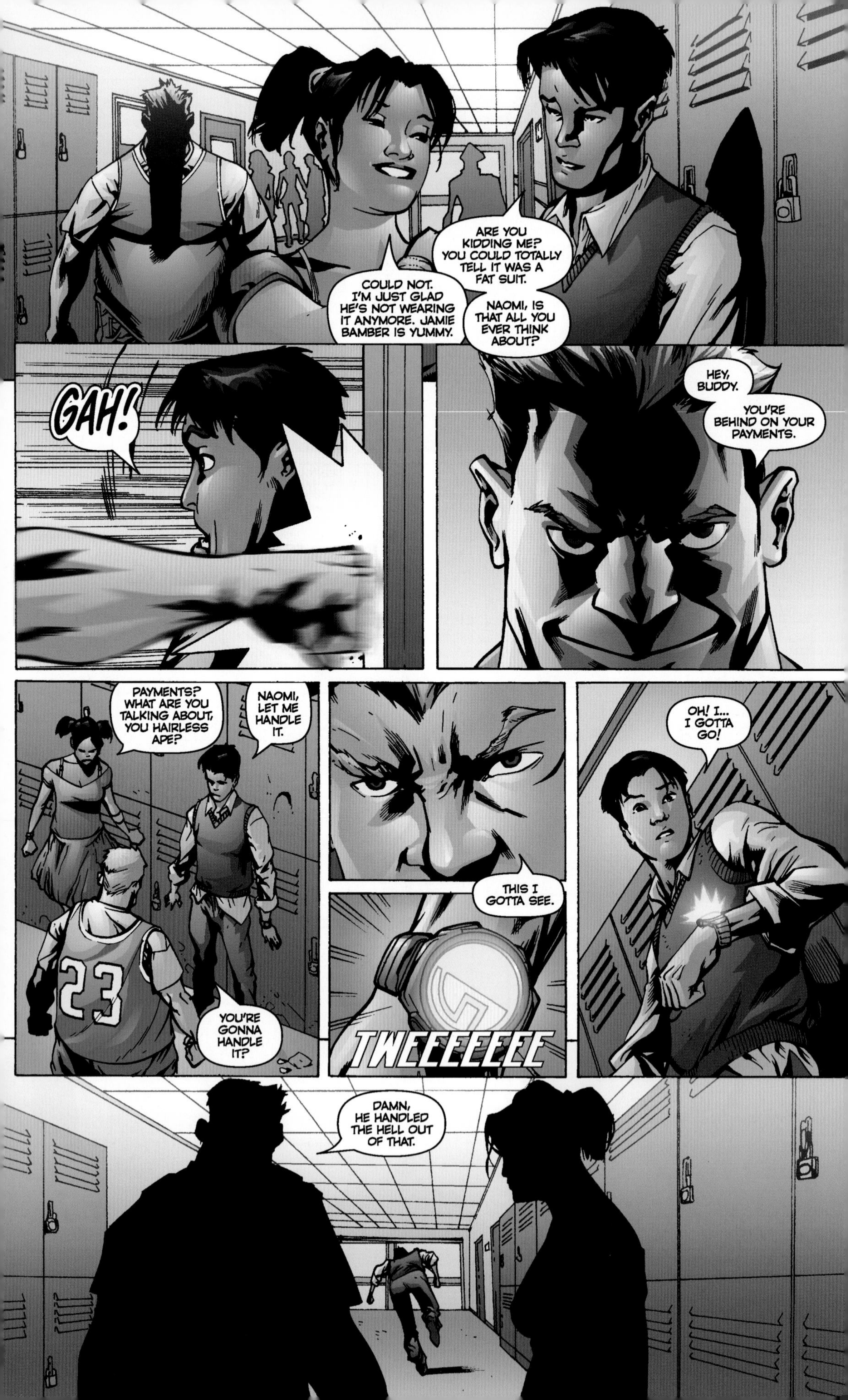
ARE YOU KIDDING ME? YOU COULD TOTALLY TELL IT WAS A FAT SUIT.
COULD NOT. I'M JUST GLAD HE'S NOT WEARING IT ANYMORE. JAMIE BAMBER IS YUMMY.
NAOMI, IS THAT ALL YOU EVER THINK ABOUT?
GAH!
HEY, BUDDY.
YOU'RE BEHIND ON YOUR PAYMENTS.
PAYMENTS? WHAT ARE YOU TALKING ABOUT, YOU HAIRLESS APE?
NAOMI, LET ME HANDLE IT.
YOU'RE GONNA HANDLE IT?
THIS I GOTTA SEE.
TWEEEEEEE
OH! I... I GOTTA GO!
DAMN, HE HANDLED THE HELL OUT OF THAT.

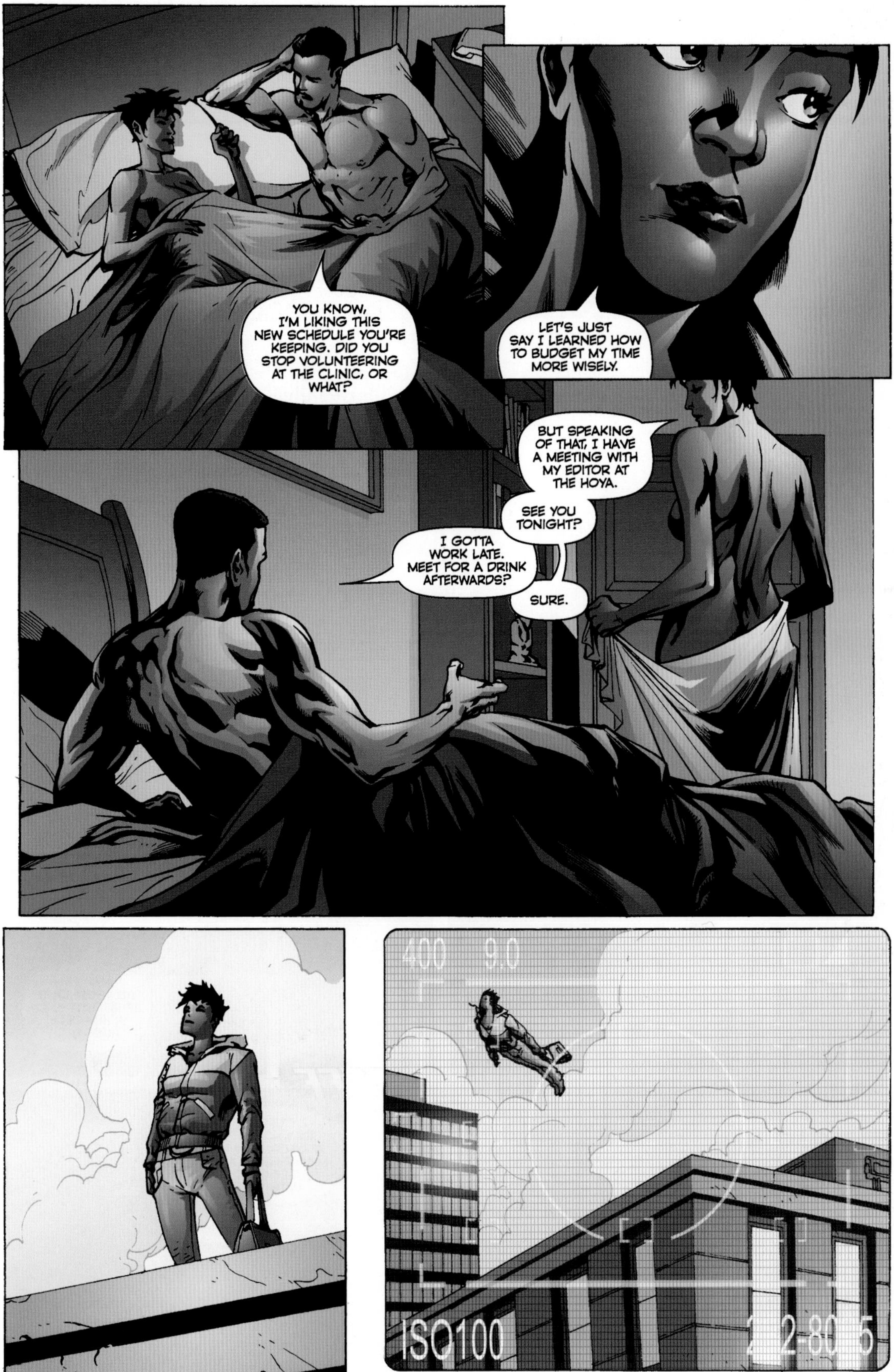
YOU KNOW, I'M LIKING THIS NEW SCHEDULE YOU'RE KEEPING. DID YOU STOP VOLUNTEERING AT THE CLINIC, OR WHAT?
LET'S JUST SAY I LEARNED HOW TO BUDGET MY TIME MORE WISELY.
BUT SPEAKING OF THAT, I HAVE A MEETING WITH MY EDITOR AT THE HOYA.
SEE YOU TONIGHT?
I GOTTA WORK LATE. MEET FOR A DRINK AFTERWARDS?
SURE.
400 9.0
ISO100

THANK YOU KINDLY, MR. MAYOR. IT'S WITH GREAT PRIDE...
...THAT I ACCEPT THIS KEY TO THE CITY.
THE PEOPLE OF TOWER CITY ARE TRULY ADMIRABLE. IF MORE PEOPLE FOLLOWED YOUR EXAMPLE OF HONESTY AND GOODWILL TOWARDS ONE ANOTHER, THE WORLD WOULDN'T NEED PEOPLE LIKE ME.
AND I'M AN ENORMOUS HYPOCRITE AND A HORRIBLE HUSBAND.
I SPEND MY WHOLE LIFE WONDERING WHO MY FATHER IS, AND I GET STUCK WITH YOU.
HOORAY FOR ME.

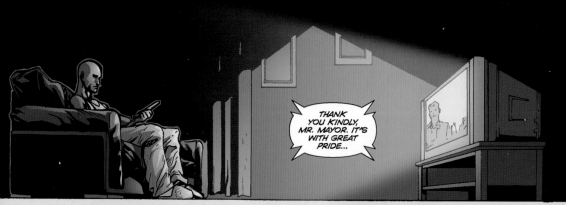

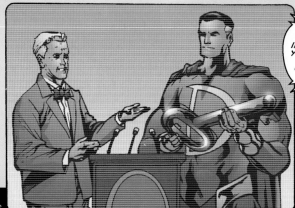

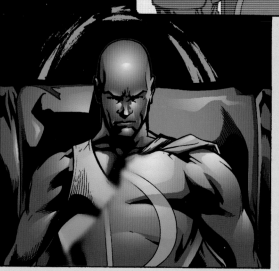

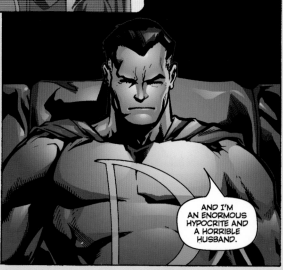

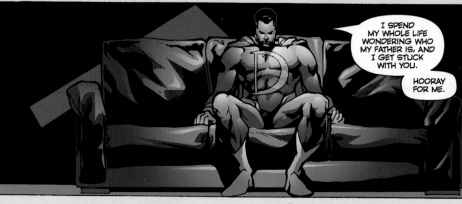

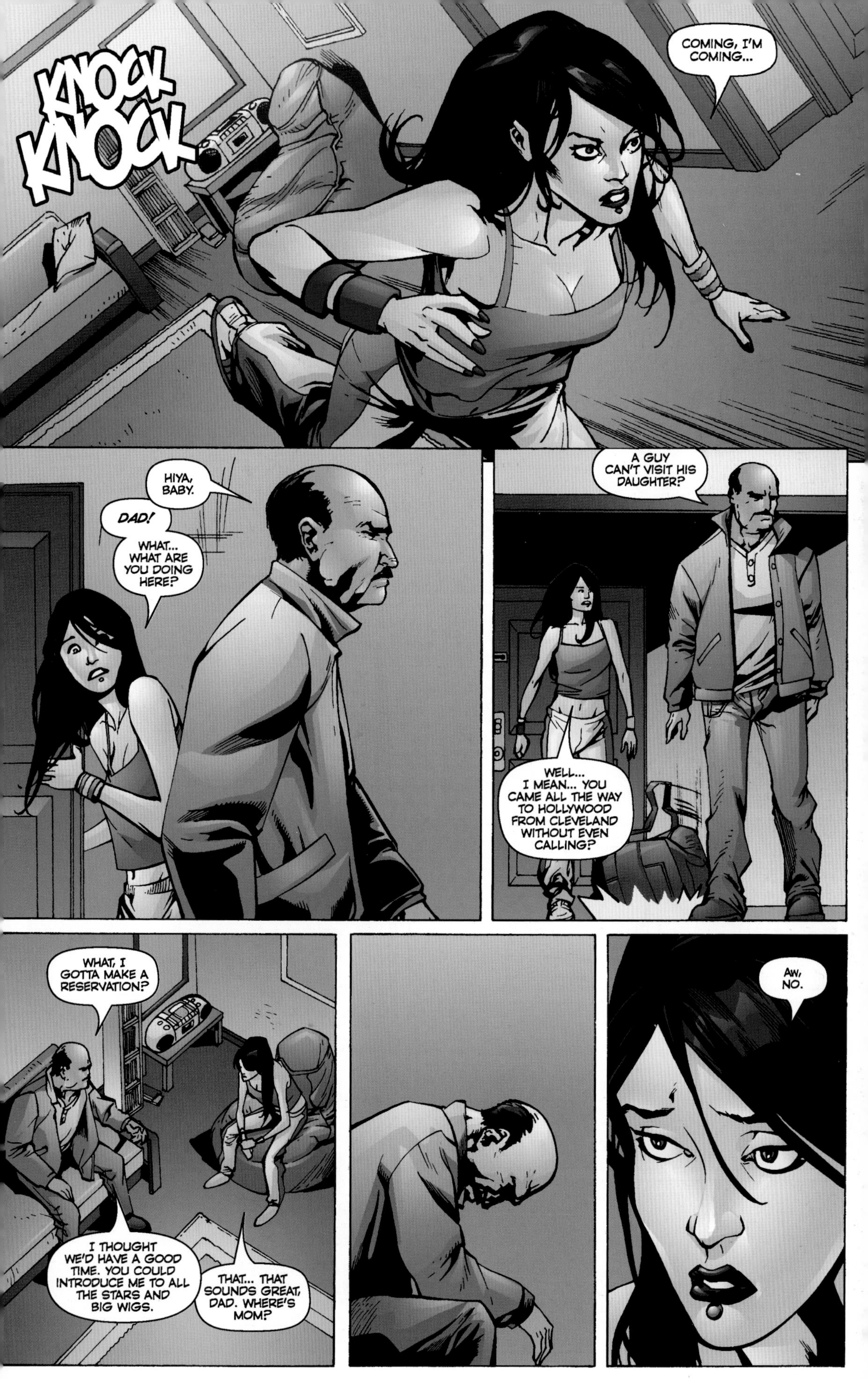
KNOCK KNOCK
COMING, I'M COMING...
HIYA, BABY.
DAD!
WHAT... WHAT ARE YOU DOING HERE?
A GUY CAN'T VISIT HIS DAUGHTER?
WELL... I MEAN... YOU CAME ALL THE WAY TO HOLLYWOOD FROM CLEVELAND WITHOUT EVEN CALLING?
WHAT, I GOTTA MAKE A RESERVATION?
I THOUGHT WE'D HAVE A GOOD TIME. YOU COULD INTRODUCE ME TO ALL THE STARS AND BIG WIGS.
THAT... THAT SOUNDS GREAT, DAD. WHERE'S MOM?
AW, NO.

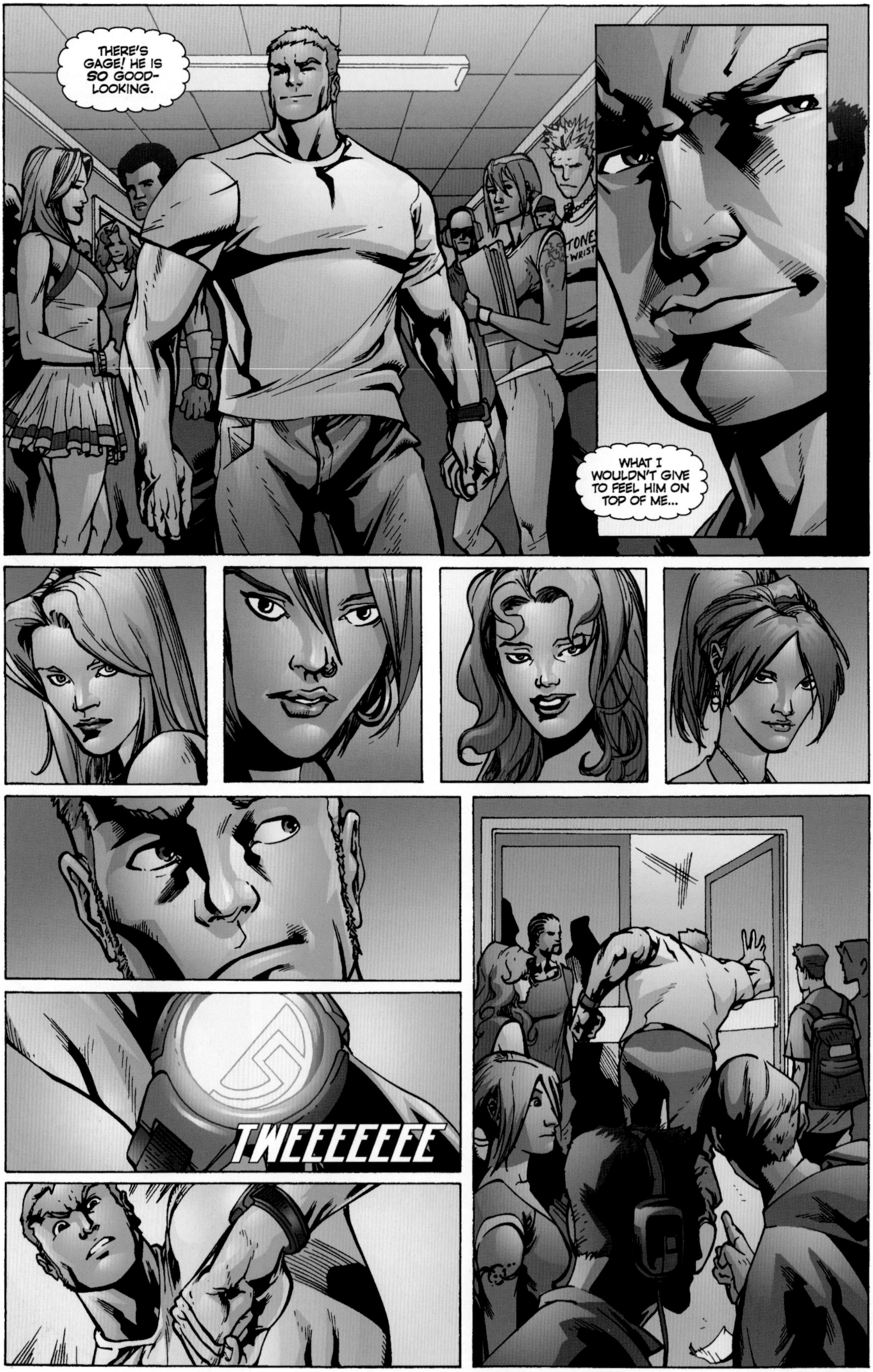

THERE'S GAGE! HE IS SO GOOD-LOOKING.
WHAT I WOULDN'T GIVE TO FEEL HIM ON TOP OF ME...
TWEEEEEEE

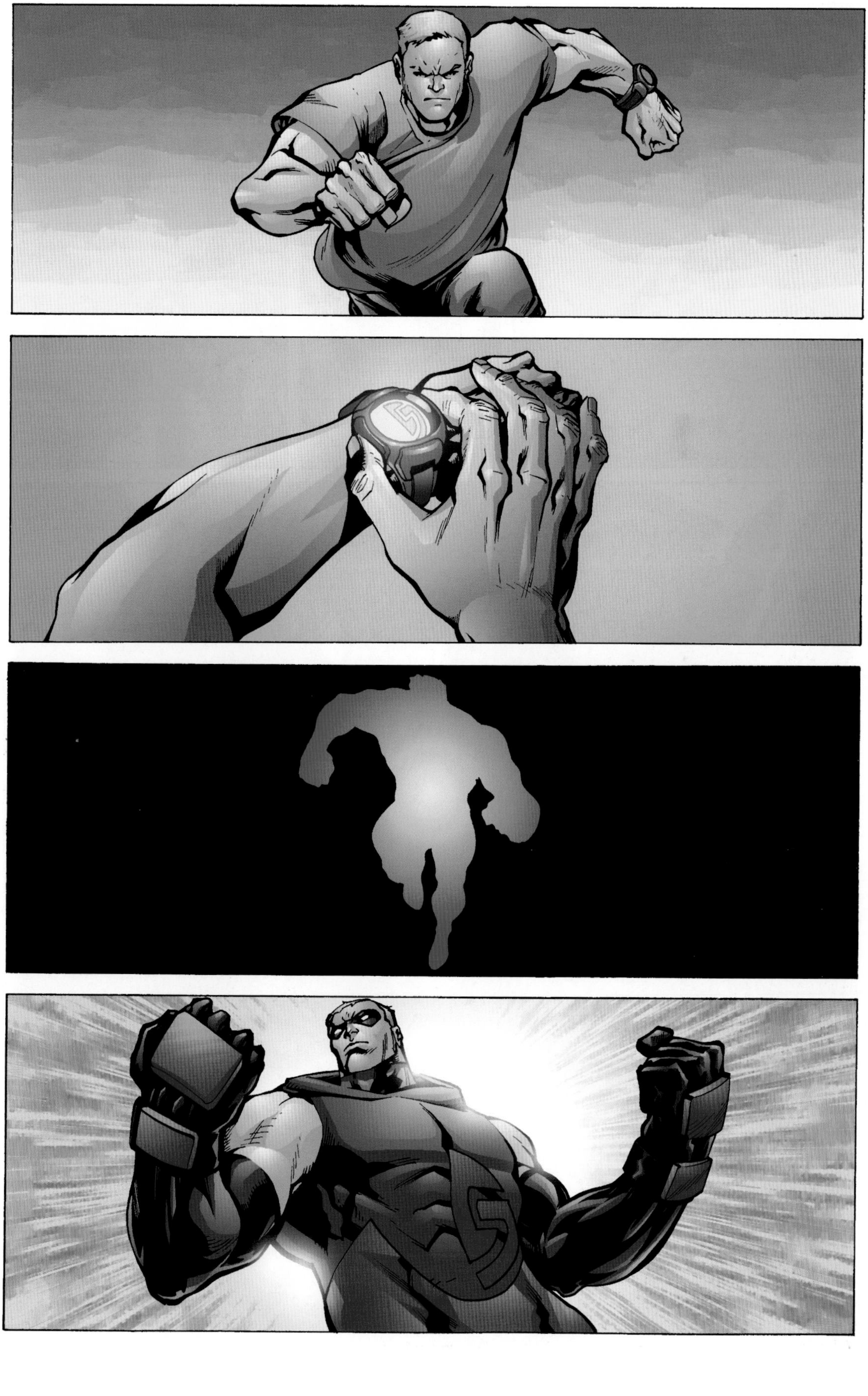

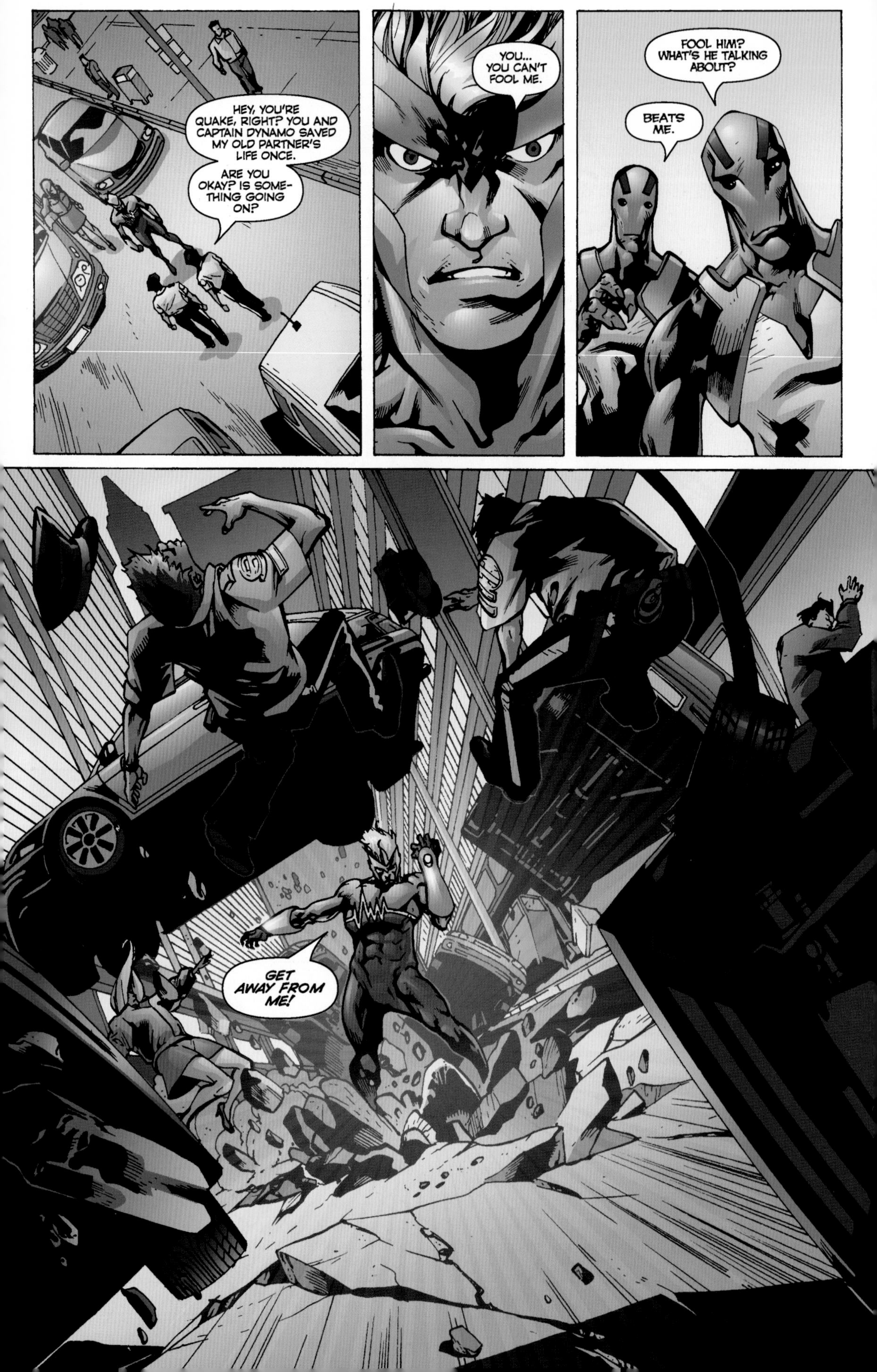
HEY, YOU'RE QUAKE, RIGHT? YOU AND CAPTAIN DYNAMO SAVED MY OLD PARTNER'S LIFE ONCE.
ARE YOU OKAY? IS SOMETHING GOING ON?
YOU... YOU CAN'T FOOL ME.
FOOL HIM? WHAT'S HE TALKING ABOUT?
BEATS ME.
GET AWAY FROM ME!

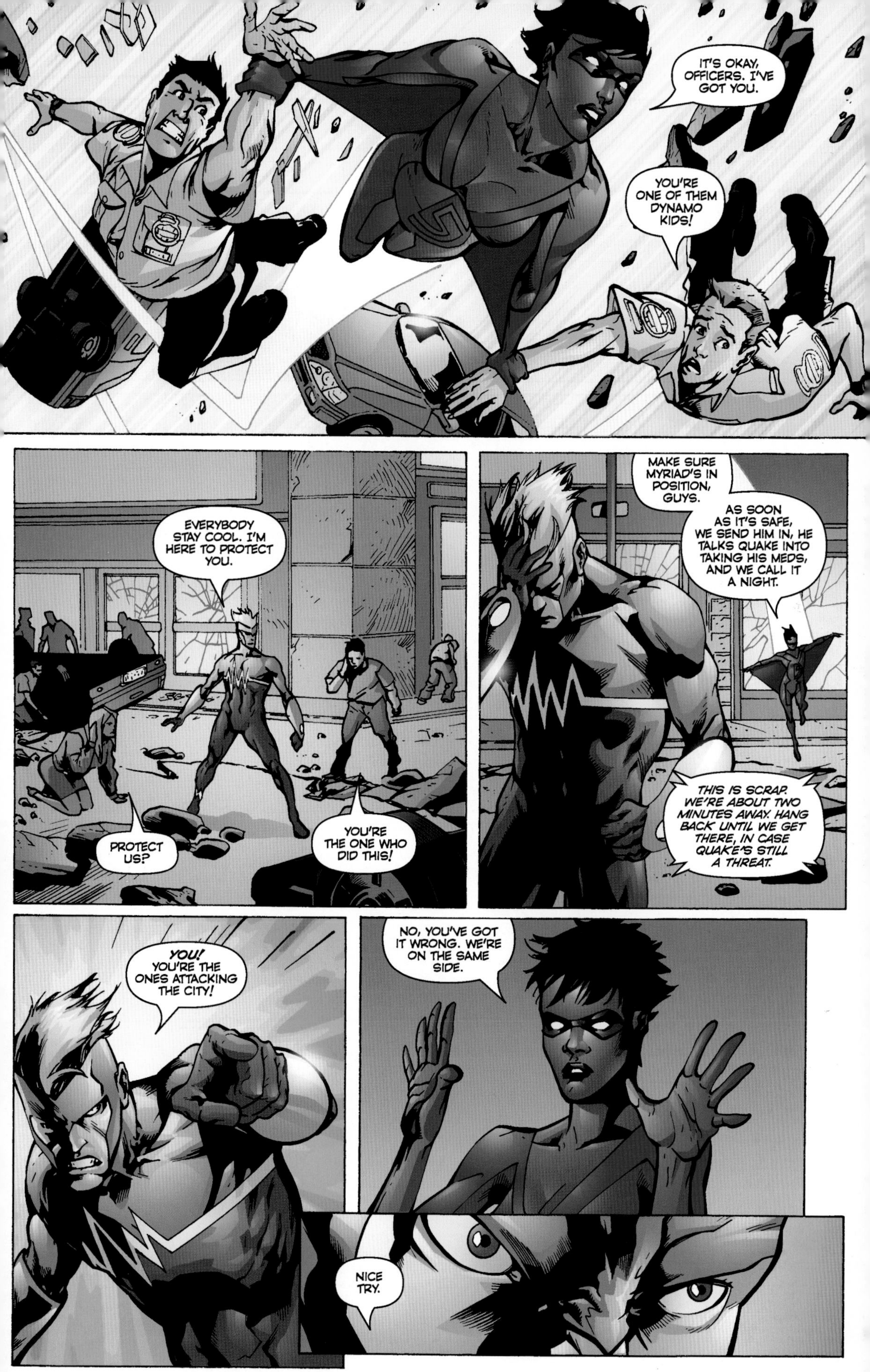
IT'S OKAY, OFFICERS. I'VE GOT YOU.
YOU'RE ONE OF THEM DYNAMO KIDS!
EVERYBODY STAY COOL. I'M HERE TO PROTECT YOU.
PROTECT US?
YOU'RE THE ONE WHO DID THIS!
MAKE SURE MYRIAD'S IN POSITION, GUYS.
AS SOON AS IT'S SAFE, WE SEND HIM IN, HE TALKS QUAKE INTO TAKING HIS MEDS, AND WE CALL IT A NIGHT.
THIS IS SCRAP. WE'RE ABOUT TWO MINUTES AWAY. HANG BACK UNTIL WE GET THERE, IN CASE QUAKE'S STILL A THREAT.
YOU! YOU'RE THE ONES ATTACKING THE CITY!
NO, YOU'VE GOT IT WRONG. WE'RE ON THE SAME SIDE.
NICE TRY.

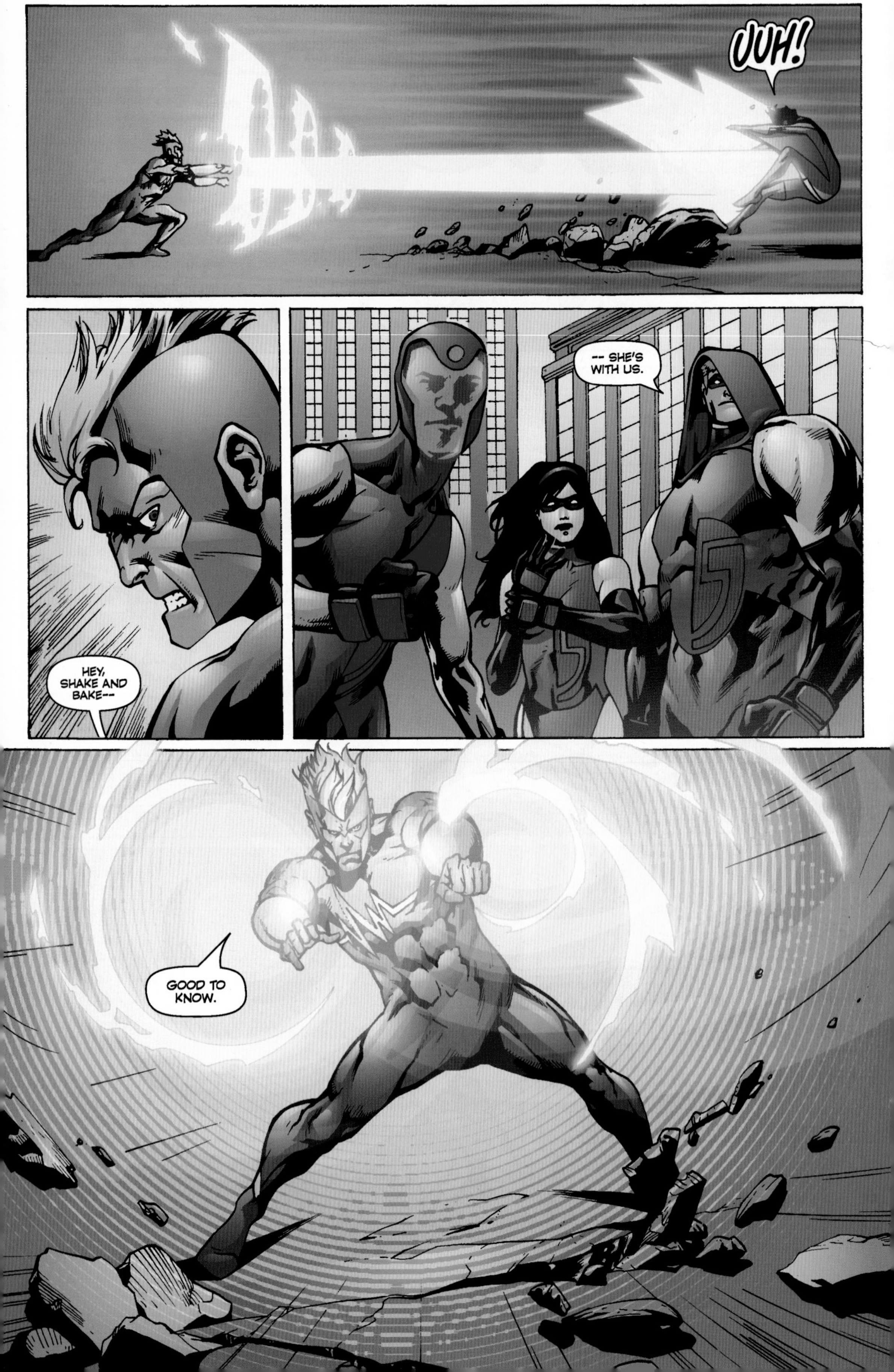
UUH!
HEY, SHAKE AND BAKE--
-- SHE'S WITH US.
GOOD TO KNOW.

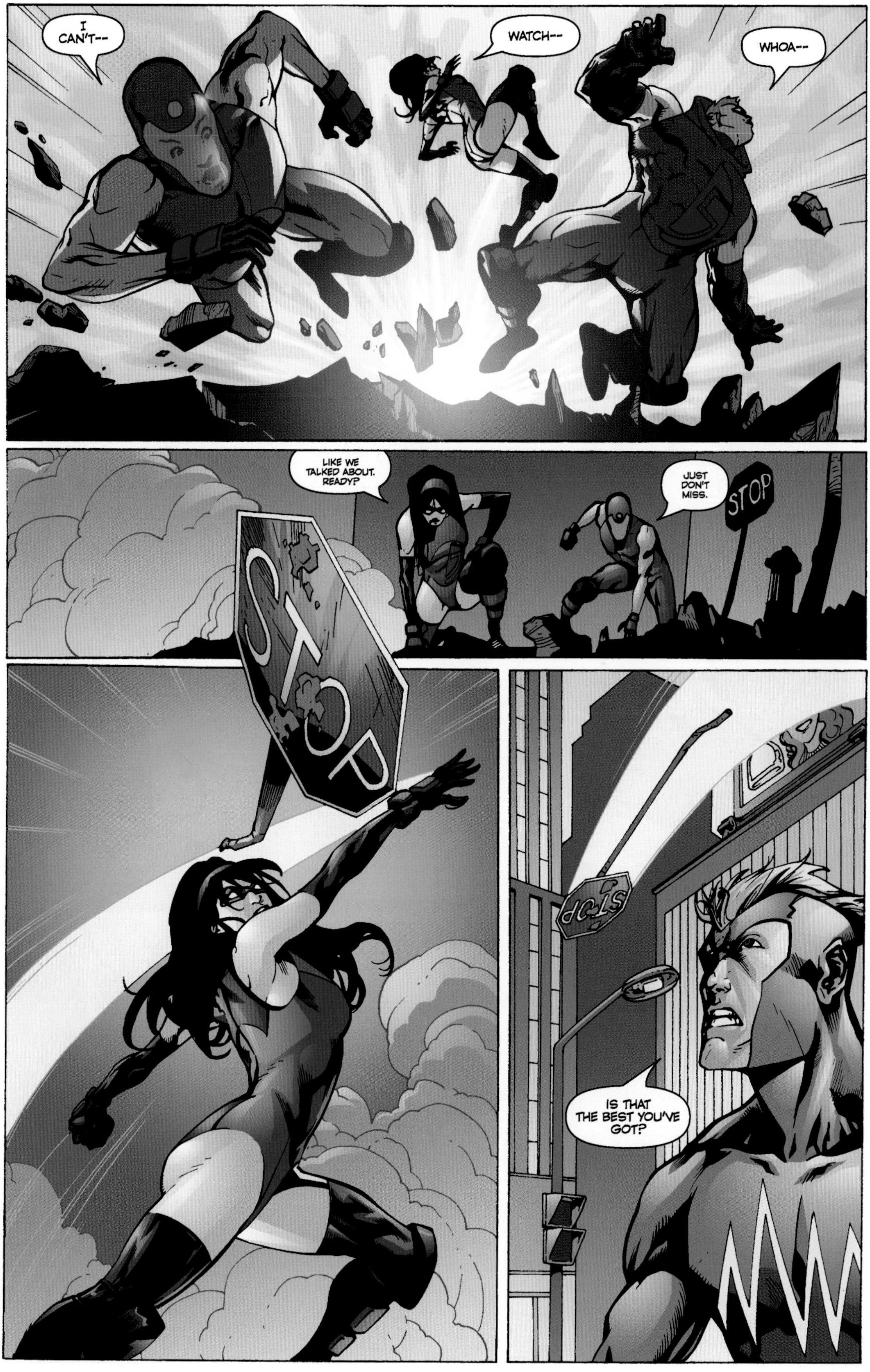
I CAN'T--
WATCH--
WHOA--
LIKE WE TALKED ABOUT. READY?
JUST DON'T MISS.
STOP
STOP
IS THAT THE BEST YOU'VE GOT?

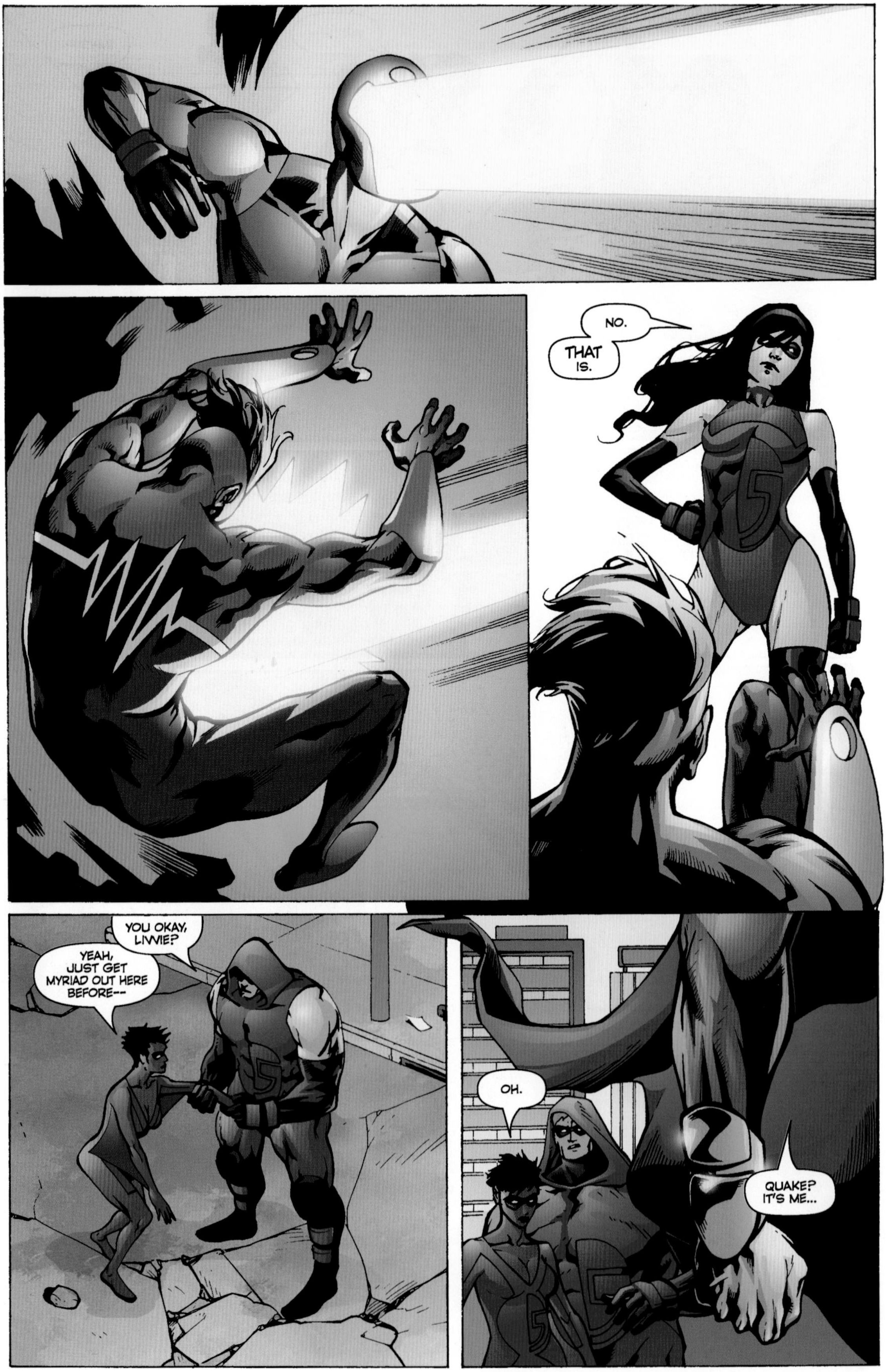
NO.
THAT IS.
YOU OKAY, LIVVIE?
YEAH, JUST GET MYRIAD OUT HERE BEFORE--
OH.
QUAKE? IT'S ME...

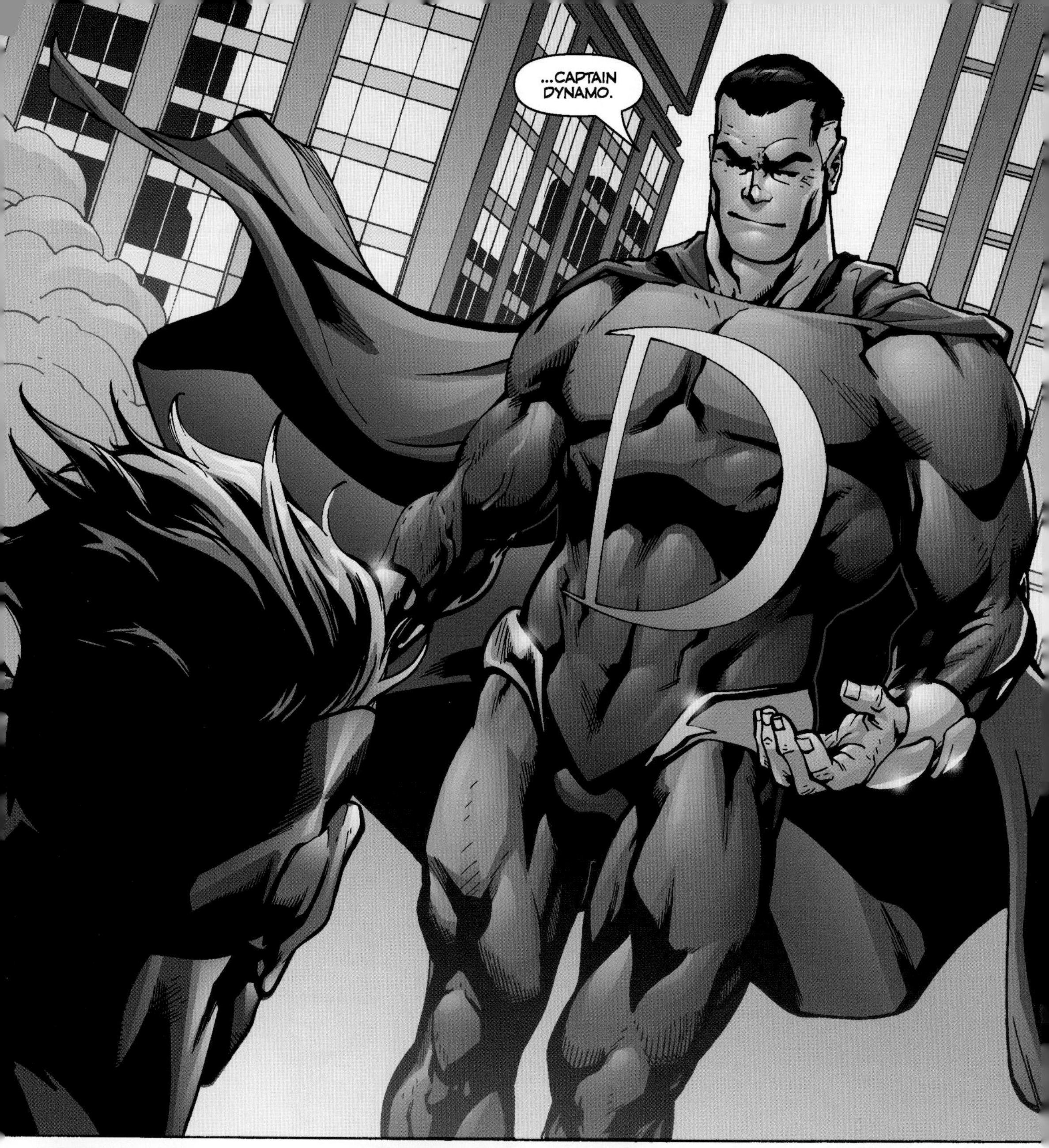
...CAPTAIN
DYNAMO.

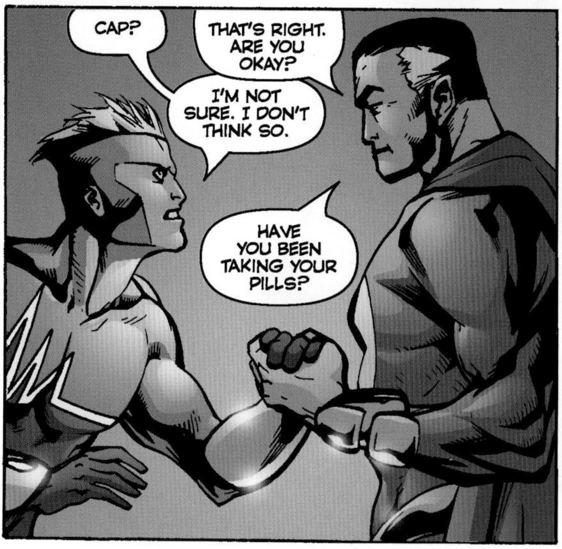
CAP?
THAT'S RIGHT. ARE YOU OKAY?
I'M NOT SURE. I DON'T THINK SO.
HAVE YOU BEEN TAKING YOUR PILLS?

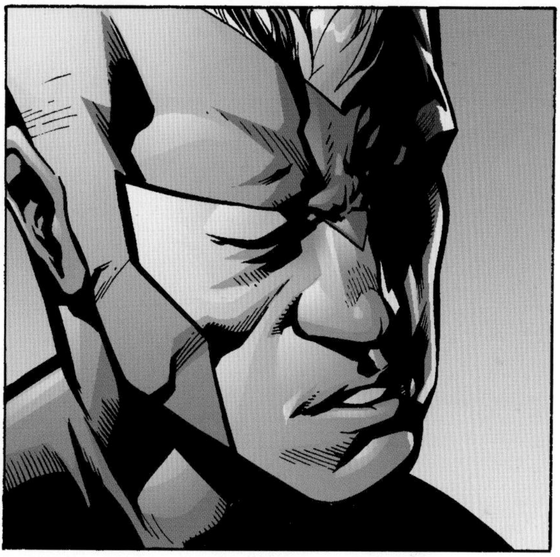

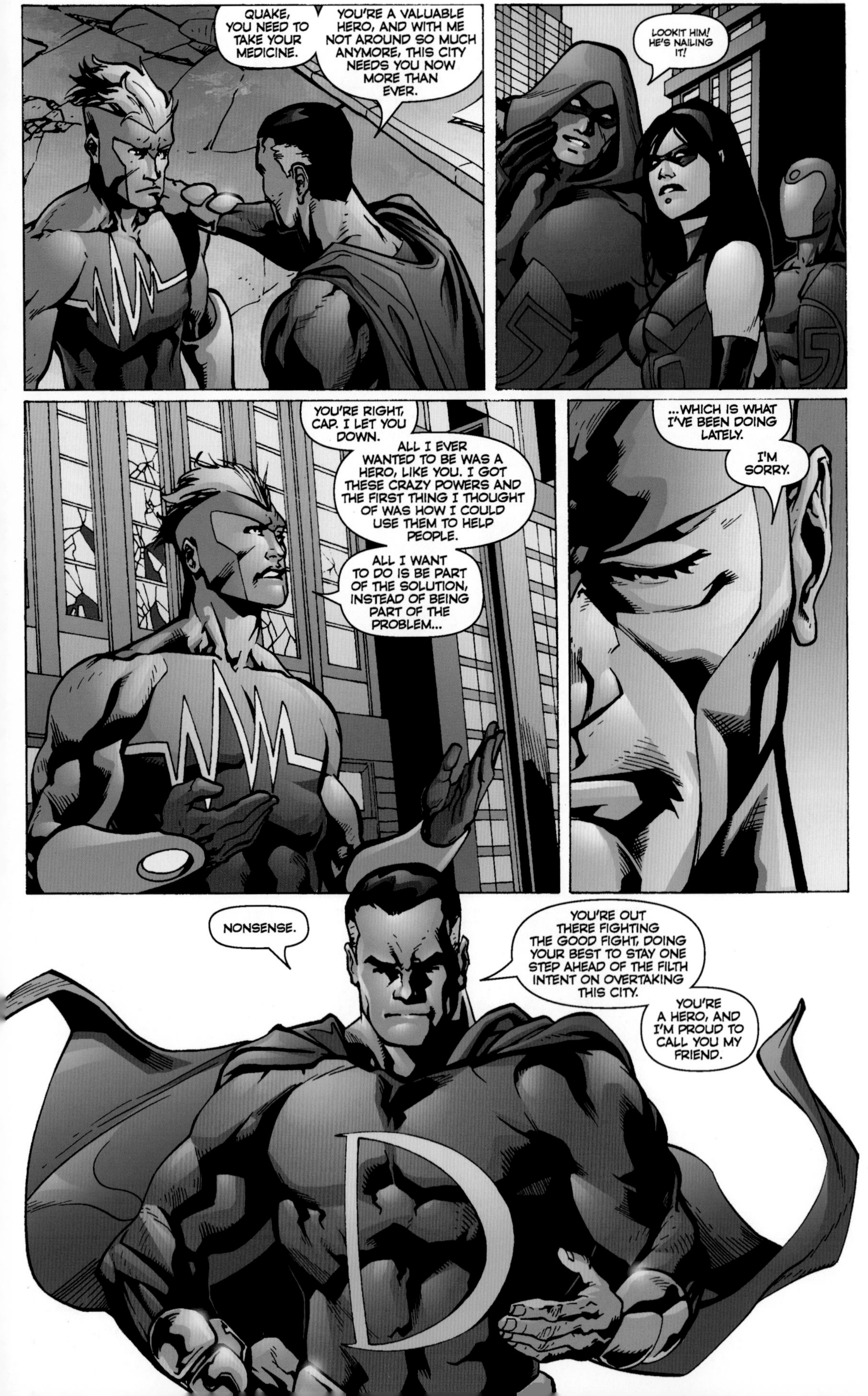
QUAKE, YOU NEED TO TAKE YOUR MEDICINE.
YOU'RE A VALUABLE HERO, AND WITH ME NOT AROUND SO MUCH ANYMORE, THIS CITY NEEDS YOU NOW MORE THAN EVER.
LOOKIT HIM! HE'S NAILING IT!
YOU'RE RIGHT, CAP. I LET YOU DOWN.
ALL I EVER WANTED TO BE WAS A HERO, LIKE YOU. I GOT THESE CRAZY POWERS AND THE FIRST THING I THOUGHT OF WAS HOW I COULD USE THEM TO HELP PEOPLE.
ALL I WANT TO DO IS BE PART OF THE SOLUTION, INSTEAD OF BEING PART OF THE PROBLEM...
...WHICH IS WHAT I'VE BEEN DOING LATELY.
I'M SORRY.
NONSENSE.
YOU'RE OUT THERE FIGHTING THE GOOD FIGHT, DOING YOUR BEST TO STAY ONE STEP AHEAD OF THE FILTH INTENT ON OVERTAKING THIS CITY.
YOU'RE A HERO, AND I'M PROUD TO CALL YOU MY FRIEND.

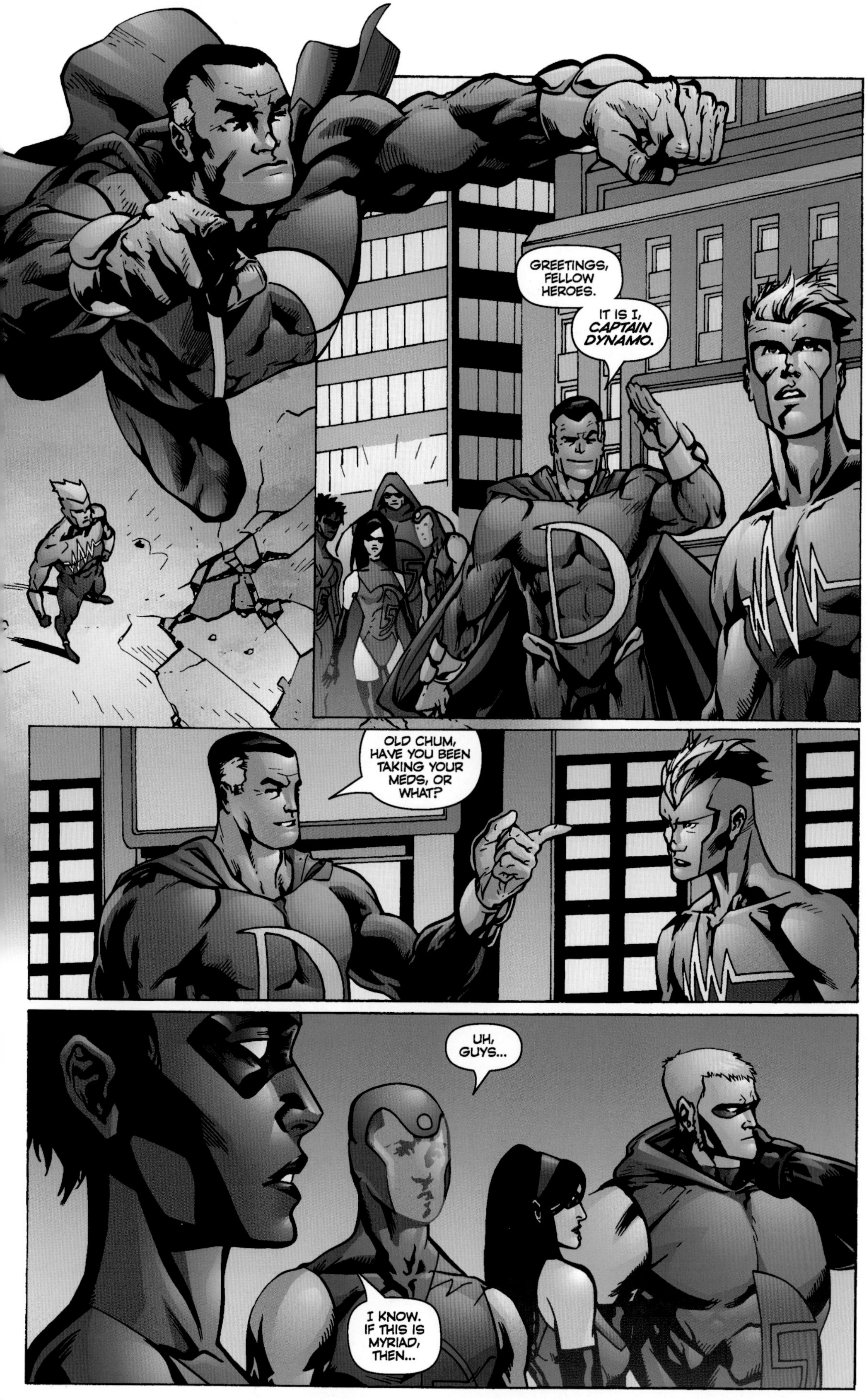
GREETINGS, FELLOW HEROES.
IT IS I, CAPTAIN DYNAMO.
OLD CHUM, HAVE YOU BEEN TAKING YOUR MEDS, OR WHAT?
UH, GUYS...
I KNOW. IF THIS IS MYRIAD, THEN...

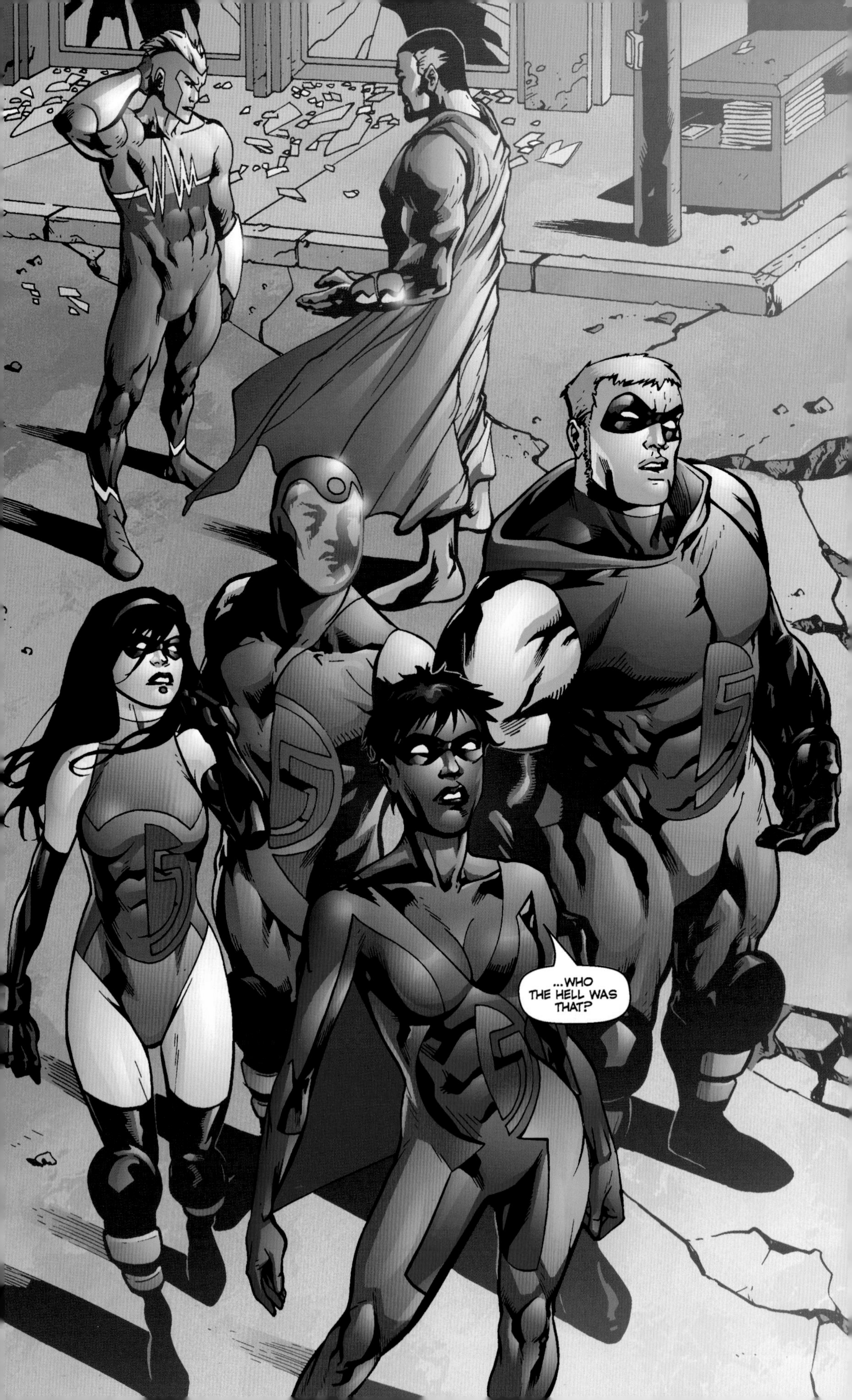
...WHO THE HELL WAS THAT?

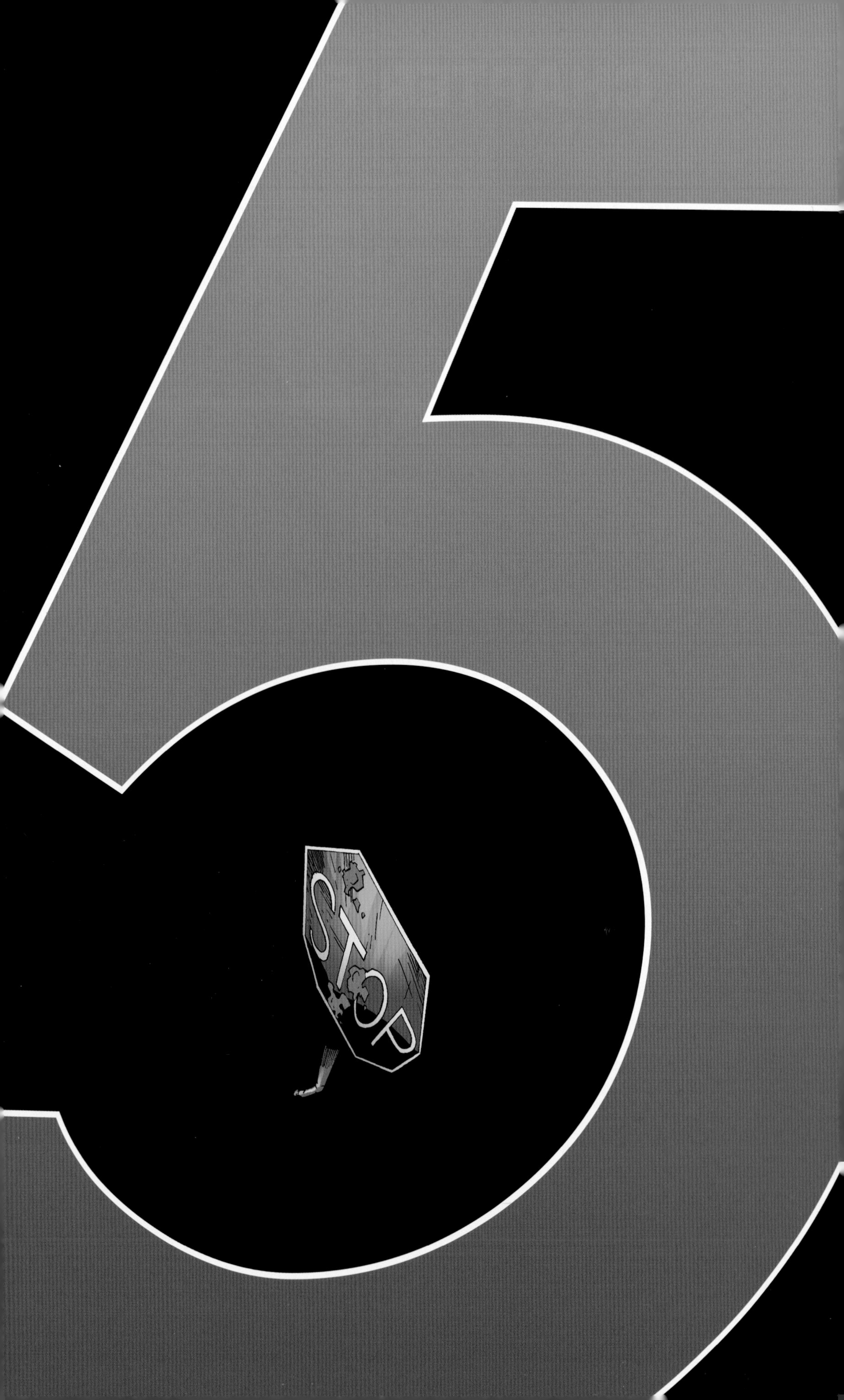
STOP

CHAPTER FOUR

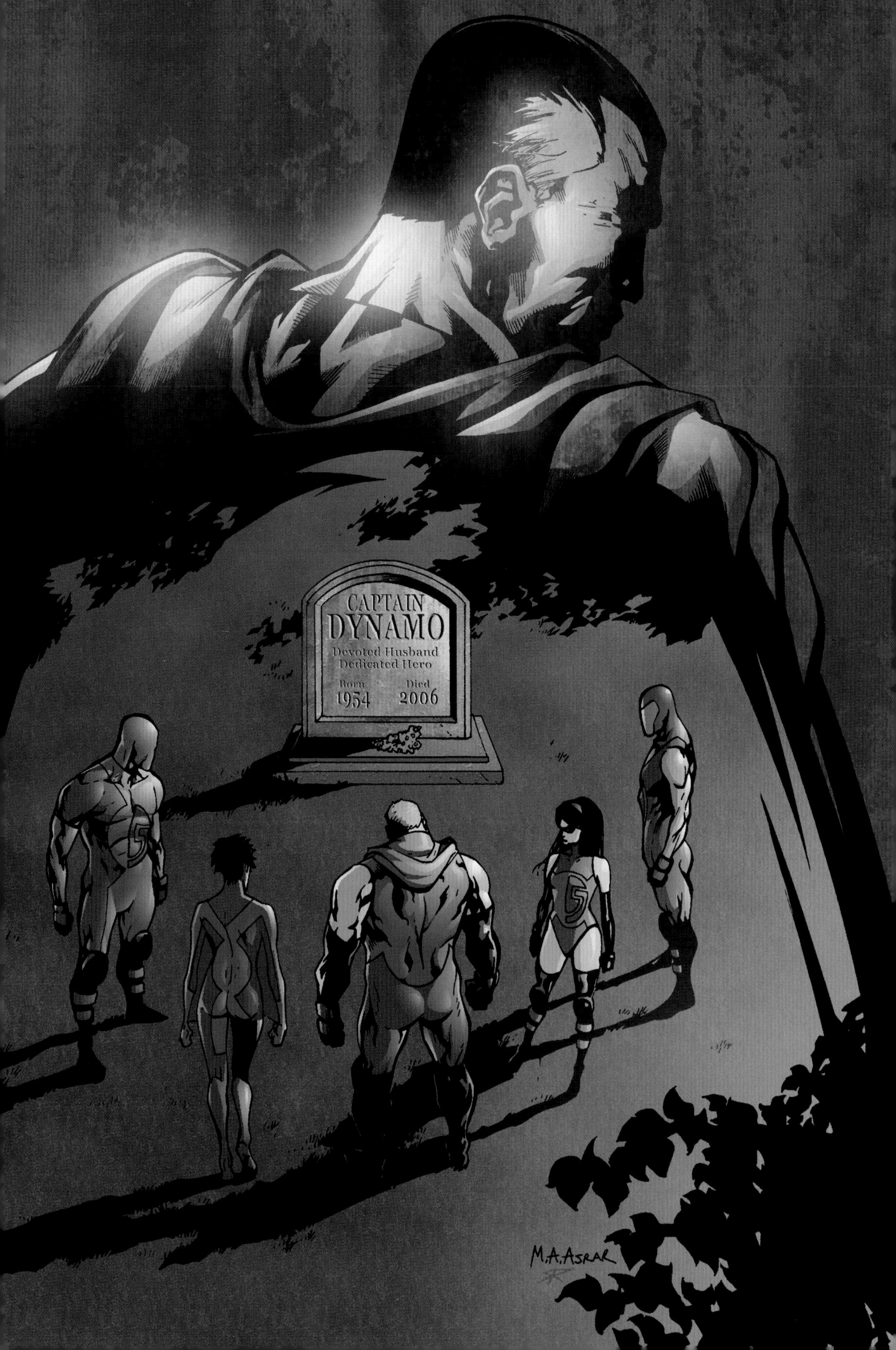
CAPTAIN
DYNAMO
Devoted Husband
Dedicated Hero
Born 1954
Died 2006
M.A.ASRAR

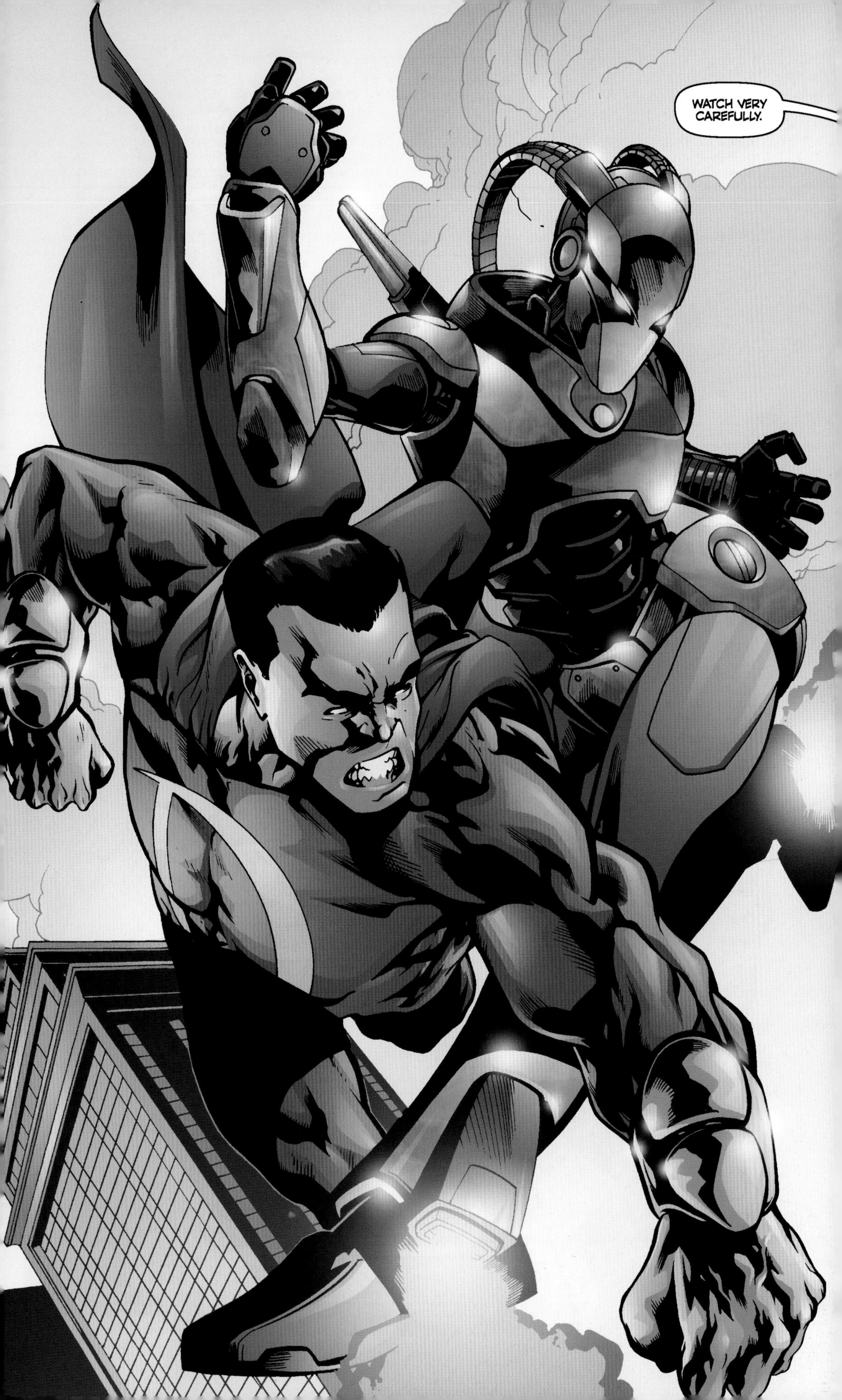
WATCH VERY CAREFULLY.

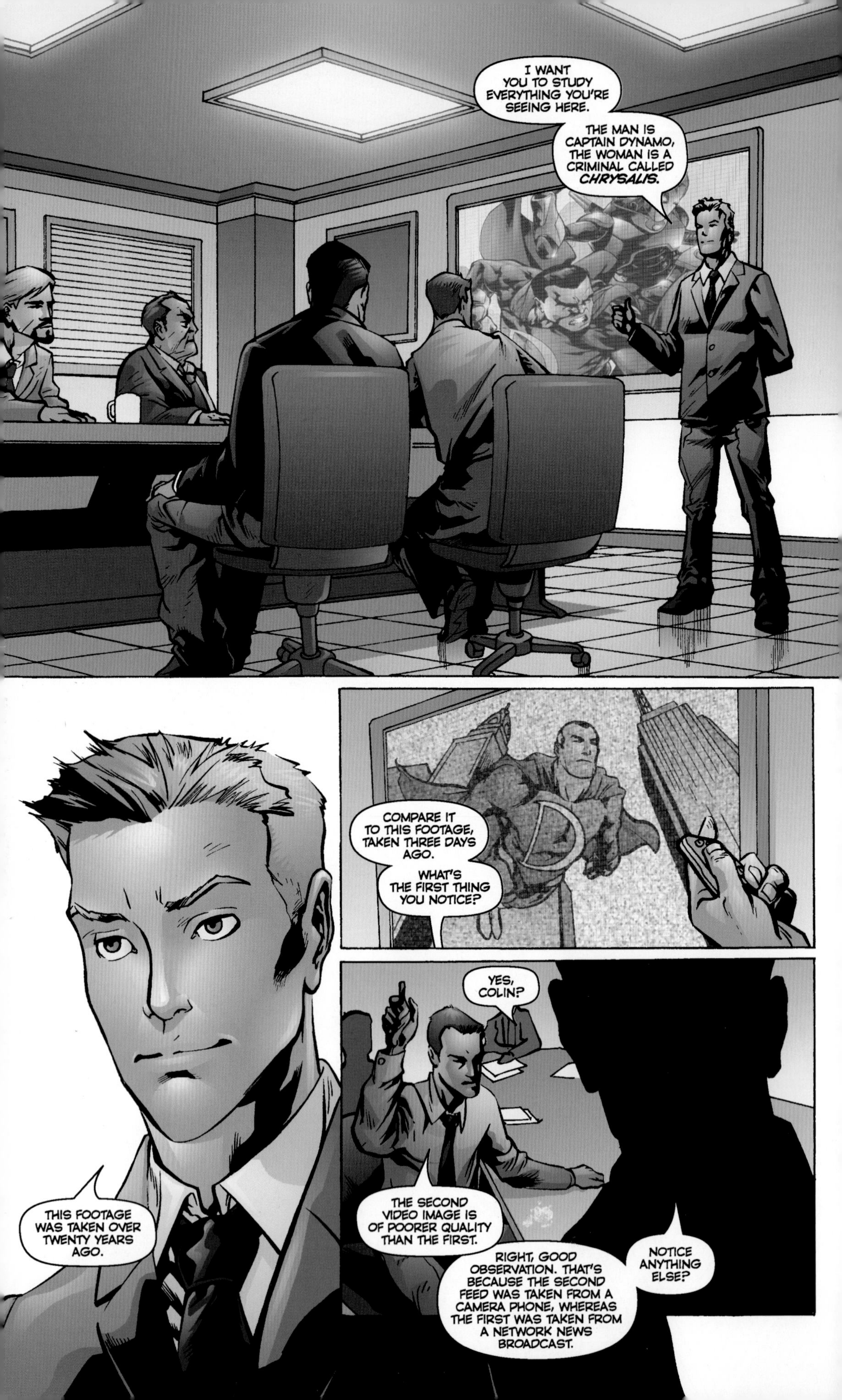
I WANT YOU TO STUDY EVERYTHING YOU'RE SEEING HERE.
THE MAN IS CAPTAIN DYNAMO, THE WOMAN IS A CRIMINAL CALLED *CHRYSALIS*.
COMPARE IT TO THIS FOOTAGE, TAKEN THREE DAYS AGO.
WHAT'S THE FIRST THING YOU NOTICE?
YES, COLIN?
THE SECOND VIDEO IMAGE IS OF POORER QUALITY THAN THE FIRST.
RIGHT, GOOD OBSERVATION. THAT'S BECAUSE THE SECOND FEED WAS TAKEN FROM A CAMERA PHONE, WHEREAS THE FIRST WAS TAKEN FROM A NETWORK NEWS BROADCAST.
NOTICE ANYTHING ELSE?
THIS FOOTAGE WAS TAKEN OVER TWENTY YEARS AGO.

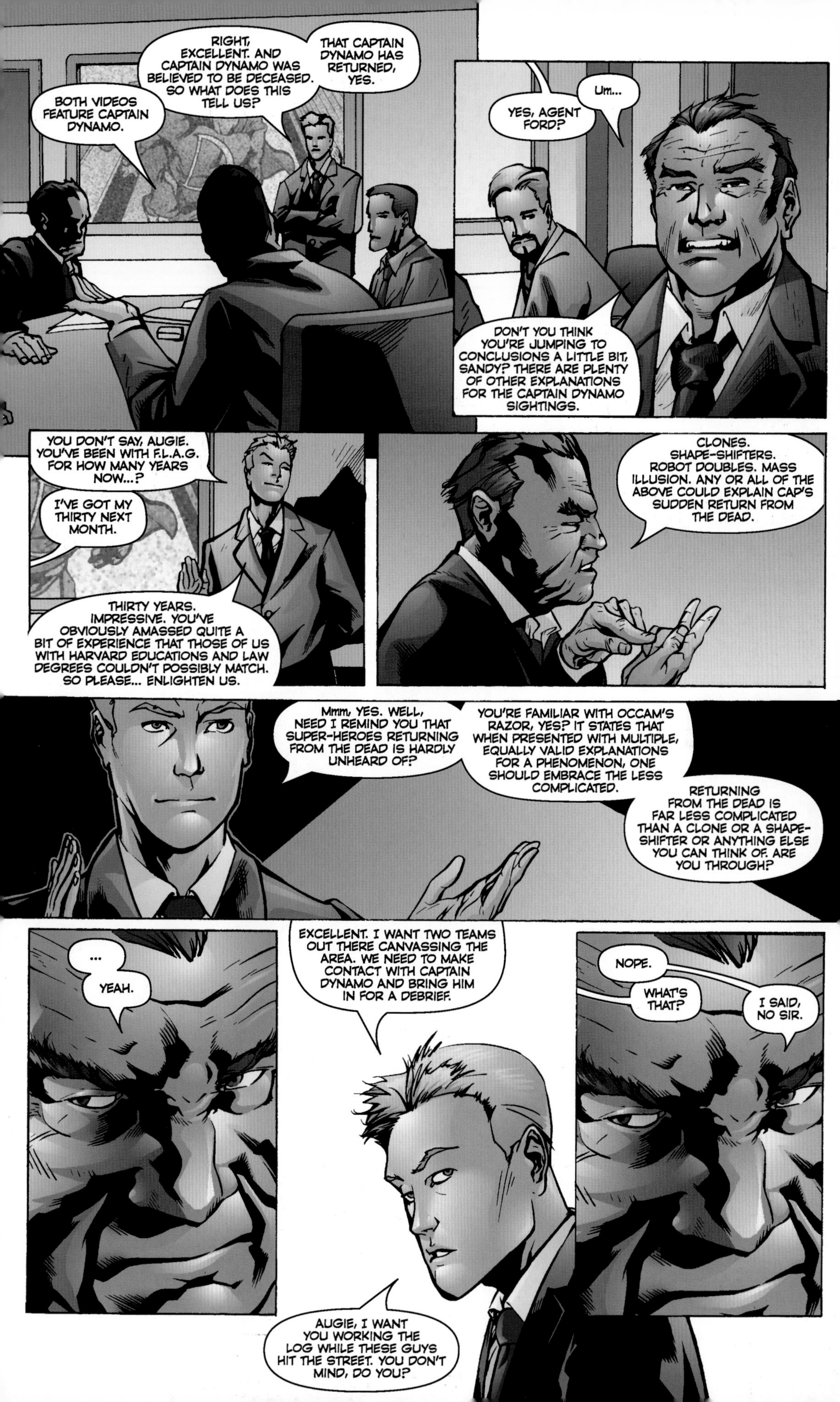

BOTH VIDEOS FEATURE CAPTAIN DYNAMO.
RIGHT, EXCELLENT. AND CAPTAIN DYNAMO WAS BELIEVED TO BE DECEASED. SO WHAT DOES THIS TELL US?
THAT CAPTAIN DYNAMO HAS RETURNED, YES.
Um...
YES, AGENT FORD?
DON'T YOU THINK YOU'RE JUMPING TO CONCLUSIONS A LITTLE BIT, SANDY? THERE ARE PLENTY OF OTHER EXPLANATIONS FOR THE CAPTAIN DYNAMO SIGHTINGS.
YOU DON'T SAY, AUGIE. YOU'VE BEEN WITH F.L.A.G. FOR HOW MANY YEARS NOW...?
I'VE GOT MY THIRTY NEXT MONTH.
THIRTY YEARS. IMPRESSIVE. YOU'VE OBVIOUSLY AMASSED QUITE A BIT OF EXPERIENCE THAT THOSE OF US WITH HARVARD EDUCATIONS AND LAW DEGREES COULDN'T POSSIBLY MATCH. SO PLEASE... ENLIGHTEN US.
CLONES. SHAPE-SHIFTERS. ROBOT DOUBLES. MASS ILLUSION. ANY OR ALL OF THE ABOVE COULD EXPLAIN CAP'S SUDDEN RETURN FROM THE DEAD.
Mmm, YES. WELL, NEED I REMIND YOU THAT SUPER-HEROES RETURNING FROM THE DEAD IS HARDLY UNHEARD OF?
YOU'RE FAMILIAR WITH OCCAM'S RAZOR, YES? IT STATES THAT WHEN PRESENTED WITH MULTIPLE, EQUALLY VALID EXPLANATIONS FOR A PHENOMENON, ONE SHOULD EMBRACE THE LESS COMPLICATED.
RETURNING FROM THE DEAD IS FAR LESS COMPLICATED THAN A CLONE OR A SHAPE-SHIFTER OR ANYTHING ELSE YOU CAN THINK OF. ARE YOU THROUGH?
...
YEAH.
EXCELLENT. I WANT TWO TEAMS OUT THERE CANVASSING THE AREA. WE NEED TO MAKE CONTACT WITH CAPTAIN DYNAMO AND BRING HIM IN FOR A DEBRIEF.
AUGIE, I WANT YOU WORKING THE LOG WHILE THESE GUYS HIT THE STREET. YOU DON'T MIND, DO YOU?
NOPE.
WHAT'S THAT?
I SAID, NO SIR.

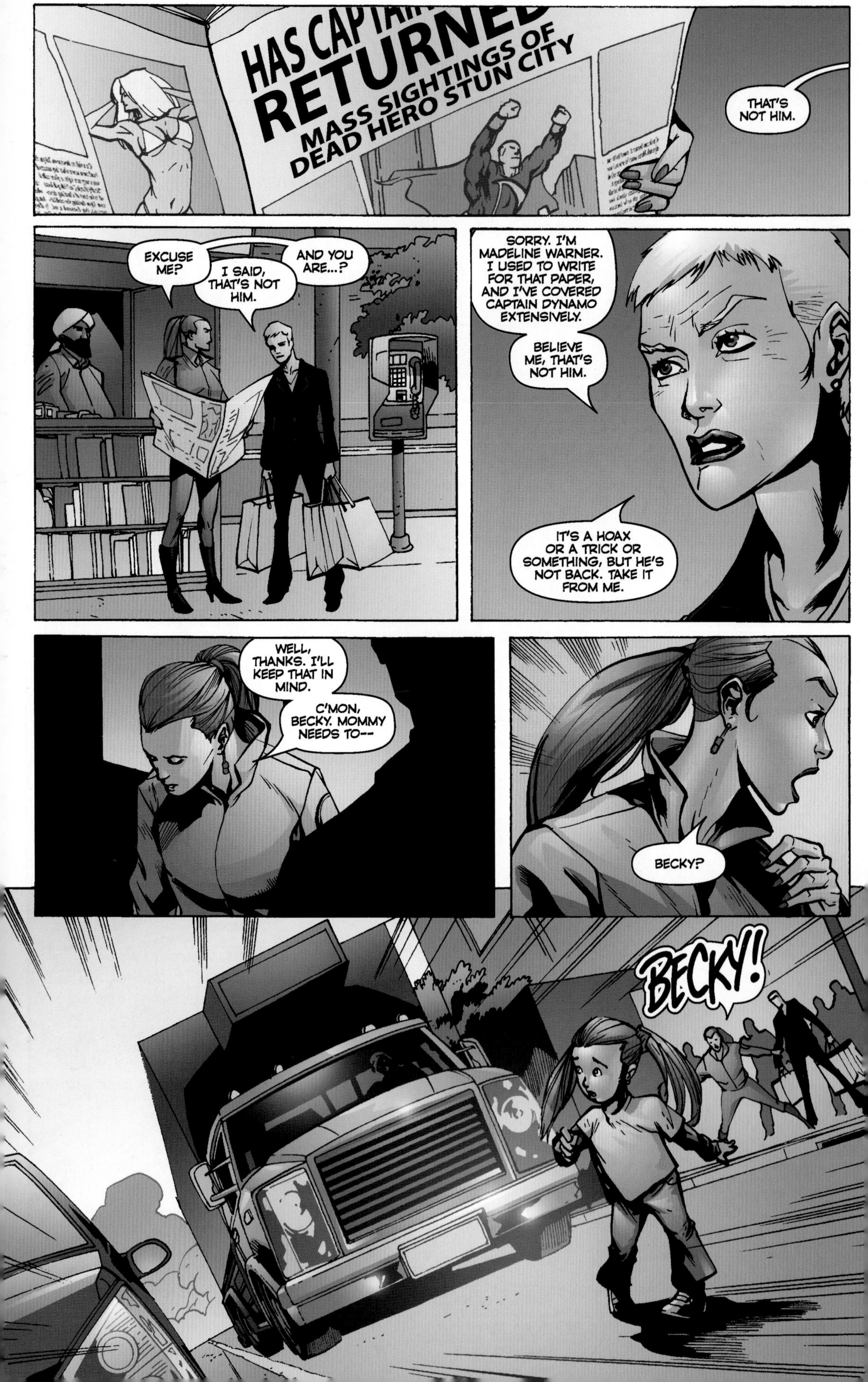
HAS CAPTAIN
RETURNED
MASS SIGHTINGS OF DEAD HERO STUN CITY
THAT'S NOT HIM.
EXCUSE ME?
I SAID, THAT'S NOT HIM.
AND YOU ARE...?
SORRY. I'M MADELINE WARNER. I USED TO WRITE FOR THAT PAPER, AND I'VE COVERED CAPTAIN DYNAMO EXTENSIVELY.
BELIEVE ME, THAT'S NOT HIM.
IT'S A HOAX OR A TRICK OR SOMETHING, BUT HE'S NOT BACK. TAKE IT FROM ME.
WELL, THANKS. I'LL KEEP THAT IN MIND.
C'MON, BECKY. MOMMY NEEDS TO--
BECKY?
BECKY!

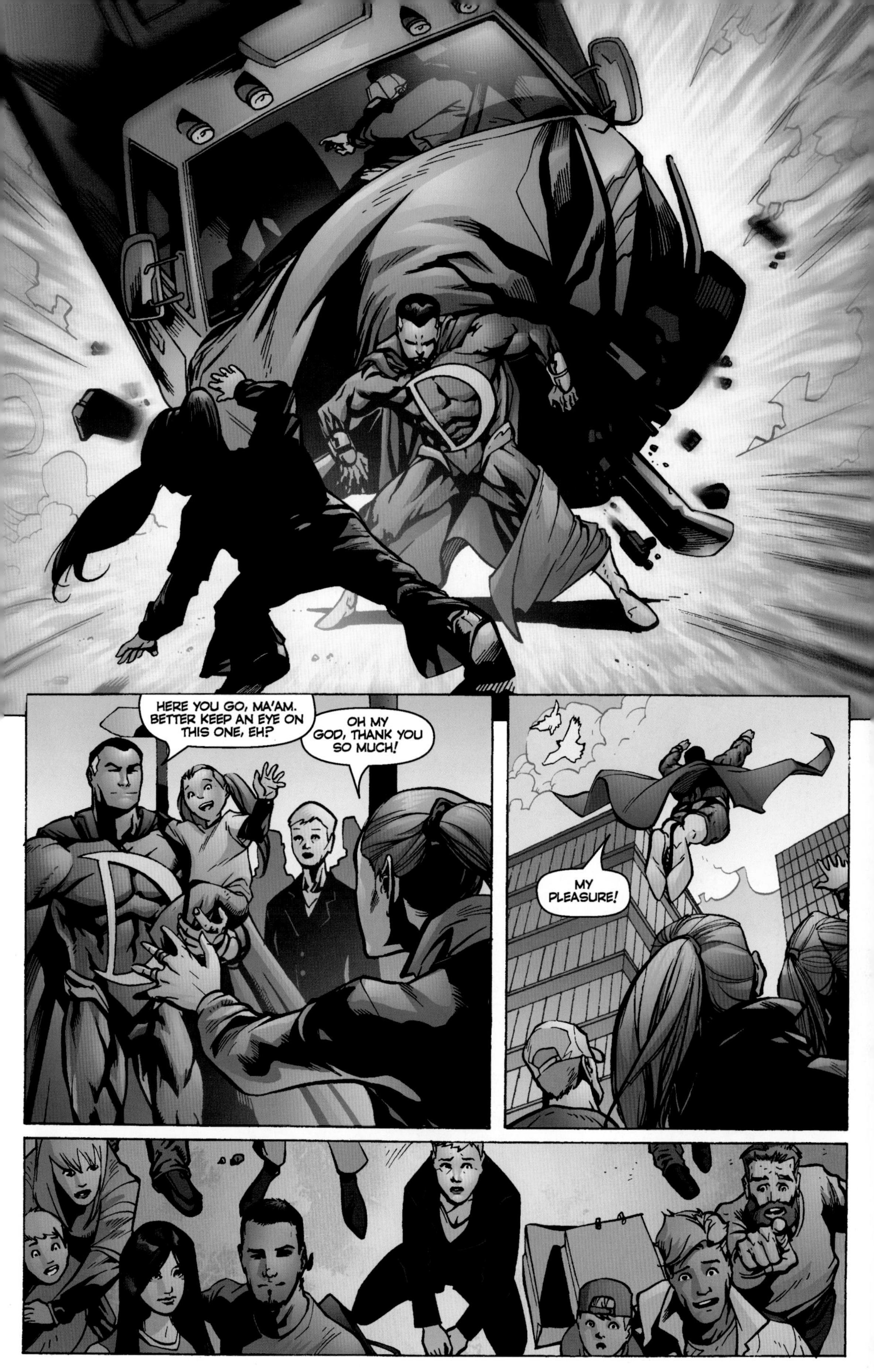
HERE YOU GO, MA'AM. BETTER KEEP AN EYE ON THIS ONE, EH?
OH MY GOD, THANK YOU SO MUCH!
MY PLEASURE!

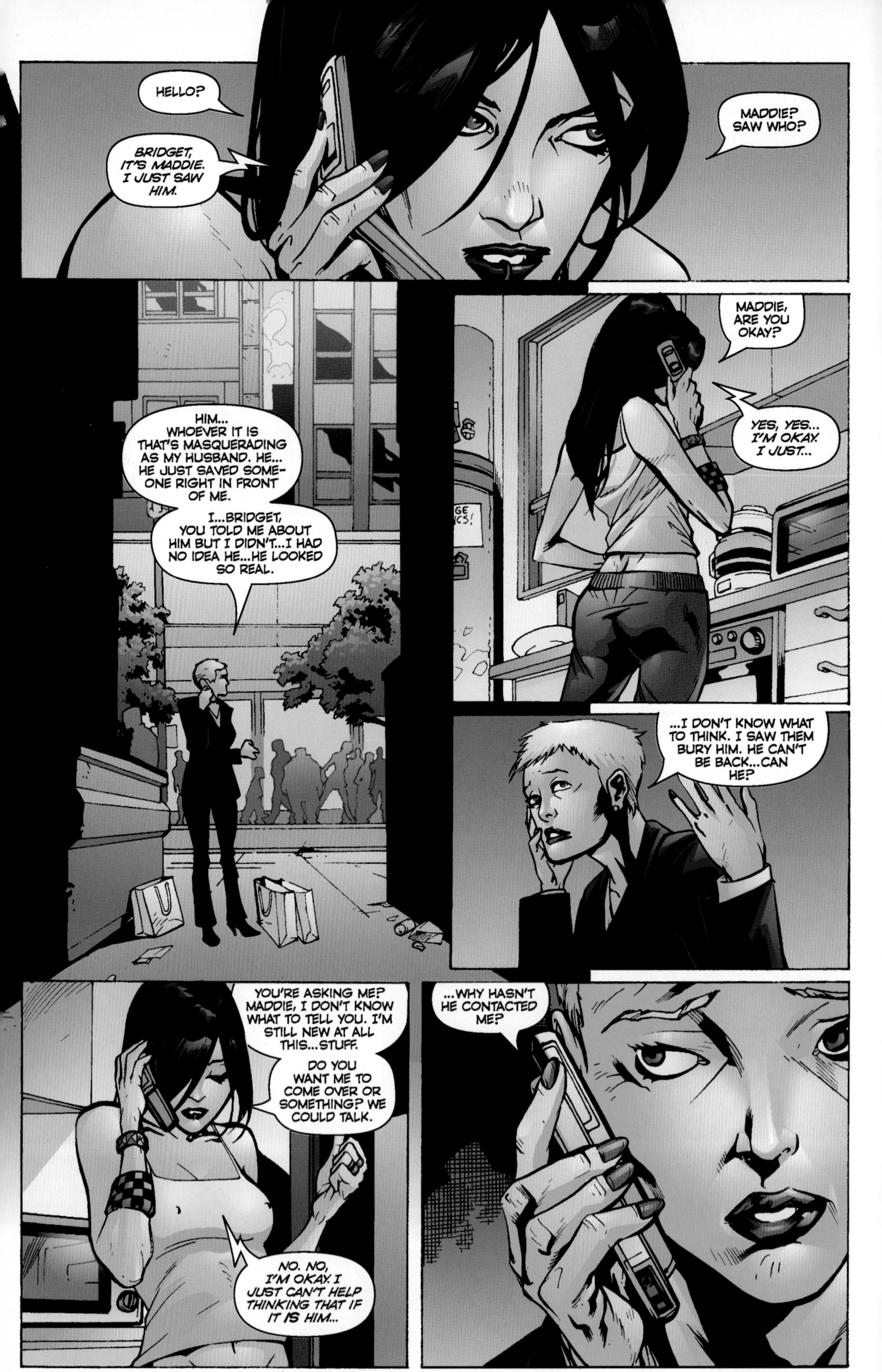
HELLO?
BRIDGET, IT'S MADDIE. I JUST SAW HIM.
MADDIE? SAW WHO?
MADDIE, ARE YOU OKAY?
YES, YES... I'M OKAY. I JUST...
HIM... WHOEVER IT IS THAT'S MASQUERADING AS MY HUSBAND. HE... HE JUST SAVED SOME-ONE RIGHT IN FRONT OF ME.
I...BRIDGET, YOU TOLD ME ABOUT HIM BUT I DIDN'T...I HAD NO IDEA HE...HE LOOKED SO REAL.
...I DON'T KNOW WHAT TO THINK. I SAW THEM BURY HIM. HE CAN'T BE BACK...CAN HE?
YOU'RE ASKING ME? MADDIE, I DON'T KNOW WHAT TO TELL YOU. I'M STILL NEW AT ALL THIS...STUFF.
DO YOU WANT ME TO COME OVER OR SOMETHING? WE COULD TALK.
NO. NO, I'M OKAY. I JUST CAN'T HELP THINKING THAT IF IT IS HIM...
...WHY HASN'T HE CONTACTED ME?

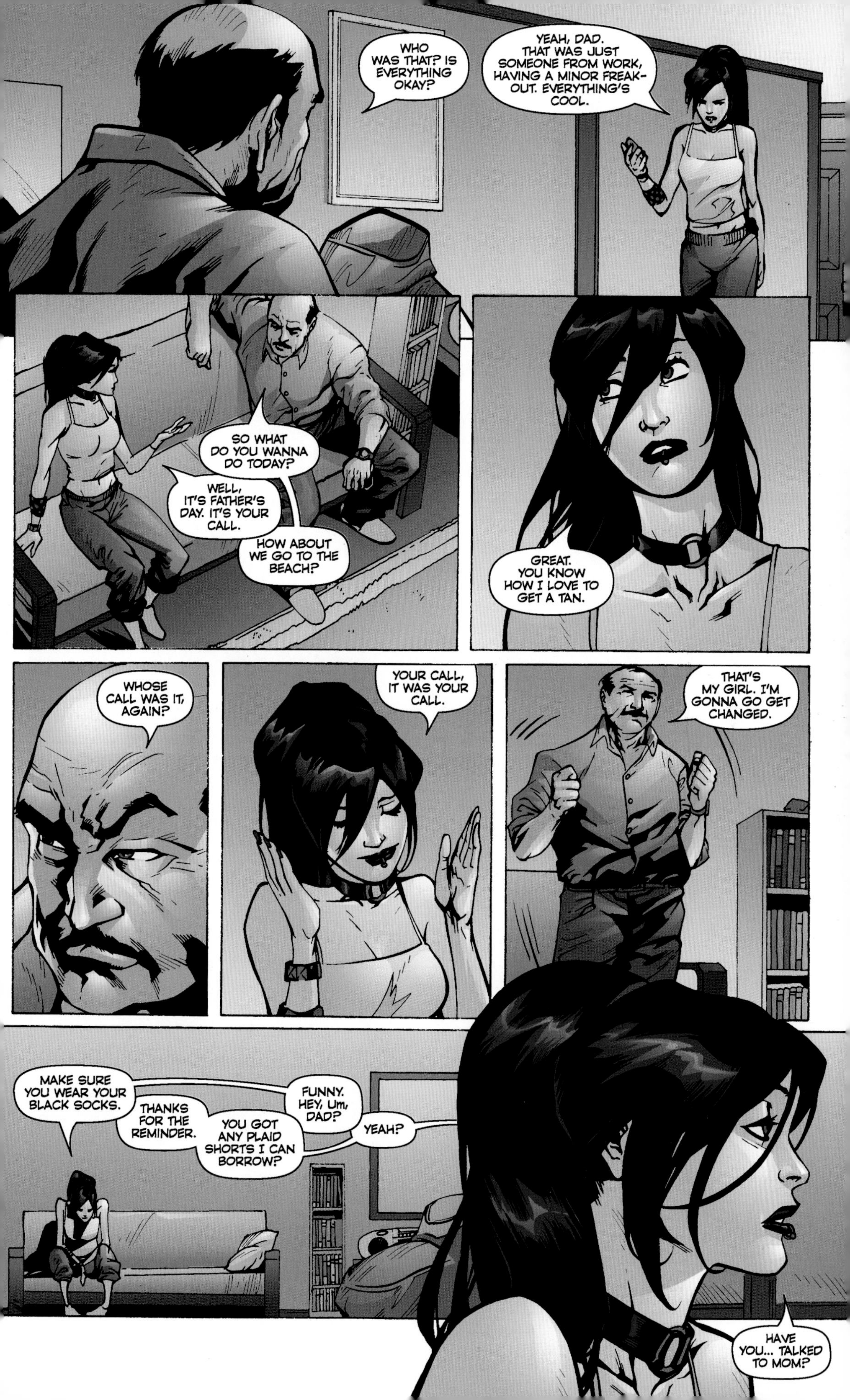
WHO WAS THAT? IS EVERYTHING OKAY?
YEAH, DAD. THAT WAS JUST SOMEONE FROM WORK, HAVING A MINOR FREAK-OUT. EVERYTHING'S COOL.
SO WHAT DO YOU WANNA DO TODAY?
WELL, IT'S FATHER'S DAY. IT'S YOUR CALL.
HOW ABOUT WE GO TO THE BEACH?
GREAT. YOU KNOW HOW I LOVE TO GET A TAN.
WHOSE CALL WAS IT, AGAIN?
YOUR CALL, IT WAS YOUR CALL.
THAT'S MY GIRL. I'M GONNA GO GET CHANGED.
MAKE SURE YOU WEAR YOUR BLACK SOCKS.
FUNNY. HEY, UM, DAD?
THANKS FOR THE REMINDER.
YOU GOT ANY PLAID SHORTS I CAN BORROW?
YEAH?
HAVE YOU... TALKED TO MOM?

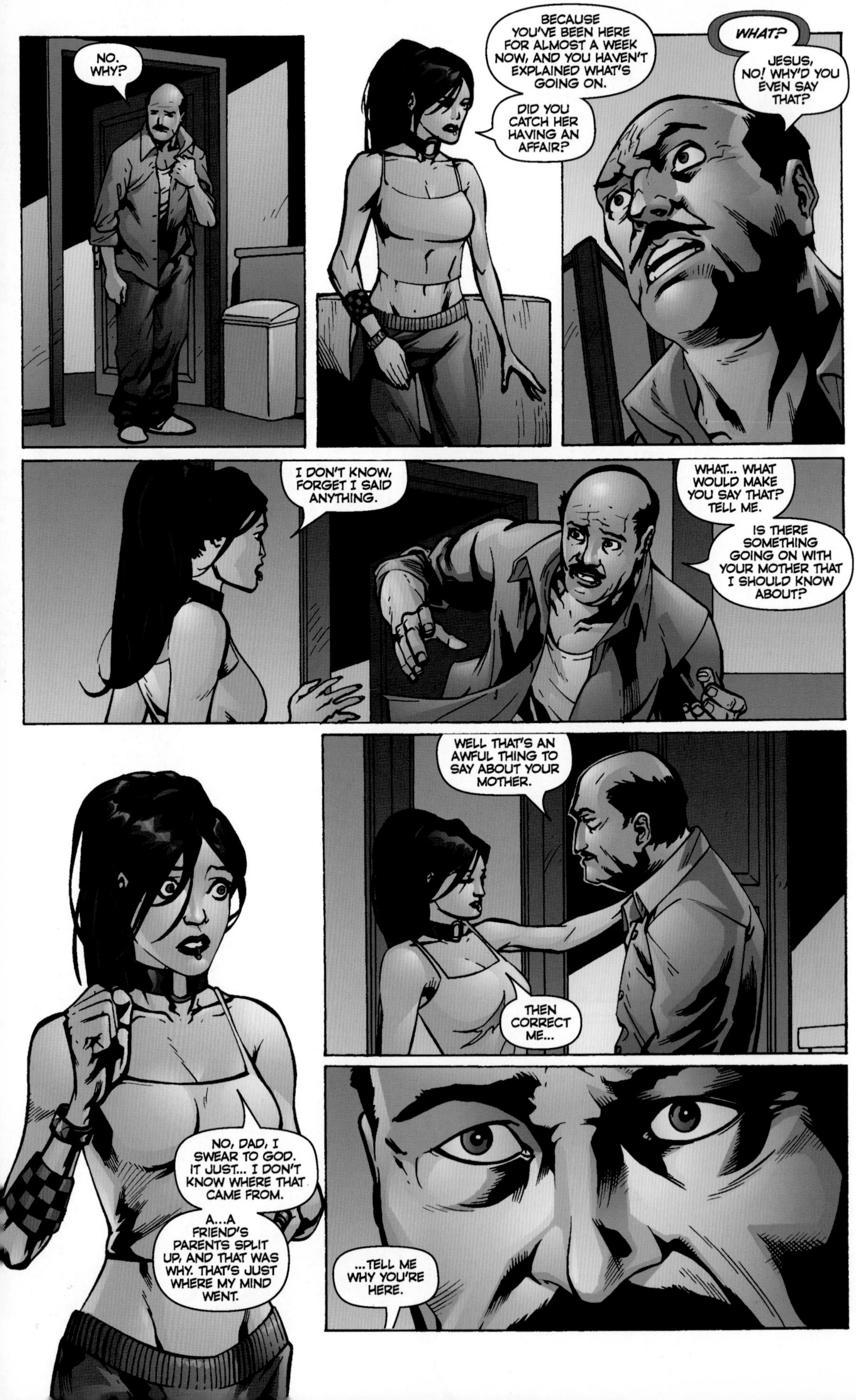
NO. WHY?
BECAUSE YOU'VE BEEN HERE FOR ALMOST A WEEK NOW, AND YOU HAVEN'T EXPLAINED WHAT'S GOING ON.
DID YOU CATCH HER HAVING AN AFFAIR?
WHAT?
JESUS, NO! WHY'D YOU EVEN SAY THAT?
I DON'T KNOW, FORGET I SAID ANYTHING.
WHAT... WHAT WOULD MAKE YOU SAY THAT? TELL ME.
IS THERE SOMETHING GOING ON WITH YOUR MOTHER THAT I SHOULD KNOW ABOUT?
NO, DAD, I SWEAR TO GOD. IT JUST... I DON'T KNOW WHERE THAT CAME FROM.
A...A FRIEND'S PARENTS SPLIT UP, AND THAT WAS WHY. THAT'S JUST WHERE MY MIND WENT.
WELL THAT'S AN AWFUL THING TO SAY ABOUT YOUR MOTHER.
THEN CORRECT ME...
...TELL ME WHY YOU'RE HERE.

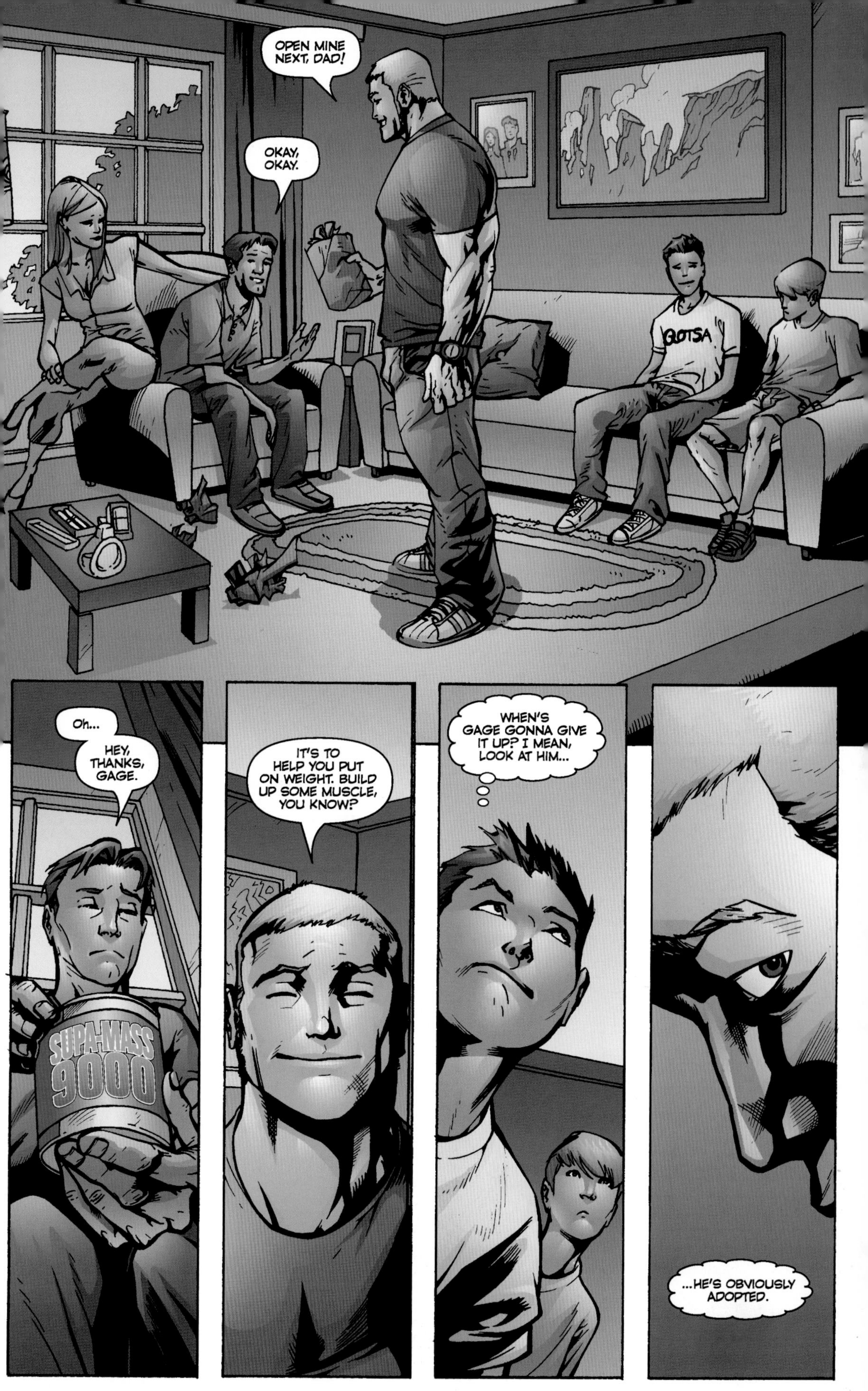
OPEN MINE NEXT, DAD!
OKAY, OKAY.
QOTSA
Oh...
HEY, THANKS, GAGE.
SUPA-MASS 9000
IT'S TO HELP YOU PUT ON WEIGHT. BUILD UP SOME MUSCLE, YOU KNOW?
WHEN'S GAGE GONNA GIVE IT UP? I MEAN, LOOK AT HIM...
...HE'S OBVIOUSLY ADOPTED.

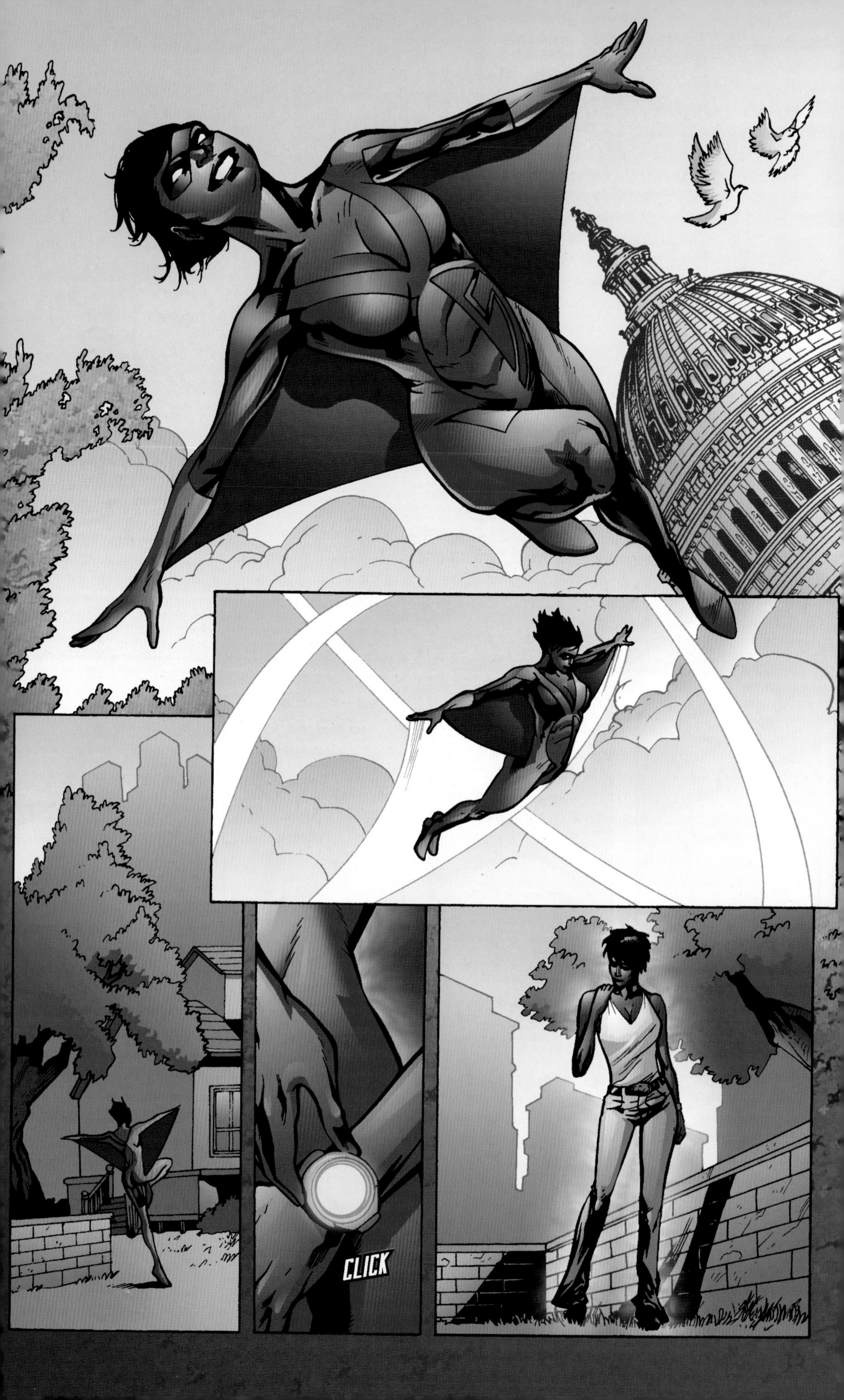
CLICK

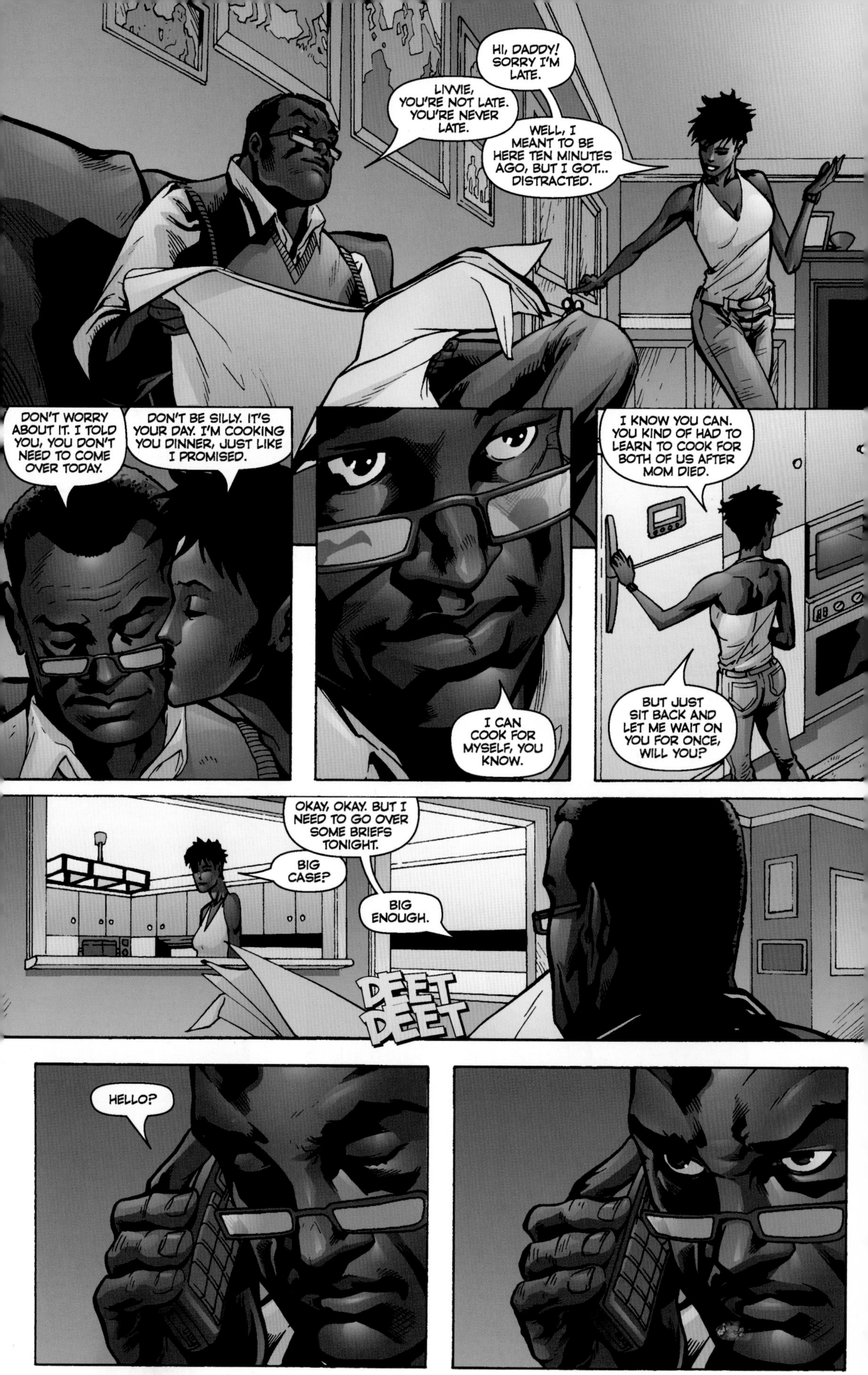
HI, DADDY! SORRY I'M LATE.
LIVVIE, YOU'RE NOT LATE. YOU'RE NEVER LATE.
WELL, I MEANT TO BE HERE TEN MINUTES AGO, BUT I GOT... DISTRACTED.
DON'T WORRY ABOUT IT. I TOLD YOU, YOU DON'T NEED TO COME OVER TODAY.
DON'T BE SILLY. IT'S YOUR DAY. I'M COOKING YOU DINNER, JUST LIKE I PROMISED.
I CAN COOK FOR MYSELF, YOU KNOW.
I KNOW YOU CAN. YOU KIND OF HAD TO LEARN TO COOK FOR BOTH OF US AFTER MOM DIED.
BUT JUST SIT BACK AND LET ME WAIT ON YOU FOR ONCE, WILL YOU?
OKAY, OKAY. BUT I NEED TO GO OVER SOME BRIEFS TONIGHT.
BIG CASE?
BIG ENOUGH.
DEET DEET
HELLO?

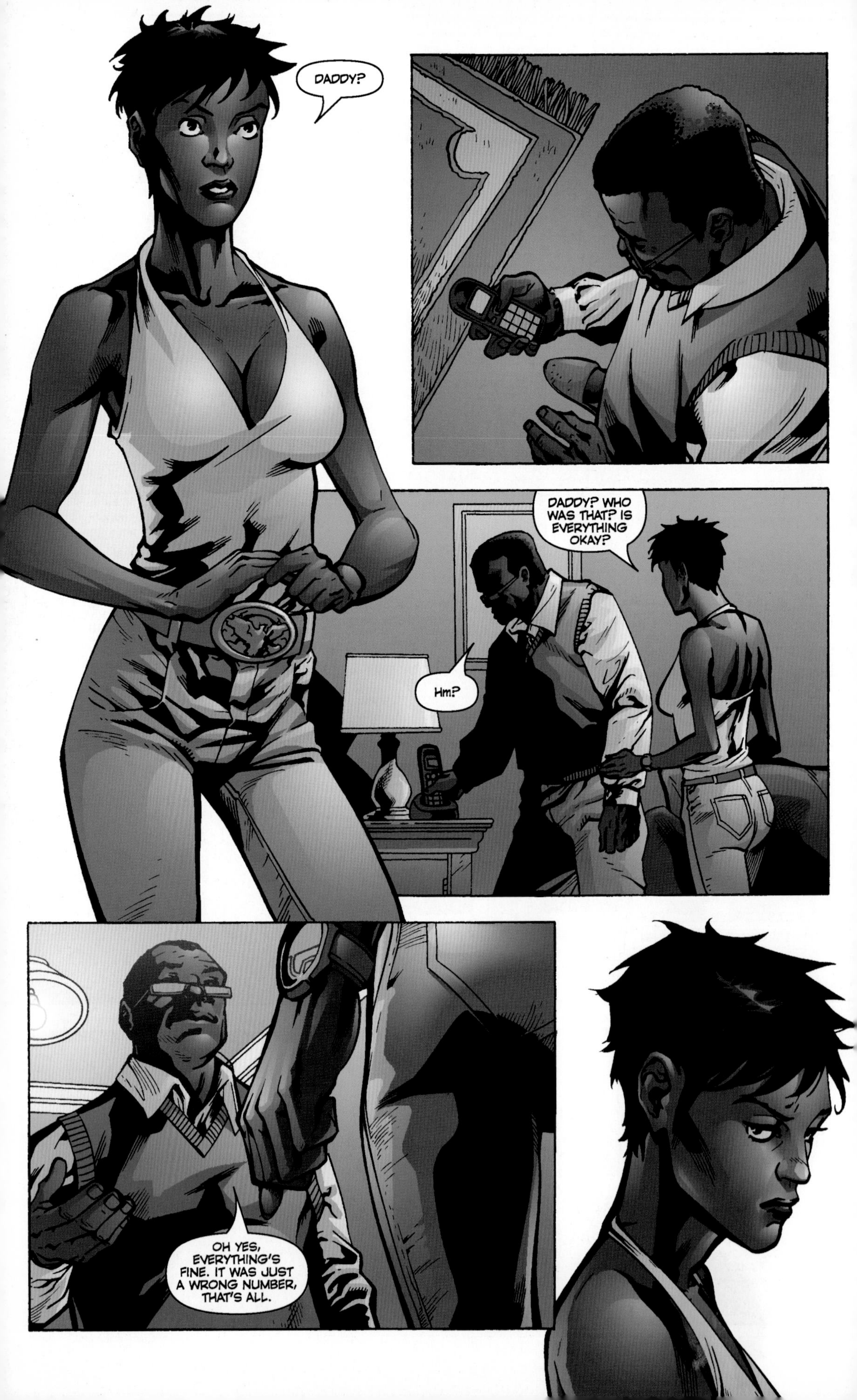
DADDY?
DADDY? WHO WAS THAT? IS EVERYTHING OKAY?
Hm?
OH YES, EVERYTHING'S FINE. IT WAS JUST A WRONG NUMBER, THAT'S ALL.

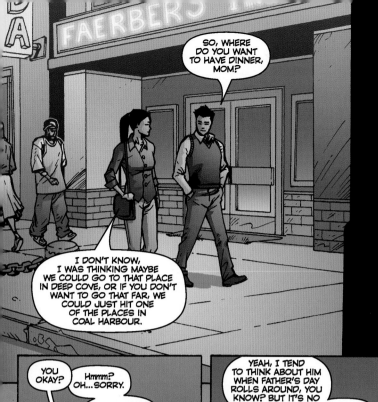

SO, WHERE DO YOU WANT TO HAVE DINNER, MOM?

I DON'T KNOW, I WAS THINKING MAYBE WE COULD GO TO THAT PLACE IN DEEP COVE, OR IF YOU DON'T WANT TO GO THAT FAR, WE COULD JUST HIT ONE OF THE PLACES IN COAL HARBOUR.

Father's Day Sale!

OR... HECTOR?

YOU OKAY?

Hmmm? OH...SORRY.

WE CAN GO WHEREVER YOU WANT.

YOU THINKING ABOUT YOUR DAD? IT'S OKAY IF YOU ARE.

YEAH, I TEND TO THINK ABOUT HIM WHEN FATHER'S DAY ROLLS AROUND, YOU KNOW? BUT IT'S NO BIG DEAL.

DON'T WORRY ABOUT IT.

IT *IS* A BIG DEAL. YOU DESERVE A FATHER... A MALE ROLE MODEL. YOU'VE GOT YOUR GRANDFATHER, BUT THAT'S NOT THE SAME THING.

I GUESS I COULD'VE TOLD YOU THAT YOUR FATHER DIED A HEROIC DEATH OR SOMETHING, BUT--

I KNOW, DAD WAS JUST SOME GUY WHO GOT YOU PREGNANT THAT YOU NEVER SAW AGAIN. IT'S OKAY, MOM.

I'M GLAD YOU TOLD ME THE TRUTH ABOUT IT.

IT WASN'T EXACTLY A SHINING MOMENT FOR ME...

... BUT I GOT *YOU* OUT OF THE DEAL, SO I GUESS I CAME OUT ON TOP.

Ugh! TOO...SAPPY... CAN'T... BREATHE!

HEY, NOW... YOU GOTTA INDULGE YOUR MOTHER EVERY ONCE IN AWHILE.

OH, ALL RIGHT.

BUT HEY, IS IT OKAY IF I BAIL ON DINNER? THERE'S SOMEWHERE I KINDA NEED TO BE.

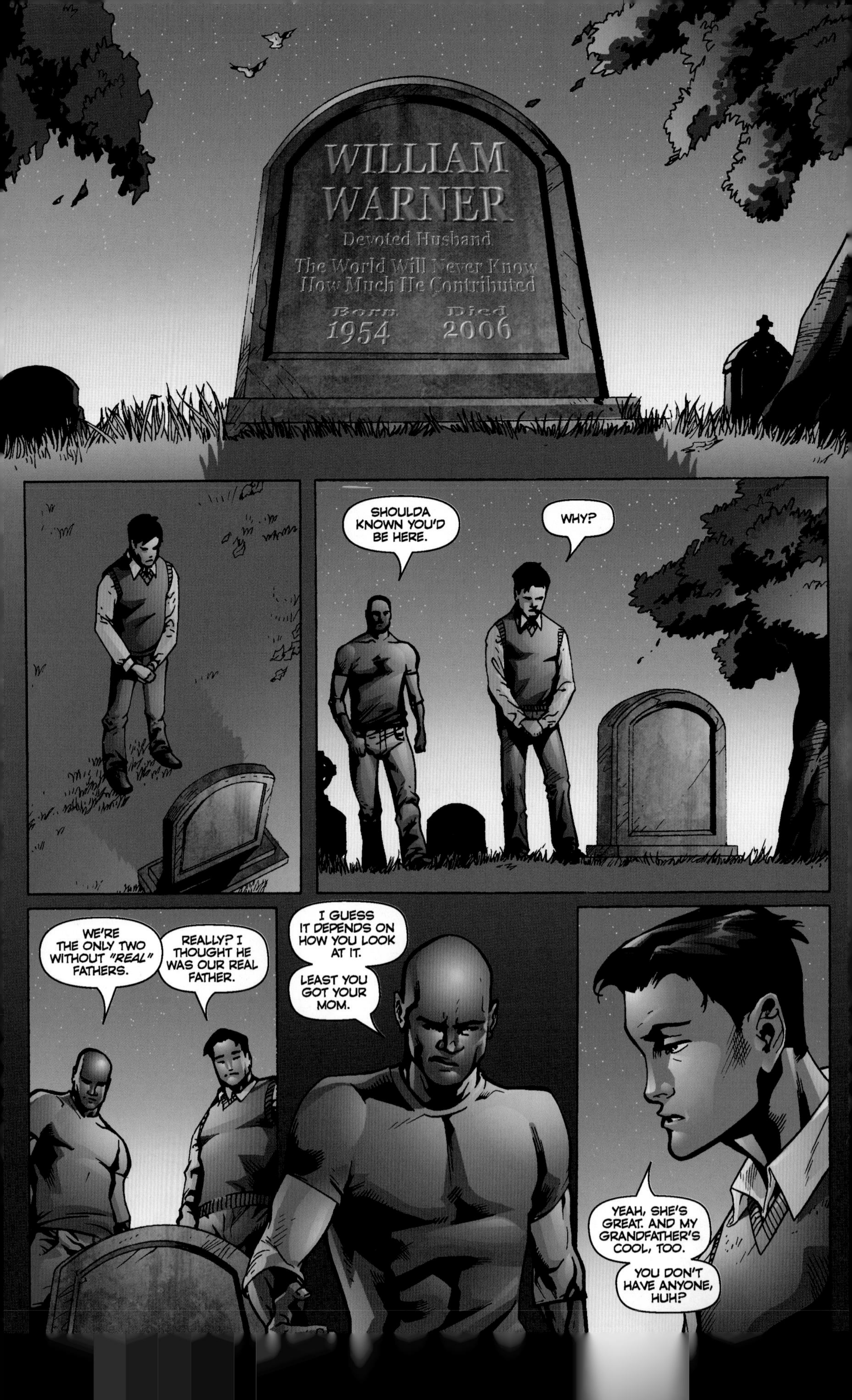
WILLIAM WARNER
Devoted Husband
The World Will Never Know How Much He Contributed
Born 1954 Died 2006
SHOULDA KNOWN YOU'D BE HERE.
WHY?
WE'RE THE ONLY TWO WITHOUT "REAL" FATHERS.
REALLY? I THOUGHT HE WAS OUR REAL FATHER.
I GUESS IT DEPENDS ON HOW YOU LOOK AT IT.
LEAST YOU GOT YOUR MOM.
YEAH, SHE'S GREAT. AND MY GRANDFATHER'S COOL, TOO.
YOU DON'T HAVE ANYONE, HUH?

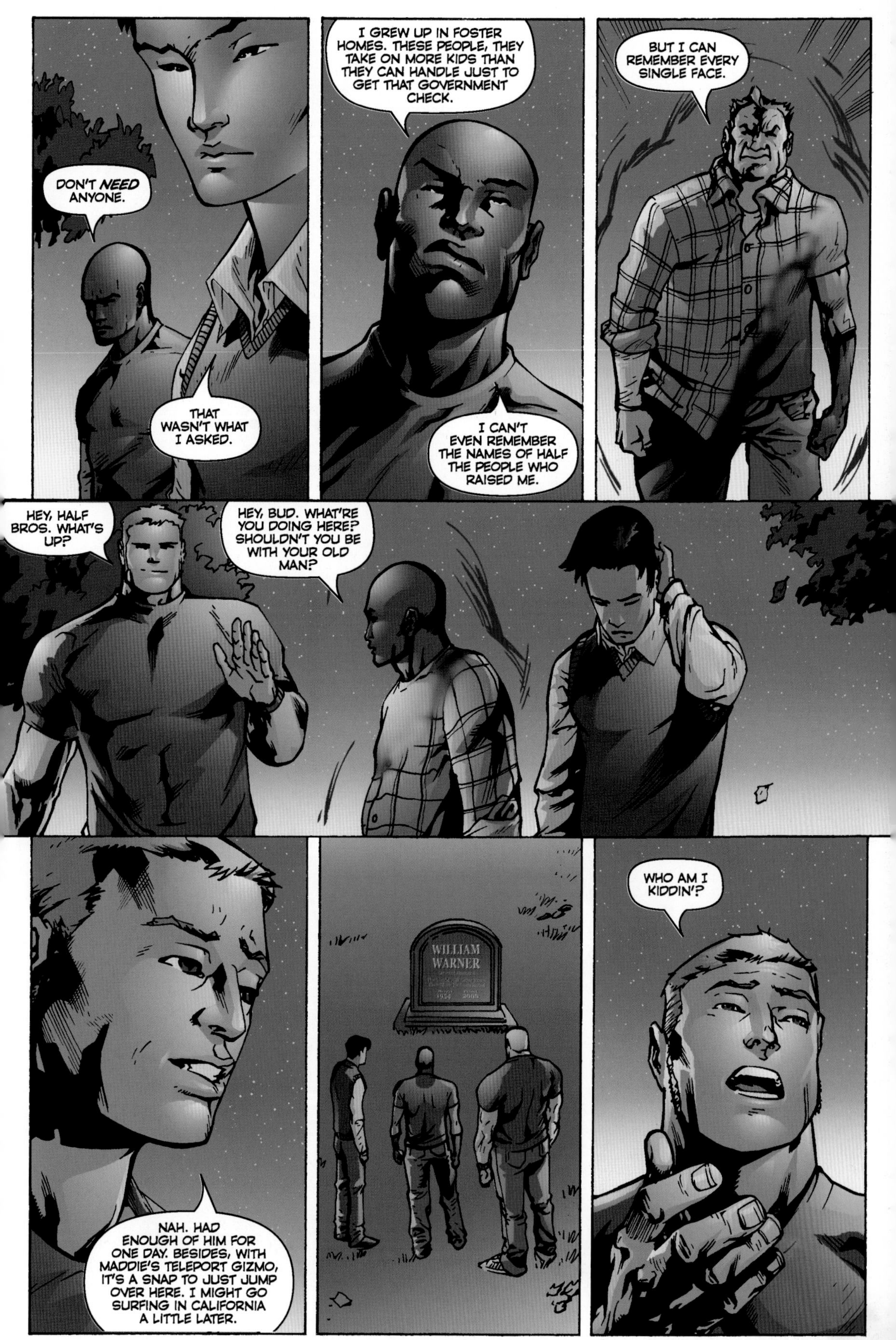
DON'T NEED ANYONE.
THAT WASN'T WHAT I ASKED.
I GREW UP IN FOSTER HOMES. THESE PEOPLE, THEY TAKE ON MORE KIDS THAN THEY CAN HANDLE JUST TO GET THAT GOVERNMENT CHECK.
I CAN'T EVEN REMEMBER THE NAMES OF HALF THE PEOPLE WHO RAISED ME.
BUT I CAN REMEMBER EVERY SINGLE FACE.
HEY, HALF BROS. WHAT'S UP?
HEY, BUD. WHAT'RE YOU DOING HERE? SHOULDN'T YOU BE WITH YOUR OLD MAN?
NAH. HAD ENOUGH OF HIM FOR ONE DAY. BESIDES, WITH MADDIE'S TELEPORT GIZMO, IT'S A SNAP TO JUST JUMP OVER HERE. I MIGHT GO SURFING IN CALIFORNIA A LITTLE LATER.
WILLIAM WARNER
WHO AM I KIDDIN'?

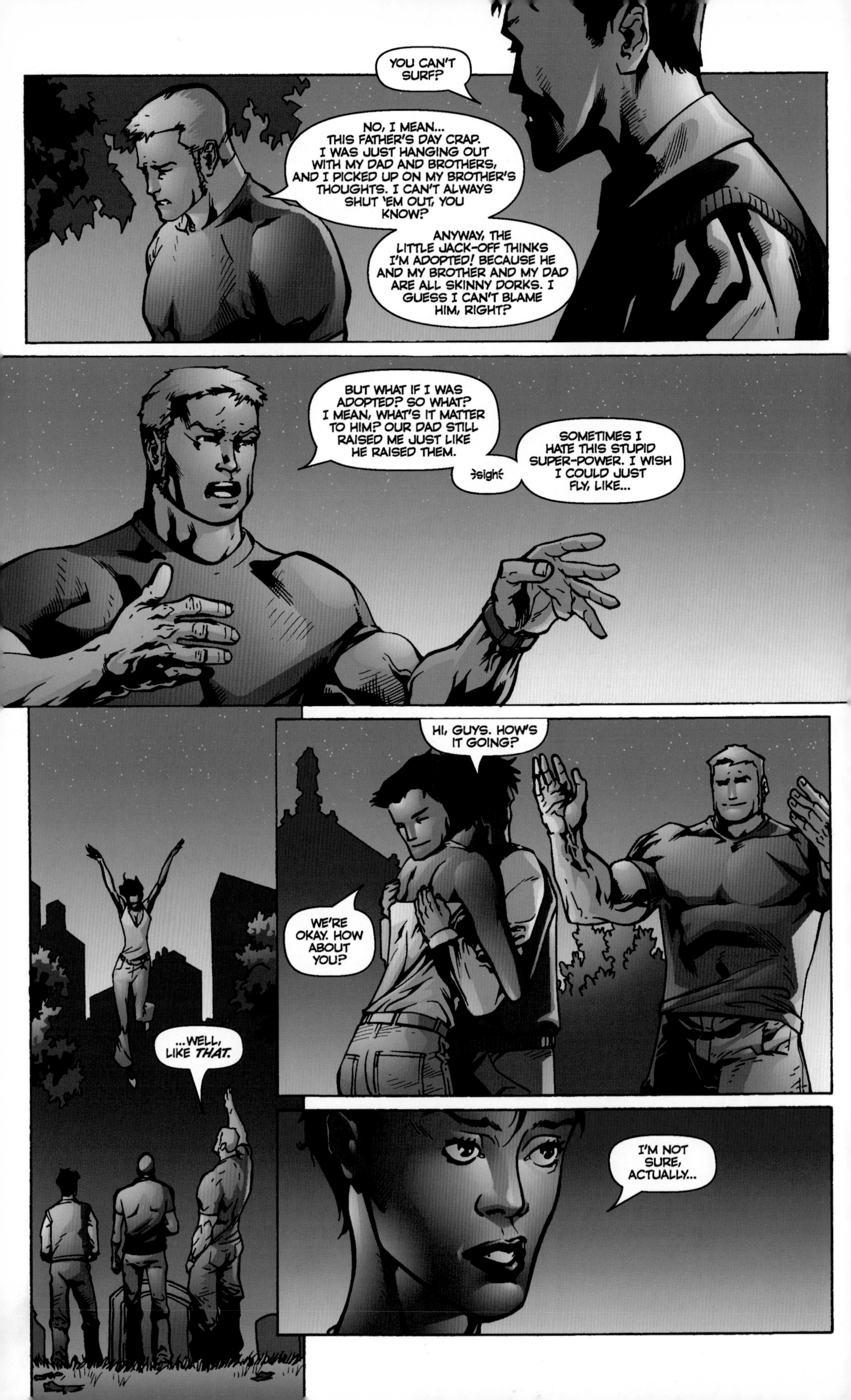
YOU CAN'T SURF?
NO, I MEAN... THIS FATHER'S DAY CRAP. I WAS JUST HANGING OUT WITH MY DAD AND BROTHERS, AND I PICKED UP ON MY BROTHER'S THOUGHTS. I CAN'T ALWAYS SHUT 'EM OUT, YOU KNOW?
ANYWAY, THE LITTLE JACK-OFF THINKS I'M ADOPTED! BECAUSE HE AND MY BROTHER AND MY DAD ARE ALL SKINNY DORKS. I GUESS I CAN'T BLAME HIM, RIGHT?
BUT WHAT IF I WAS ADOPTED? SO WHAT? I MEAN, WHAT'S IT MATTER TO HIM? OUR DAD STILL RAISED ME JUST LIKE HE RAISED THEM.
sigh
SOMETIMES I HATE THIS STUPID SUPER-POWER. I WISH I COULD JUST FLY, LIKE...
...WELL, LIKE *THAT.*
HI, GUYS. HOW'S IT GOING?
WE'RE OKAY. HOW ABOUT YOU?
I'M NOT SURE, ACTUALLY...

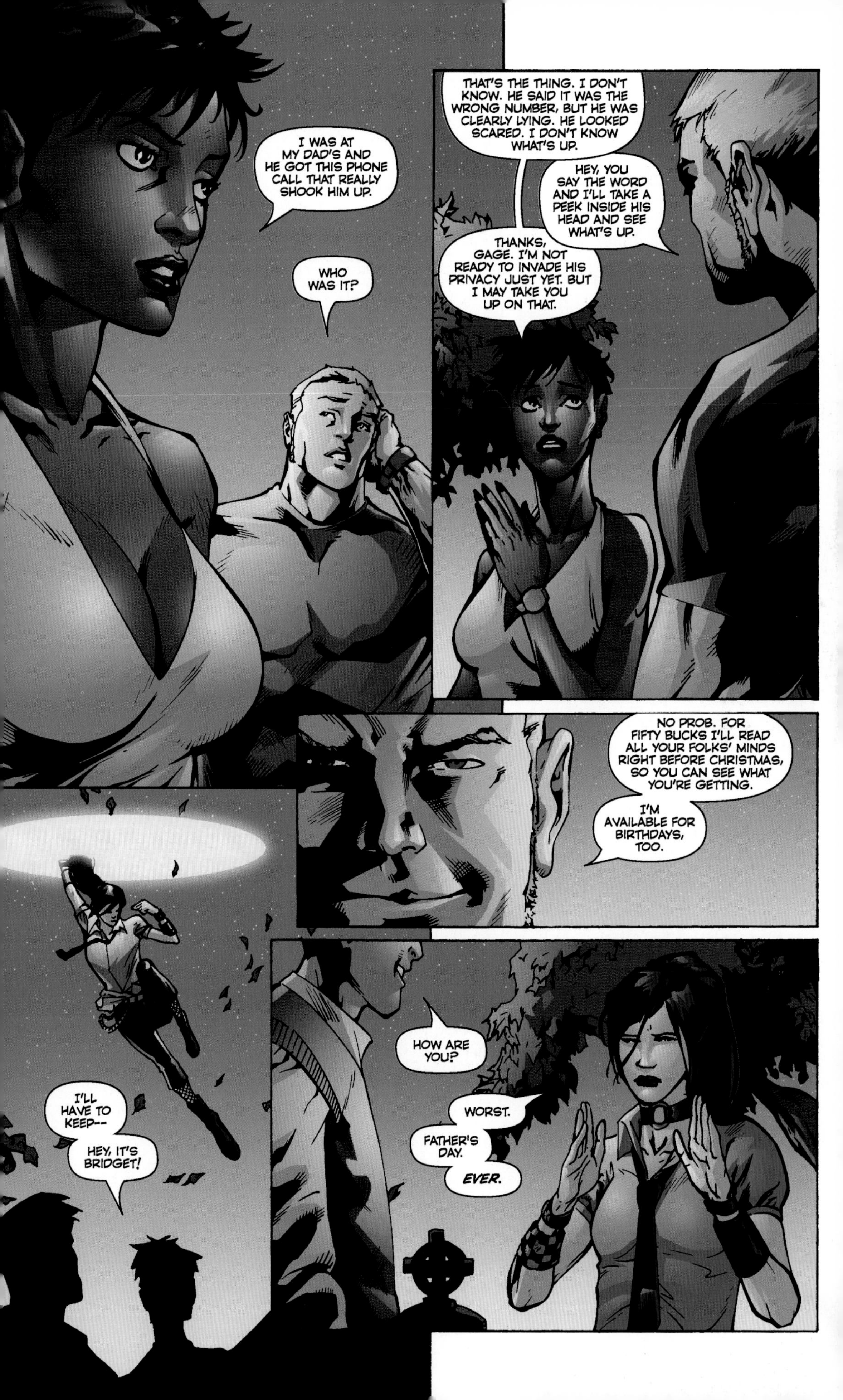

I WAS AT MY DAD'S AND HE GOT THIS PHONE CALL THAT REALLY SHOOK HIM UP.
WHO WAS IT?
THAT'S THE THING. I DON'T KNOW. HE SAID IT WAS THE WRONG NUMBER, BUT HE WAS CLEARLY LYING. HE LOOKED SCARED. I DON'T KNOW WHAT'S UP.
HEY, YOU SAY THE WORD AND I'LL TAKE A PEEK INSIDE HIS HEAD AND SEE WHAT'S UP.
THANKS, GAGE. I'M NOT READY TO INVADE HIS PRIVACY JUST YET. BUT I MAY TAKE YOU UP ON THAT.
NO PROB. FOR FIFTY BUCKS I'LL READ ALL YOUR FOLKS' MINDS RIGHT BEFORE CHRISTMAS, SO YOU CAN SEE WHAT YOU'RE GETTING.
I'M AVAILABLE FOR BIRTHDAYS, TOO.
I'LL HAVE TO KEEP--
HEY, IT'S BRIDGET!
HOW ARE YOU?
WORST.
FATHER'S DAY.
EVER.

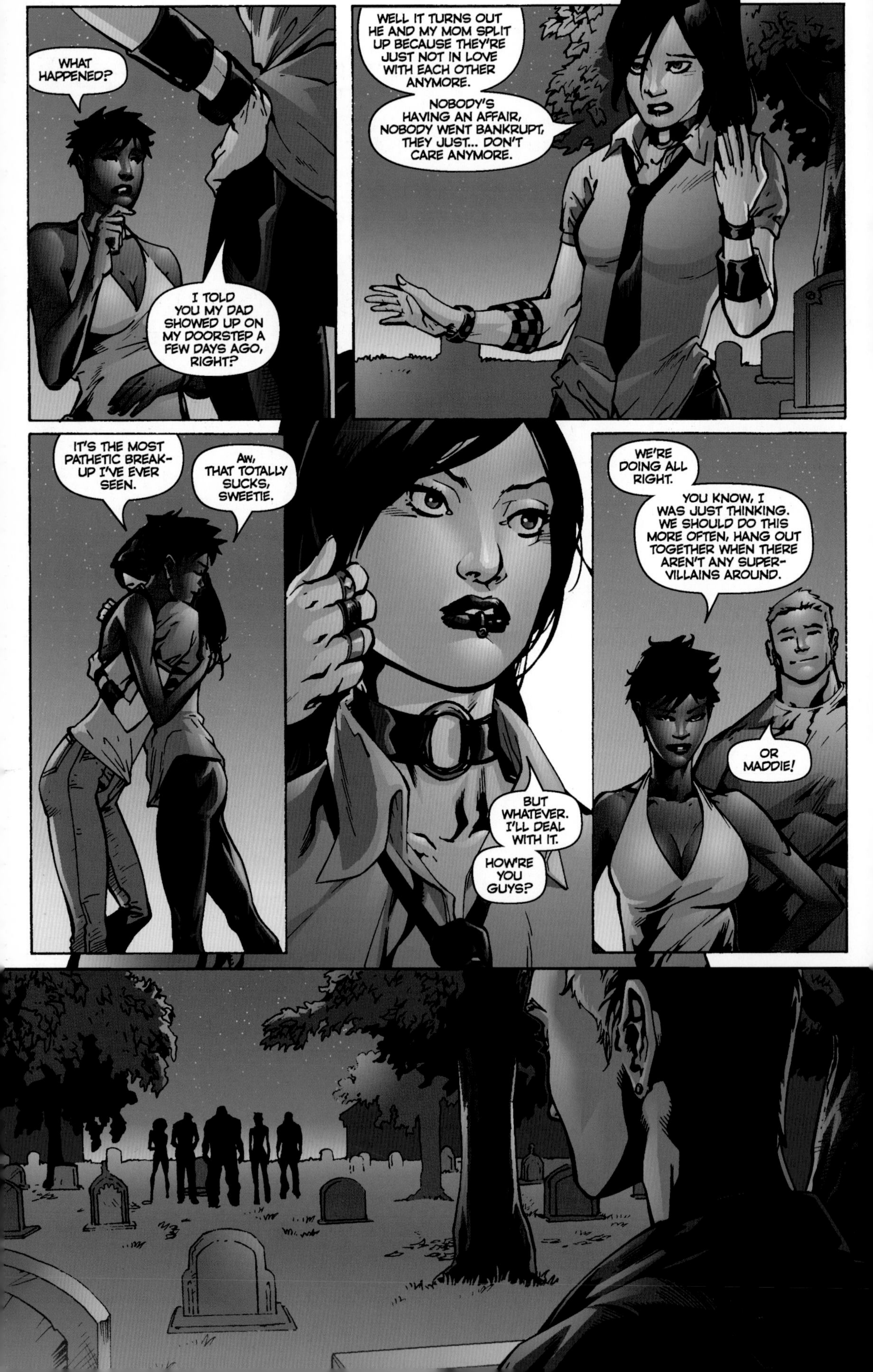
WHAT HAPPENED?
I TOLD YOU MY DAD SHOWED UP ON MY DOORSTEP A FEW DAYS AGO, RIGHT?
WELL IT TURNS OUT HE AND MY MOM SPLIT UP BECAUSE THEY'RE JUST NOT IN LOVE WITH EACH OTHER ANYMORE.
NOBODY'S HAVING AN AFFAIR, NOBODY WENT BANKRUPT, THEY JUST... DON'T CARE ANYMORE.
IT'S THE MOST PATHETIC BREAK-UP I'VE EVER SEEN.
AW, THAT TOTALLY SUCKS, SWEETIE.
BUT WHATEVER. I'LL DEAL WITH IT.
HOW'RE YOU GUYS?
WE'RE DOING ALL RIGHT.
YOU KNOW, I WAS JUST THINKING. WE SHOULD DO THIS MORE OFTEN, HANG OUT TOGETHER WHEN THERE AREN'T ANY SUPER-VILLAINS AROUND.
OR MADDIE!

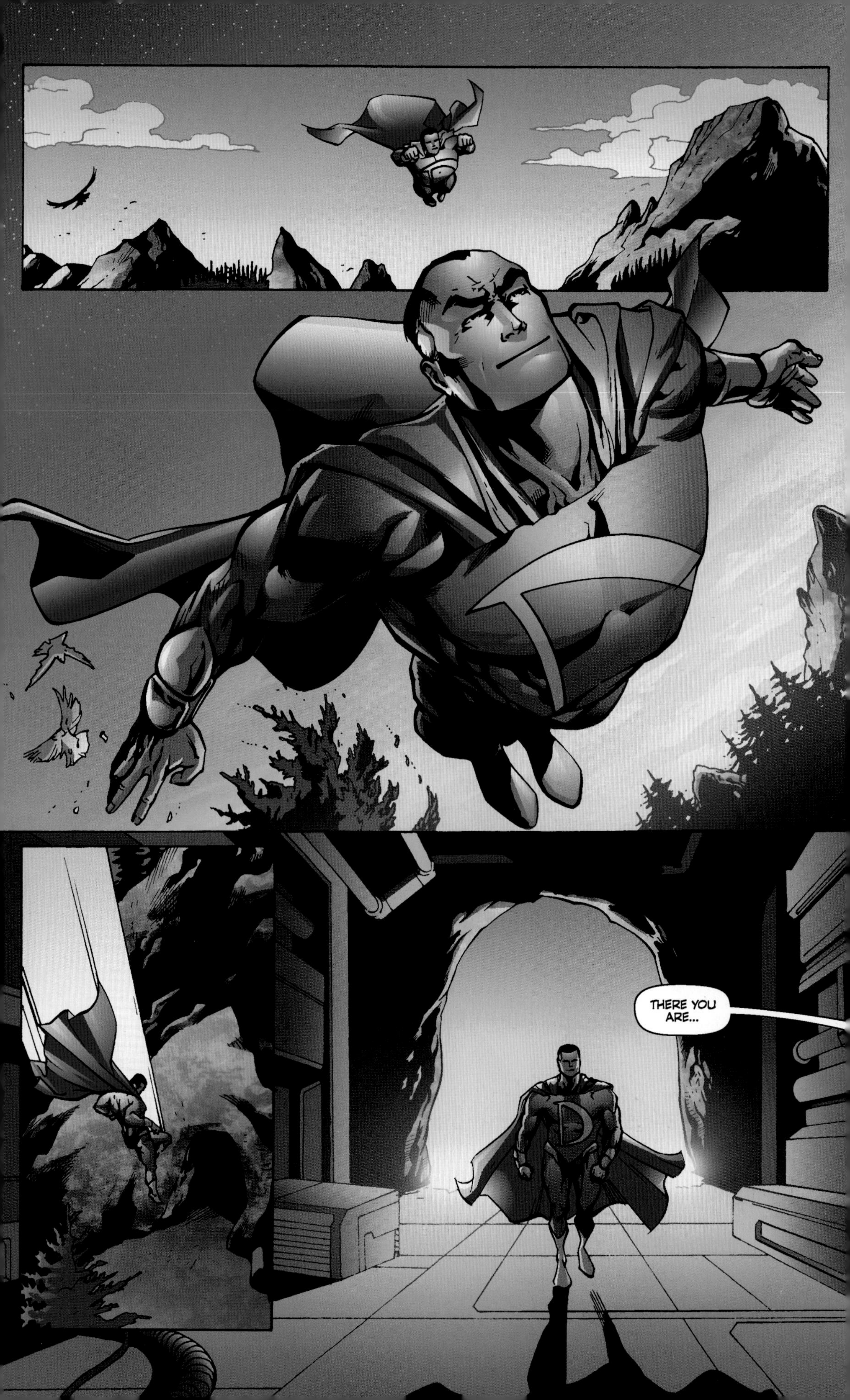
THERE YOU ARE...

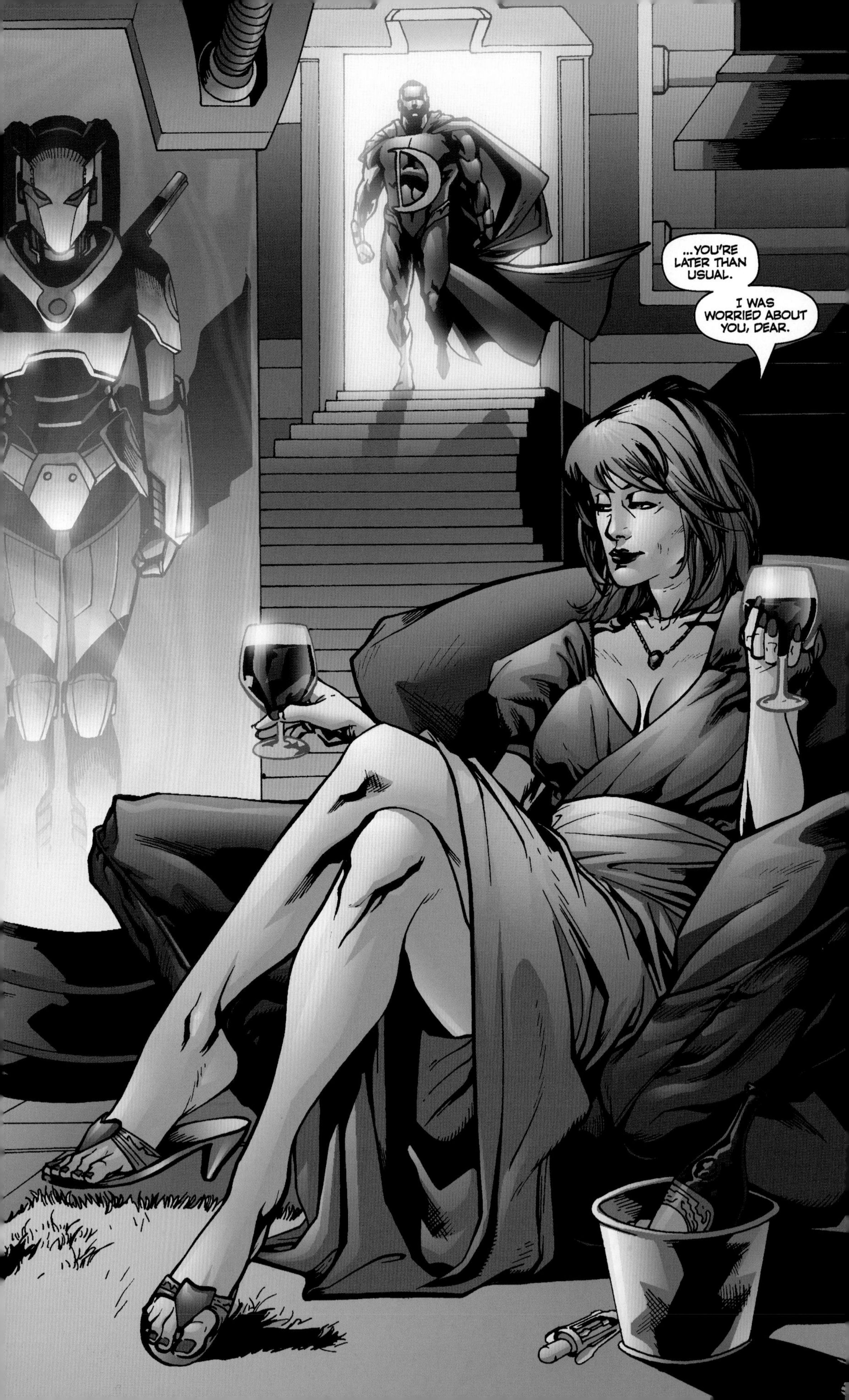
...YOU'RE LATER THAN USUAL.
I WAS WORRIED ABOUT YOU, DEAR.

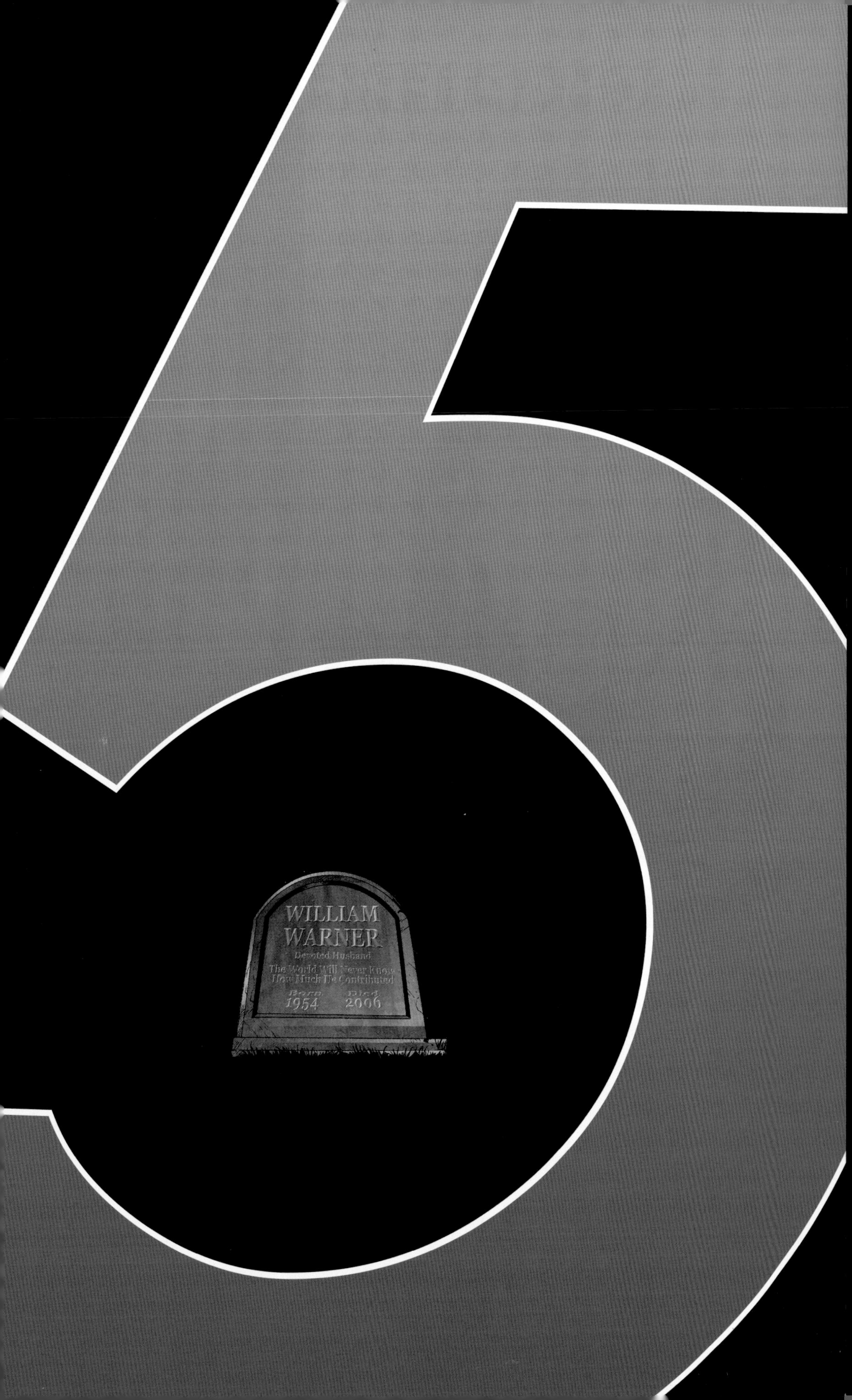
5
WILLIAM WARNER
Devoted Husband
The World Will Never Know How Much He Contributed
Born 1954
Died 2006

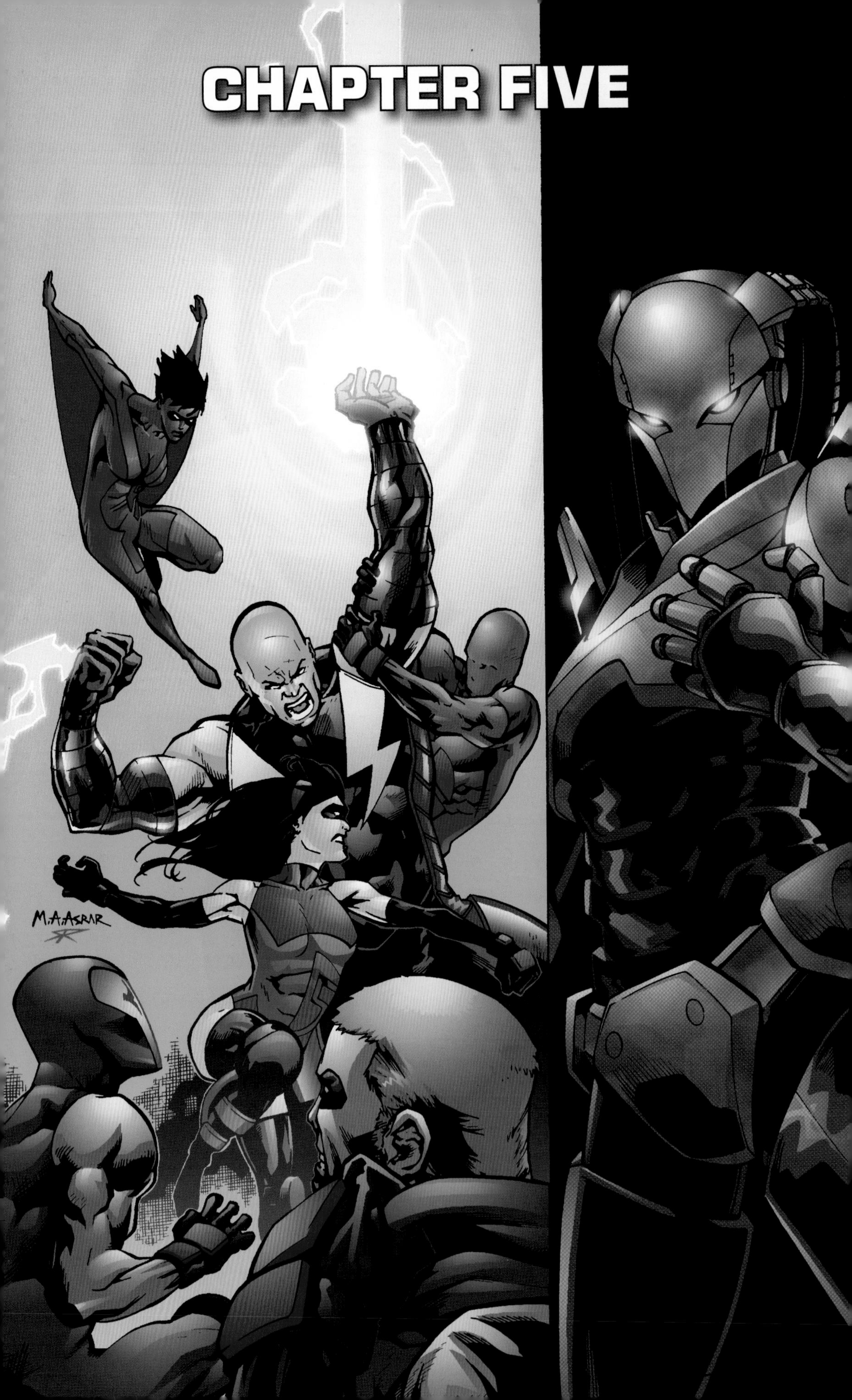
CHAPTER FIVE
M.A.ASRAR

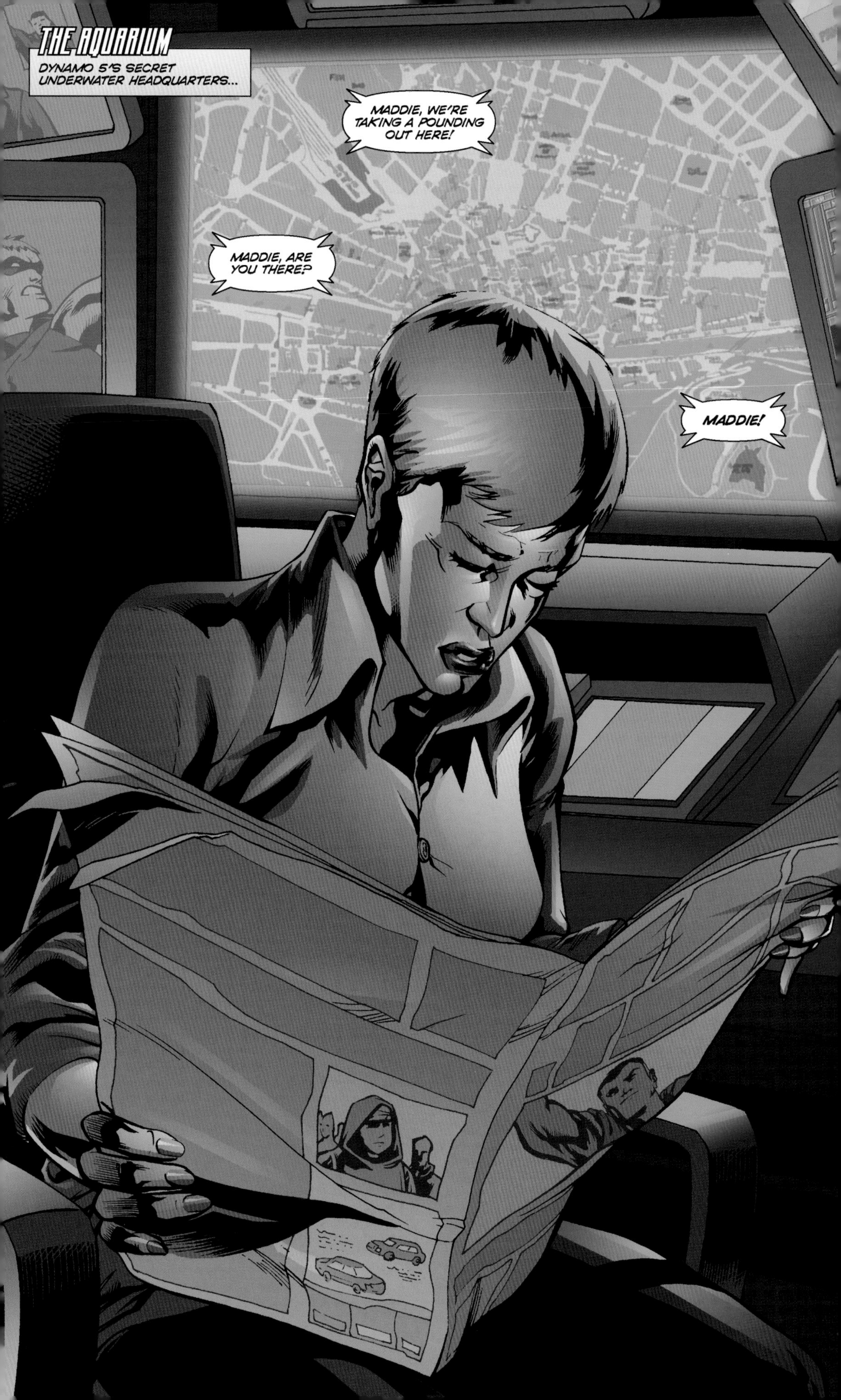
THE AQUARIUM
DYNAMO 5'S SECRET UNDERWATER HEADQUARTERS...
MADDIE, WE'RE TAKING A POUNDING OUT HERE!
MADDIE, ARE YOU THERE?
MADDIE!

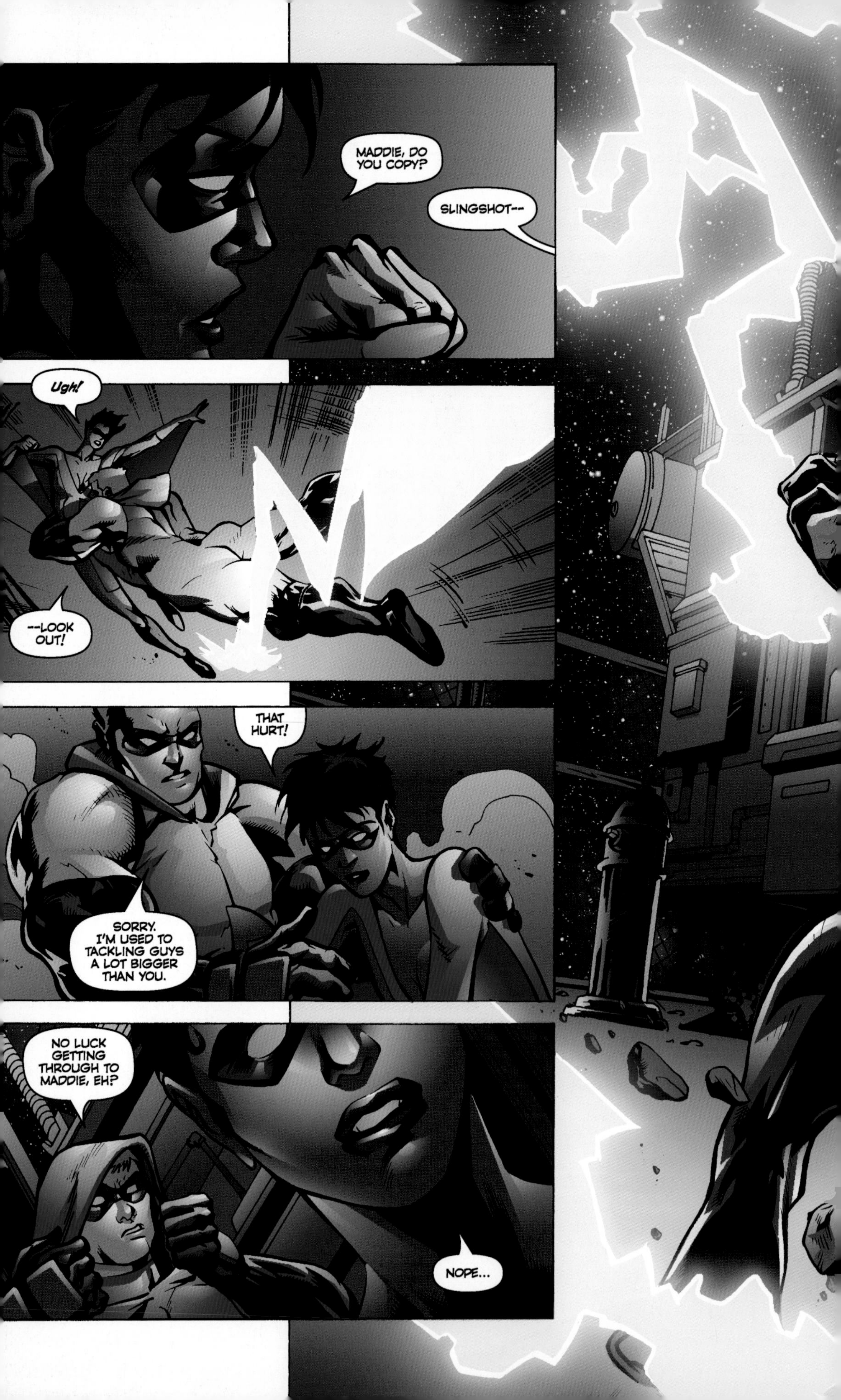
MADDIE, DO YOU COPY?
SLINGSHOT--
Ugh!
--LOOK OUT!
THAT HURT!
SORRY. I'M USED TO TACKLING GUYS A LOT BIGGER THAN YOU.
NO LUCK GETTING THROUGH TO MADDIE, EH?
NOPE...

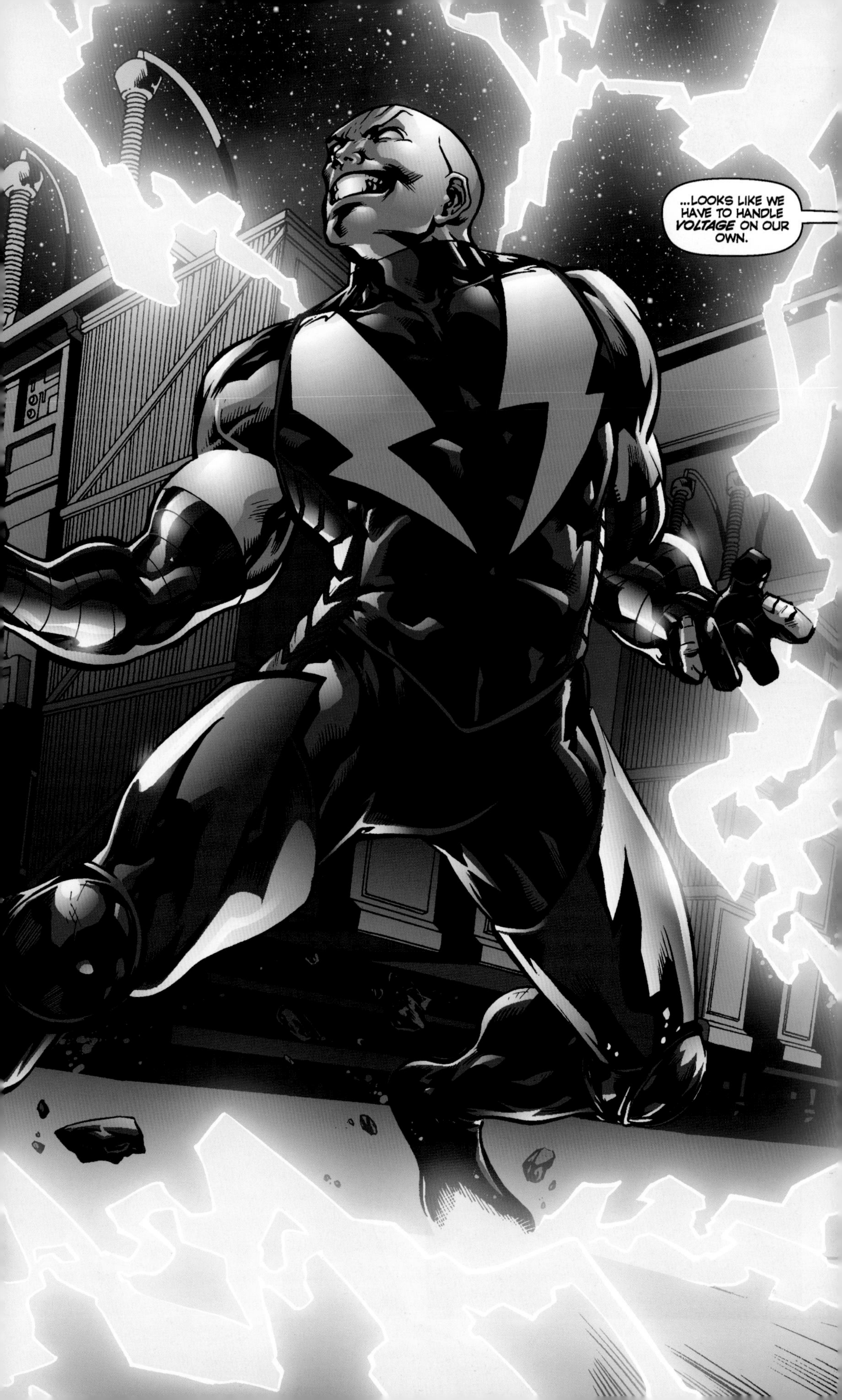
...LOOKS LIKE WE HAVE TO HANDLE VOLTAGE ON OUR OWN.

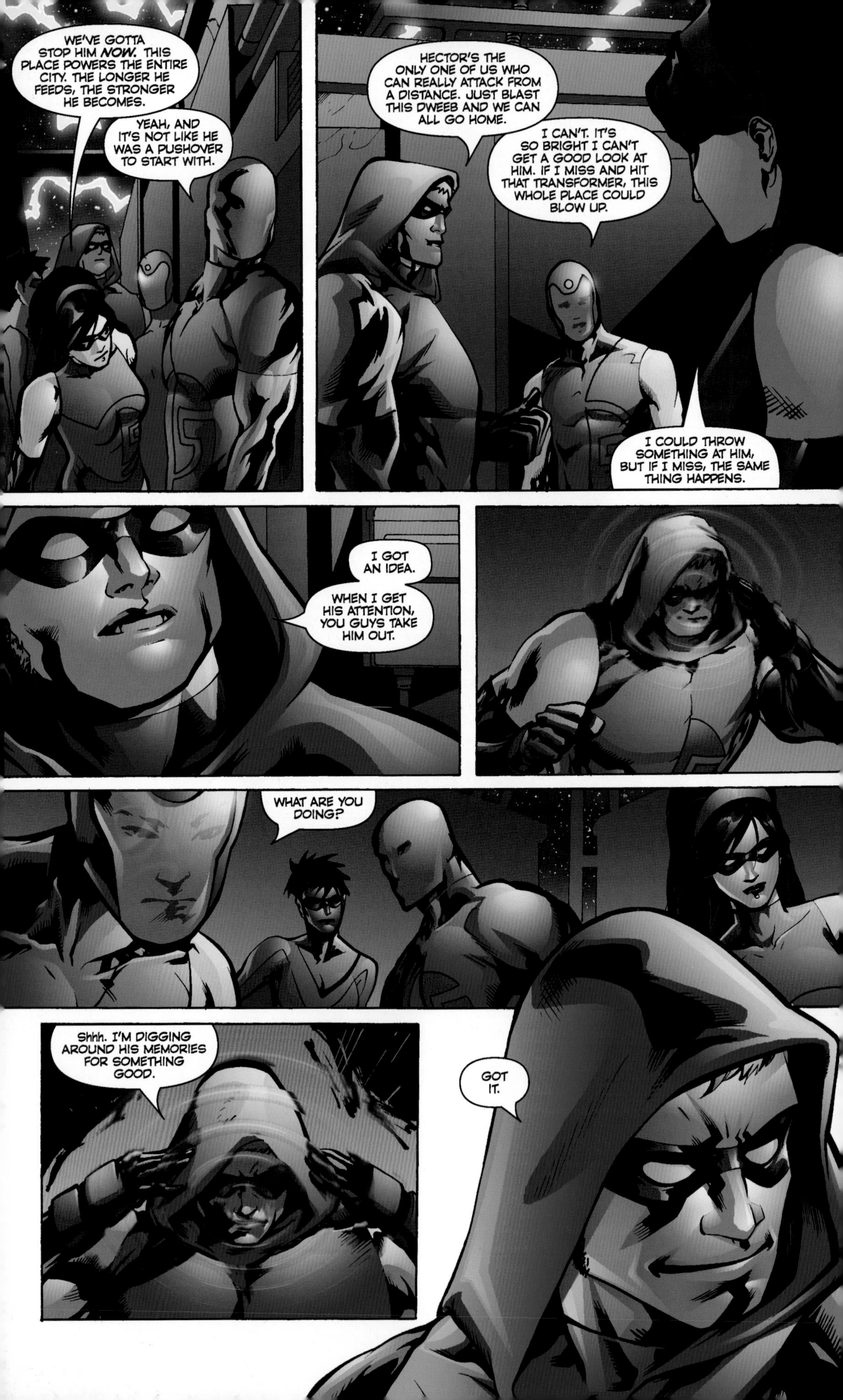
WE'VE GOTTA STOP HIM NOW. THIS PLACE POWERS THE ENTIRE CITY. THE LONGER HE FEEDS, THE STRONGER HE BECOMES.
YEAH, AND IT'S NOT LIKE HE WAS A PUSHOVER TO START WITH.
HECTOR'S THE ONLY ONE OF US WHO CAN REALLY ATTACK FROM A DISTANCE. JUST BLAST THIS DWEEB AND WE CAN ALL GO HOME.
I CAN'T. IT'S SO BRIGHT I CAN'T GET A GOOD LOOK AT HIM. IF I MISS AND HIT THAT TRANSFORMER, THIS WHOLE PLACE COULD BLOW UP.
I COULD THROW SOMETHING AT HIM, BUT IF I MISS, THE SAME THING HAPPENS.
I GOT AN IDEA.
WHEN I GET HIS ATTENTION, YOU GUYS TAKE HIM OUT.
WHAT ARE YOU DOING?
Shhh. I'M DIGGING AROUND HIS MEMORIES FOR SOMETHING GOOD.
GOT IT.

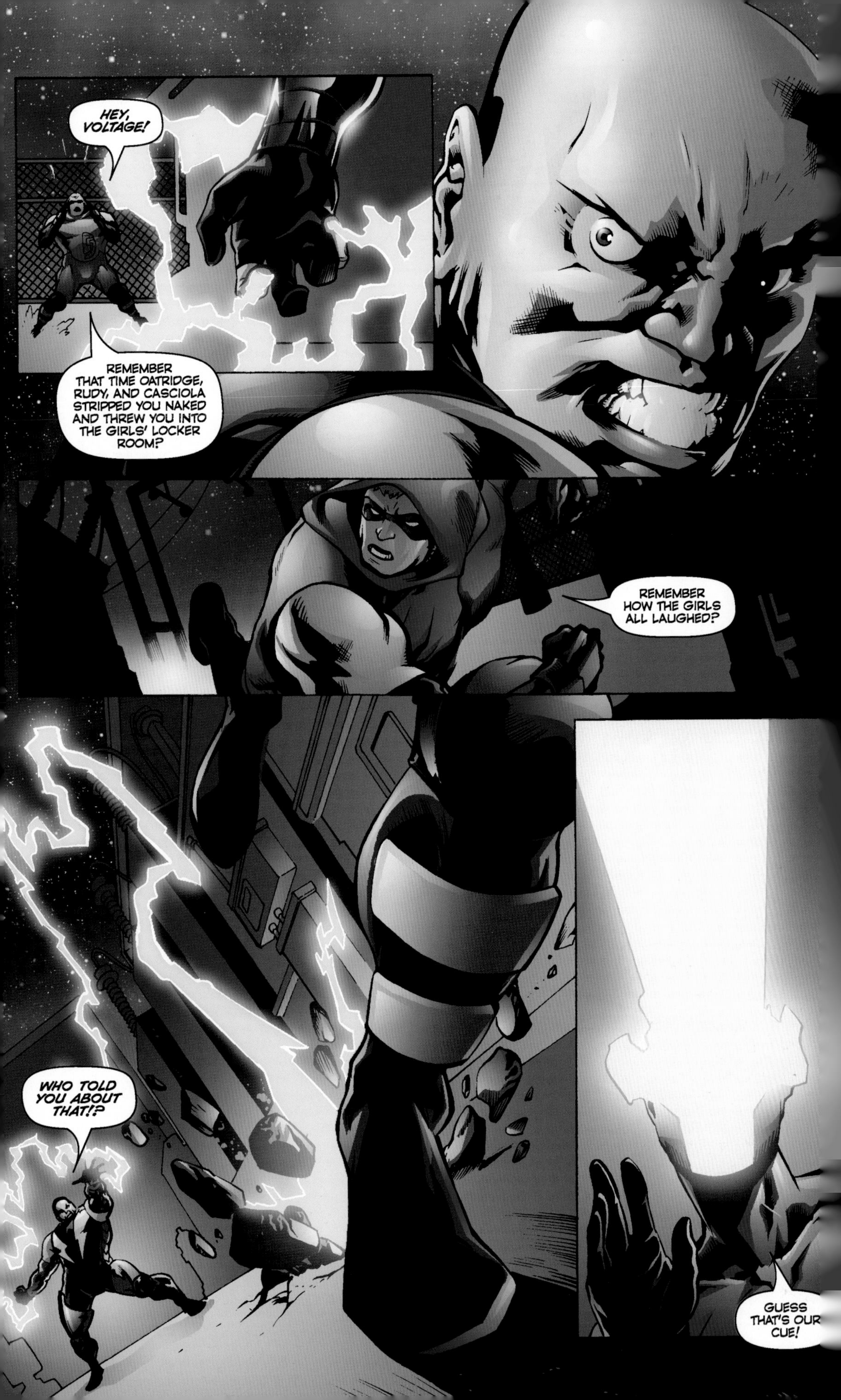

HEY, VOLTAGE!
REMEMBER THAT TIME OATRIDGE, RUDY, AND CASCIOLA STRIPPED YOU NAKED AND THREW YOU INTO THE GIRLS' LOCKER ROOM?
REMEMBER HOW THE GIRLS ALL LAUGHED?
WHO TOLD YOU ABOUT THAT!?
GUESS THAT'S OUR CUE!

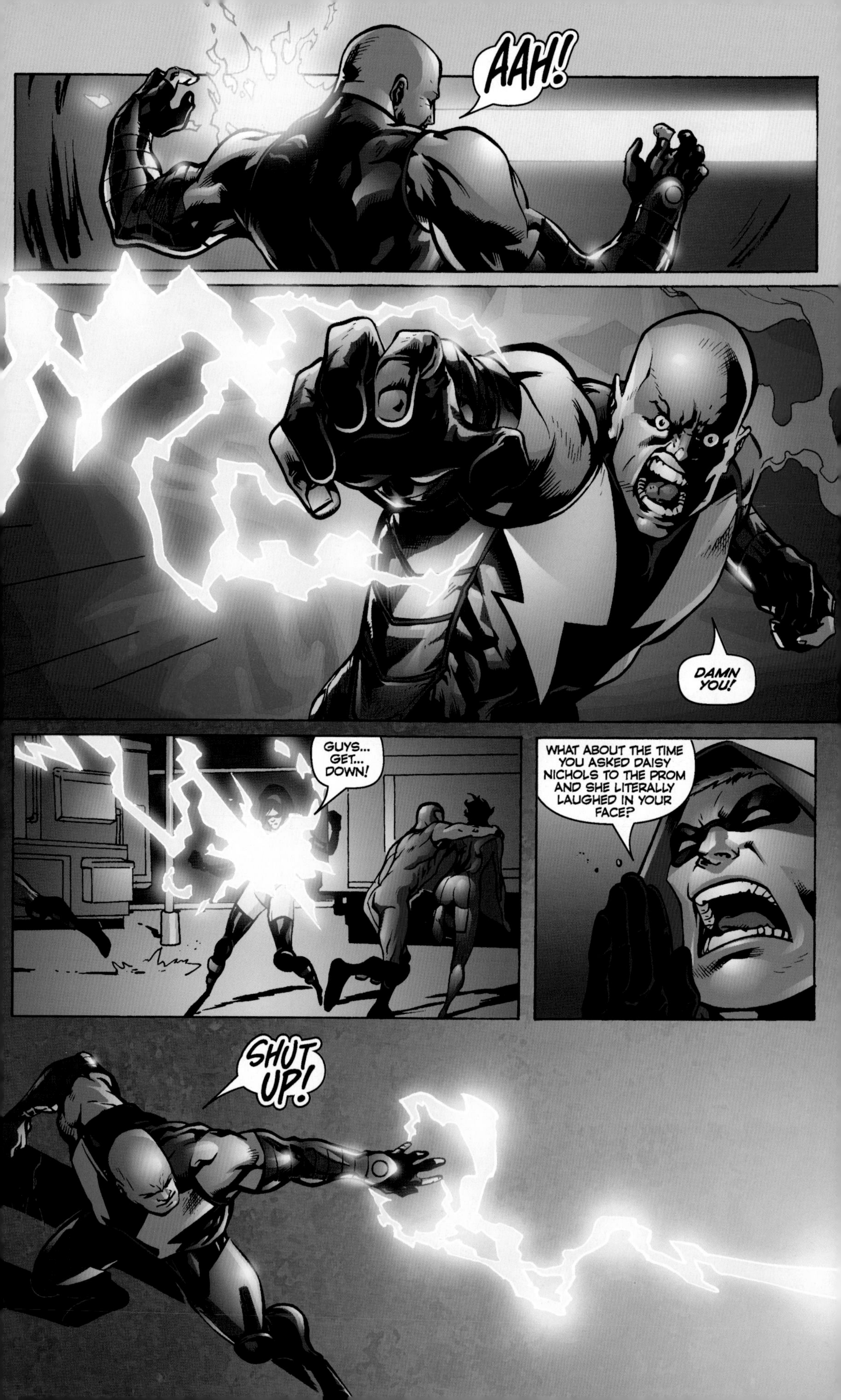
AAH!
DAMN YOU!
GUYS... GET... DOWN!
WHAT ABOUT THE TIME YOU ASKED DAISY NICHOLS TO THE PROM AND SHE LITERALLY LAUGHED IN YOUR FACE?
SHUT UP!

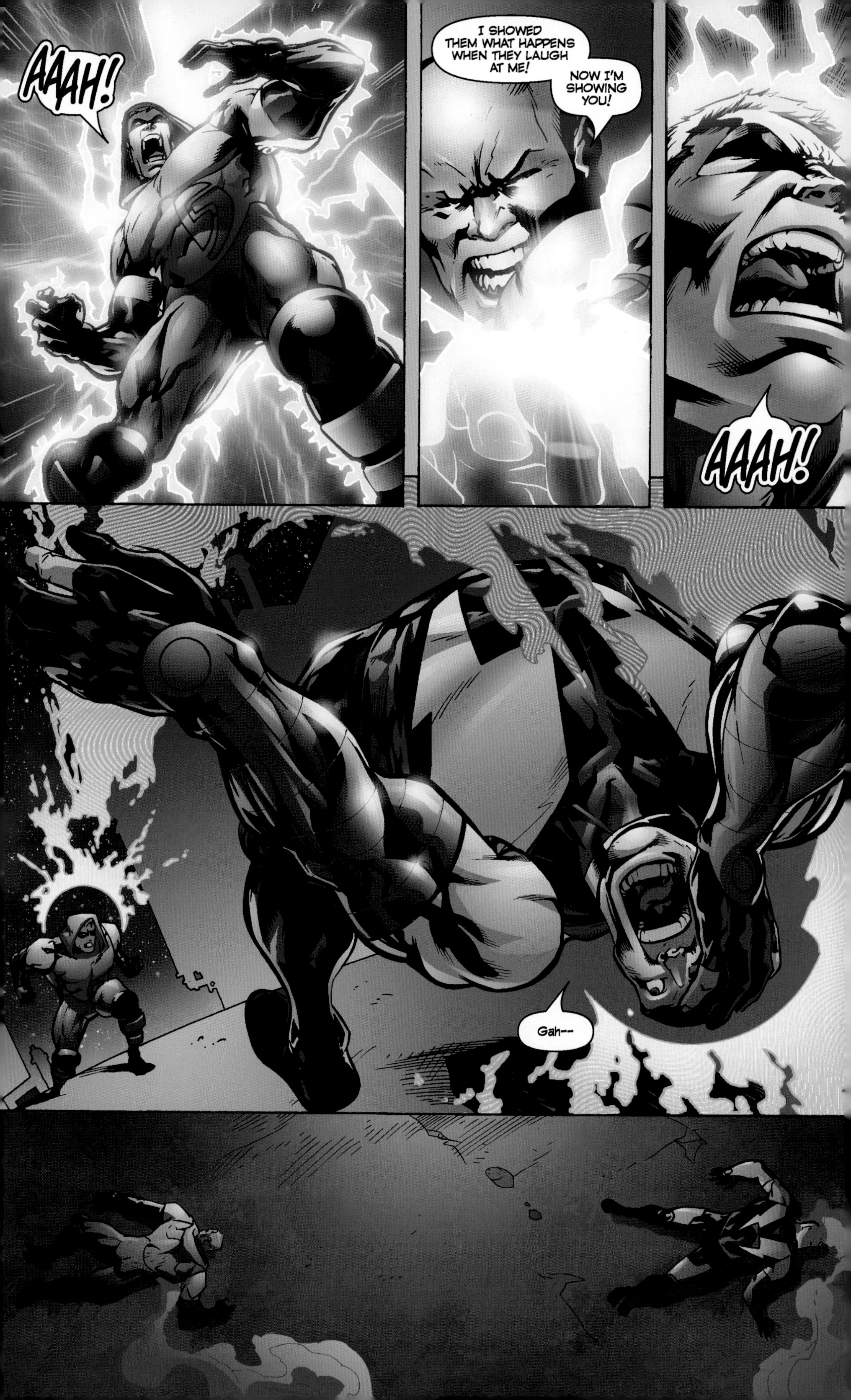

AAAH!
I SHOWED THEM WHAT HAPPENS WHEN THEY LAUGH AT ME!
NOW I'M SHOWING YOU!
AAAH!
Gah--

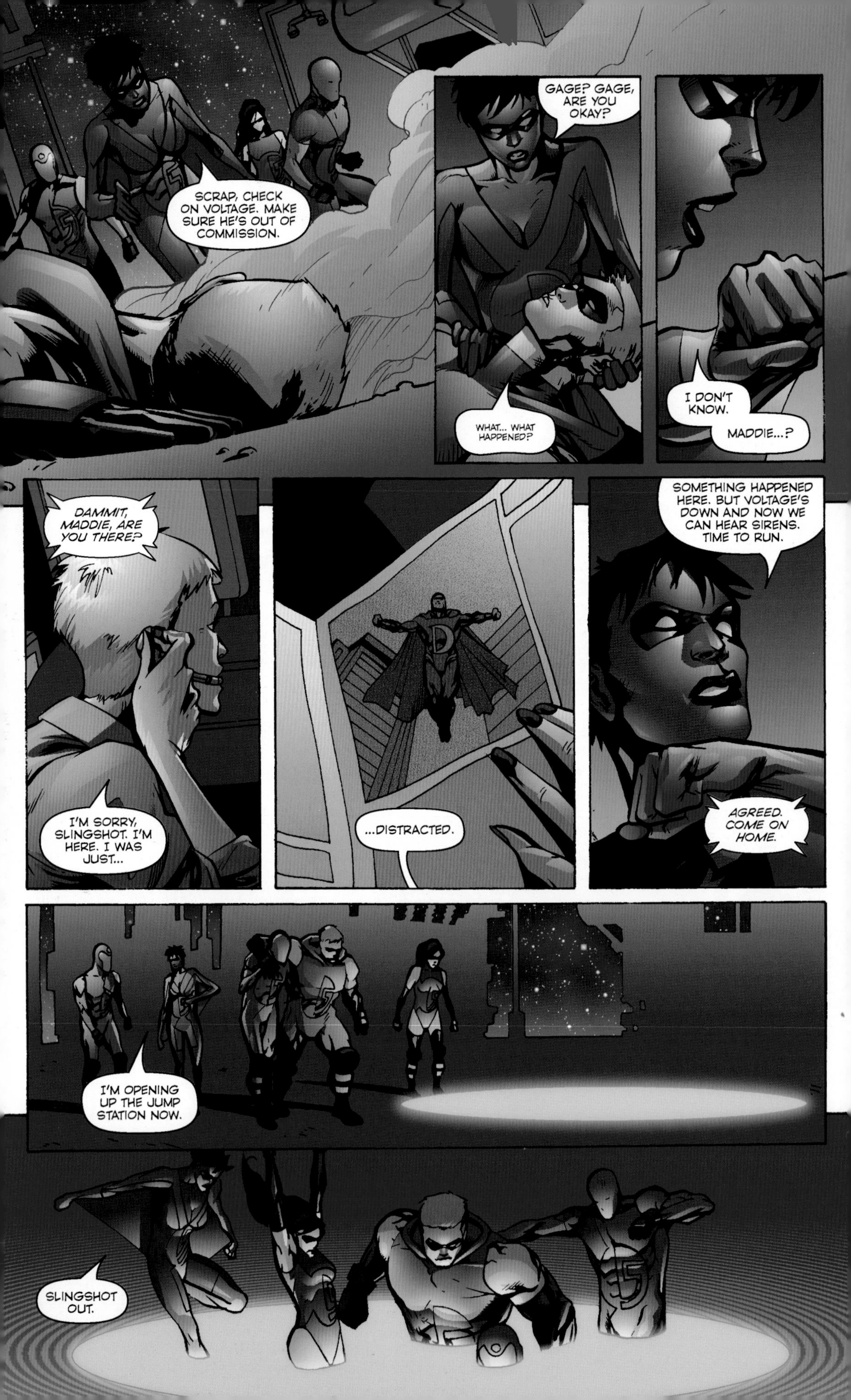
SCRAP, CHECK ON VOLTAGE. MAKE SURE HE'S OUT OF COMMISSION.
GAGE? GAGE, ARE YOU OKAY?
WHAT... WHAT HAPPENED?
I DON'T KNOW.
MADDIE...?
DAMMIT, MADDIE, ARE YOU THERE?
I'M SORRY, SLINGSHOT. I'M HERE. I WAS JUST...
...DISTRACTED.
SOMETHING HAPPENED HERE. BUT VOLTAGE'S DOWN AND NOW WE CAN HEAR SIRENS. TIME TO RUN.
AGREED. COME ON HOME.
I'M OPENING UP THE JUMP STATION NOW.
SLINGSHOT OUT.

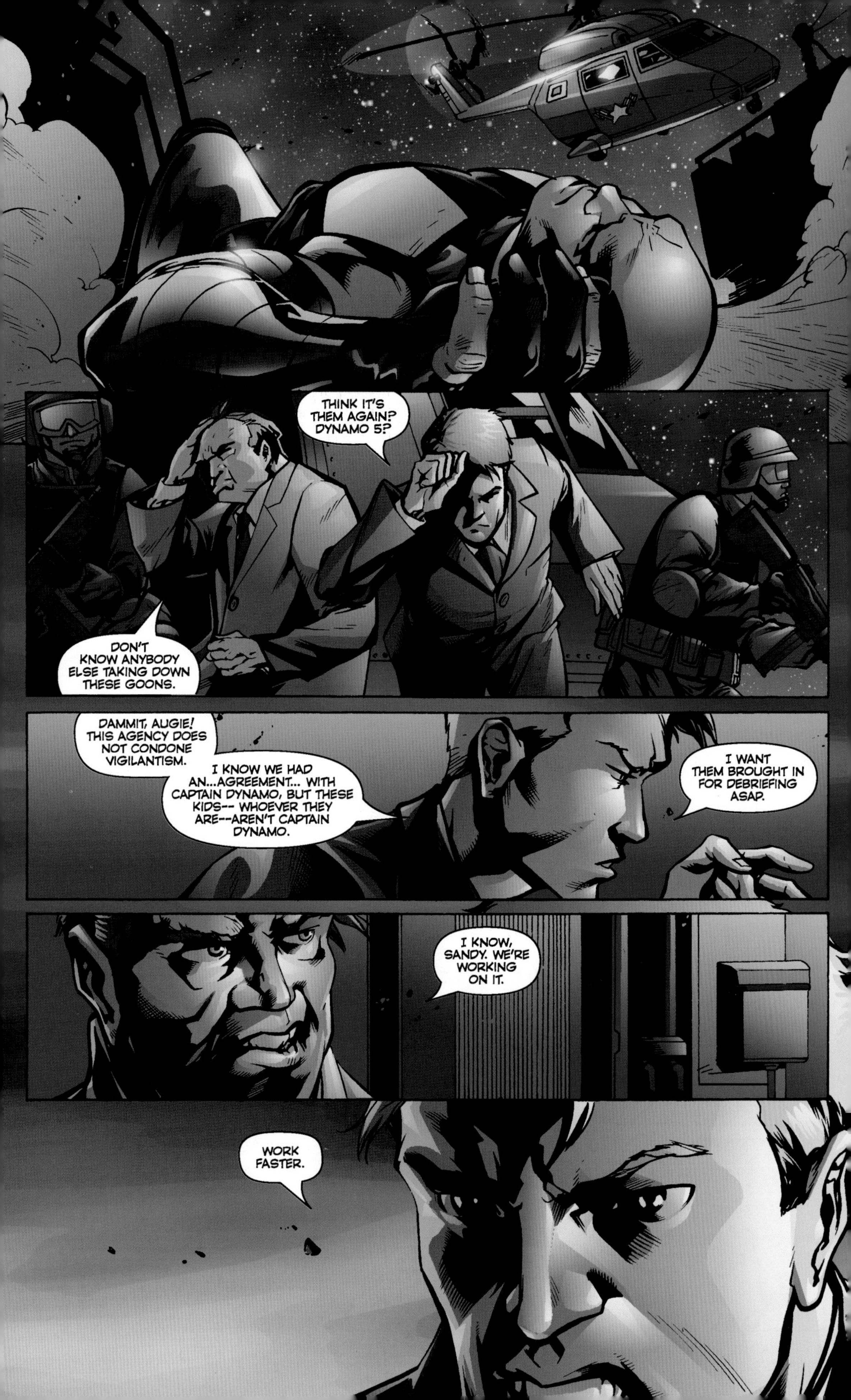
THINK IT'S THEM AGAIN? DYNAMO 5?
DON'T KNOW ANYBODY ELSE TAKING DOWN THESE GOONS.
DAMMIT, AUGIE! THIS AGENCY DOES NOT CONDONE VIGILANTISM.
I KNOW WE HAD AN...AGREEMENT... WITH CAPTAIN DYNAMO, BUT THESE KIDS-- WHOEVER THEY ARE--AREN'T CAPTAIN DYNAMO.
I WANT THEM BROUGHT IN FOR DEBRIEFING ASAP.
I KNOW, SANDY. WE'RE WORKING ON IT.
WORK FASTER.

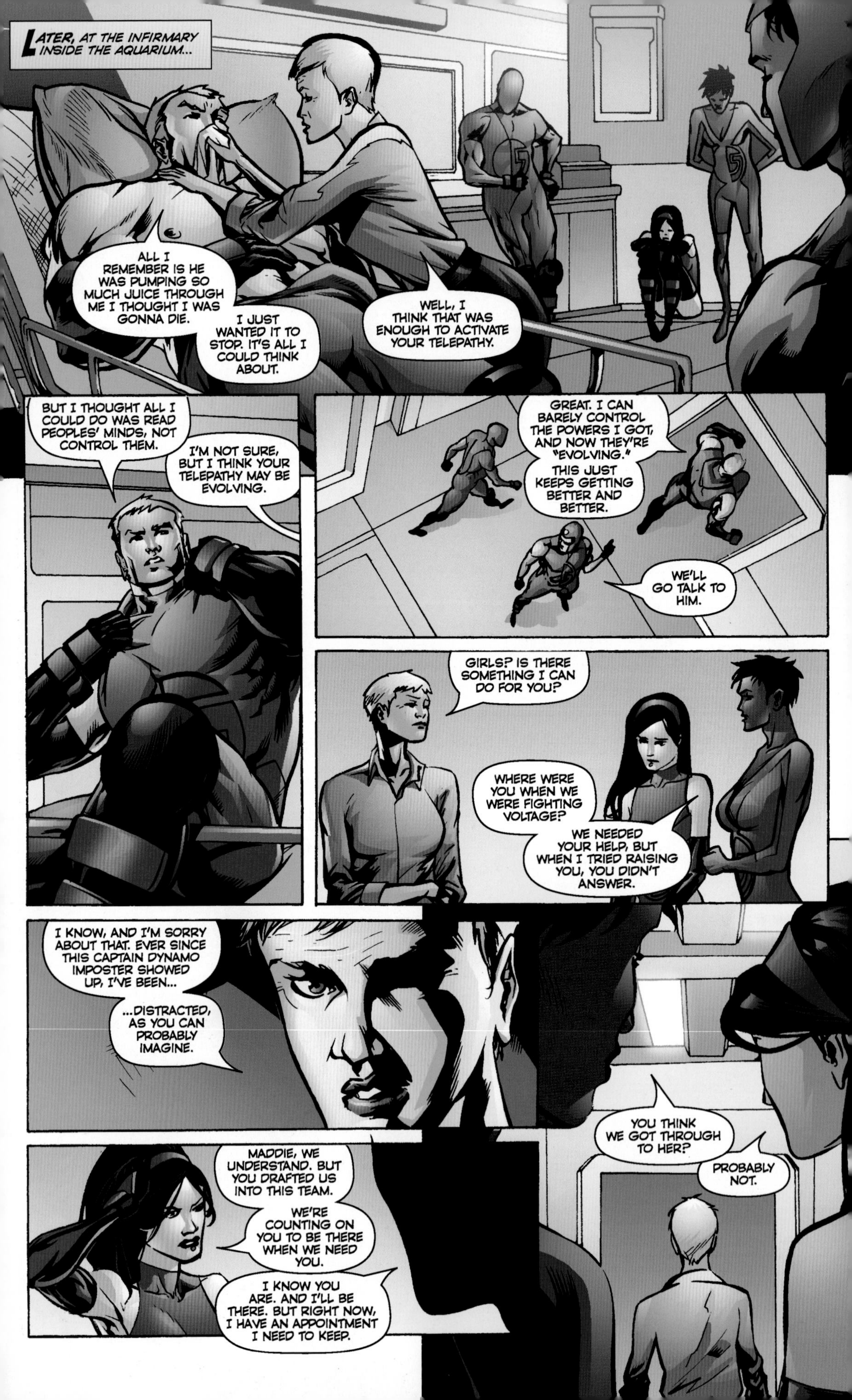
LATER, AT THE INFIRMARY INSIDE THE AQUARIUM...
ALL I REMEMBER IS HE WAS PUMPING SO MUCH JUICE THROUGH ME I THOUGHT I WAS GONNA DIE.
I JUST WANTED IT TO STOP. IT'S ALL I COULD THINK ABOUT.
WELL, I THINK THAT WAS ENOUGH TO ACTIVATE YOUR TELEPATHY.
BUT I THOUGHT ALL I COULD DO WAS READ PEOPLES' MINDS, NOT CONTROL THEM.
I'M NOT SURE, BUT I THINK YOUR TELEPATHY MAY BE EVOLVING.
GREAT. I CAN BARELY CONTROL THE POWERS I GOT, AND NOW THEY'RE "EVOLVING."
THIS JUST KEEPS GETTING BETTER AND BETTER.
WE'LL GO TALK TO HIM.
GIRLS? IS THERE SOMETHING I CAN DO FOR YOU?
WHERE WERE YOU WHEN WE WERE FIGHTING VOLTAGE?
WE NEEDED YOUR HELP, BUT WHEN I TRIED RAISING YOU, YOU DIDN'T ANSWER.
I KNOW, AND I'M SORRY ABOUT THAT. EVER SINCE THIS CAPTAIN DYNAMO IMPOSTER SHOWED UP, I'VE BEEN...
...DISTRACTED, AS YOU CAN PROBABLY IMAGINE.
MADDIE, WE UNDERSTAND. BUT YOU DRAFTED US INTO THIS TEAM.
WE'RE COUNTING ON YOU TO BE THERE WHEN WE NEED YOU.
I KNOW YOU ARE. AND I'LL BE THERE. BUT RIGHT NOW, I HAVE AN APPOINTMENT I NEED TO KEEP.
YOU THINK WE GOT THROUGH TO HER?
PROBABLY NOT.

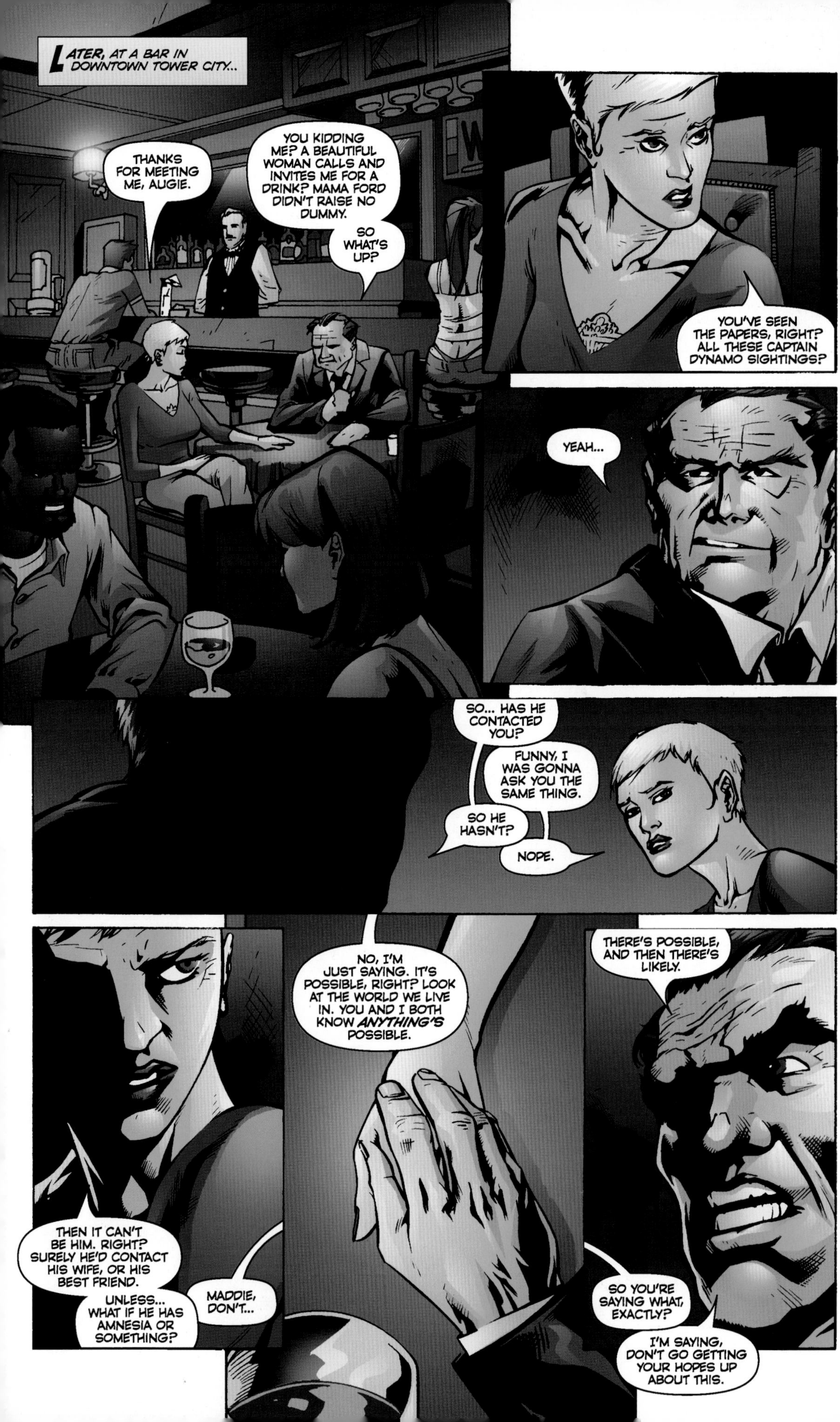
LATER, AT A BAR IN DOWNTOWN TOWER CITY...
THANKS FOR MEETING ME, AUGIE.
YOU KIDDING ME? A BEAUTIFUL WOMAN CALLS AND INVITES ME FOR A DRINK? MAMA FORD DIDN'T RAISE NO DUMMY.
SO WHAT'S UP?
YOU'VE SEEN THE PAPERS, RIGHT? ALL THESE CAPTAIN DYNAMO SIGHTINGS?
YEAH...
SO... HAS HE CONTACTED YOU?
FUNNY, I WAS GONNA ASK YOU THE SAME THING.
SO HE HASN'T?
NOPE.
THEN IT CAN'T BE HIM. RIGHT? SURELY HE'D CONTACT HIS WIFE, OR HIS BEST FRIEND.
UNLESS... WHAT IF HE HAS AMNESIA OR SOMETHING?
MADDIE, DON'T...
NO, I'M JUST SAYING. IT'S POSSIBLE, RIGHT? LOOK AT THE WORLD WE LIVE IN. YOU AND I BOTH KNOW *ANYTHING'S* POSSIBLE.
THERE'S POSSIBLE, AND THEN THERE'S LIKELY.
SO YOU'RE SAYING WHAT, EXACTLY?
I'M SAYING, DON'T GO GETTING YOUR HOPES UP ABOUT THIS.

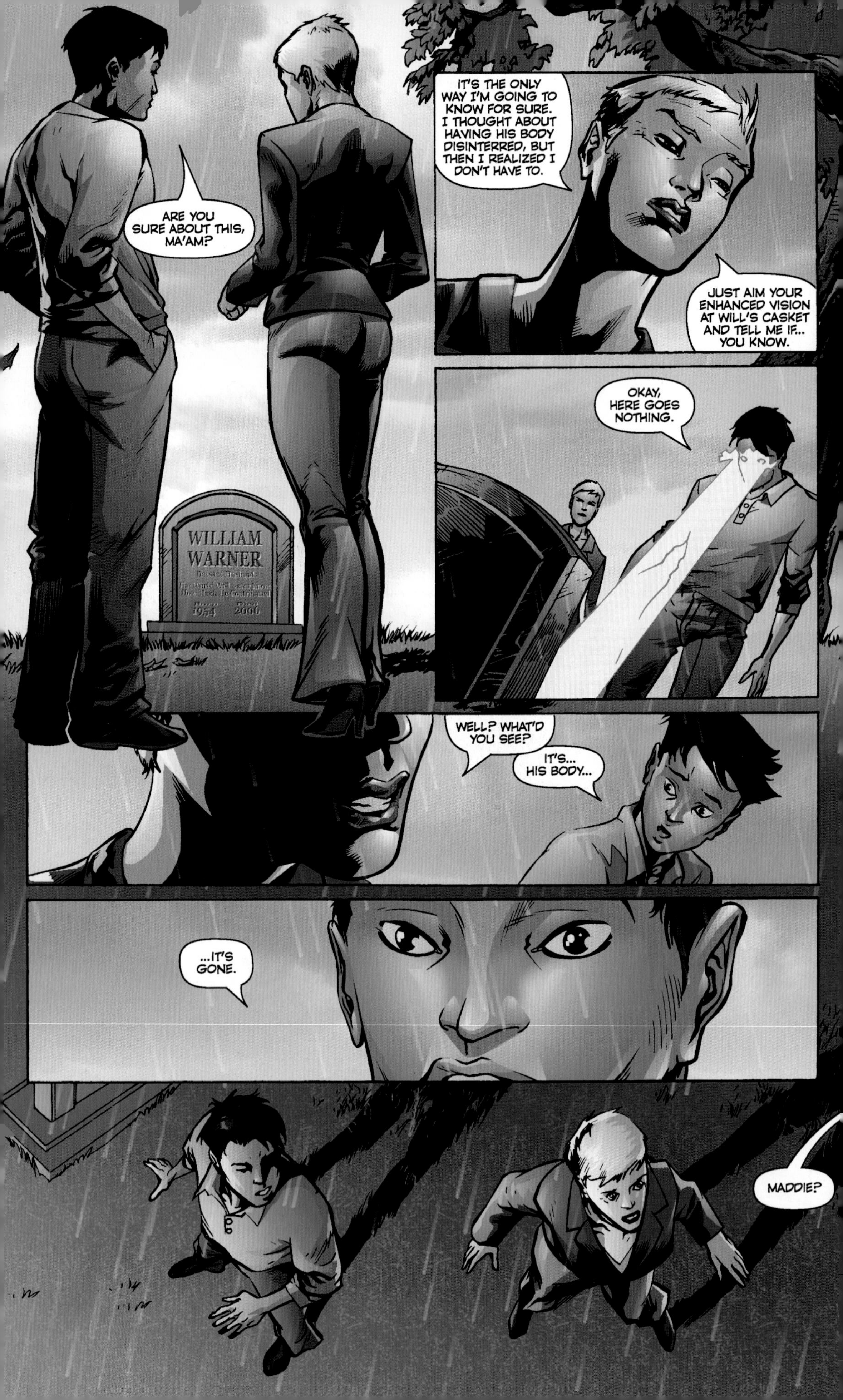
ARE YOU SURE ABOUT THIS, MA'AM?
IT'S THE ONLY WAY I'M GOING TO KNOW FOR SURE. I THOUGHT ABOUT HAVING HIS BODY DISINTERRED, BUT THEN I REALIZED I DON'T HAVE TO.
JUST AIM YOUR ENHANCED VISION AT WILL'S CASKET AND TELL ME IF... YOU KNOW.
WILLIAM WARNER
1954 2006
OKAY, HERE GOES NOTHING.
WELL? WHAT'D YOU SEE?
IT'S... HIS BODY...
...IT'S GONE.
MADDIE?

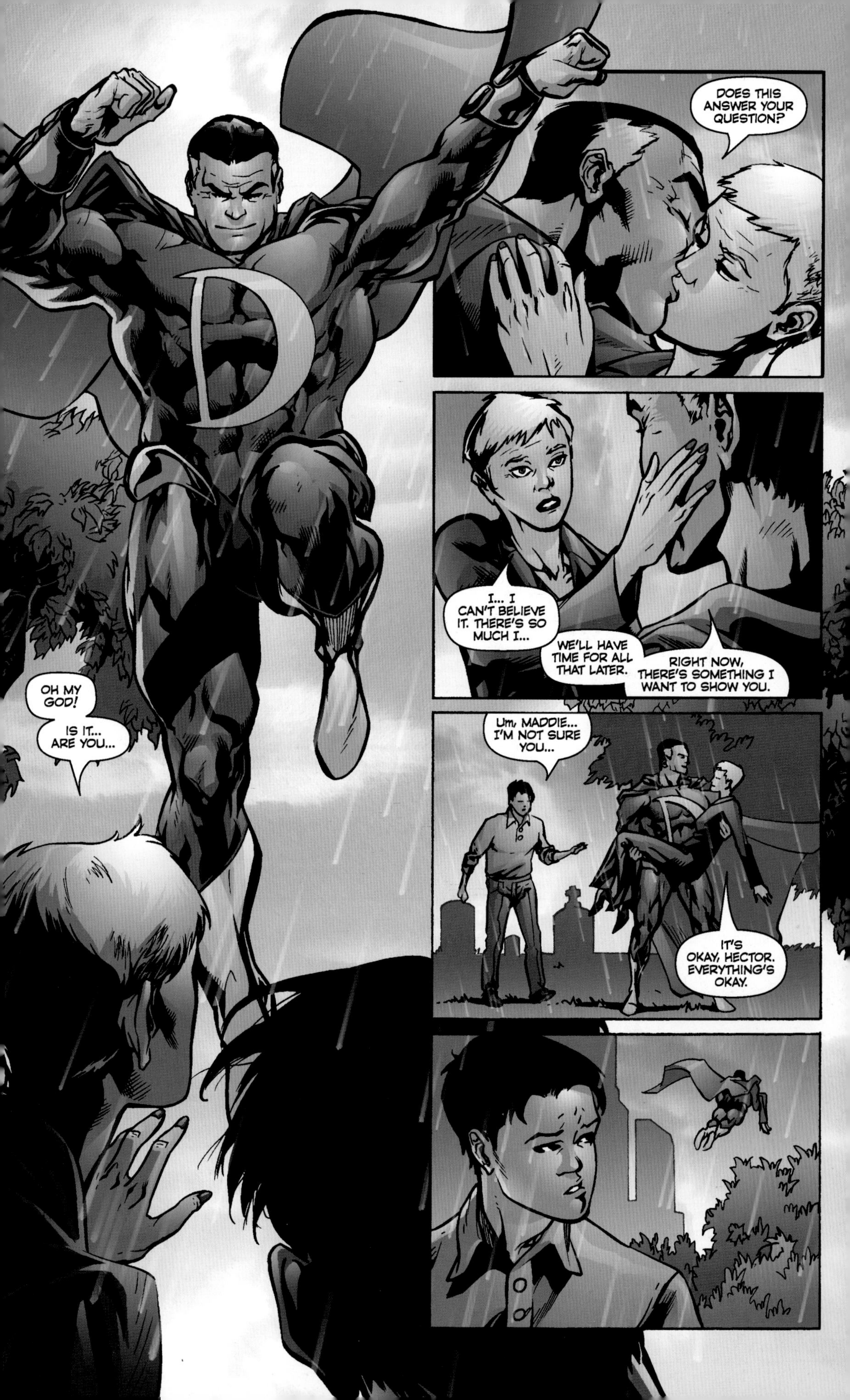
DOES THIS ANSWER YOUR QUESTION?
OH MY GOD!
IS IT... ARE YOU...
I... I CAN'T BELIEVE IT. THERE'S SO MUCH I...
WE'LL HAVE TIME FOR ALL THAT LATER.
RIGHT NOW, THERE'S SOMETHING I WANT TO SHOW YOU.
Um, MADDIE... I'M NOT SURE YOU...
IT'S OKAY, HECTOR. EVERYTHING'S OKAY.

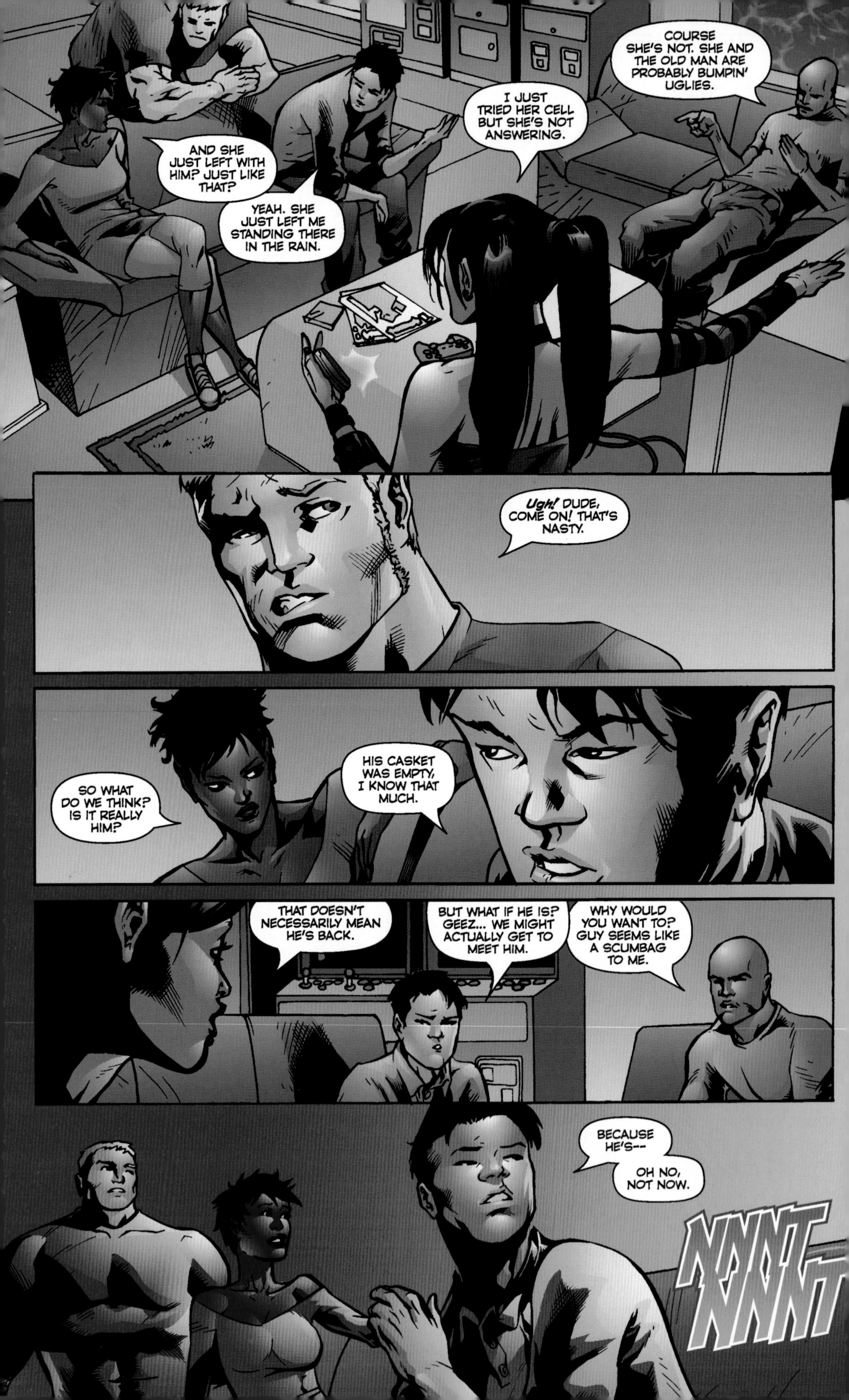

AND SHE JUST LEFT WITH HIM? JUST LIKE THAT?
YEAH. SHE JUST LEFT ME STANDING THERE IN THE RAIN.
I JUST TRIED HER CELL BUT SHE'S NOT ANSWERING.
COURSE SHE'S NOT. SHE AND THE OLD MAN ARE PROBABLY BUMPIN' UGLIES.
Ugh! DUDE, COME ON! THAT'S NASTY.
SO WHAT DO WE THINK? IS IT REALLY HIM?
HIS CASKET WAS EMPTY, I KNOW THAT MUCH.
THAT DOESN'T NECESSARILY MEAN HE'S BACK.
BUT WHAT IF HE IS? GEEZ... WE MIGHT ACTUALLY GET TO MEET HIM.
WHY WOULD YOU WANT TO? GUY SEEMS LIKE A SCUMBAG TO ME.
BECAUSE HE'S--
OH NO, NOT NOW.
NNNT NNNT

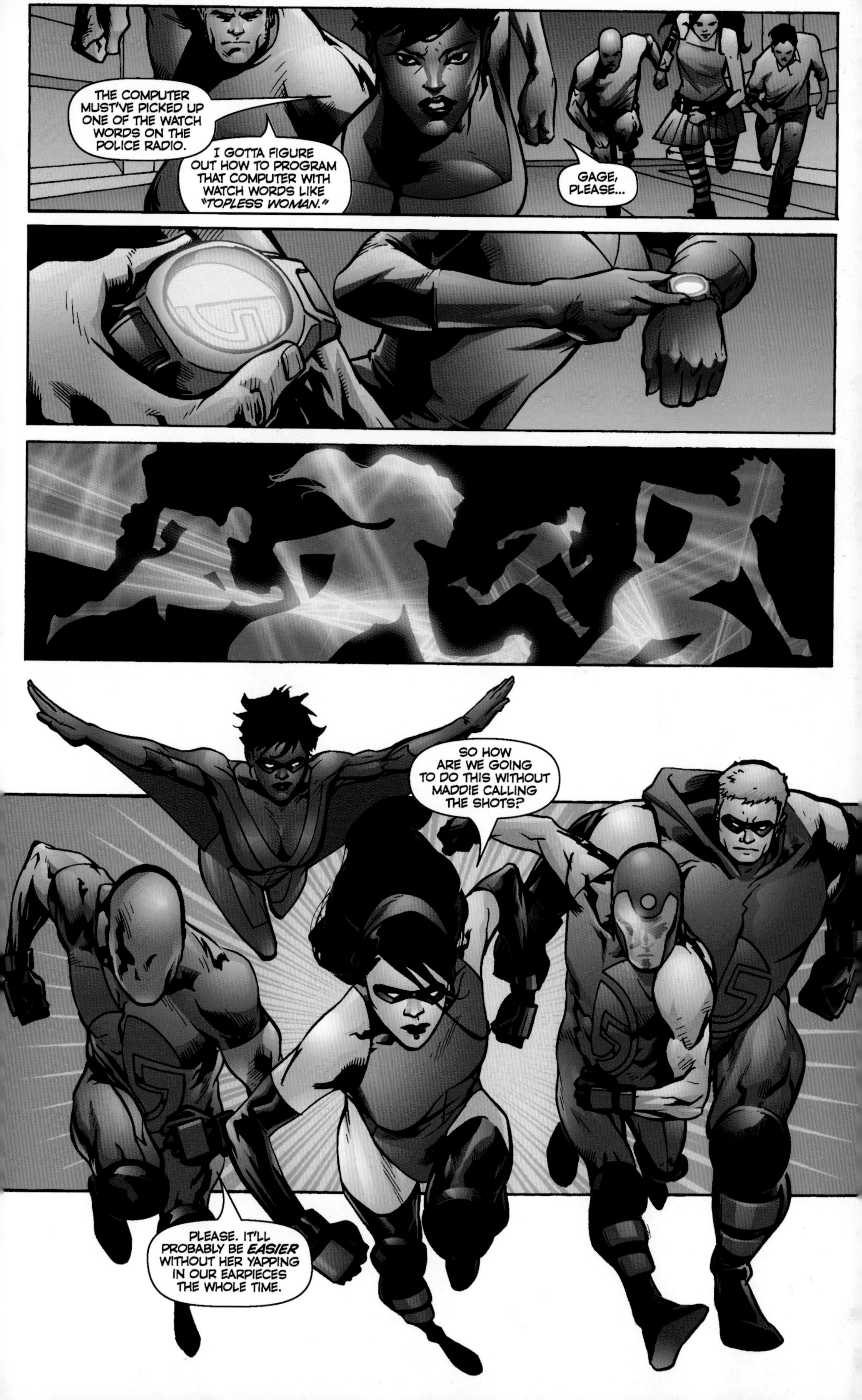
THE COMPUTER MUST'VE PICKED UP ONE OF THE WATCH WORDS ON THE POLICE RADIO.
I GOTTA FIGURE OUT HOW TO PROGRAM THAT COMPUTER WITH WATCH WORDS LIKE "TOPLESS WOMAN."
GAGE, PLEASE...
SO HOW ARE WE GOING TO DO THIS WITHOUT MADDIE CALLING THE SHOTS?
PLEASE. IT'LL PROBABLY BE EASIER WITHOUT HER YAPPING IN OUR EARPIECES THE WHOLE TIME.

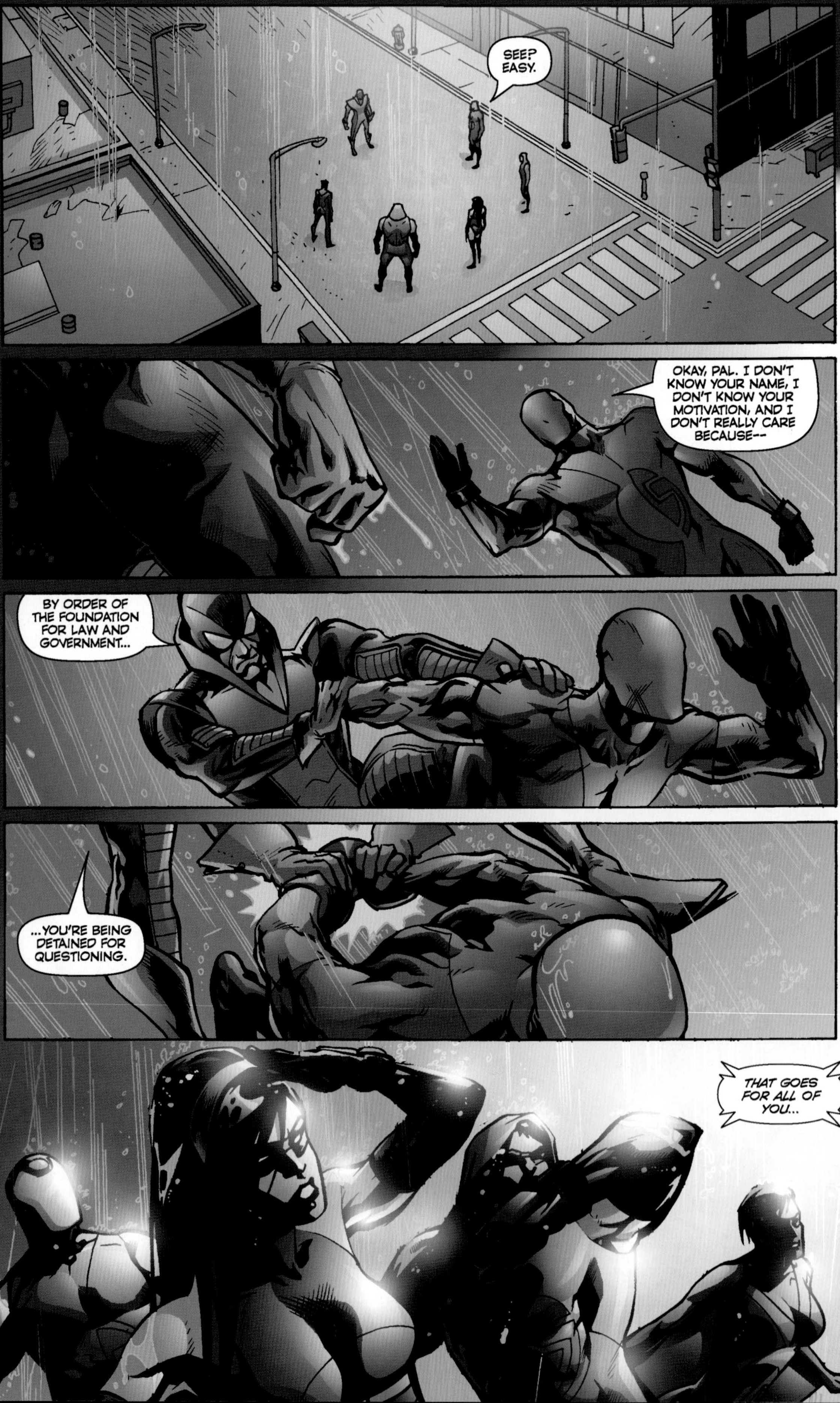
SEE? EASY.
OKAY, PAL. I DON'T KNOW YOUR NAME, I DON'T KNOW YOUR MOTIVATION, AND I DON'T REALLY CARE BECAUSE--
BY ORDER OF THE FOUNDATION FOR LAW AND GOVERNMENT...
...YOU'RE BEING DETAINED FOR QUESTIONING.
THAT GOES FOR ALL OF YOU...

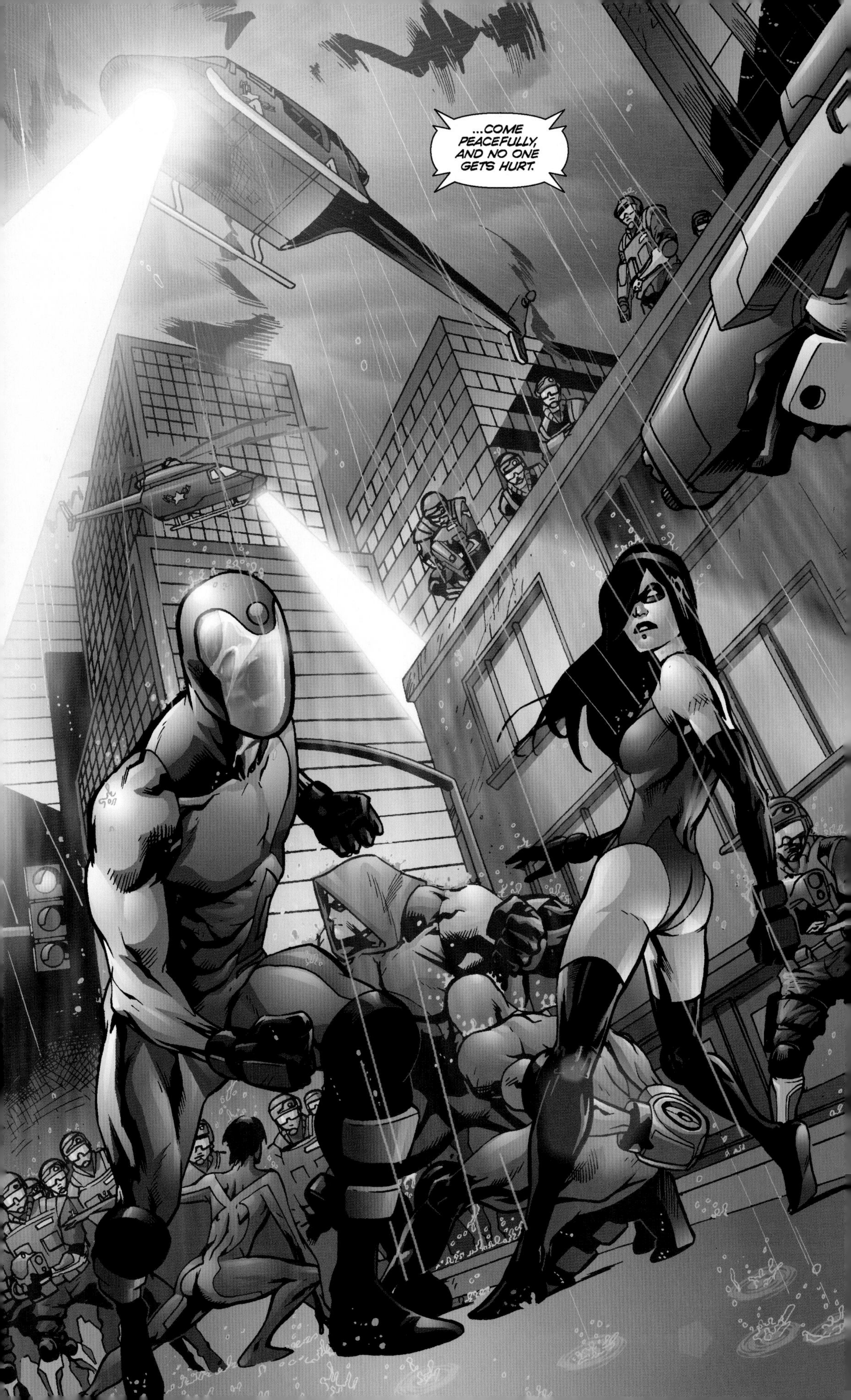
...COME PEACEFULLY, AND NO ONE GETS HURT.

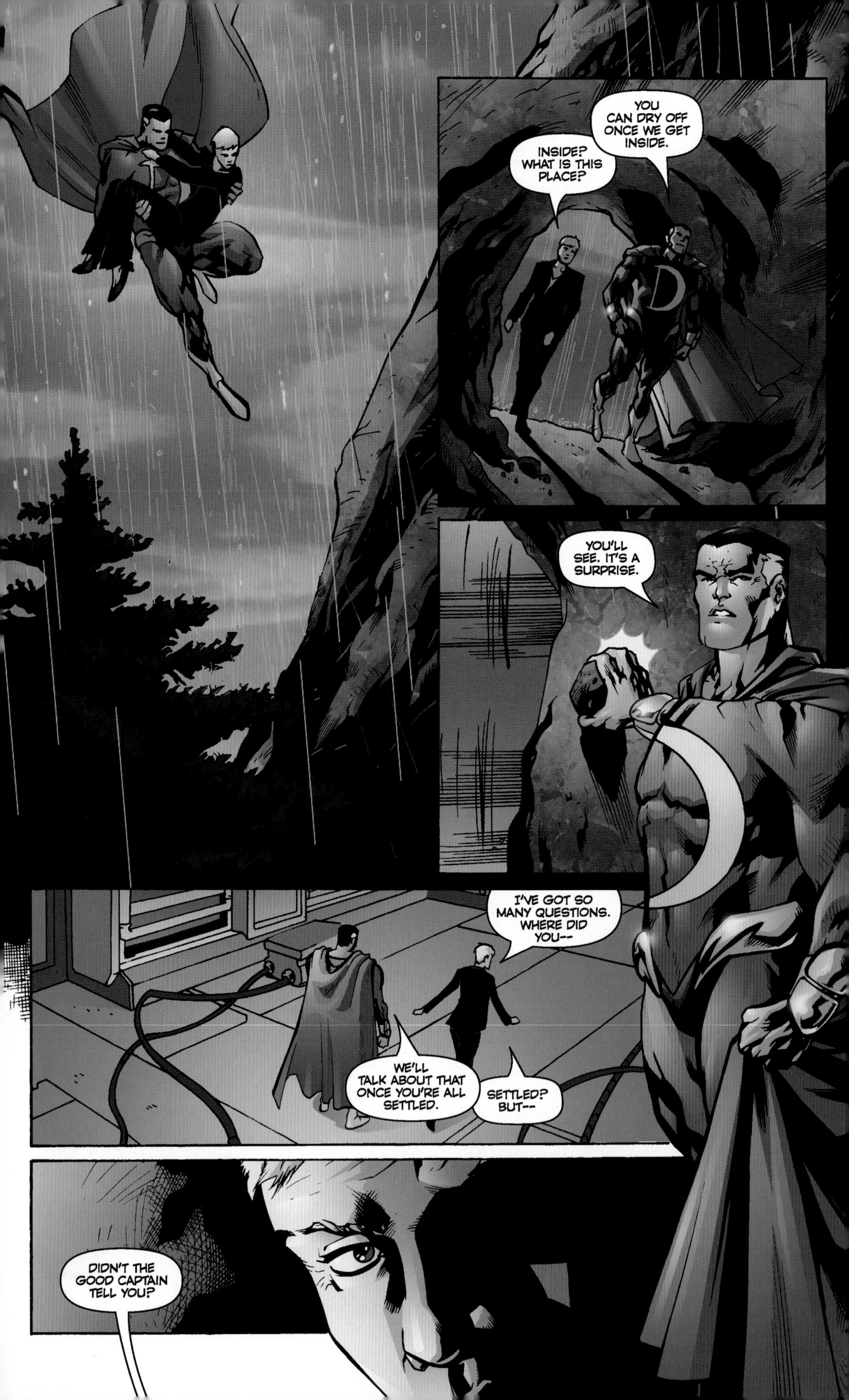
INSIDE? WHAT IS THIS PLACE?
YOU CAN DRY OFF ONCE WE GET INSIDE.
YOU'LL SEE. IT'S A SURPRISE.
I'VE GOT SO MANY QUESTIONS. WHERE DID YOU--
WE'LL TALK ABOUT THAT ONCE YOU'RE ALL SETTLED.
SETTLED? BUT--
DIDN'T THE GOOD CAPTAIN TELL YOU?

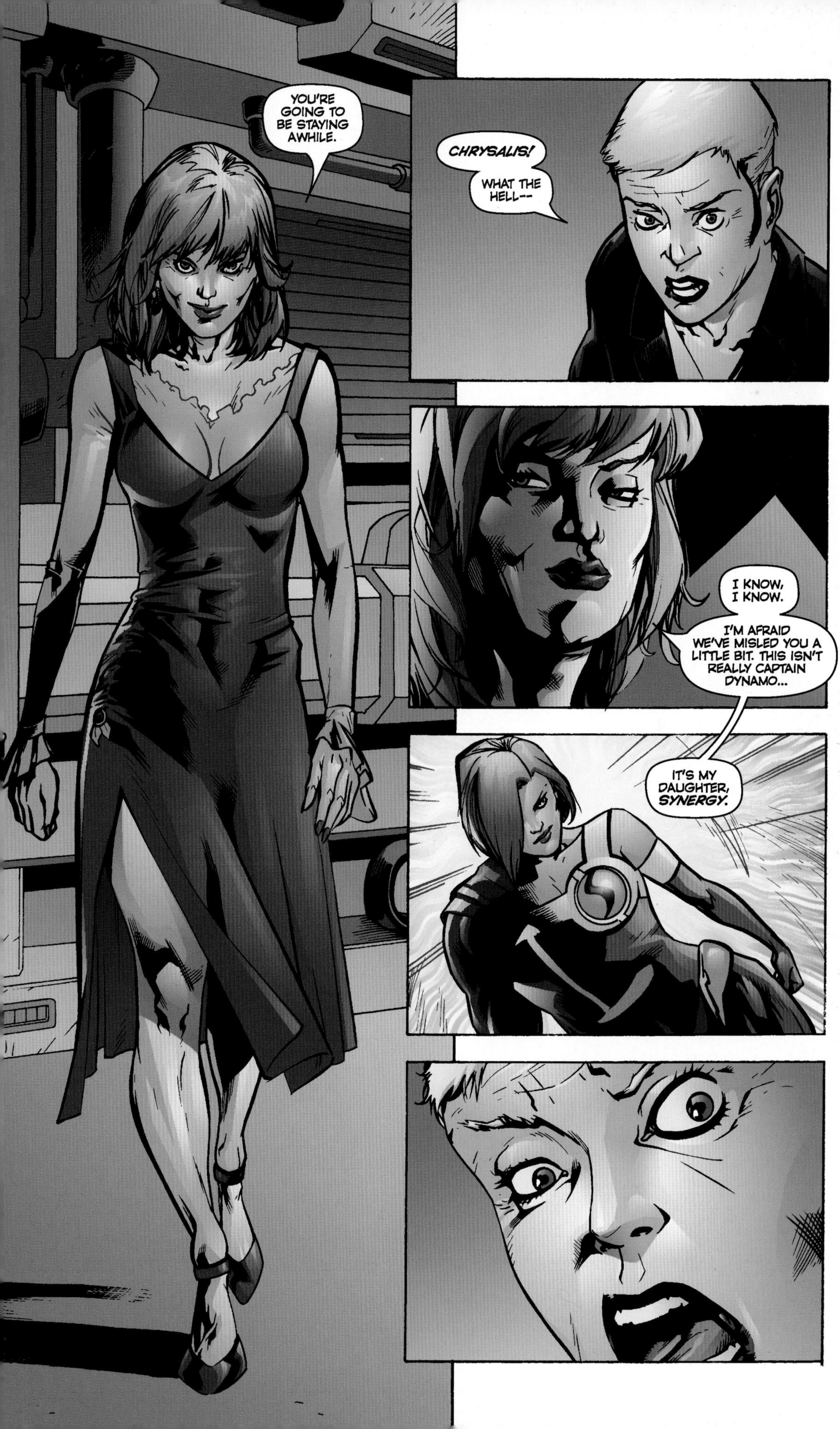

YOU'RE GOING TO BE STAYING AWHILE.
CHRYSALIS!
WHAT THE HELL--
I KNOW, I KNOW.
I'M AFRAID WE'VE MISLED YOU A LITTLE BIT. THIS ISN'T REALLY CAPTAIN DYNAMO...
IT'S MY DAUGHTER, SYNERGY.

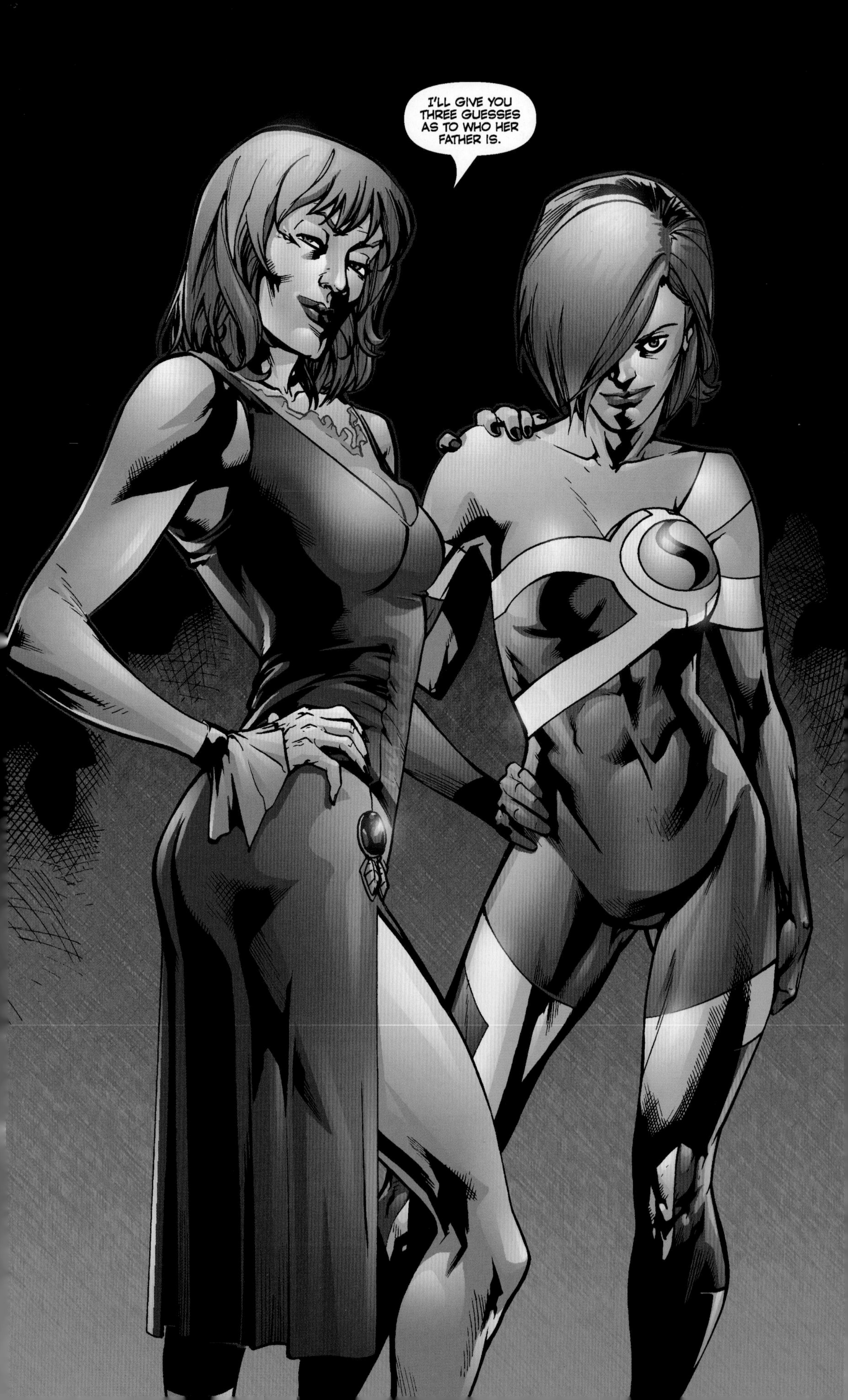
I'LL GIVE YOU THREE GUESSES AS TO WHO HER FATHER IS.

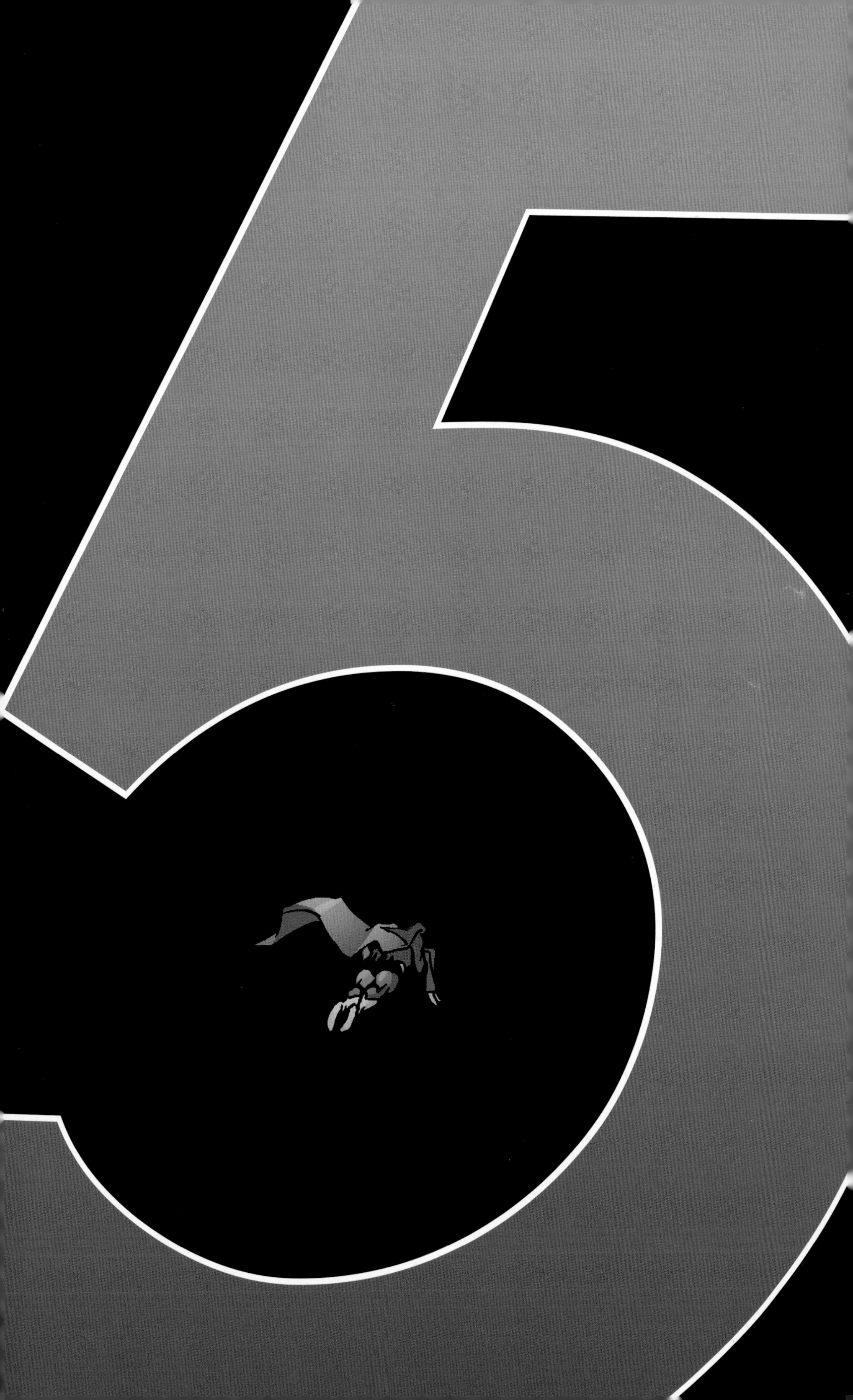

CHAPTER SIX

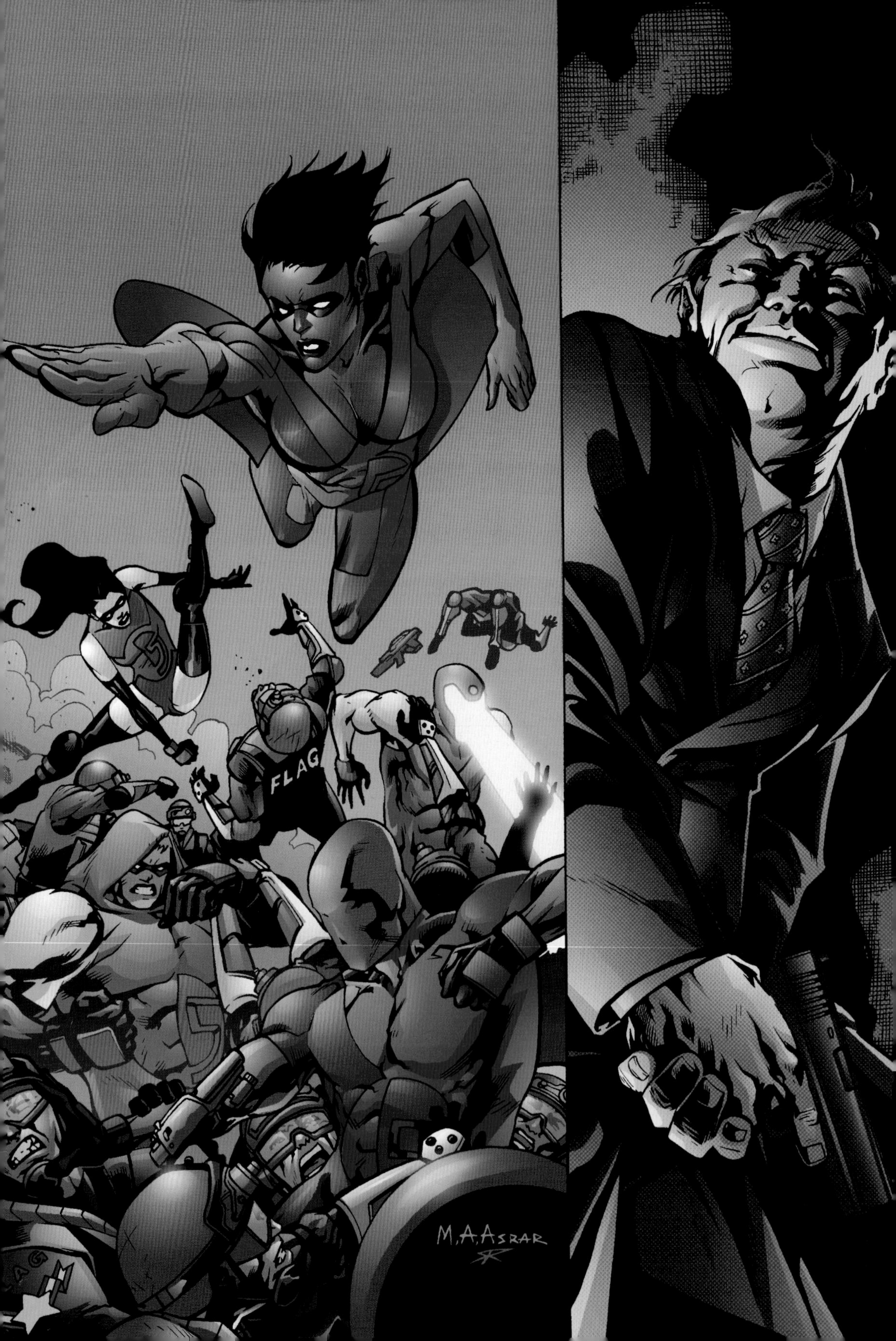
FLAG
M.A.Asrar

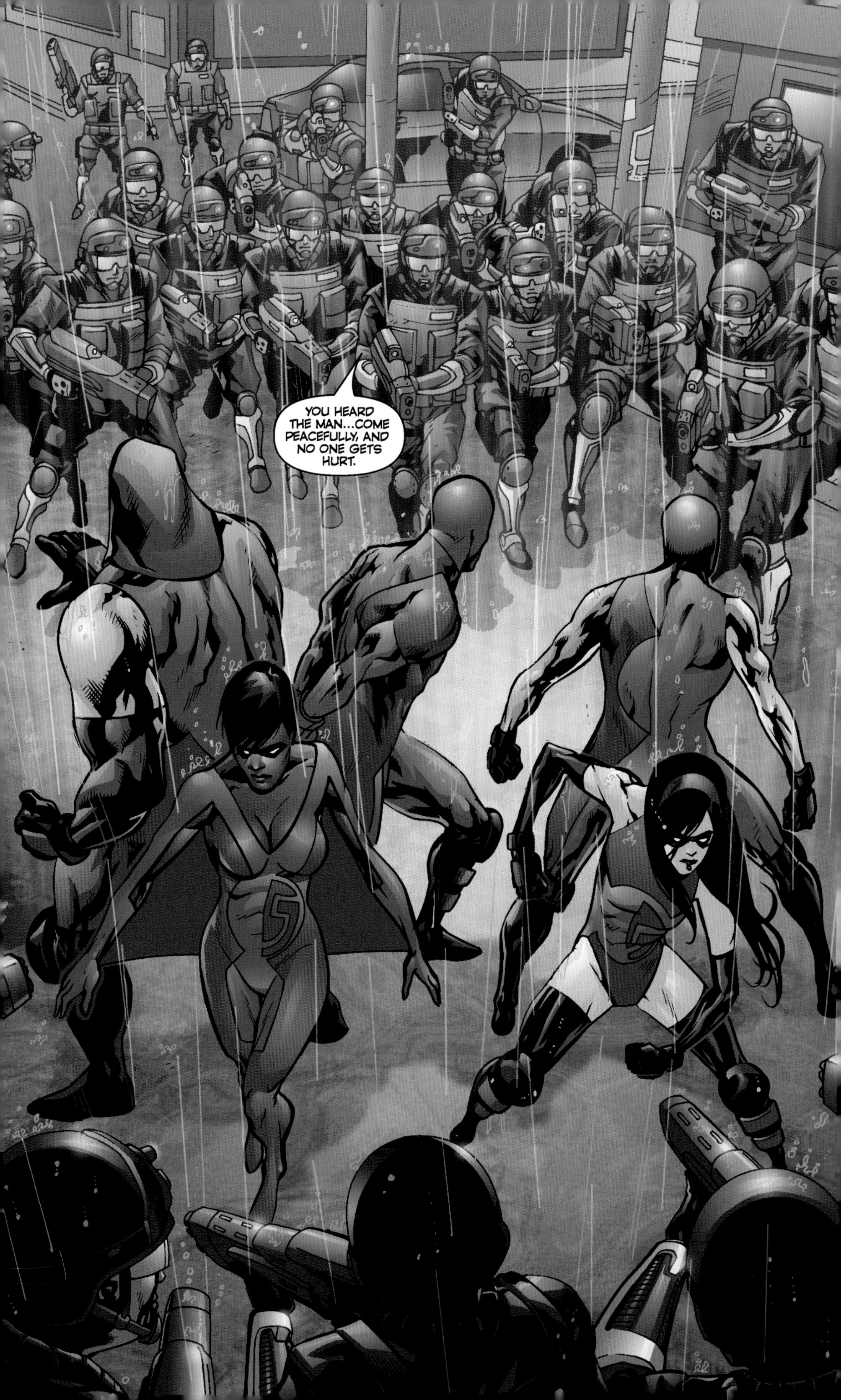
YOU HEARD THE MAN...COME PEACEFULLY, AND NO ONE GETS HURT.

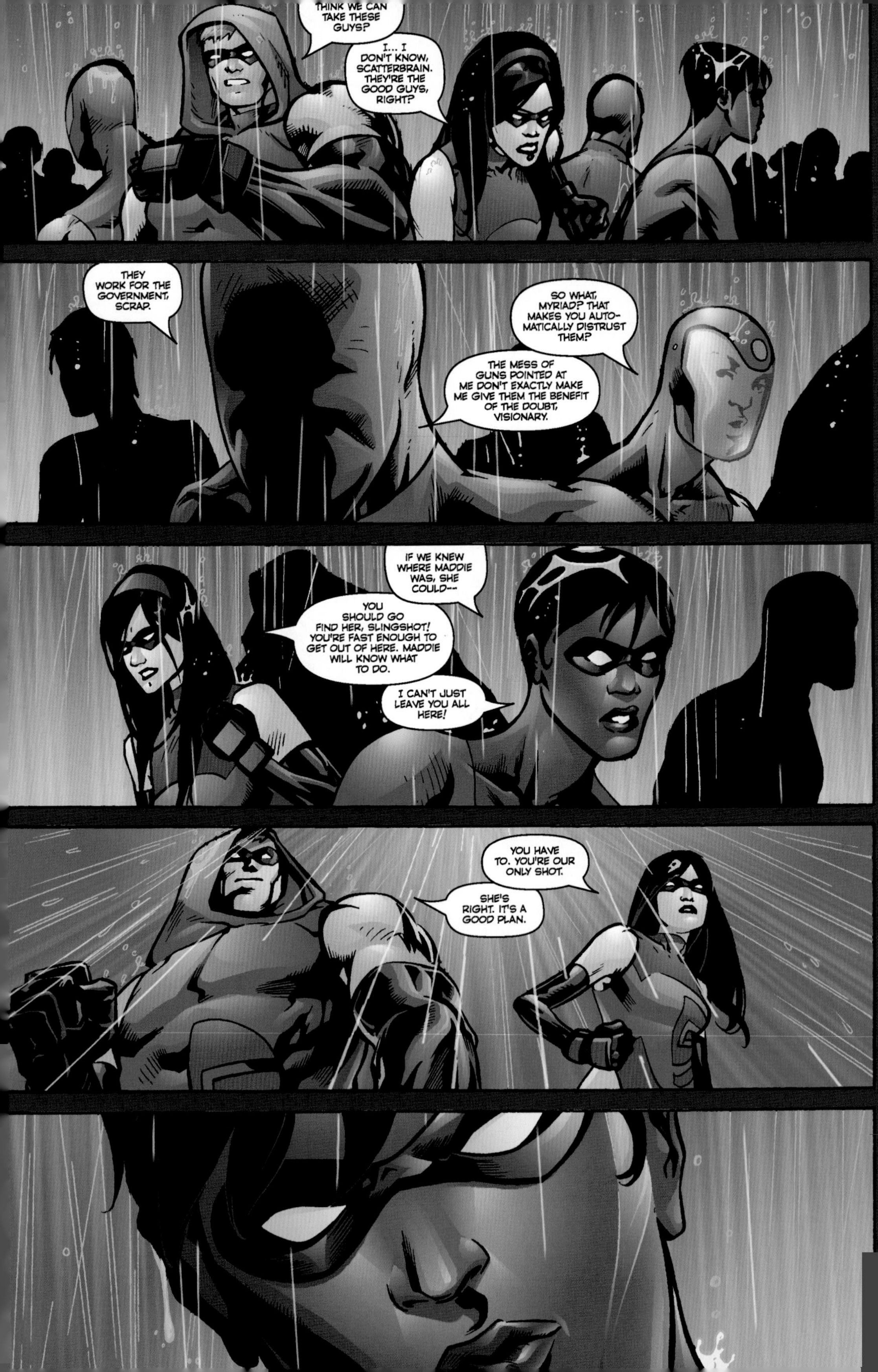

THINK WE CAN TAKE THESE GUYS?
I... I DON'T KNOW, SCATTERBRAIN. THEY'RE THE GOOD GUYS, RIGHT?
THEY WORK FOR THE GOVERNMENT, SCRAP.
SO WHAT, MYRIAD? THAT MAKES YOU AUTOMATICALLY DISTRUST THEM?
THE MESS OF GUNS POINTED AT ME DON'T EXACTLY MAKE ME GIVE THEM THE BENEFIT OF THE DOUBT, VISIONARY.
IF WE KNEW WHERE MADDIE WAS, SHE COULD--
YOU SHOULD GO FIND HER, SLINGSHOT! YOU'RE FAST ENOUGH TO GET OUT OF HERE. MADDIE WILL KNOW WHAT TO DO.
I CAN'T JUST LEAVE YOU ALL HERE!
YOU HAVE TO. YOU'RE OUR ONLY SHOT.
SHE'S RIGHT. IT'S A GOOD PLAN.

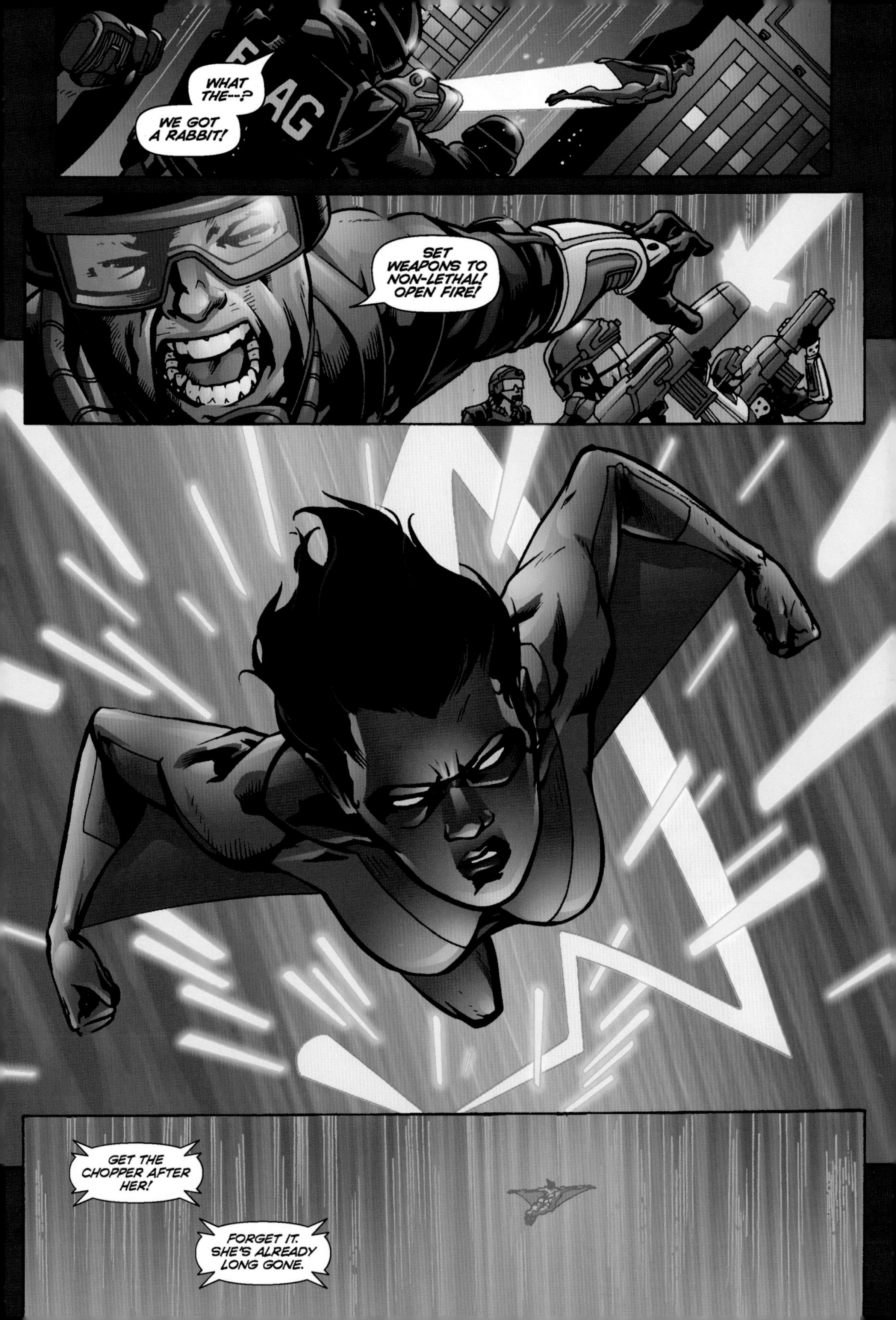

WHAT THE--?
WE GOT A RABBIT!
SET WEAPONS TO NON-LETHAL! OPEN FIRE!
GET THE CHOPPER AFTER HER!
FORGET IT. SHE'S ALREADY LONG GONE.

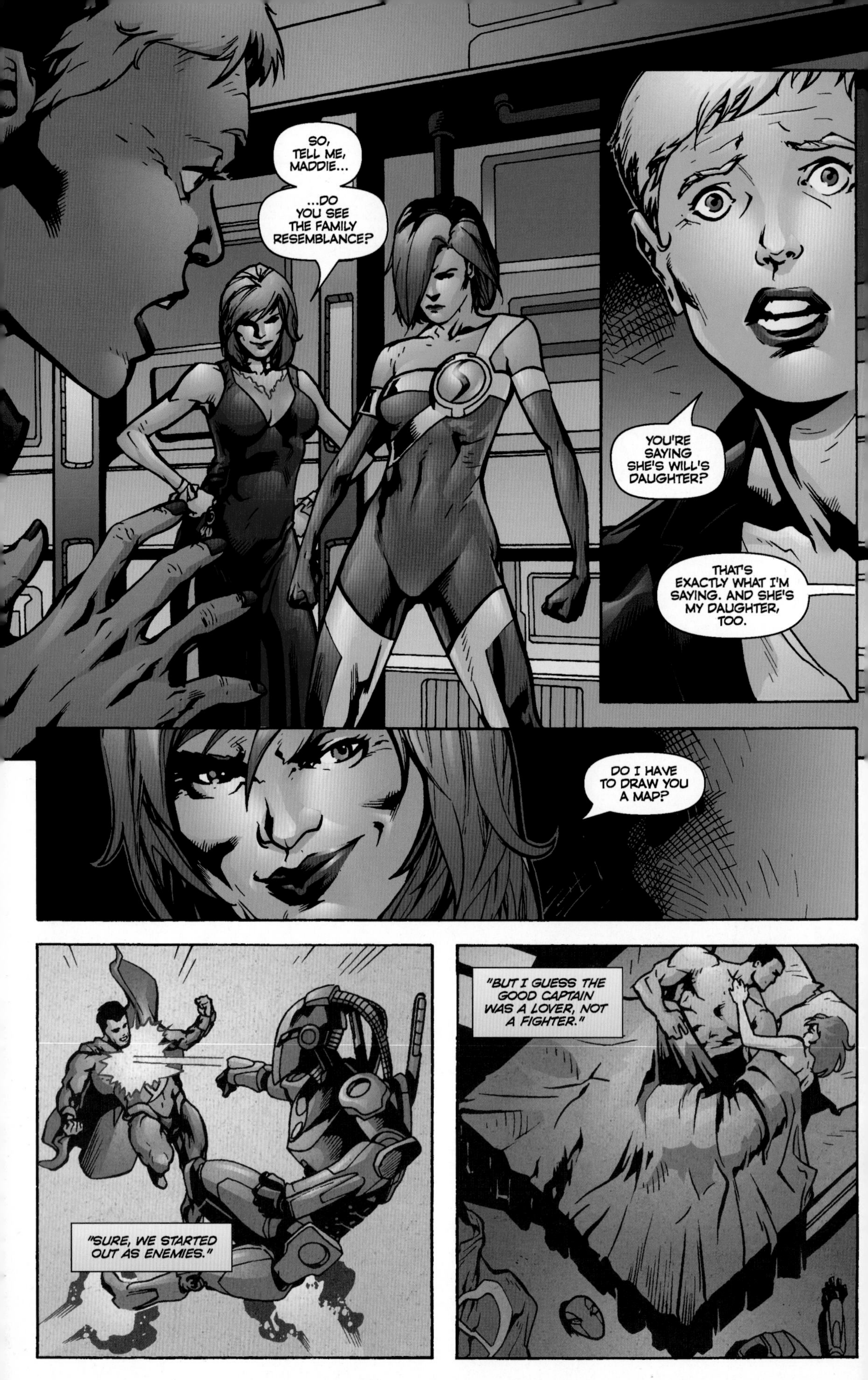
SO, TELL ME, MADDIE...
...DO YOU SEE THE FAMILY RESEMBLANCE?
YOU'RE SAYING SHE'S WILL'S DAUGHTER?
THAT'S EXACTLY WHAT I'M SAYING. AND SHE'S MY DAUGHTER, TOO.
DO I HAVE TO DRAW YOU A MAP?
"SURE, WE STARTED OUT AS ENEMIES."
"BUT I GUESS THE GOOD CAPTAIN WAS A LOVER, NOT A FIGHTER."

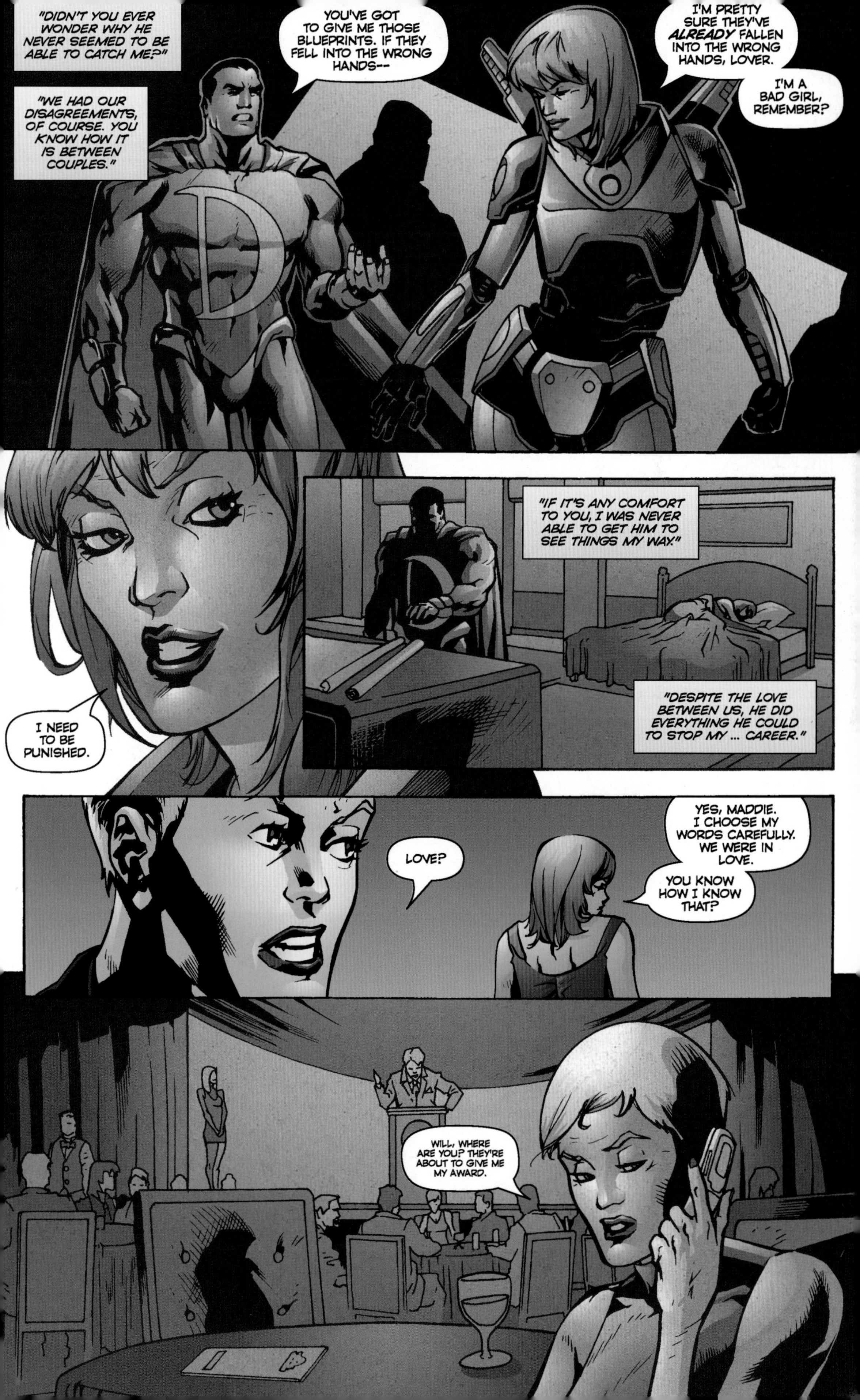
"DIDN'T YOU EVER WONDER WHY HE NEVER SEEMED TO BE ABLE TO CATCH ME?"
"WE HAD OUR DISAGREEMENTS, OF COURSE. YOU KNOW HOW IT IS BETWEEN COUPLES."
YOU'VE GOT TO GIVE ME THOSE BLUEPRINTS. IF THEY FELL INTO THE WRONG HANDS--
I'M PRETTY SURE THEY'VE ALREADY FALLEN INTO THE WRONG HANDS, LOVER.
I'M A BAD GIRL, REMEMBER?
I NEED TO BE PUNISHED.
"IF IT'S ANY COMFORT TO YOU, I WAS NEVER ABLE TO GET HIM TO SEE THINGS MY WAY."
"DESPITE THE LOVE BETWEEN US, HE DID EVERYTHING HE COULD TO STOP MY ... CAREER."
LOVE?
YES, MADDIE. I CHOOSE MY WORDS CAREFULLY. WE WERE IN LOVE.
YOU KNOW HOW I KNOW THAT?
WILL, WHERE ARE YOU? THEY'RE ABOUT TO GIVE ME MY AWARD.

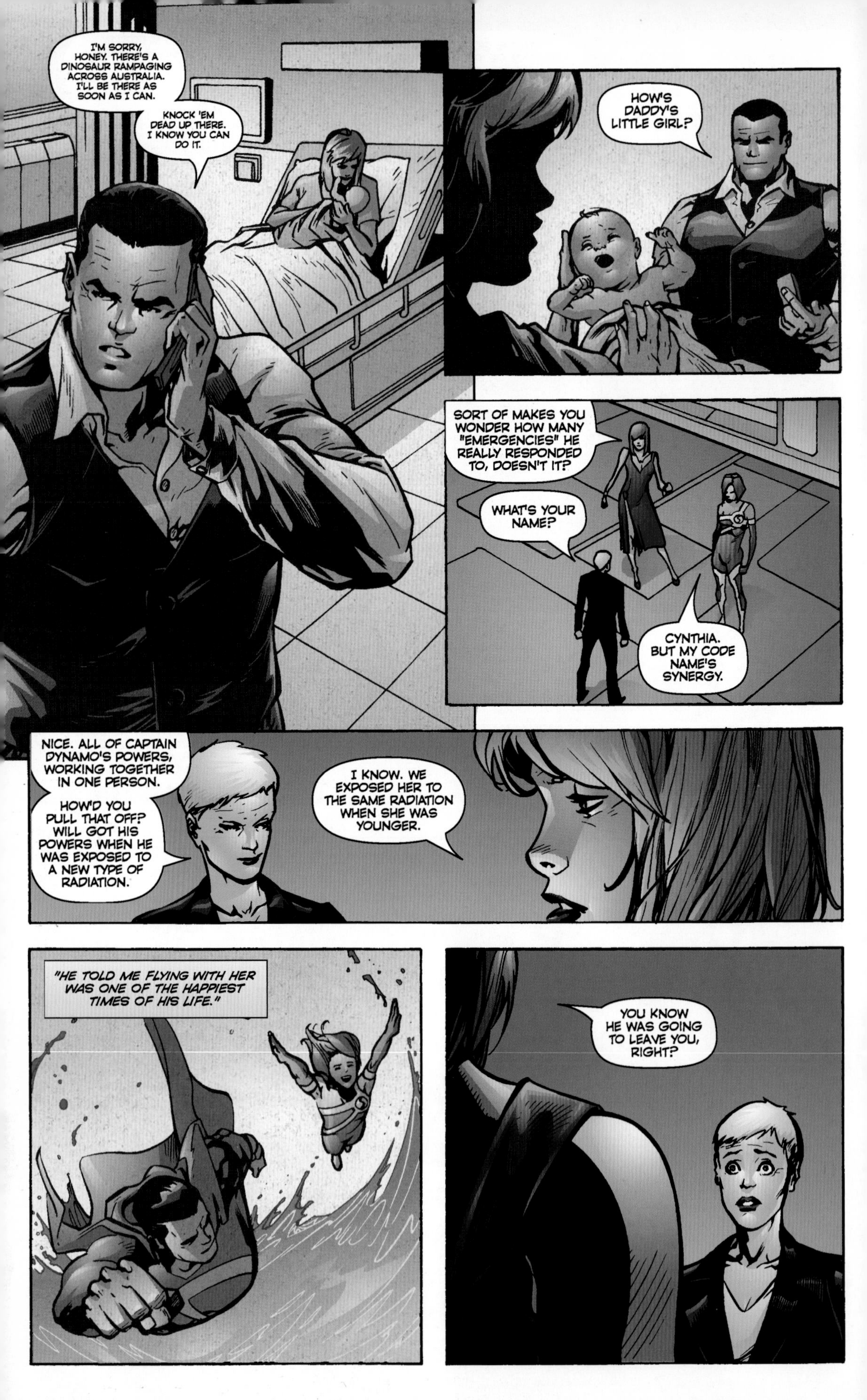
I'M SORRY, HONEY. THERE'S A DINOSAUR RAMPAGING ACROSS AUSTRALIA. I'LL BE THERE AS SOON AS I CAN.
KNOCK 'EM DEAD UP THERE. I KNOW YOU CAN DO IT.
HOW'S DADDY'S LITTLE GIRL?
SORT OF MAKES YOU WONDER HOW MANY "EMERGENCIES" HE REALLY RESPONDED TO, DOESN'T IT?
WHAT'S YOUR NAME?
CYNTHIA. BUT MY CODE NAME'S SYNERGY.
NICE. ALL OF CAPTAIN DYNAMO'S POWERS, WORKING TOGETHER IN ONE PERSON.
HOW'D YOU PULL THAT OFF? WILL GOT HIS POWERS WHEN HE WAS EXPOSED TO A NEW TYPE OF RADIATION.
I KNOW. WE EXPOSED HER TO THE SAME RADIATION WHEN SHE WAS YOUNGER.
"HE TOLD ME FLYING WITH HER WAS ONE OF THE HAPPIEST TIMES OF HIS LIFE."
YOU KNOW HE WAS GOING TO LEAVE YOU, RIGHT?

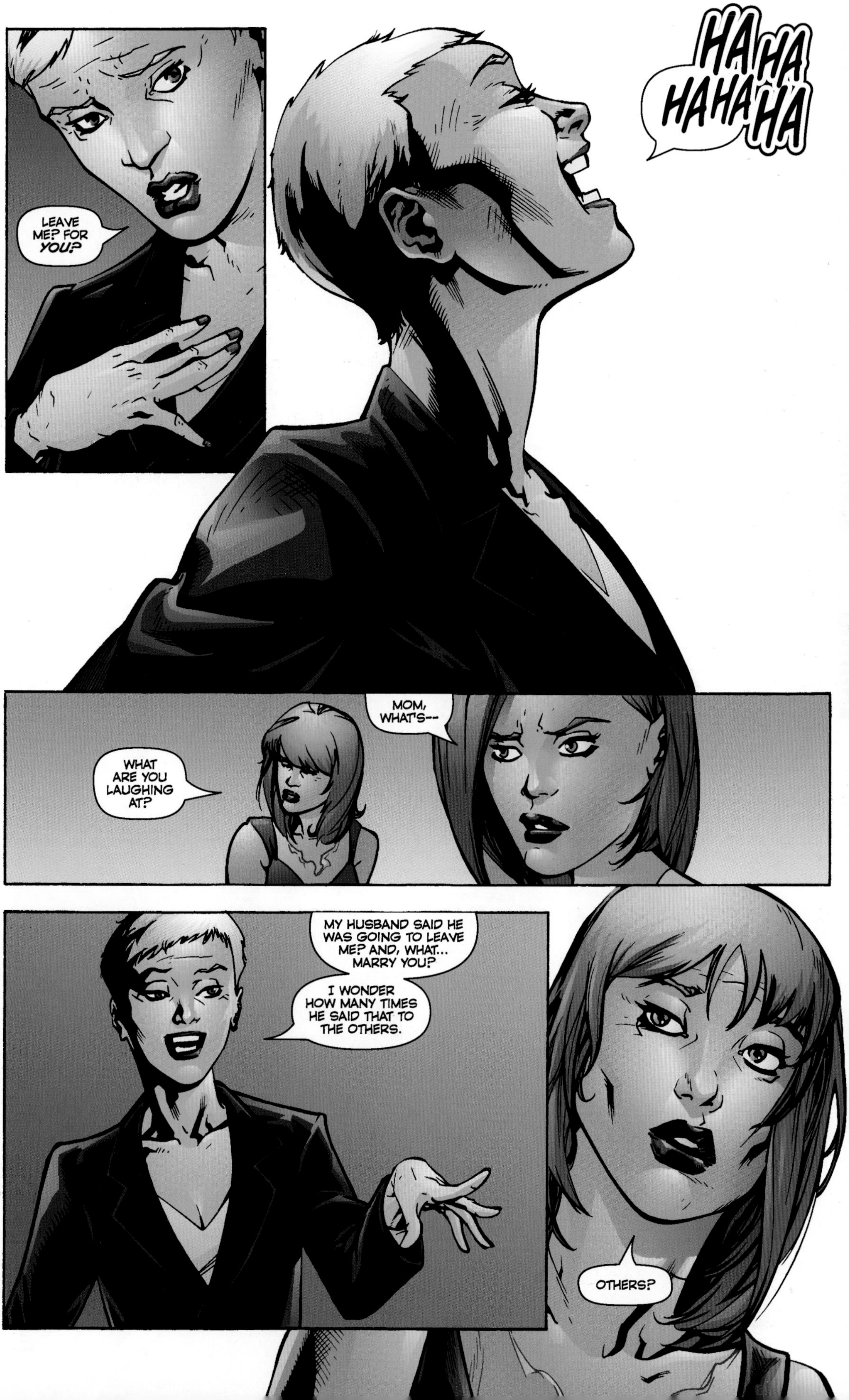
LEAVE ME? FOR YOU?
HA HA HAHAHA HA
MOM, WHAT'S--
WHAT ARE YOU LAUGHING AT?
MY HUSBAND SAID HE WAS GOING TO LEAVE ME? AND, WHAT... MARRY YOU?
I WONDER HOW MANY TIMES HE SAID THAT TO THE OTHERS.
OTHERS?

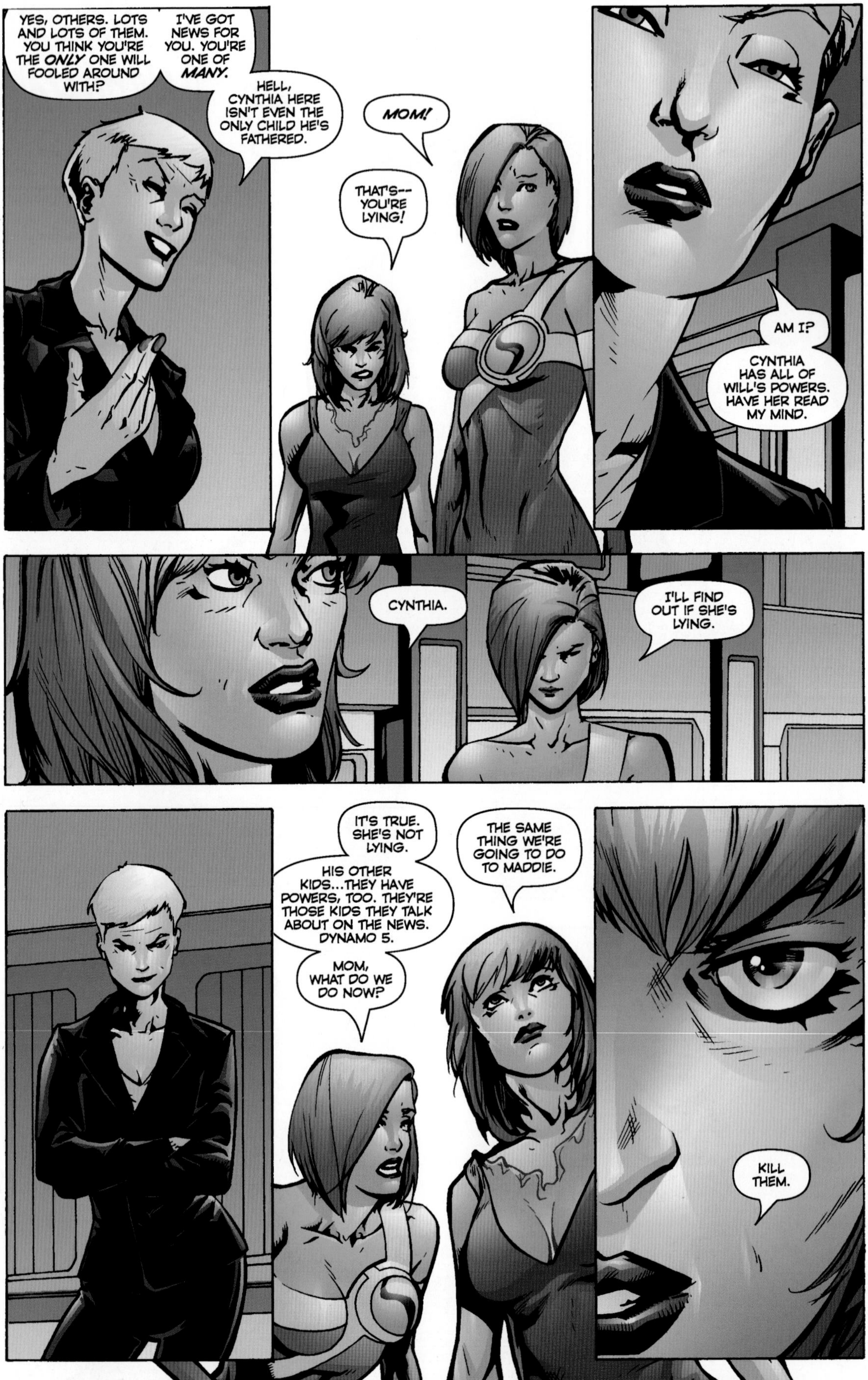
YES, OTHERS. LOTS AND LOTS OF THEM. YOU THINK YOU'RE THE *ONLY* ONE WILL FOOLED AROUND WITH?
I'VE GOT NEWS FOR YOU. YOU'RE ONE OF *MANY*.
HELL, CYNTHIA HERE ISN'T EVEN THE ONLY CHILD HE'S FATHERED.
MOM!
THAT'S-- YOU'RE LYING!
AM I?
CYNTHIA HAS ALL OF WILL'S POWERS. HAVE HER READ MY MIND.
CYNTHIA.
I'LL FIND OUT IF SHE'S LYING.
IT'S TRUE. SHE'S NOT LYING.
HIS OTHER KIDS...THEY HAVE POWERS, TOO. THEY'RE THOSE KIDS THEY TALK ABOUT ON THE NEWS. DYNAMO 5.
MOM, WHAT DO WE DO NOW?
THE SAME THING WE'RE GOING TO DO TO MADDIE.
KILL THEM.

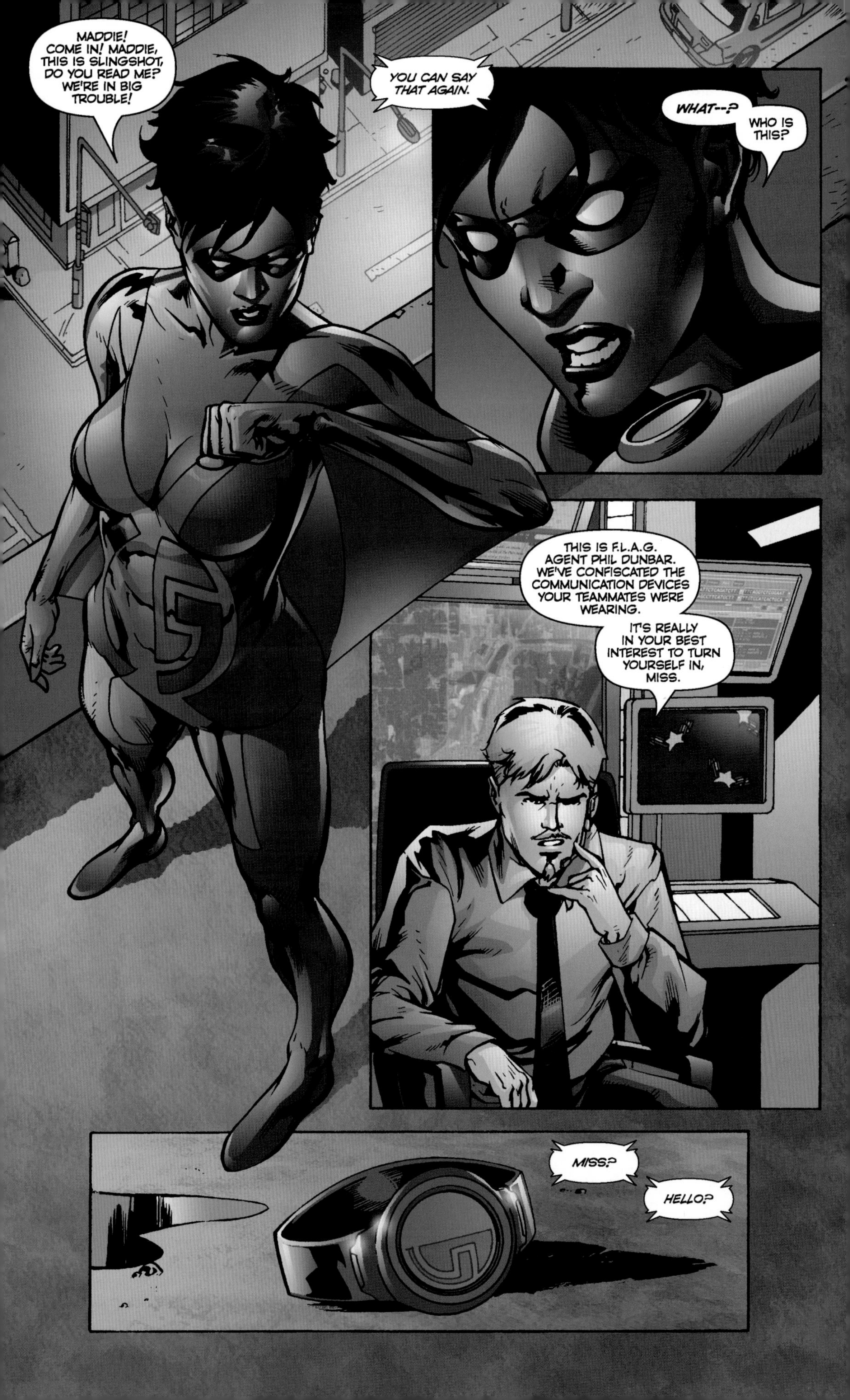
MADDIE! COME IN! MADDIE, THIS IS SLINGSHOT, DO YOU READ ME? WE'RE IN BIG TROUBLE!
YOU CAN SAY THAT AGAIN.
WHAT--?
WHO IS THIS?
THIS IS F.L.A.G. AGENT PHIL DUNBAR. WE'VE CONFISCATED THE COMMUNICATION DEVICES YOUR TEAMMATES WERE WEARING.
IT'S REALLY IN YOUR BEST INTEREST TO TURN YOURSELF IN, MISS.
MISS?
HELLO?

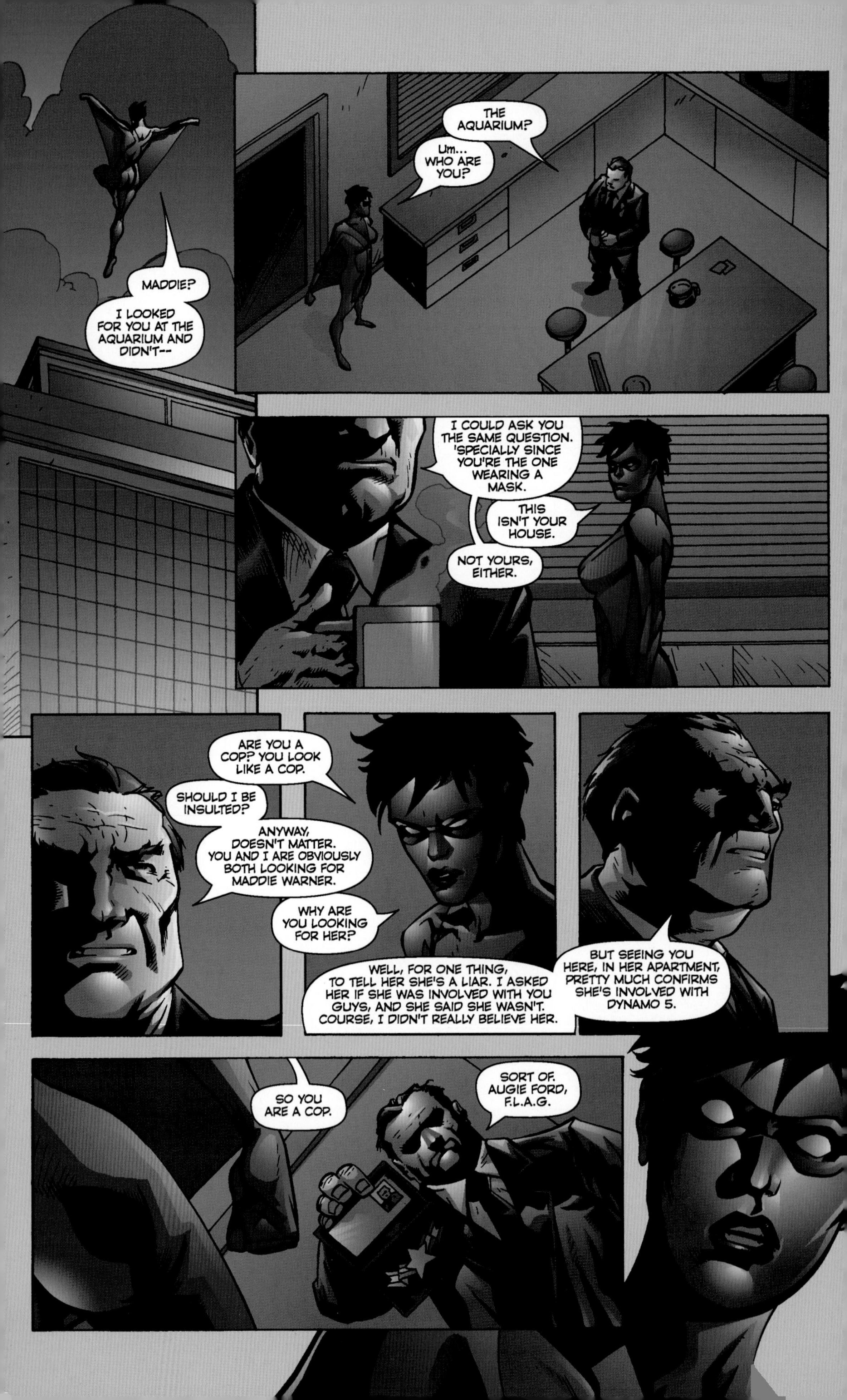
MADDIE?
I LOOKED FOR YOU AT THE AQUARIUM AND DIDN'T--
THE AQUARIUM?
Um... WHO ARE YOU?
I COULD ASK YOU THE SAME QUESTION. 'SPECIALLY SINCE YOU'RE THE ONE WEARING A MASK.
THIS ISN'T YOUR HOUSE.
NOT YOURS, EITHER.
ARE YOU A COP? YOU LOOK LIKE A COP.
SHOULD I BE INSULTED?
ANYWAY, DOESN'T MATTER. YOU AND I ARE OBVIOUSLY BOTH LOOKING FOR MADDIE WARNER.
WHY ARE YOU LOOKING FOR HER?
WELL, FOR ONE THING, TO TELL HER SHE'S A LIAR. I ASKED HER IF SHE WAS INVOLVED WITH YOU GUYS, AND SHE SAID SHE WASN'T. COURSE, I DIDN'T REALLY BELIEVE HER.
BUT SEEING YOU HERE, IN HER APARTMENT, PRETTY MUCH CONFIRMS SHE'S INVOLVED WITH DYNAMO 5.
SO YOU ARE A COP.
SORT OF. AUGIE FORD, F.L.A.G.

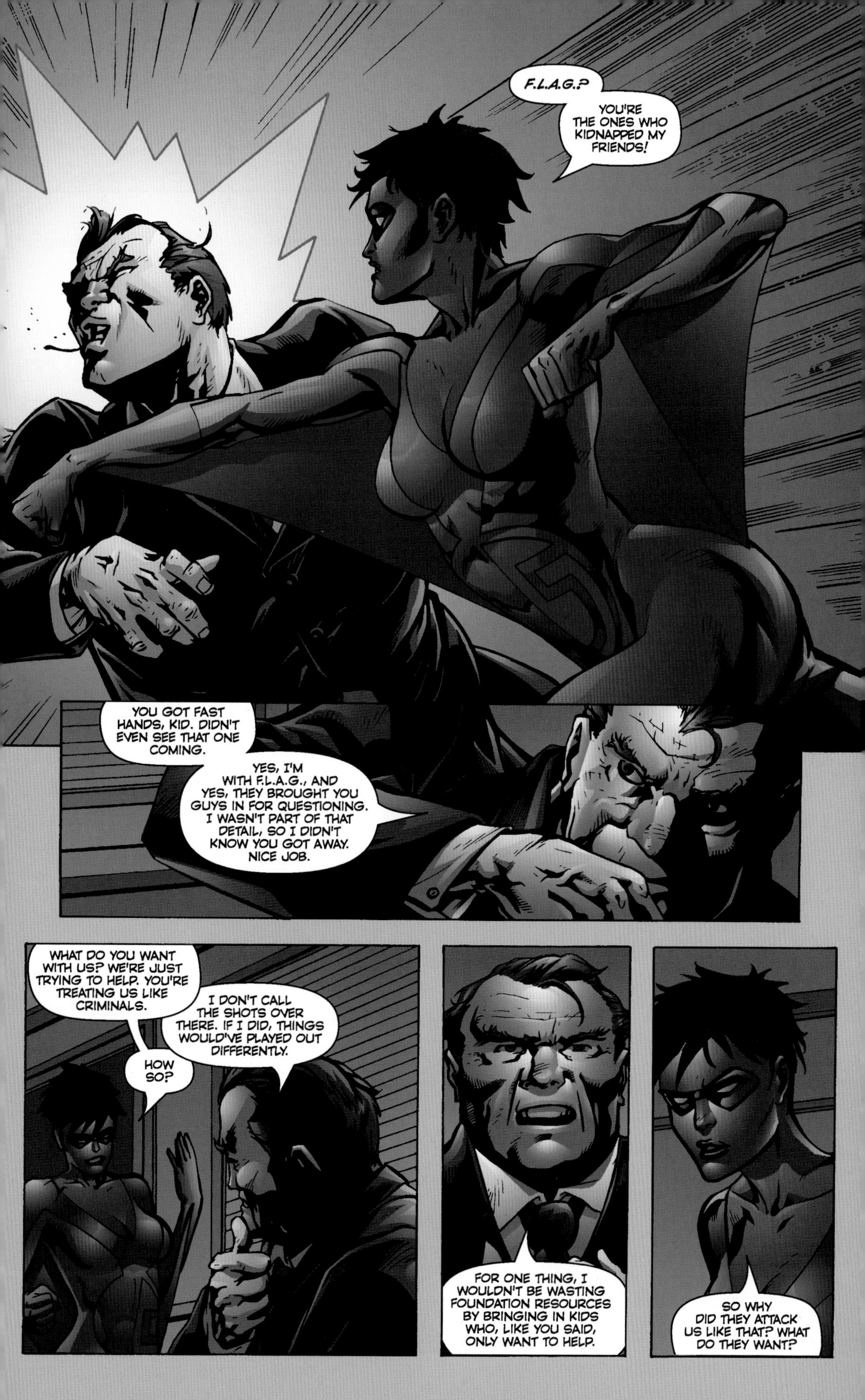
F.L.A.G.?
YOU'RE THE ONES WHO KIDNAPPED MY FRIENDS!
YOU GOT FAST HANDS, KID. DIDN'T EVEN SEE THAT ONE COMING.
YES, I'M WITH F.L.A.G., AND YES, THEY BROUGHT YOU GUYS IN FOR QUESTIONING. I WASN'T PART OF THAT DETAIL, SO I DIDN'T KNOW YOU GOT AWAY. NICE JOB.
WHAT DO YOU WANT WITH US? WE'RE JUST TRYING TO HELP. YOU'RE TREATING US LIKE CRIMINALS.
I DON'T CALL THE SHOTS OVER THERE. IF I DID, THINGS WOULD'VE PLAYED OUT DIFFERENTLY.
HOW SO?
FOR ONE THING, I WOULDN'T BE WASTING FOUNDATION RESOURCES BY BRINGING IN KIDS WHO, LIKE YOU SAID, ONLY WANT TO HELP.
SO WHY DID THEY ATTACK US LIKE THAT? WHAT DO THEY WANT?

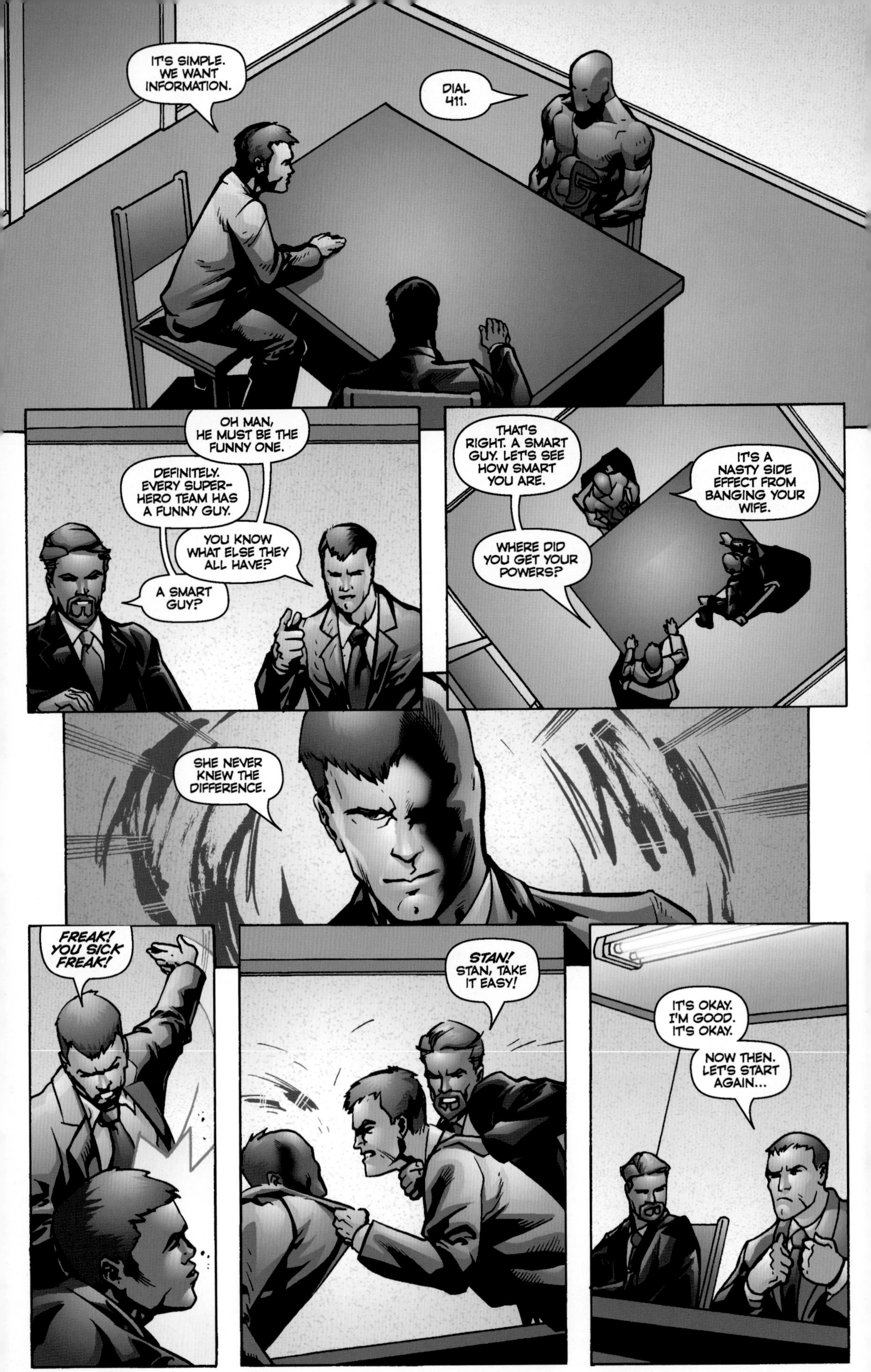
IT'S SIMPLE. WE WANT INFORMATION.
DIAL 411.
OH MAN, HE MUST BE THE FUNNY ONE.
DEFINITELY. EVERY SUPER-HERO TEAM HAS A FUNNY GUY.
YOU KNOW WHAT ELSE THEY ALL HAVE?
A SMART GUY?
THAT'S RIGHT. A SMART GUY. LET'S SEE HOW SMART YOU ARE.
WHERE DID YOU GET YOUR POWERS?
IT'S A NASTY SIDE EFFECT FROM BANGING YOUR WIFE.
SHE NEVER KNEW THE DIFFERENCE.
FREAK! YOU SICK FREAK!
STAN! STAN, TAKE IT EASY!
IT'S OKAY. I'M GOOD. IT'S OKAY.
NOW THEN. LET'S START AGAIN...

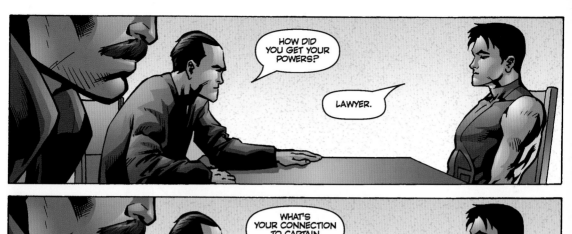

HOW DID YOU GET YOUR POWERS?

LAWYER.

WHAT'S YOUR CONNECTION TO CAPTAIN DYNAMO?

LAWYER.

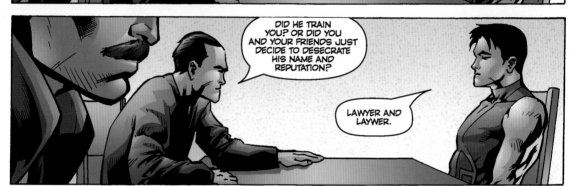

DID HE TRAIN YOU? OR DID YOU AND YOUR FRIENDS JUST DECIDE TO DESECRATE HIS NAME AND REPUTATION?

LAWYER AND LAYWER.

HE DOESN'T GET IT. HE THINKS WE'RE THE POLICE AND HE'S A REGULAR CITIZEN.

POOR BASTARD DOESN'T REALIZE WE'RE LIVING IN THE POST-9/11 WORLD. A WORLD WHERE WE CAN HOLD ANYONE WITH SUSPECTED TERRORIST TIES INDEFINITELY. NO CHARGES. NO TRIAL.

NO LAWYER.

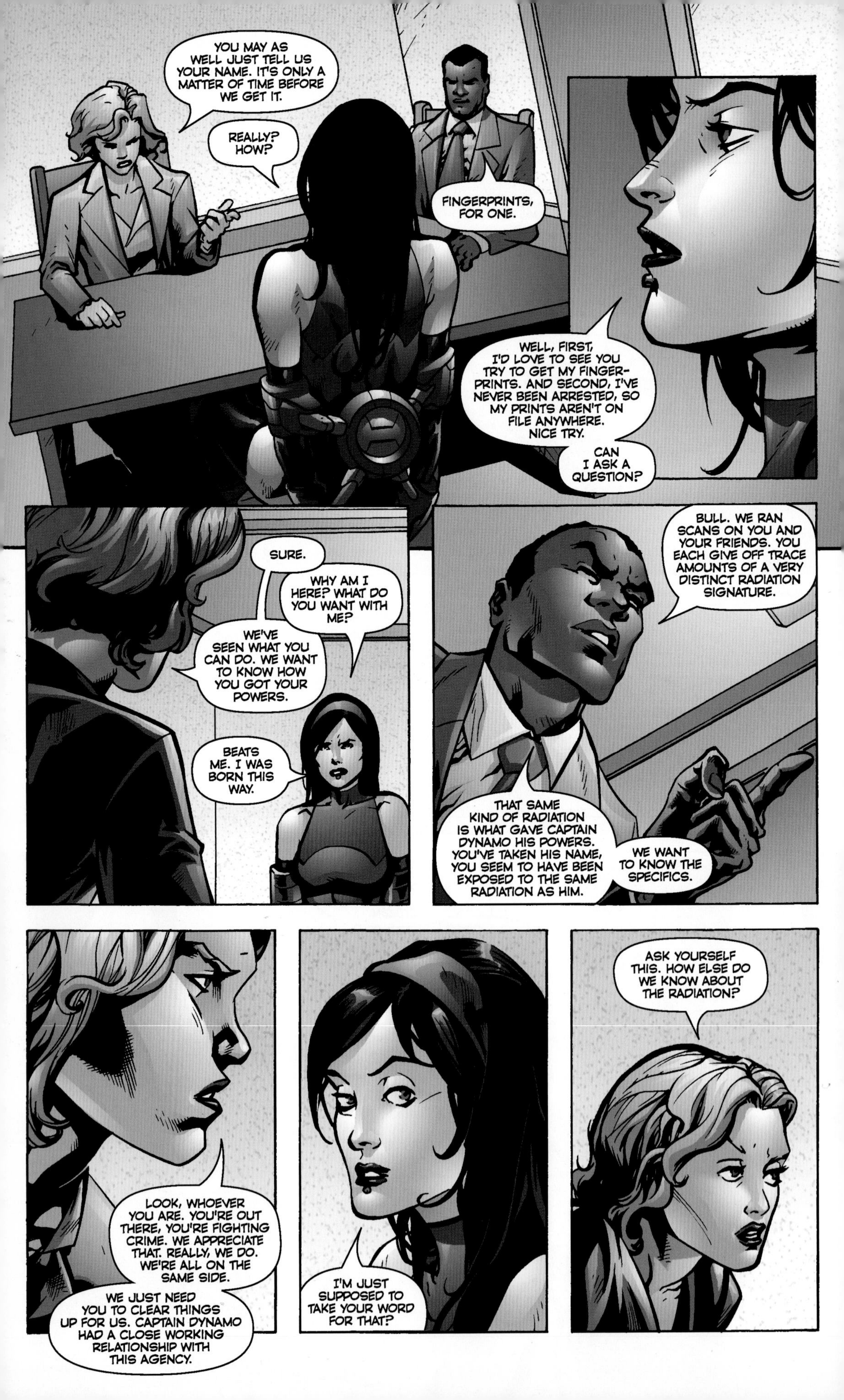
YOU MAY AS WELL JUST TELL US YOUR NAME. IT'S ONLY A MATTER OF TIME BEFORE WE GET IT.
REALLY? HOW?
FINGERPRINTS, FOR ONE.
WELL, FIRST, I'D LOVE TO SEE YOU TRY TO GET MY FINGER-PRINTS. AND SECOND, I'VE NEVER BEEN ARRESTED, SO MY PRINTS AREN'T ON FILE ANYWHERE. NICE TRY.
CAN I ASK A QUESTION?
SURE.
WHY AM I HERE? WHAT DO YOU WANT WITH ME?
WE'VE SEEN WHAT YOU CAN DO. WE WANT TO KNOW HOW YOU GOT YOUR POWERS.
BEATS ME. I WAS BORN THIS WAY.
BULL. WE RAN SCANS ON YOU AND YOUR FRIENDS. YOU EACH GIVE OFF TRACE AMOUNTS OF A VERY DISTINCT RADIATION SIGNATURE.
THAT SAME KIND OF RADIATION IS WHAT GAVE CAPTAIN DYNAMO HIS POWERS. YOU'VE TAKEN HIS NAME, YOU SEEM TO HAVE BEEN EXPOSED TO THE SAME RADIATION AS HIM.
WE WANT TO KNOW THE SPECIFICS.
LOOK, WHOEVER YOU ARE. YOU'RE OUT THERE, YOU'RE FIGHTING CRIME. WE APPRECIATE THAT. REALLY, WE DO. WE'RE ALL ON THE SAME SIDE.
WE JUST NEED YOU TO CLEAR THINGS UP FOR US. CAPTAIN DYNAMO HAD A CLOSE WORKING RELATIONSHIP WITH THIS AGENCY.
I'M JUST SUPPOSED TO TAKE YOUR WORD FOR THAT?
ASK YOURSELF THIS. HOW ELSE DO WE KNOW ABOUT THE RADIATION?

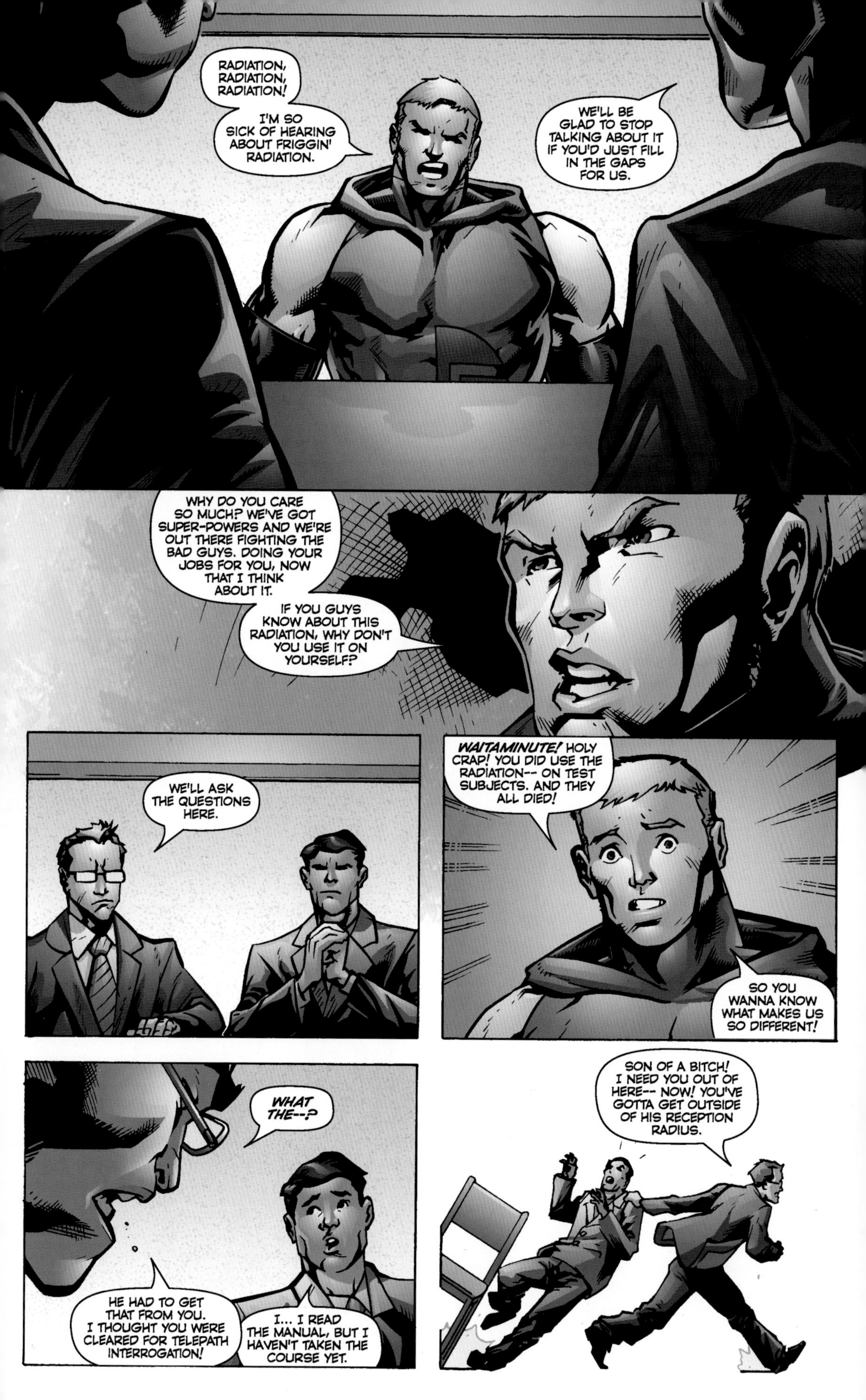
RADIATION, RADIATION, RADIATION!
I'M SO SICK OF HEARING ABOUT FRIGGIN' RADIATION.
WE'LL BE GLAD TO STOP TALKING ABOUT IT IF YOU'D JUST FILL IN THE GAPS FOR US.
WHY DO YOU CARE SO MUCH? WE'VE GOT SUPER-POWERS AND WE'RE OUT THERE FIGHTING THE BAD GUYS. DOING YOUR JOBS FOR YOU, NOW THAT I THINK ABOUT IT.
IF YOU GUYS KNOW ABOUT THIS RADIATION, WHY DON'T YOU USE IT ON YOURSELF?
WE'LL ASK THE QUESTIONS HERE.
WAITAMINUTE! HOLY CRAP! YOU DID USE THE RADIATION-- ON TEST SUBJECTS. AND THEY ALL DIED!
SO YOU WANNA KNOW WHAT MAKES US SO DIFFERENT!
WHAT THE--?
HE HAD TO GET THAT FROM YOU. I THOUGHT YOU WERE CLEARED FOR TELEPATH INTERROGATION!
I... I READ THE MANUAL, BUT I HAVEN'T TAKEN THE COURSE YET.
SON OF A BITCH! I NEED YOU OUT OF HERE-- NOW! YOU'VE GOTTA GET OUTSIDE OF HIS RECEPTION RADIUS.

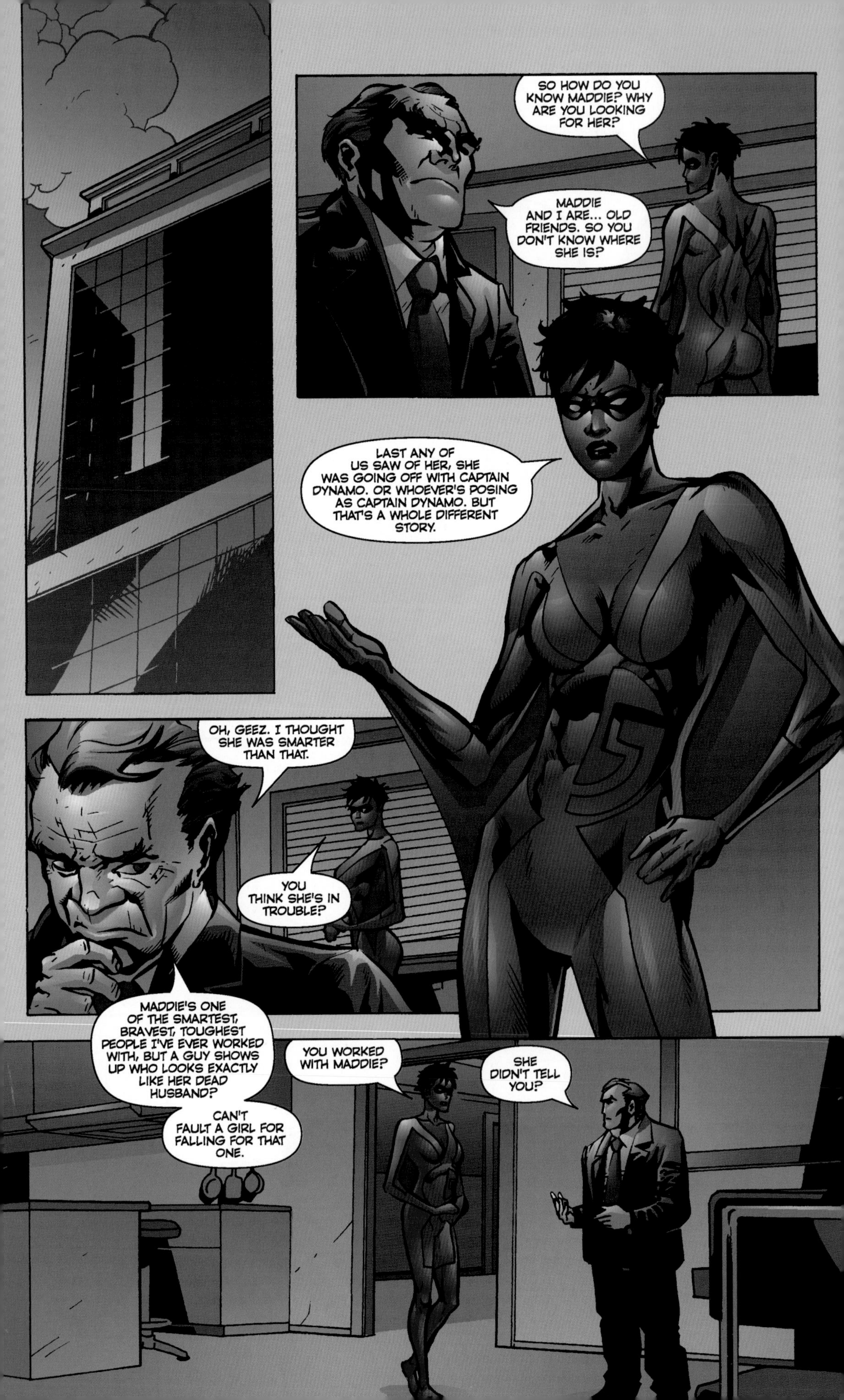
SO HOW DO YOU KNOW MADDIE? WHY ARE YOU LOOKING FOR HER?
MADDIE AND I ARE... OLD FRIENDS. SO YOU DON'T KNOW WHERE SHE IS?
LAST ANY OF US SAW OF HER, SHE WAS GOING OFF WITH CAPTAIN DYNAMO. OR WHOEVER'S POSING AS CAPTAIN DYNAMO. BUT THAT'S A WHOLE DIFFERENT STORY.
OH, GEEZ. I THOUGHT SHE WAS SMARTER THAN THAT.
YOU THINK SHE'S IN TROUBLE?
MADDIE'S ONE OF THE SMARTEST, BRAVEST, TOUGHEST PEOPLE I'VE EVER WORKED WITH, BUT A GUY SHOWS UP WHO LOOKS EXACTLY LIKE HER DEAD HUSBAND?
CAN'T FAULT A GIRL FOR FALLING FOR THAT ONE.
YOU WORKED WITH MADDIE?
SHE DIDN'T TELL YOU?

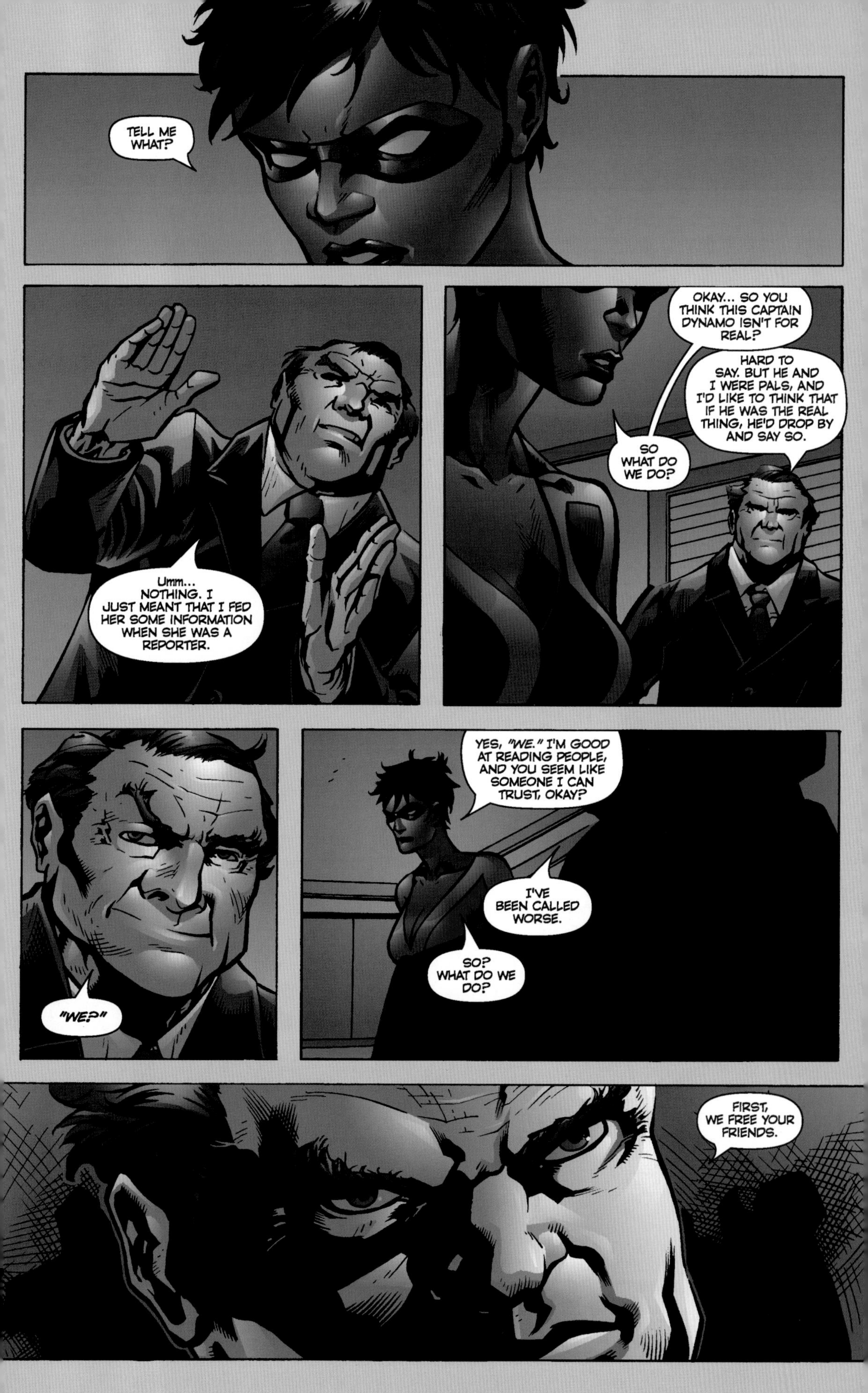
TELL ME WHAT?
Umm... NOTHING. I JUST MEANT THAT I FED HER SOME INFORMATION WHEN SHE WAS A REPORTER.
OKAY... SO YOU THINK THIS CAPTAIN DYNAMO ISN'T FOR REAL?
HARD TO SAY. BUT HE AND I WERE PALS, AND I'D LIKE TO THINK THAT IF HE WAS THE REAL THING, HE'D DROP BY AND SAY SO.
SO WHAT DO WE DO?
"WE?"
YES, "WE." I'M GOOD AT READING PEOPLE, AND YOU SEEM LIKE SOMEONE I CAN TRUST, OKAY?
I'VE BEEN CALLED WORSE.
SO? WHAT DO WE DO?
FIRST, WE FREE YOUR FRIENDS.

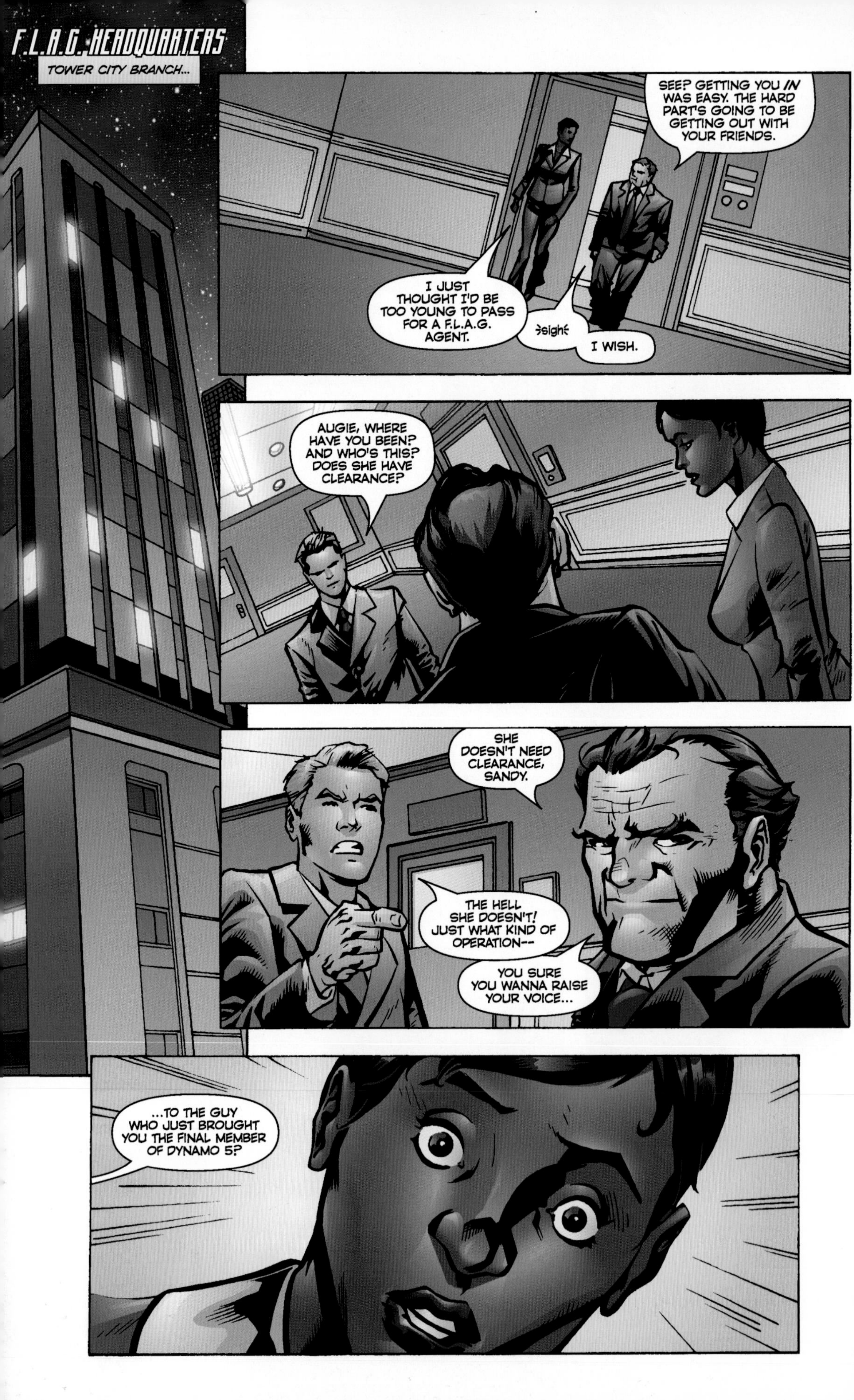
F.L.A.G. HEADQUARTERS
TOWER CITY BRANCH...
SEE? GETTING YOU *IN* WAS EASY. THE HARD PART'S GOING TO BE GETTING OUT WITH YOUR FRIENDS.
I JUST THOUGHT I'D BE TOO YOUNG TO PASS FOR A F.L.A.G. AGENT.
sigh
I WISH.
AUGIE, WHERE HAVE YOU BEEN? AND WHO'S THIS? DOES SHE HAVE CLEARANCE?
SHE DOESN'T NEED CLEARANCE, SANDY.
THE HELL SHE DOESN'T! JUST WHAT KIND OF OPERATION--
YOU SURE YOU WANNA RAISE YOUR VOICE...
...TO THE GUY WHO JUST BROUGHT YOU THE FINAL MEMBER OF DYNAMO 5?

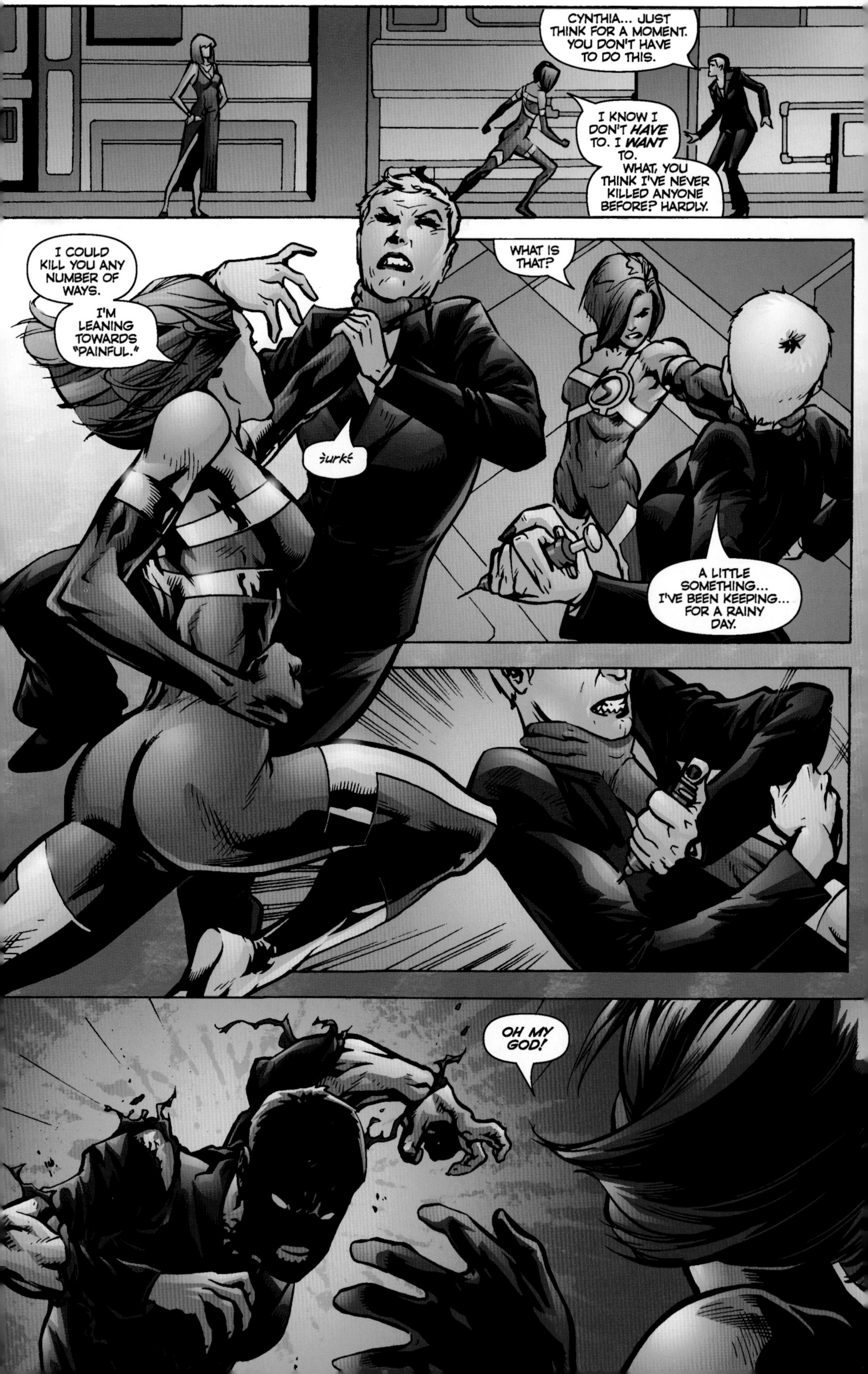
CYNTHIA... JUST THINK FOR A MOMENT. YOU DON'T HAVE TO DO THIS.
I KNOW I DON'T *HAVE* TO. I *WANT* TO.
WHAT, YOU THINK I'VE NEVER KILLED ANYONE BEFORE? HARDLY.
I COULD KILL YOU ANY NUMBER OF WAYS.
I'M LEANING TOWARDS "PAINFUL."
urk
WHAT IS THAT?
A LITTLE SOMETHING... I'VE BEEN KEEPING... FOR A RAINY DAY.
OH MY GOD!

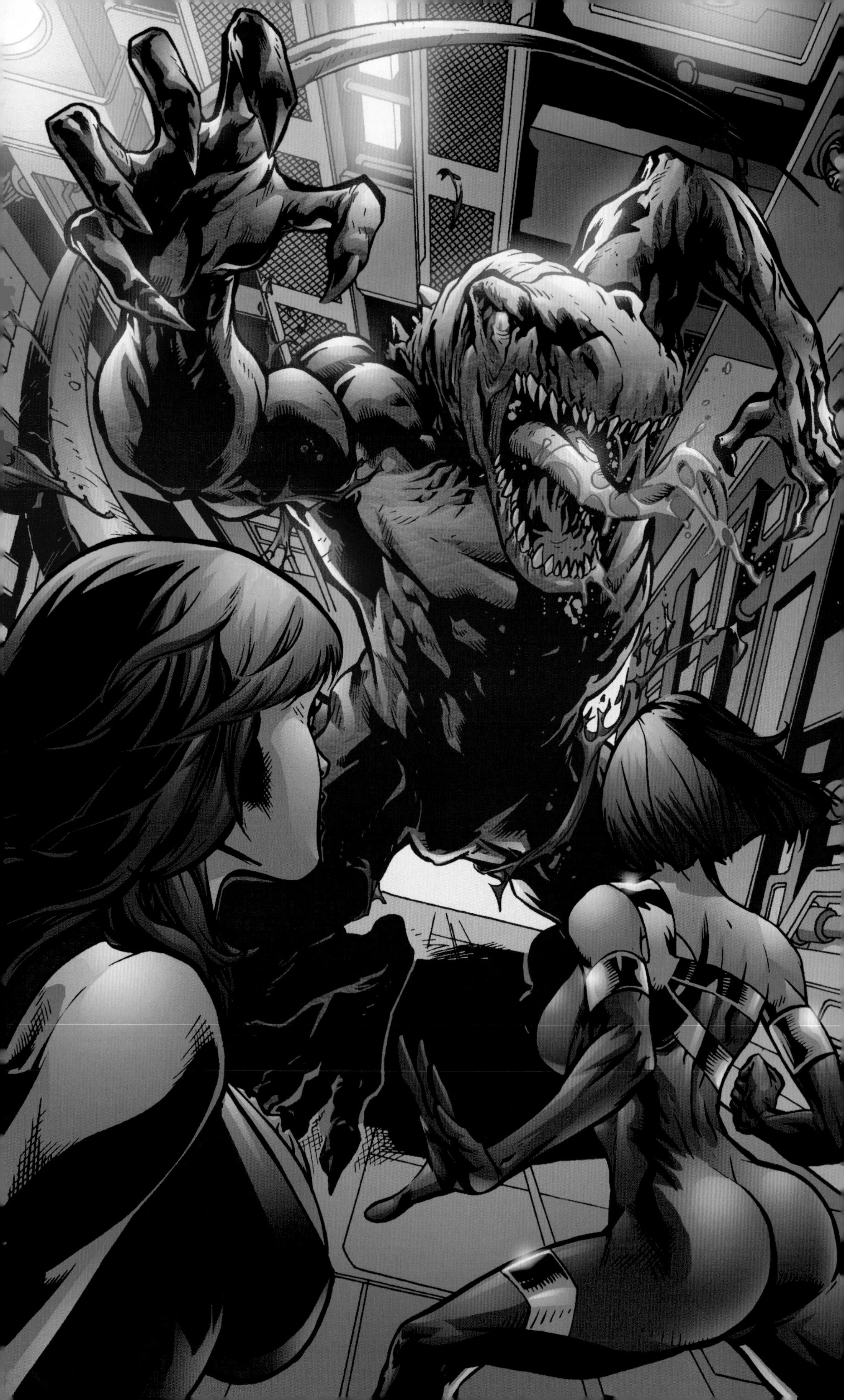

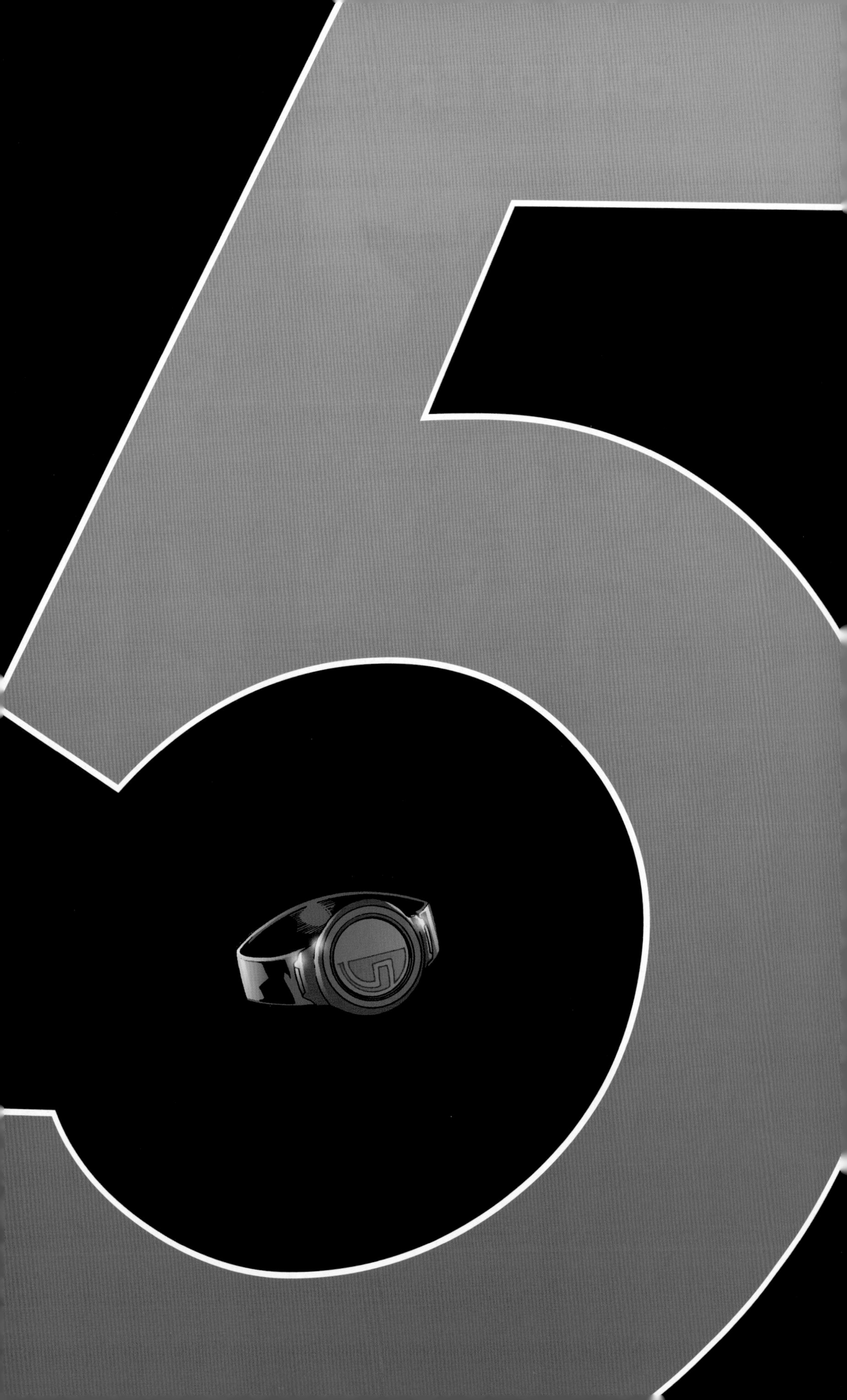

CHAPTER SEVEN

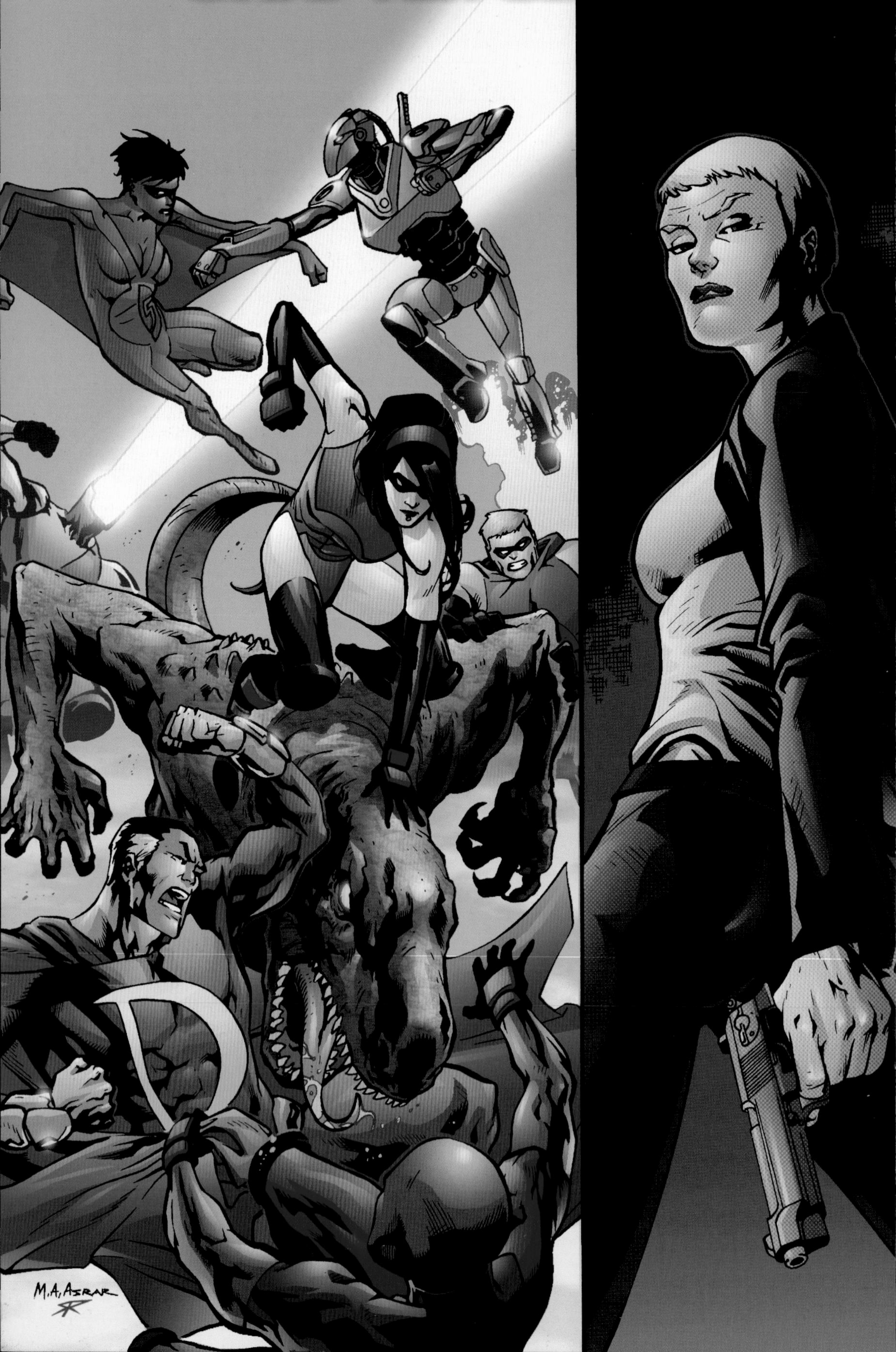
M.A. ASRAR

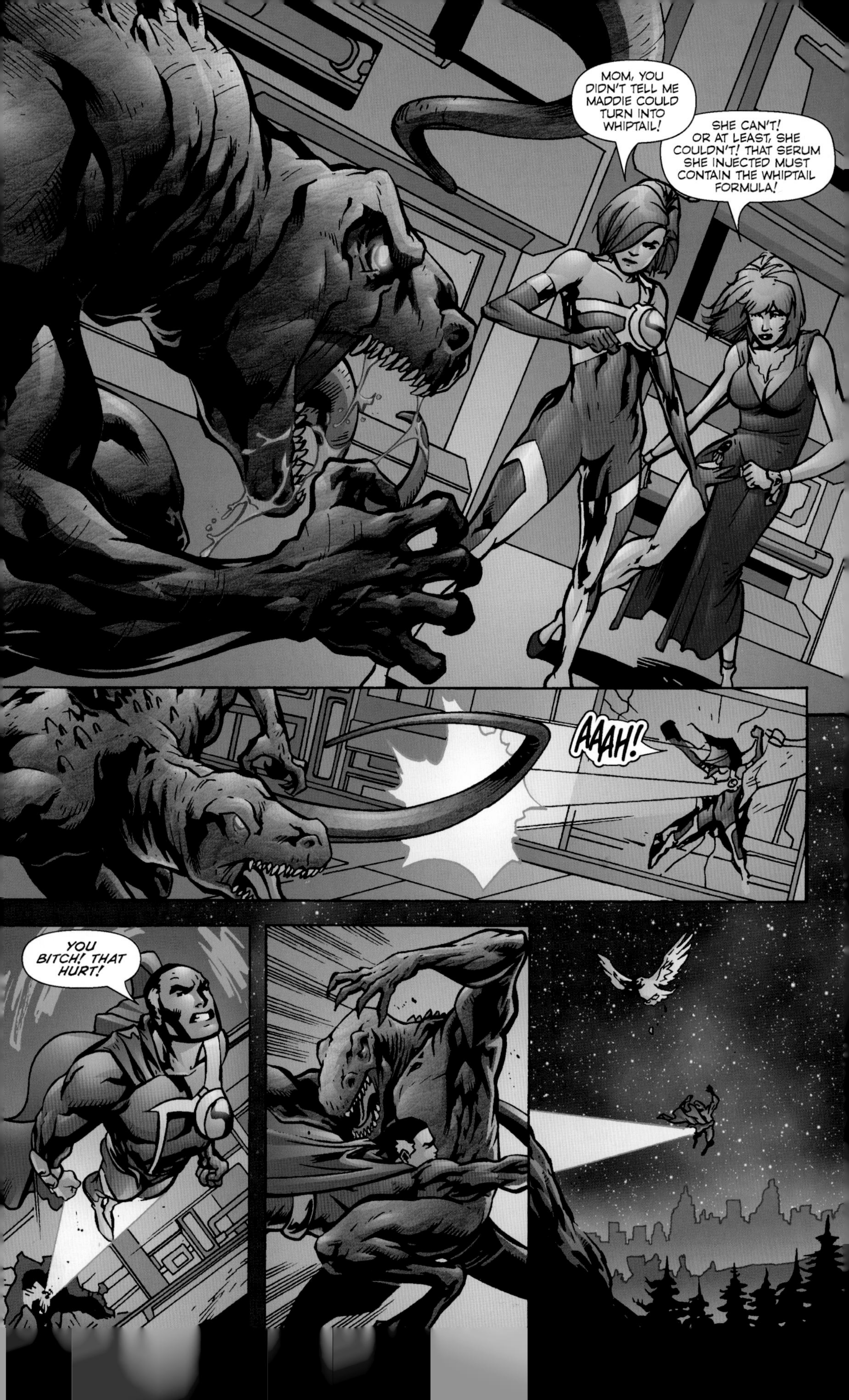
MOM, YOU DIDN'T TELL ME MADDIE COULD TURN INTO WHIPTAIL!
SHE CAN'T! OR AT LEAST, SHE COULDN'T! THAT SERUM SHE INJECTED MUST CONTAIN THE WHIPTAIL FORMULA!
AAAH!
YOU BITCH! THAT HURT!

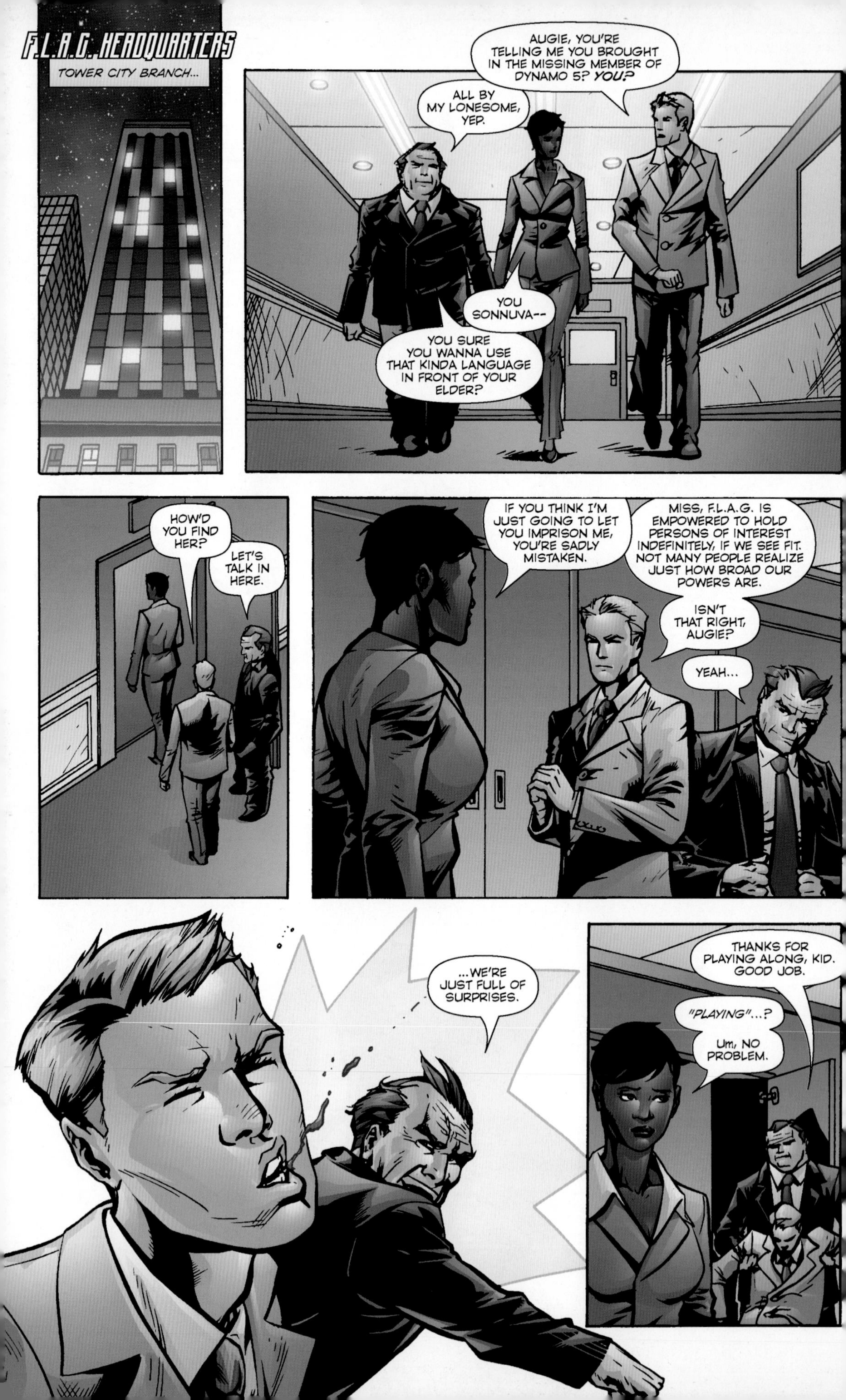
F.L.A.G. HEADQUARTERS
TOWER CITY BRANCH...
AUGIE, YOU'RE TELLING ME YOU BROUGHT IN THE MISSING MEMBER OF DYNAMO 5? YOU?
ALL BY MY LONESOME, YEP.
YOU SONNUVA--
YOU SURE YOU WANNA USE THAT KINDA LANGUAGE IN FRONT OF YOUR ELDER?
HOW'D YOU FIND HER?
LET'S TALK IN HERE.
IF YOU THINK I'M JUST GOING TO LET YOU IMPRISON ME, YOU'RE SADLY MISTAKEN.
MISS, F.L.A.G. IS EMPOWERED TO HOLD PERSONS OF INTEREST INDEFINITELY, IF WE SEE FIT. NOT MANY PEOPLE REALIZE JUST HOW BROAD OUR POWERS ARE.
ISN'T THAT RIGHT, AUGIE?
YEAH...
...WE'RE JUST FULL OF SURPRISES.
THANKS FOR PLAYING ALONG, KID. GOOD JOB.
"PLAYING"...?
Um, NO PROBLEM.

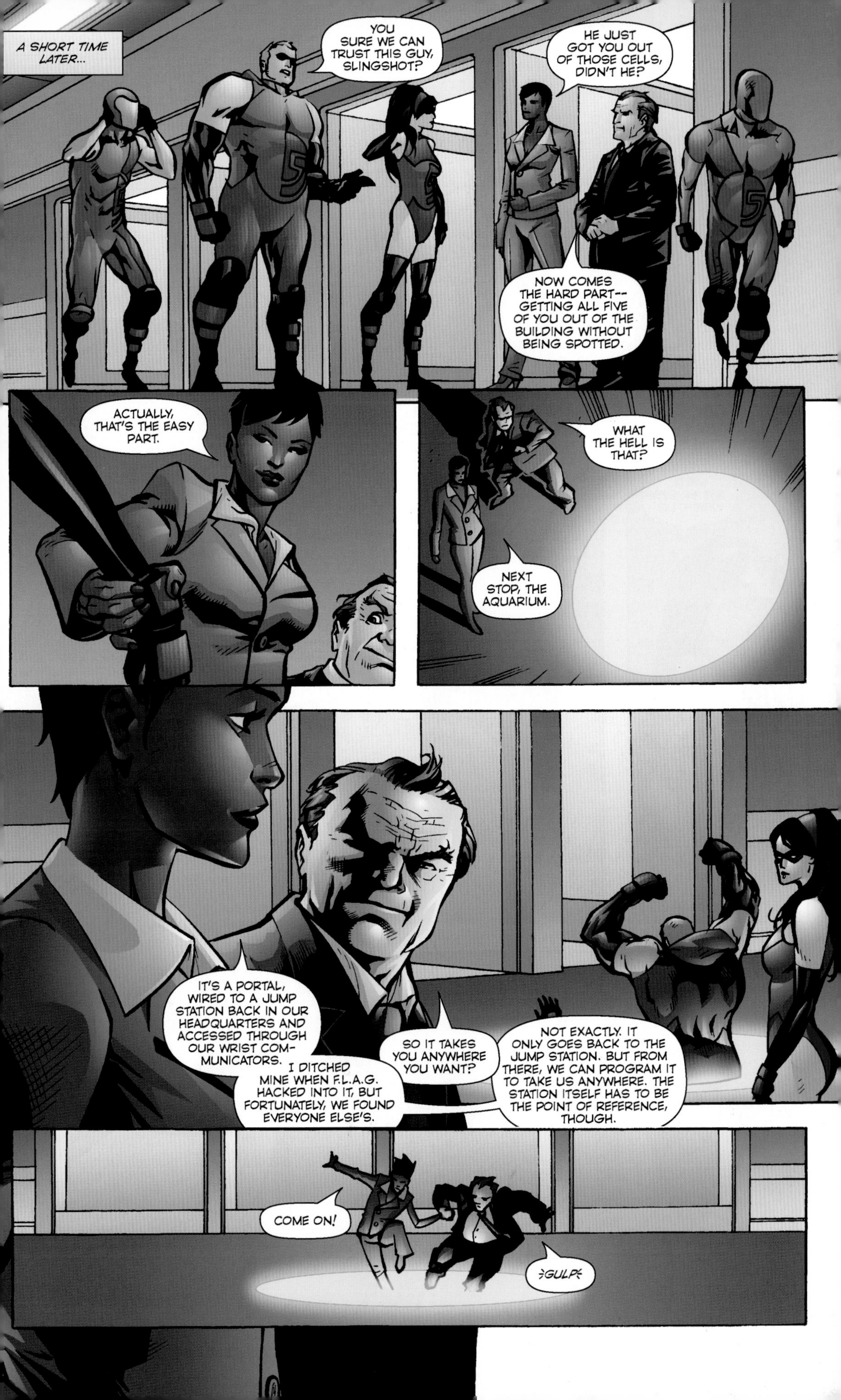
A SHORT TIME LATER...
YOU SURE WE CAN TRUST THIS GUY, SLINGSHOT?
HE JUST GOT YOU OUT OF THOSE CELLS, DIDN'T HE?
NOW COMES THE HARD PART-- GETTING ALL FIVE OF YOU OUT OF THE BUILDING WITHOUT BEING SPOTTED.
ACTUALLY, THAT'S THE EASY PART.
WHAT THE HELL IS THAT?
NEXT STOP, THE AQUARIUM.
IT'S A PORTAL, WIRED TO A JUMP STATION BACK IN OUR HEADQUARTERS AND ACCESSED THROUGH OUR WRIST COM-MUNICATORS.
I DITCHED MINE WHEN F.L.A.G. HACKED INTO IT, BUT FORTUNATELY, WE FOUND EVERYONE ELSE'S.
SO IT TAKES YOU ANYWHERE YOU WANT?
NOT EXACTLY. IT ONLY GOES BACK TO THE JUMP STATION. BUT FROM THERE, WE CAN PROGRAM IT TO TAKE US ANYWHERE. THE STATION ITSELF HAS TO BE THE POINT OF REFERENCE, THOUGH.
COME ON!
GULP

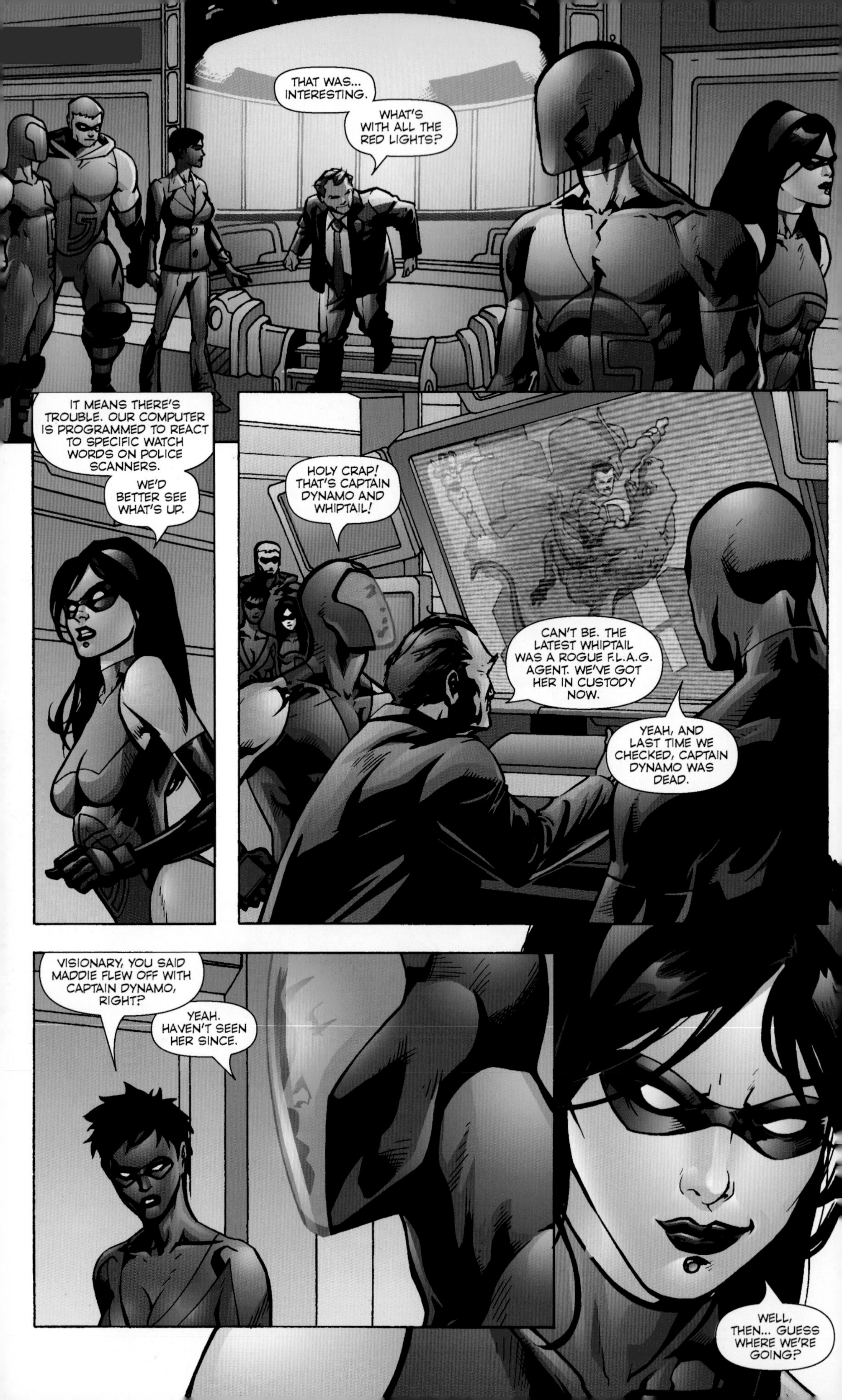
THAT WAS... INTERESTING.
WHAT'S WITH ALL THE RED LIGHTS?
IT MEANS THERE'S TROUBLE. OUR COMPUTER IS PROGRAMMED TO REACT TO SPECIFIC WATCH WORDS ON POLICE SCANNERS.
WE'D BETTER SEE WHAT'S UP.
HOLY CRAP! THAT'S CAPTAIN DYNAMO AND WHIPTAIL!
CAN'T BE. THE LATEST WHIPTAIL WAS A ROGUE F.L.A.G. AGENT. WE'VE GOT HER IN CUSTODY NOW.
YEAH, AND LAST TIME WE CHECKED, CAPTAIN DYNAMO WAS DEAD.
VISIONARY, YOU SAID MADDIE FLEW OFF WITH CAPTAIN DYNAMO, RIGHT?
YEAH. HAVEN'T SEEN HER SINCE.
WELL, THEN... GUESS WHERE WE'RE GOING?

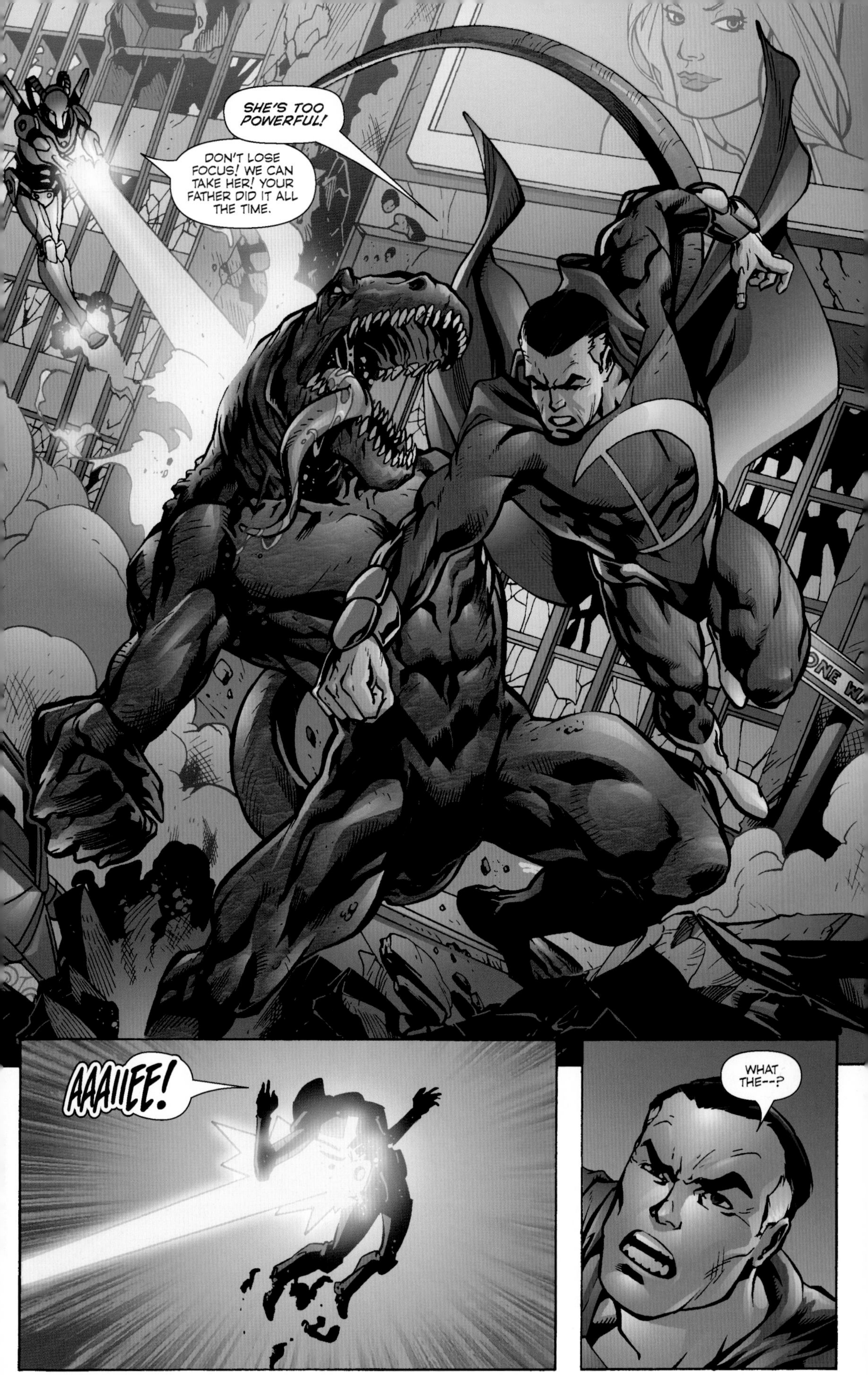
SHE'S TOO POWERFUL!
DON'T LOSE FOCUS! WE CAN TAKE HER! YOUR FATHER DID IT ALL THE TIME.
AAAIIEE!
WHAT THE--?

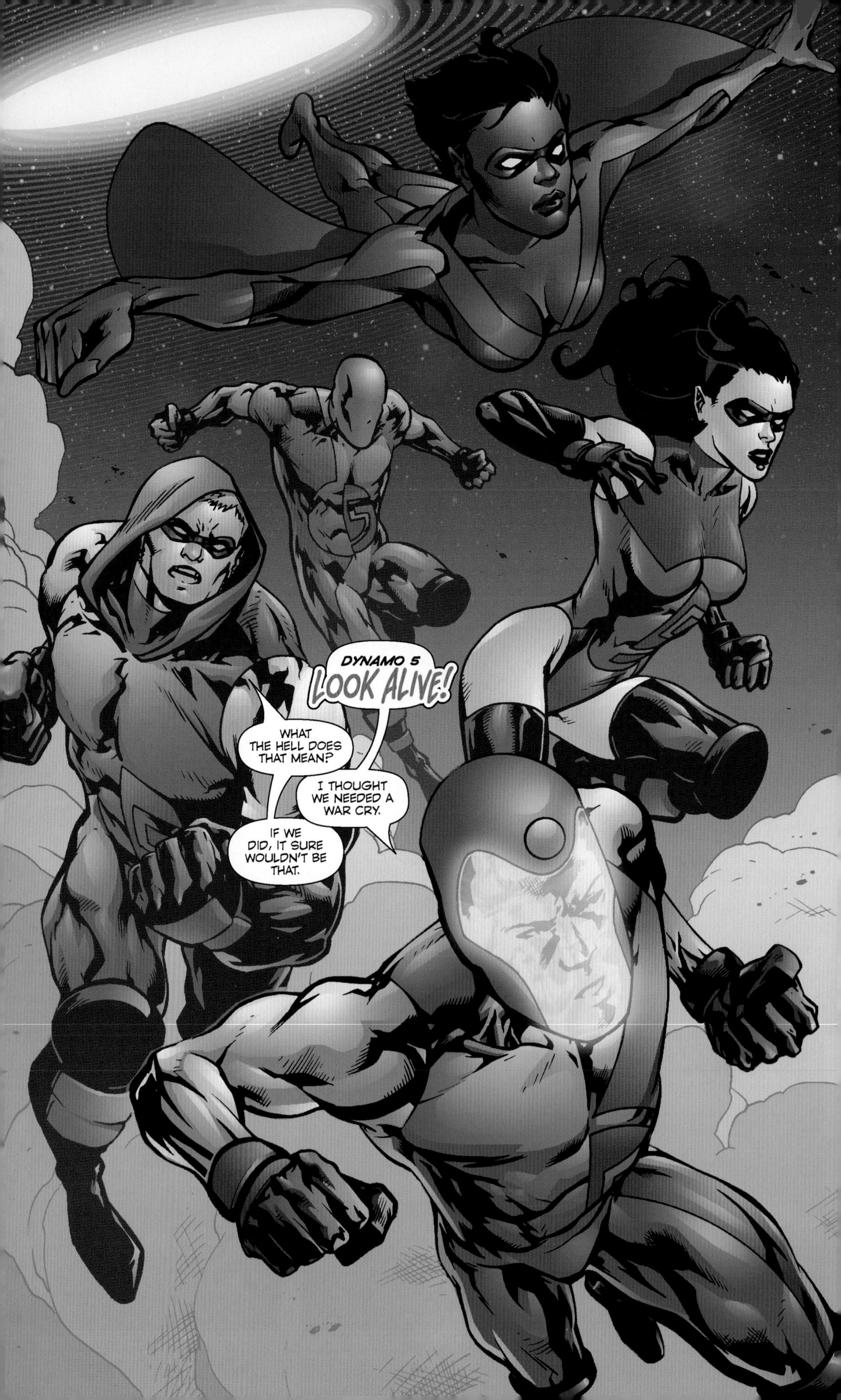
DYNAMO 5
LOOK ALIVE!
WHAT THE HELL DOES THAT MEAN?
I THOUGHT WE NEEDED A WAR CRY.
IF WE DID, IT SURE WOULDN'T BE THAT.

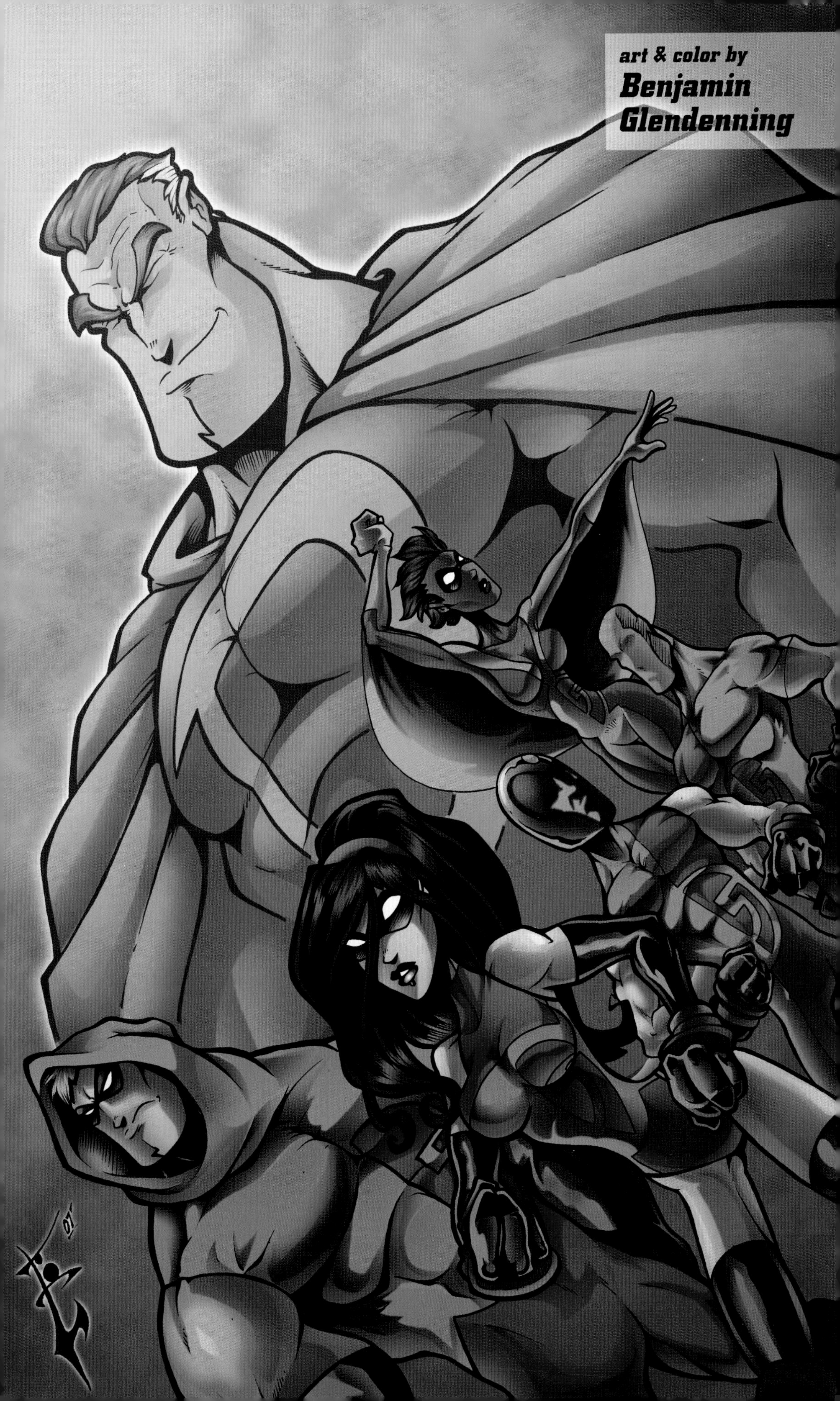
art & color by
Benjamin
Glendenning

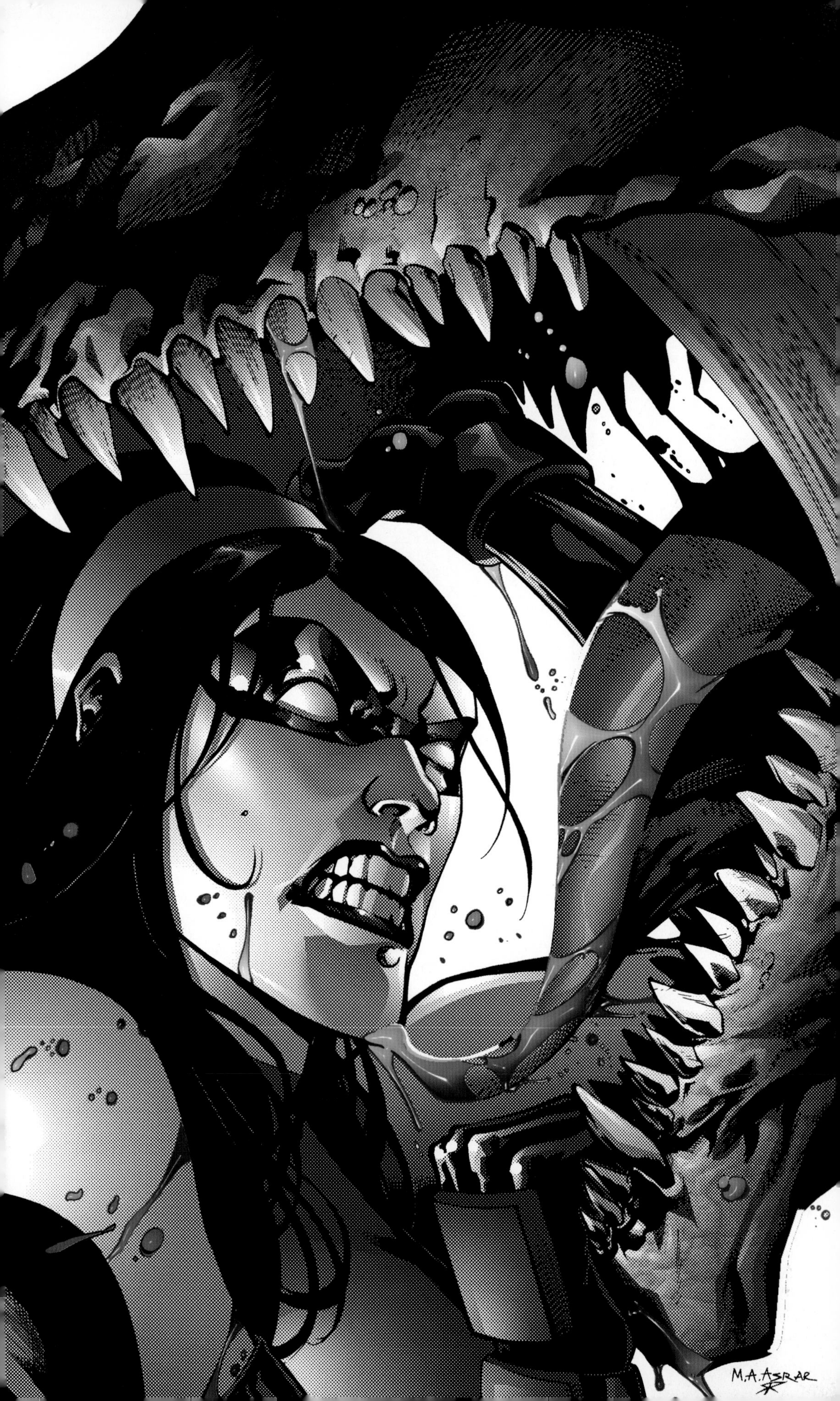
M.A. ASRAR

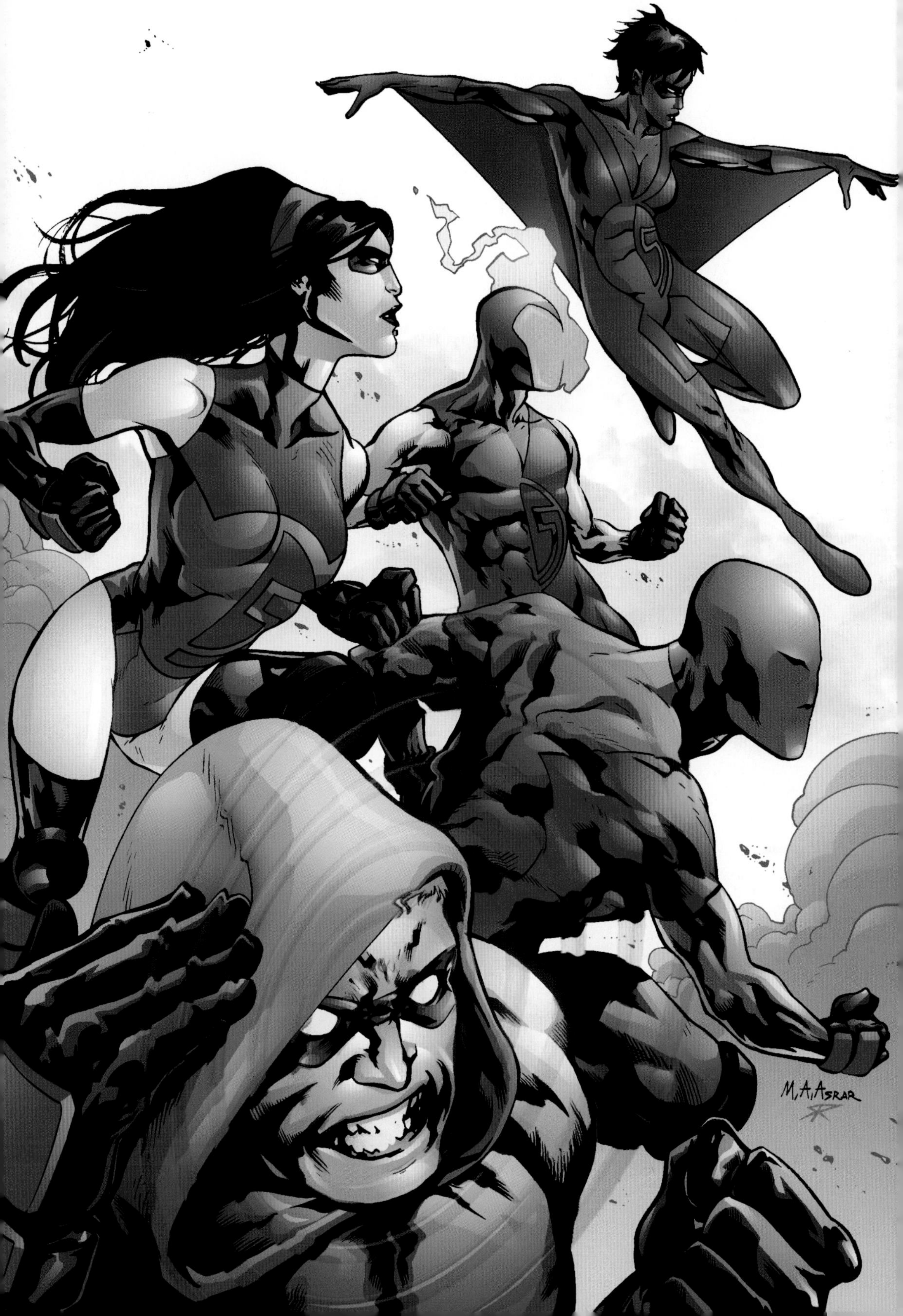
M.A.Asrar

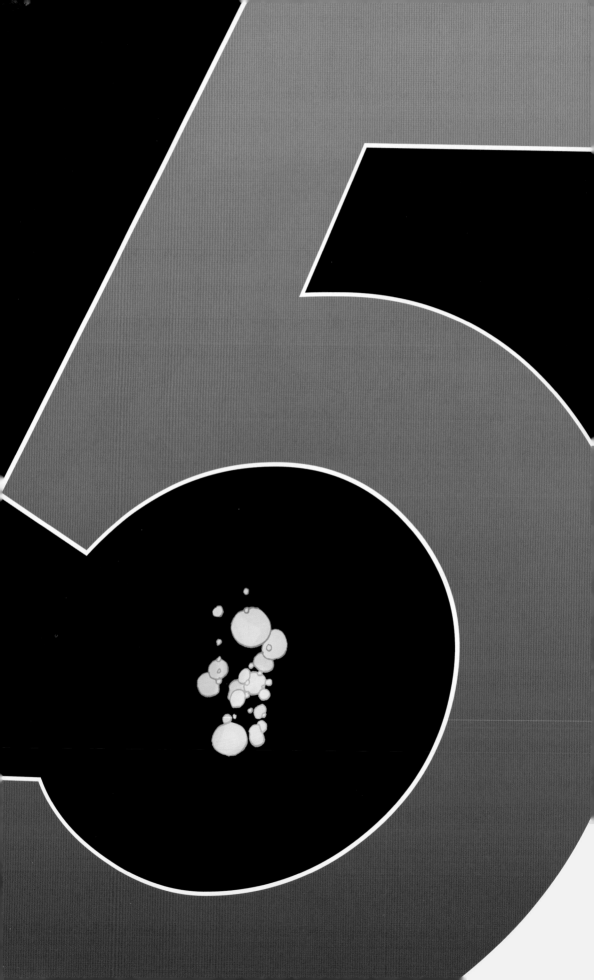

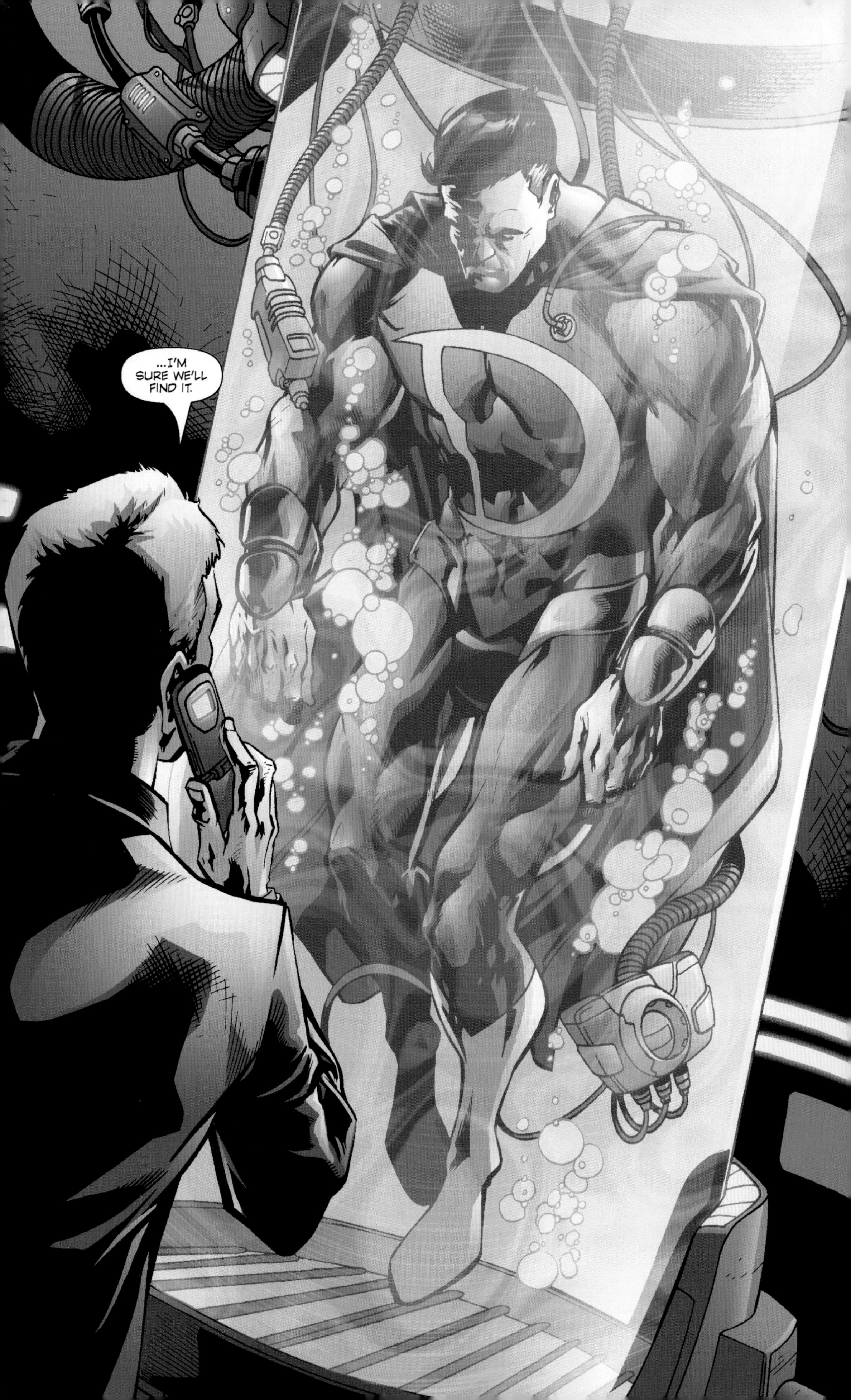
...I'M SURE WE'LL FIND IT.

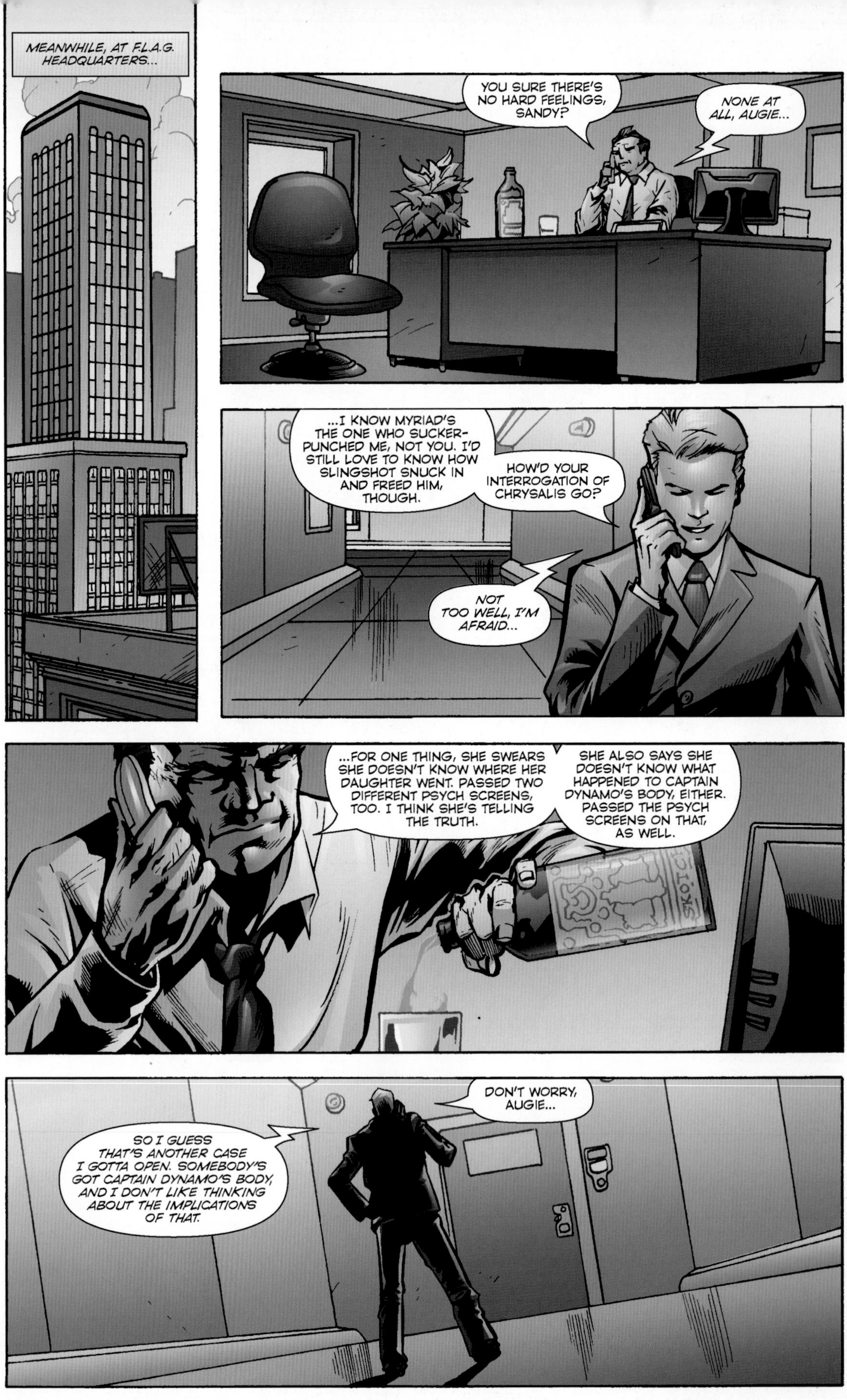
MEANWHILE, AT F.L.A.G. HEADQUARTERS...
YOU SURE THERE'S NO HARD FEELINGS, SANDY?
NONE AT ALL, AUGIE...
...I KNOW MYRIAD'S THE ONE WHO SUCKER-PUNCHED ME, NOT YOU. I'D STILL LOVE TO KNOW HOW SLINGSHOT SNUCK IN AND FREED HIM, THOUGH.
HOW'D YOUR INTERROGATION OF CHRYSALIS GO?
NOT TOO WELL, I'M AFRAID...
...FOR ONE THING, SHE SWEARS SHE DOESN'T KNOW WHERE HER DAUGHTER WENT. PASSED TWO DIFFERENT PSYCH SCREENS, TOO. I THINK SHE'S TELLING THE TRUTH.
SHE ALSO SAYS SHE DOESN'T KNOW WHAT HAPPENED TO CAPTAIN DYNAMO'S BODY, EITHER. PASSED THE PSYCH SCREENS ON THAT, AS WELL.
SKOTCH
DON'T WORRY, AUGIE...
SO I GUESS THAT'S ANOTHER CASE I GOTTA OPEN. SOMEBODY'S GOT CAPTAIN DYNAMO'S BODY, AND I DON'T LIKE THINKING ABOUT THE IMPLICATIONS OF THAT.

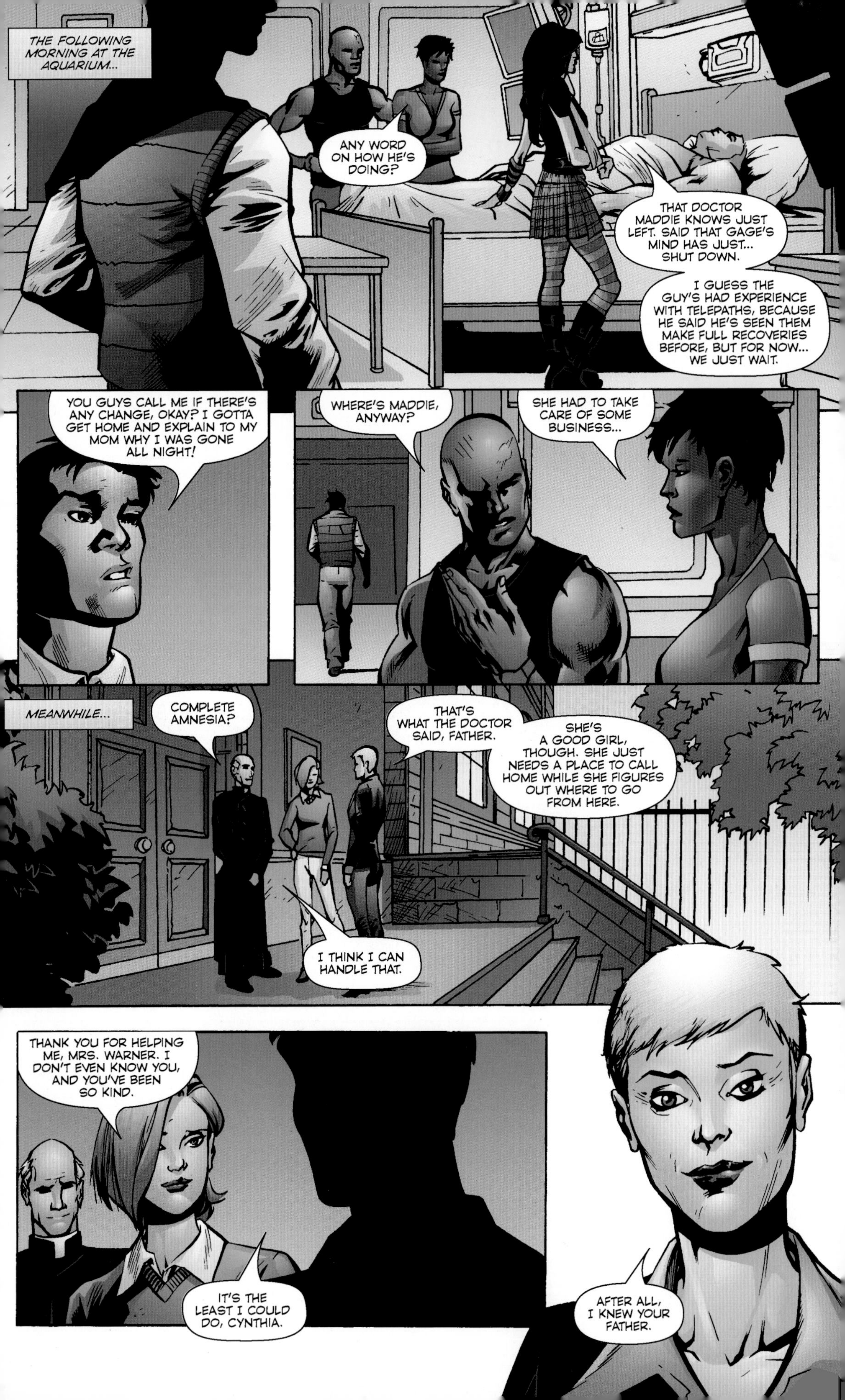
THE FOLLOWING MORNING AT THE AQUARIUM...
ANY WORD ON HOW HE'S DOING?
THAT DOCTOR MADDIE KNOWS JUST LEFT. SAID THAT GAGE'S MIND HAS JUST... SHUT DOWN.
I GUESS THE GUY'S HAD EXPERIENCE WITH TELEPATHS, BECAUSE HE SAID HE'S SEEN THEM MAKE FULL RECOVERIES BEFORE, BUT FOR NOW... WE JUST WAIT.
YOU GUYS CALL ME IF THERE'S ANY CHANGE, OKAY? I GOTTA GET HOME AND EXPLAIN TO MY MOM WHY I WAS GONE ALL NIGHT!
WHERE'S MADDIE, ANYWAY?
SHE HAD TO TAKE CARE OF SOME BUSINESS...
MEANWHILE...
COMPLETE AMNESIA?
THAT'S WHAT THE DOCTOR SAID, FATHER.
SHE'S A GOOD GIRL, THOUGH. SHE JUST NEEDS A PLACE TO CALL HOME WHILE SHE FIGURES OUT WHERE TO GO FROM HERE.
I THINK I CAN HANDLE THAT.
THANK YOU FOR HELPING ME, MRS. WARNER. I DON'T EVEN KNOW YOU, AND YOU'VE BEEN SO KIND.
IT'S THE LEAST I COULD DO, CYNTHIA.
AFTER ALL, I KNEW YOUR FATHER.

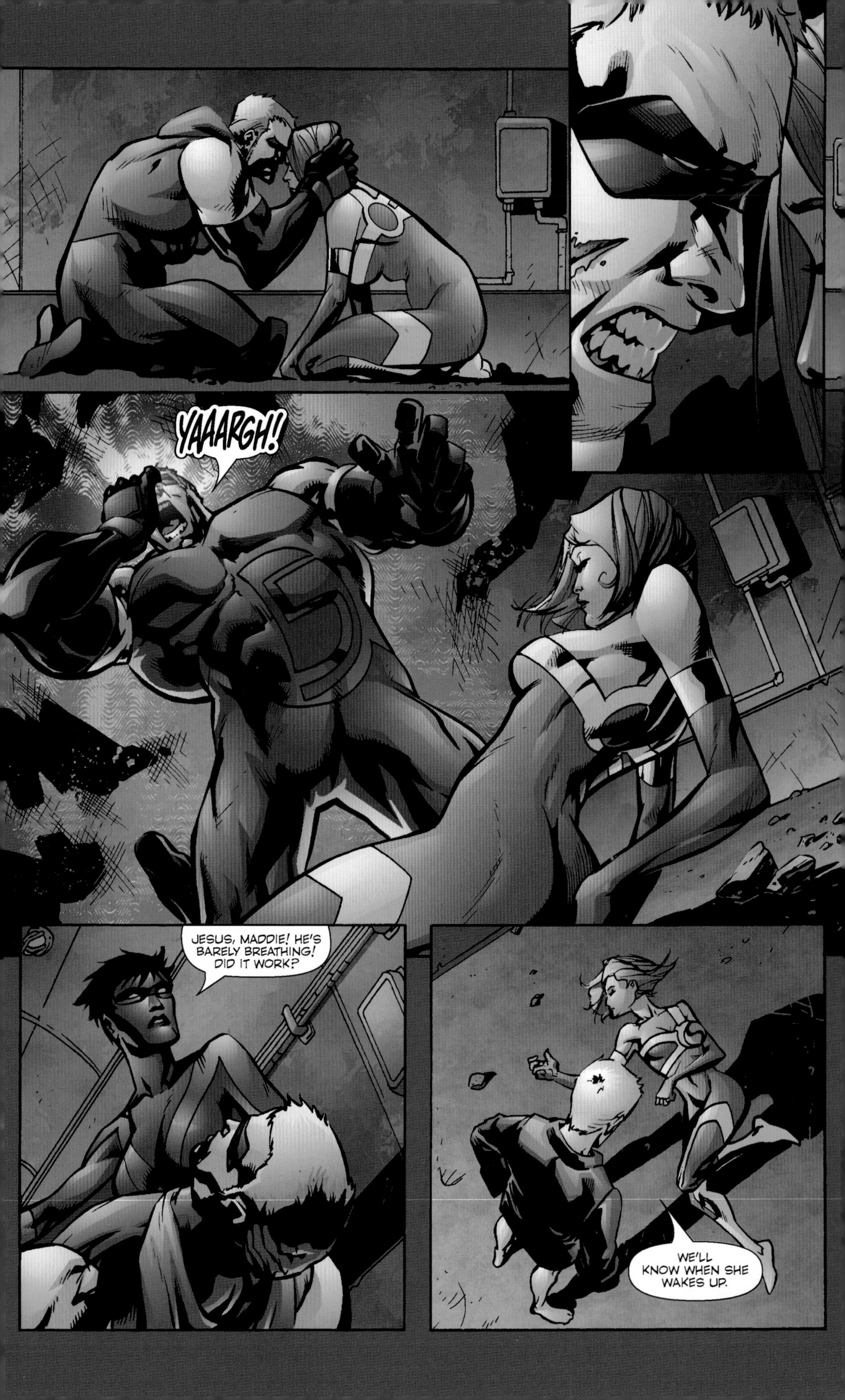
YAAARGH!
JESUS, MADDIE! HE'S BARELY BREATHING! DID IT WORK?
WE'LL KNOW WHEN SHE WAKES UP.

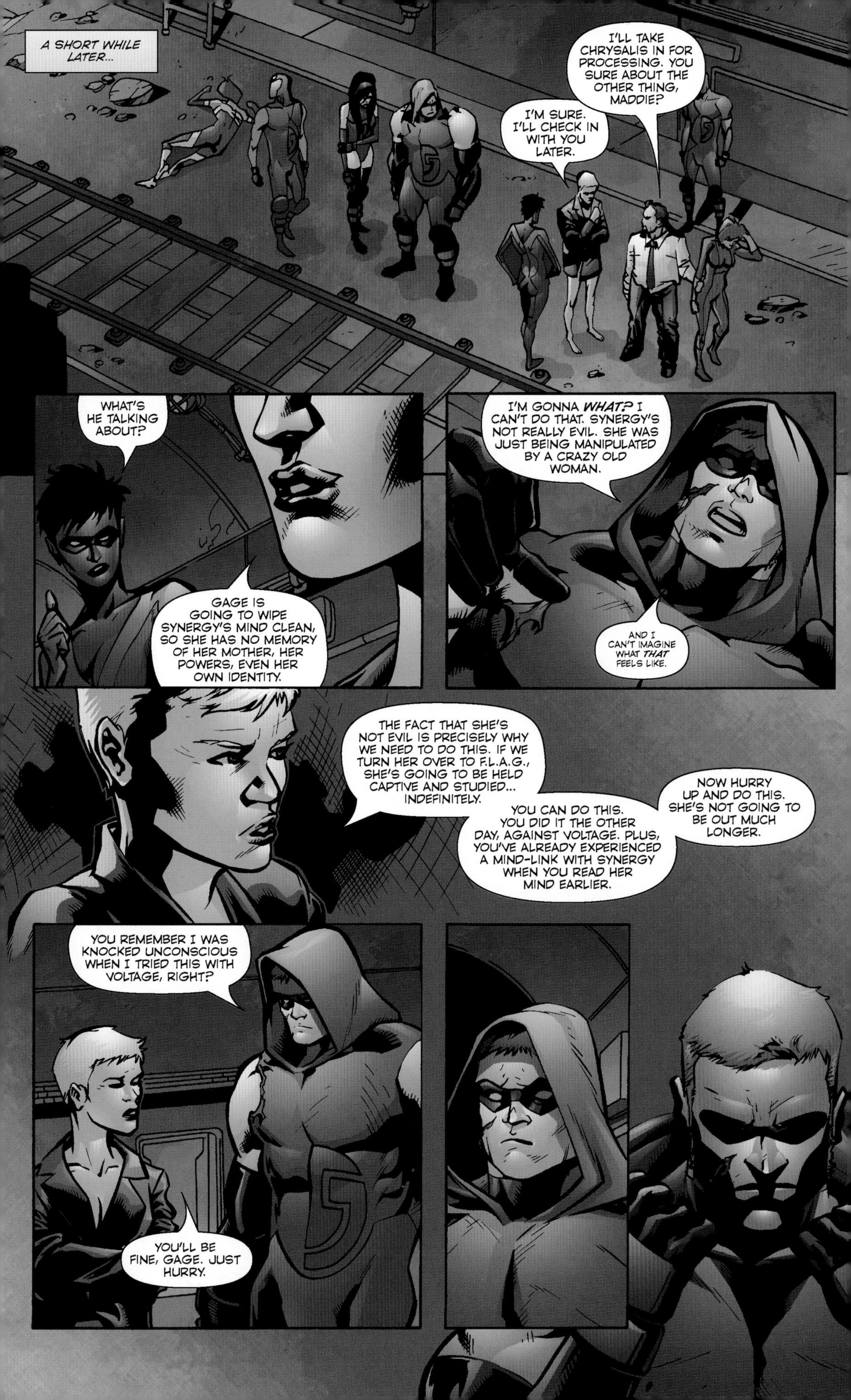
A SHORT WHILE LATER...
I'LL TAKE CHRYSALIS IN FOR PROCESSING. YOU SURE ABOUT THE OTHER THING, MADDIE?
I'M SURE. I'LL CHECK IN WITH YOU LATER.
WHAT'S HE TALKING ABOUT?
GAGE IS GOING TO WIPE SYNERGY'S MIND CLEAN, SO SHE HAS NO MEMORY OF HER MOTHER, HER POWERS, EVEN HER OWN IDENTITY.
I'M GONNA *WHAT?* I CAN'T DO THAT. SYNERGY'S NOT REALLY EVIL. SHE WAS JUST BEING MANIPULATED BY A CRAZY OLD WOMAN.
AND I CAN'T IMAGINE WHAT *THAT* FEELS LIKE.
THE FACT THAT SHE'S NOT EVIL IS PRECISELY WHY WE NEED TO DO THIS. IF WE TURN HER OVER TO F.L.A.G., SHE'S GOING TO BE HELD CAPTIVE AND STUDIED... INDEFINITELY.
YOU CAN DO THIS. YOU DID IT THE OTHER DAY, AGAINST VOLTAGE. PLUS, YOU'VE ALREADY EXPERIENCED A MIND-LINK WITH SYNERGY WHEN YOU READ HER MIND EARLIER.
NOW HURRY UP AND DO THIS. SHE'S NOT GOING TO BE OUT MUCH LONGER.
YOU REMEMBER I WAS KNOCKED UNCONSCIOUS WHEN I TRIED THIS WITH VOLTAGE, RIGHT?
YOU'LL BE FINE, GAGE. JUST HURRY.

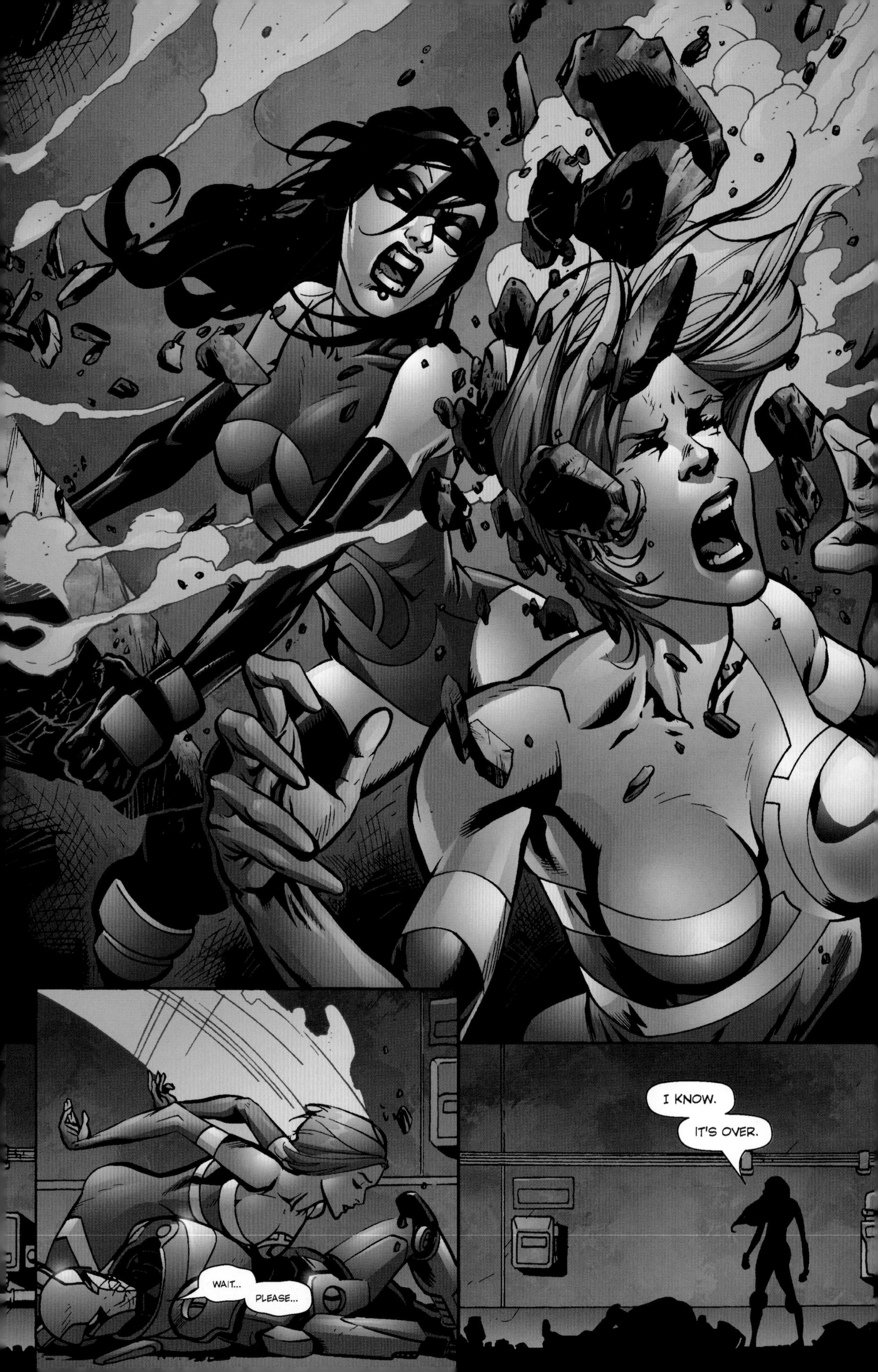
WAIT...
PLEASE...
I KNOW.
IT'S OVER.

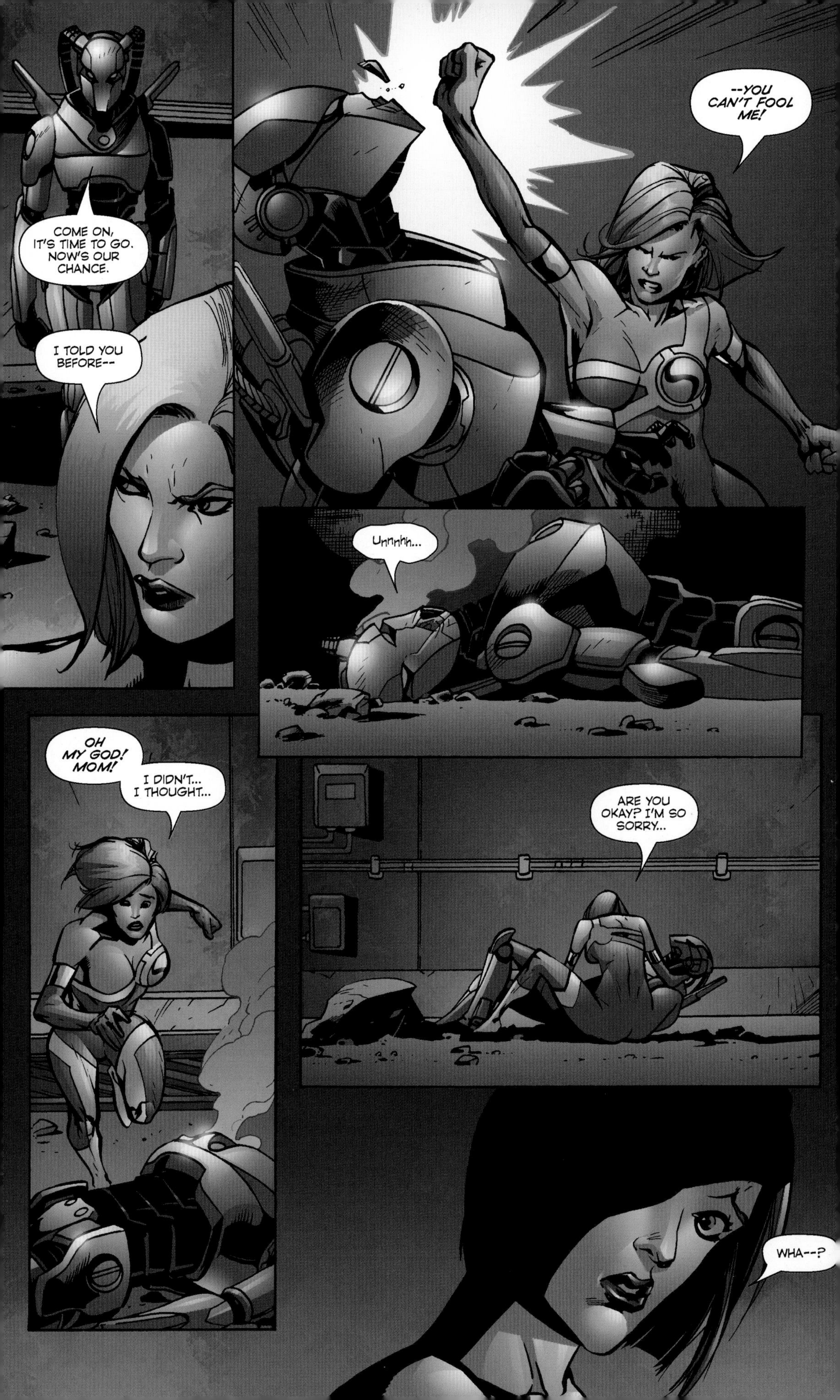

COME ON, IT'S TIME TO GO. NOW'S OUR CHANCE.
I TOLD YOU BEFORE--
--YOU CAN'T FOOL ME!
Unnnhh...
OH MY GOD! MOM!
I DIDN'T... I THOUGHT...
ARE YOU OKAY? I'M SO SORRY...
WHA--?

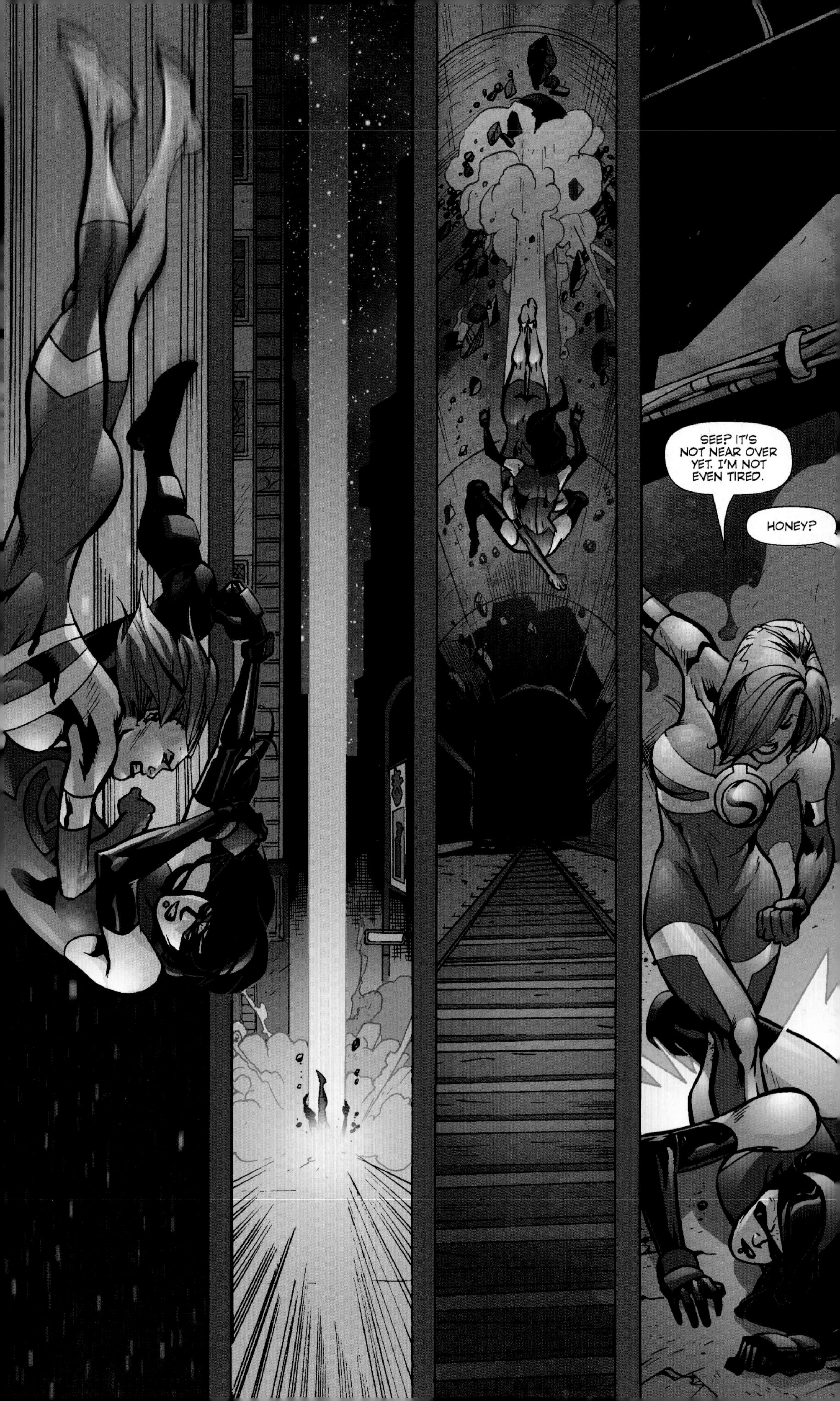
SEE? IT'S NOT NEAR OVER YET. I'M NOT EVEN TIRED.
HONEY?

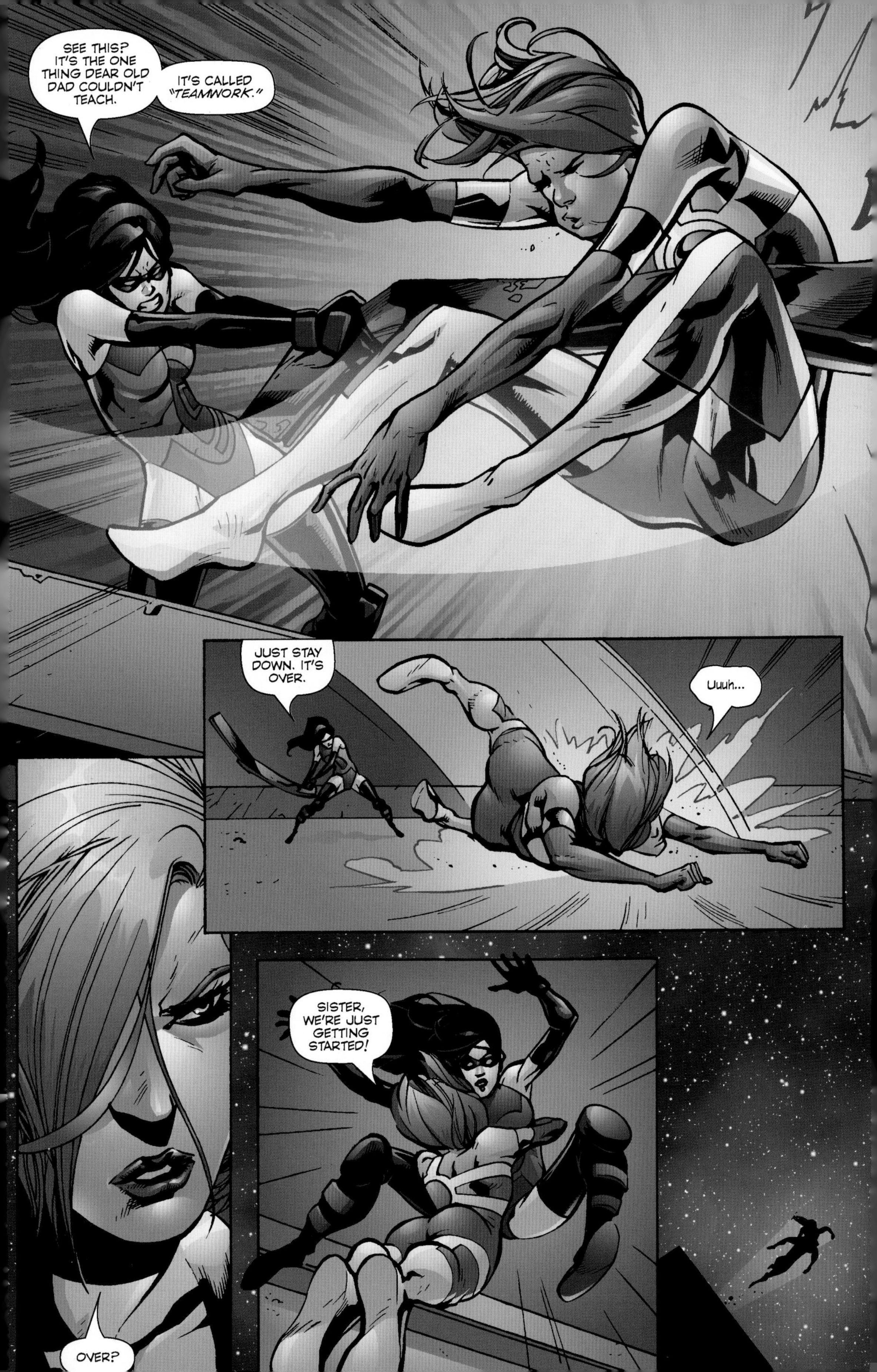
SEE THIS? IT'S THE ONE THING DEAR OLD DAD COULDN'T TEACH.
IT'S CALLED "TEAMWORK."
JUST STAY DOWN. IT'S OVER.
Uuuh...
OVER?
SISTER, WE'RE JUST GETTING STARTED!

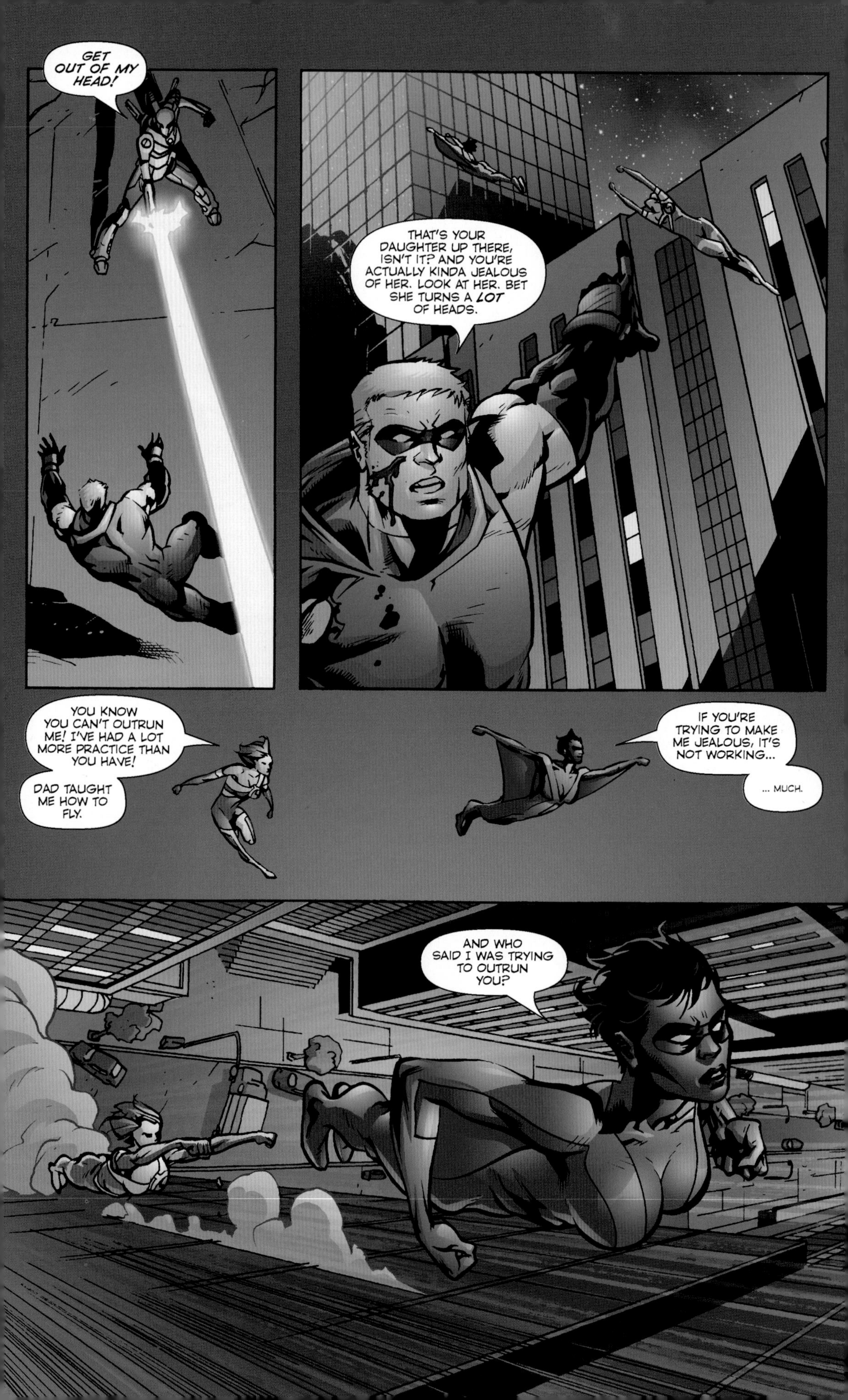
GET OUT OF MY HEAD!
THAT'S YOUR DAUGHTER UP THERE, ISN'T IT? AND YOU'RE ACTUALLY KINDA JEALOUS OF HER. LOOK AT HER. BET SHE TURNS A *LOT* OF HEADS.
YOU KNOW YOU CAN'T OUTRUN ME! I'VE HAD A LOT MORE PRACTICE THAN YOU HAVE!
DAD TAUGHT ME HOW TO FLY.
IF YOU'RE TRYING TO MAKE ME JEALOUS, IT'S NOT WORKING...
... MUCH.
AND WHO SAID I WAS TRYING TO OUTRUN YOU?

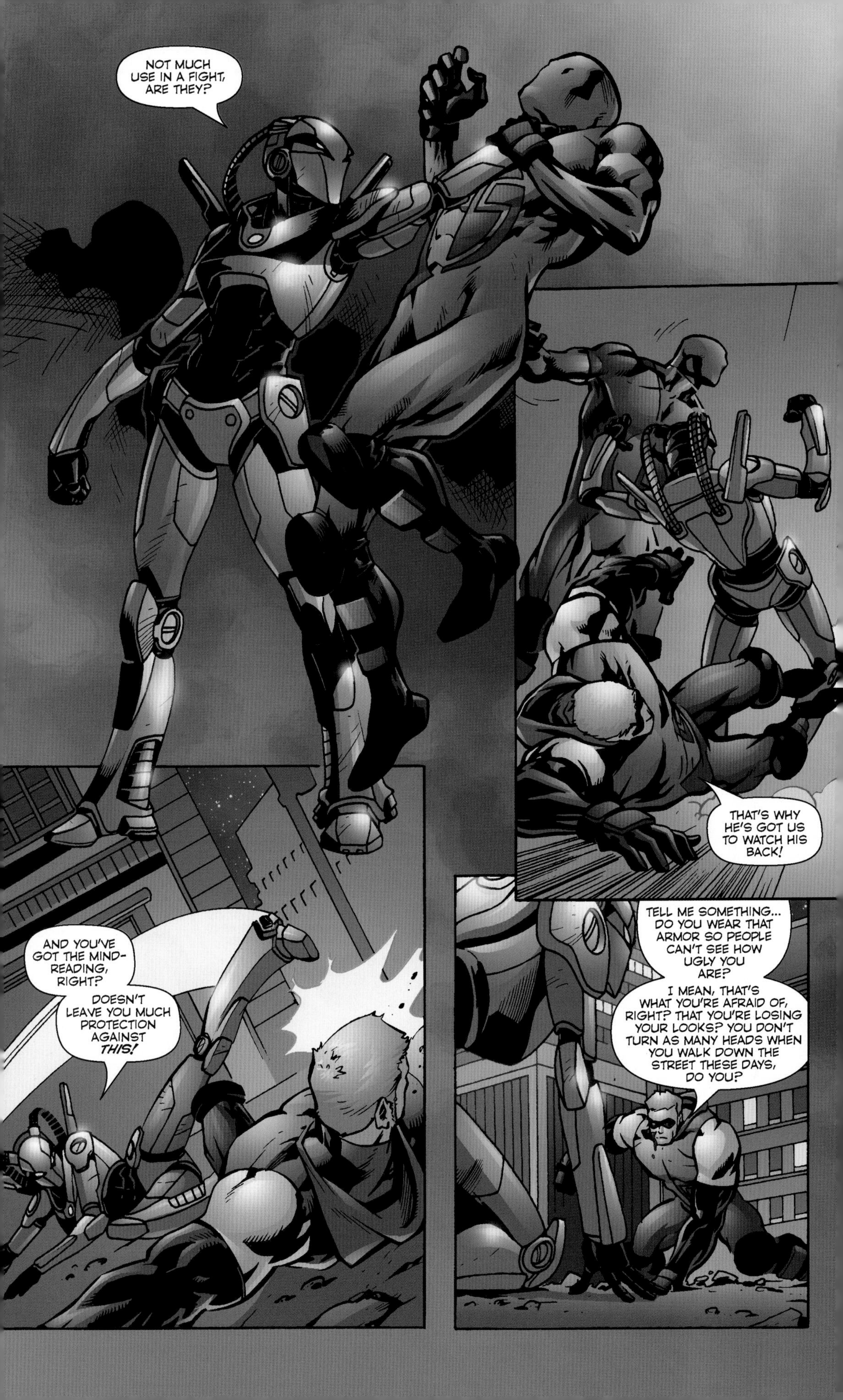
NOT MUCH USE IN A FIGHT, ARE THEY?
THAT'S WHY HE'S GOT US TO WATCH HIS BACK!
AND YOU'VE GOT THE MIND-READING, RIGHT?
DOESN'T LEAVE YOU MUCH PROTECTION AGAINST THIS!
TELL ME SOMETHING... DO YOU WEAR THAT ARMOR SO PEOPLE CAN'T SEE HOW UGLY YOU ARE?
I MEAN, THAT'S WHAT YOU'RE AFRAID OF, RIGHT? THAT YOU'RE LOSING YOUR LOOKS? YOU DON'T TURN AS MANY HEADS WHEN YOU WALK DOWN THE STREET THESE DAYS, DO YOU?

WE COULD GO ON LIKE THIS FOREVER.

MAYBE...

...BUT THIS VISOR ISN'T JUST FOR DECORATION. IT HELPS TO FOCUS MY BLASTS, MAKES THEM MORE CONCENTRATED.

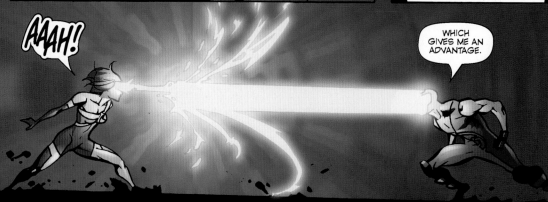

AAAH!

WHICH GIVES ME AN ADVANTAGE.

Unh!

GET AWAY FROM HER! YOU'RE RUINING EVERYTHING!

SYNERGY WAS GOING TO GIVE CAPTAIN DYNAMO BACK TO THE WORLD!

YEAH, RIGHT-- ALL THE WHILE USING HIS GOOD REPUTATION TO CEMENT YOUR OWN POWER BASE, RIGHT?

YOU MUST BE THE ONE WHO INHERITED THE IMPERSONATION POWERS.

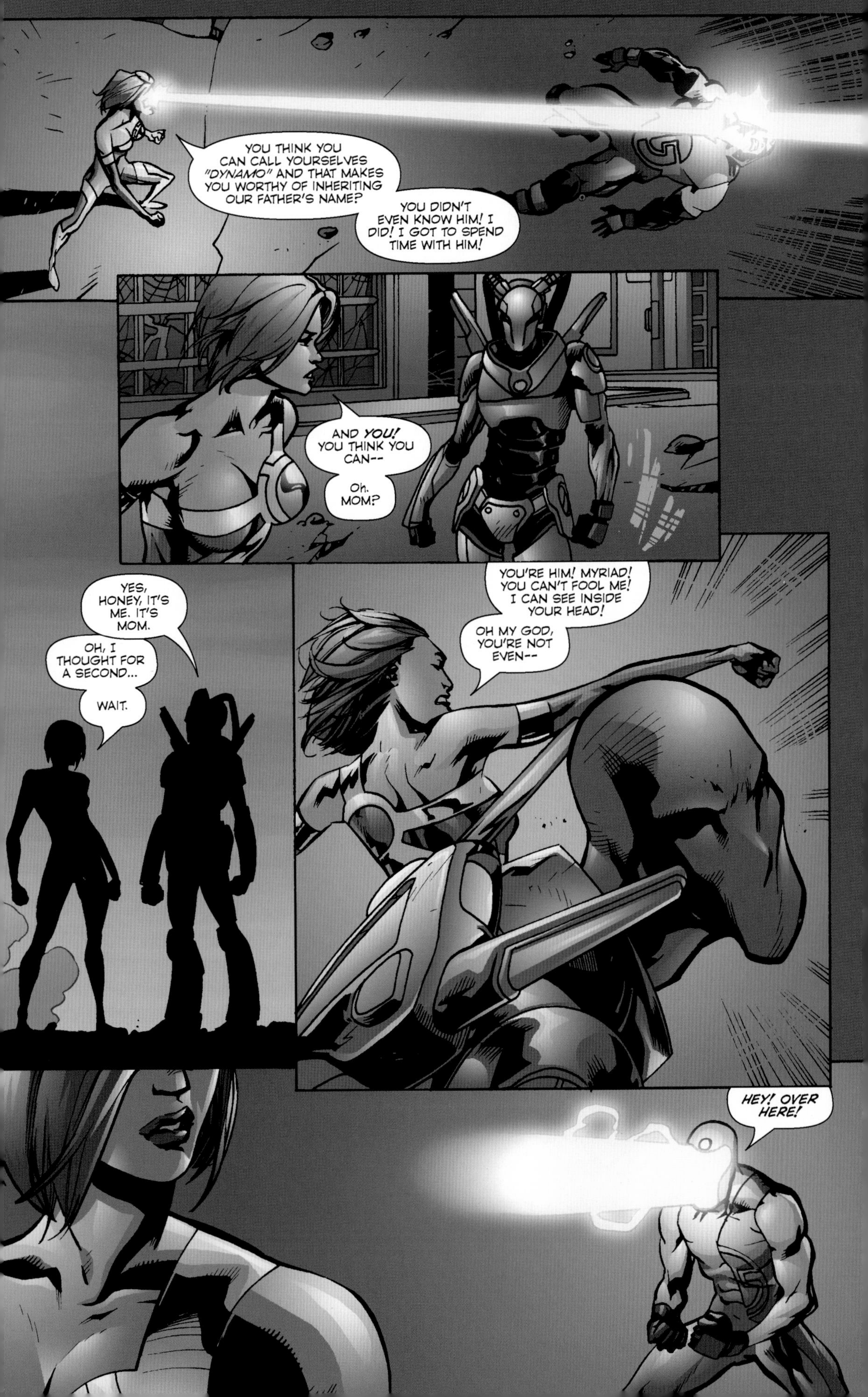
YOU THINK YOU CAN CALL YOURSELVES "DYNAMO" AND THAT MAKES YOU WORTHY OF INHERITING OUR FATHER'S NAME?
YOU DIDN'T EVEN KNOW HIM! I DID! I GOT TO SPEND TIME WITH HIM!
AND YOU! YOU THINK YOU CAN--
Oh. MOM?
YES, HONEY, IT'S ME. IT'S MOM.
OH, I THOUGHT FOR A SECOND...
WAIT.
YOU'RE HIM! MYRIAD! YOU CAN'T FOOL ME! I CAN SEE INSIDE YOUR HEAD!
OH MY GOD, YOU'RE NOT EVEN--
HEY! OVER HERE!

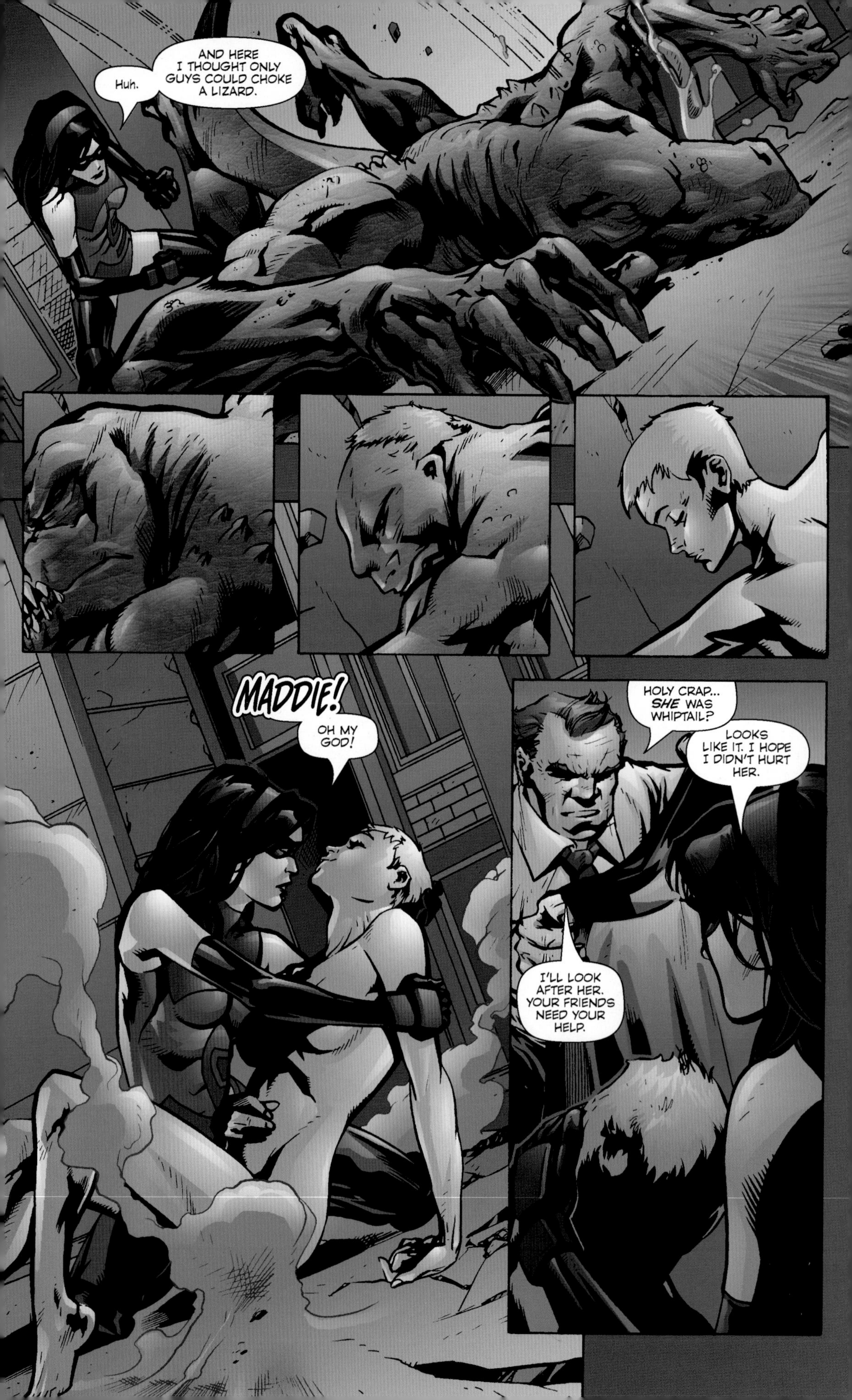
Huh.
AND HERE I THOUGHT ONLY GUYS COULD CHOKE A LIZARD.
MADDIE!
OH MY GOD!
HOLY CRAP... SHE WAS WHIPTAIL?
LOOKS LIKE IT. I HOPE I DIDN'T HURT HER.
I'LL LOOK AFTER HER. YOUR FRIENDS NEED YOUR HELP.

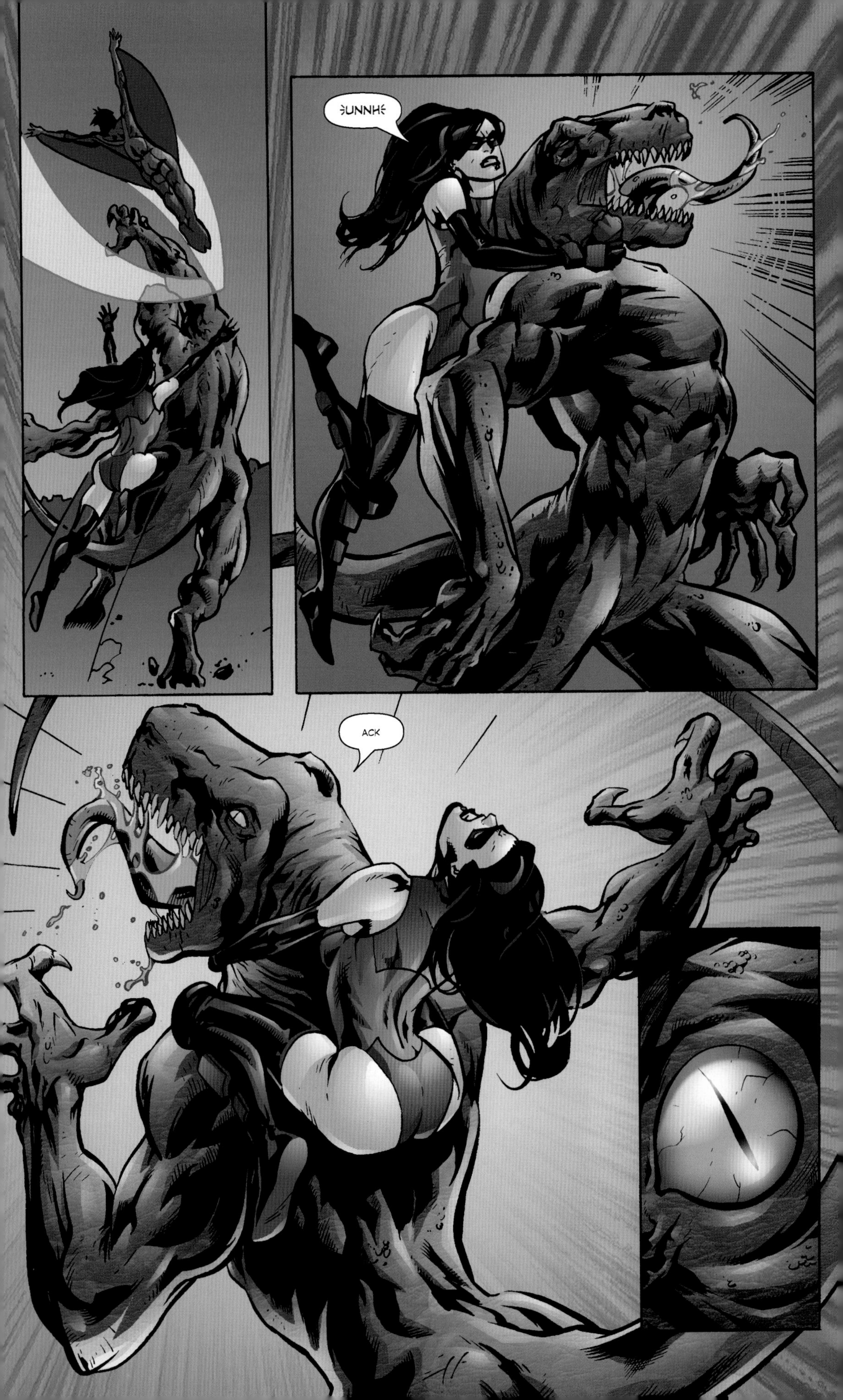
UNNH
ACK

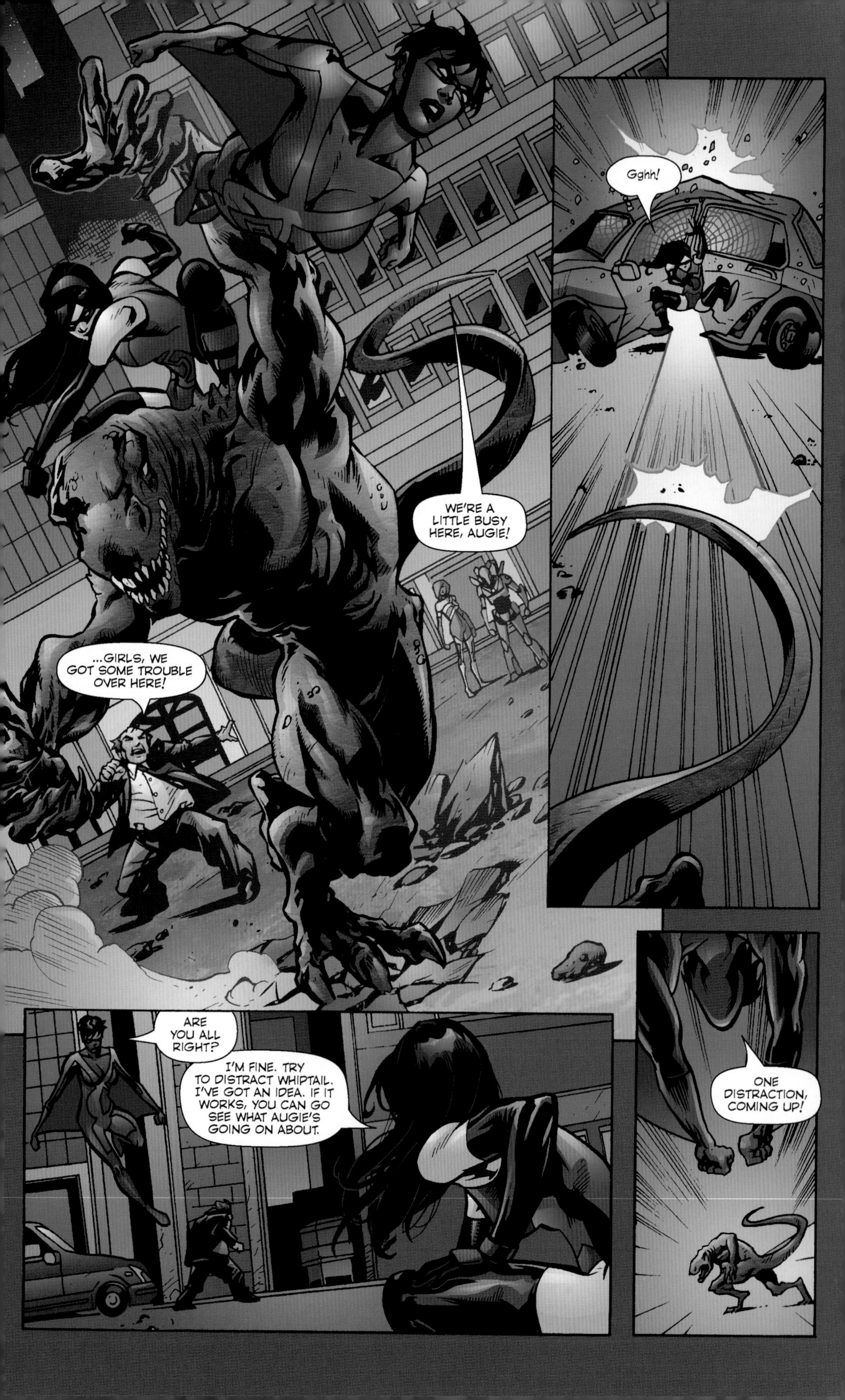
Gghh!
WE'RE A LITTLE BUSY HERE, AUGIE!
...GIRLS, WE GOT SOME TROUBLE OVER HERE!
ARE YOU ALL RIGHT?
I'M FINE. TRY TO DISTRACT WHIPTAIL. I'VE GOT AN IDEA. IF IT WORKS, YOU CAN GO SEE WHAT AUGIE'S GOING ON ABOUT.
ONE DISTRACTION, COMING UP!

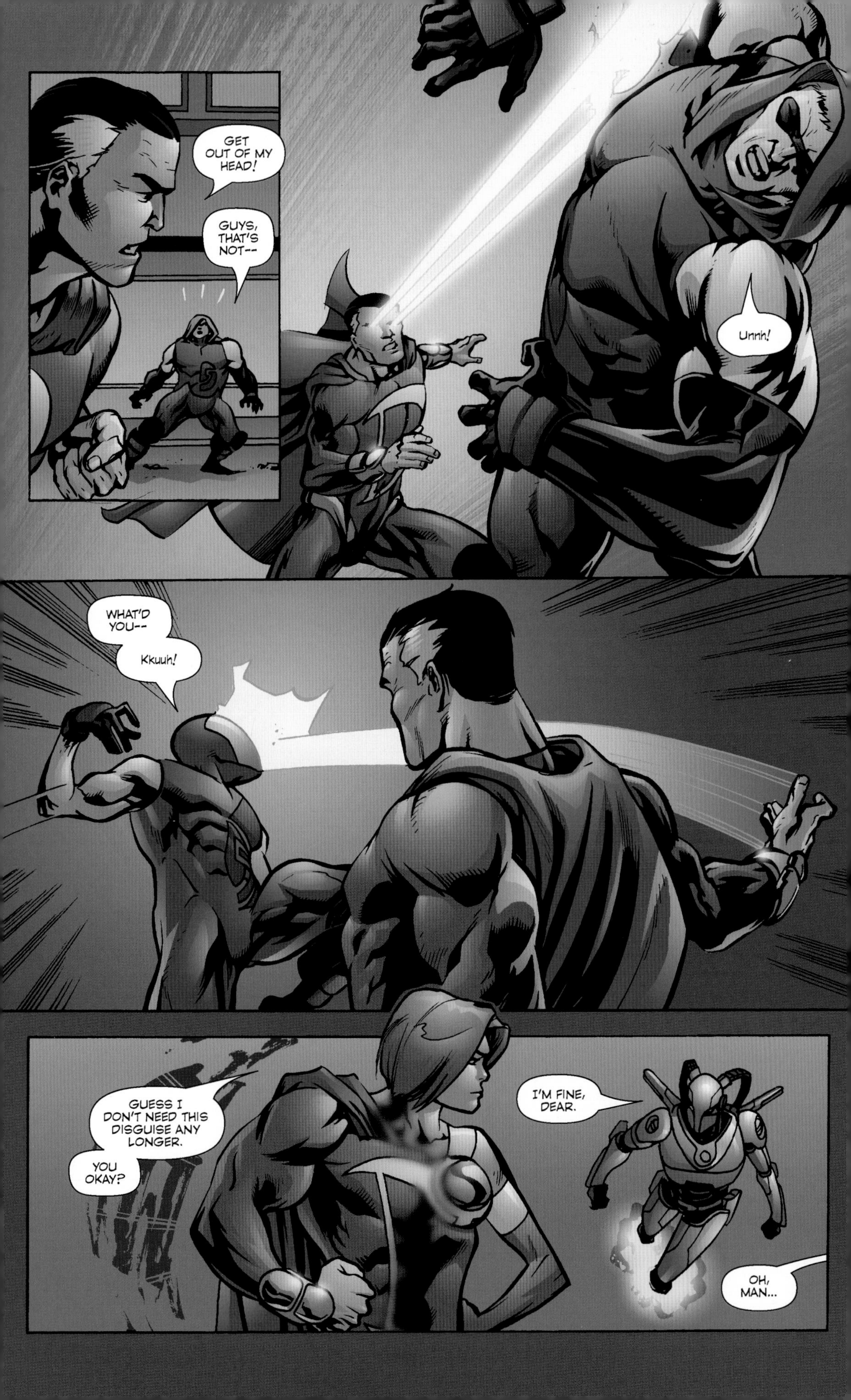
GET OUT OF MY HEAD!
GUYS, THAT'S NOT--
Unnh!
WHAT'D YOU--
Kkuuh!
GUESS I DON'T NEED THIS DISGUISE ANY LONGER.
YOU OKAY?
I'M FINE, DEAR.
OH, MAN...

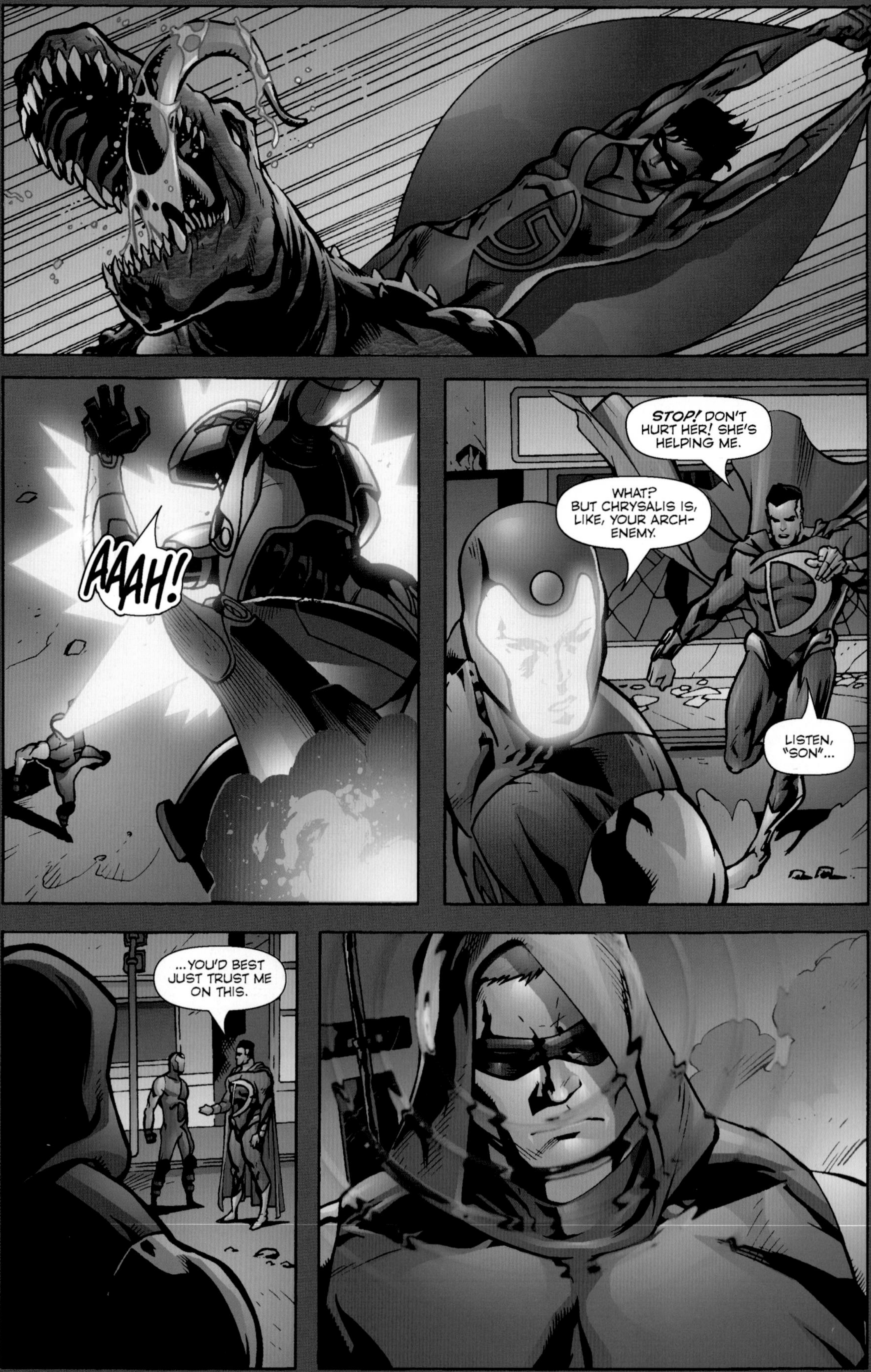
AAAH!
STOP! DON'T HURT HER! SHE'S HELPING ME.
WHAT? BUT CHRYSALIS IS, LIKE, YOUR ARCH-ENEMY.
LISTEN, "SON"...
...YOU'D BEST JUST TRUST ME ON THIS.

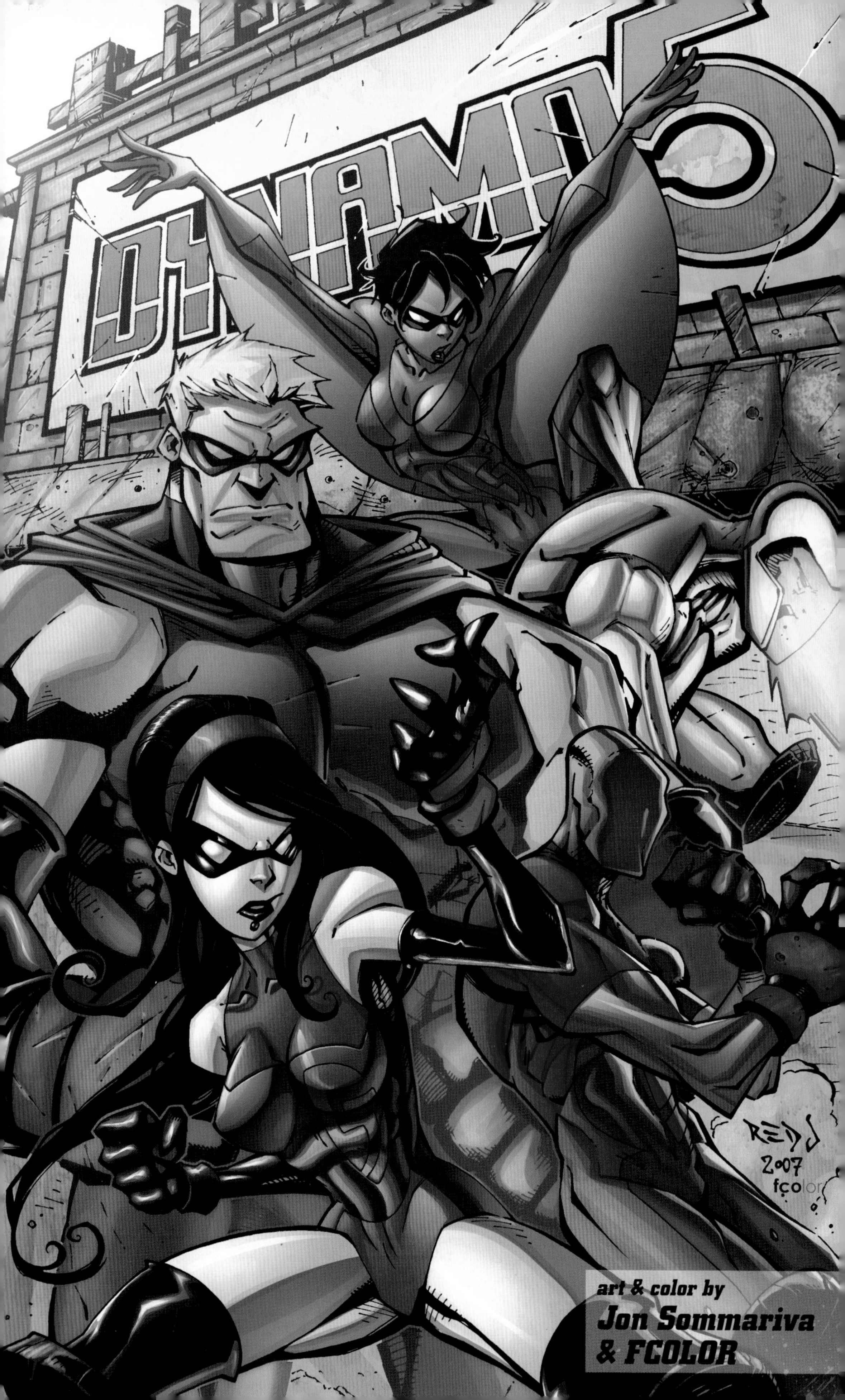
REDJ
2007
fcolor

art & color by
Jon Sommariva & FCOLOR

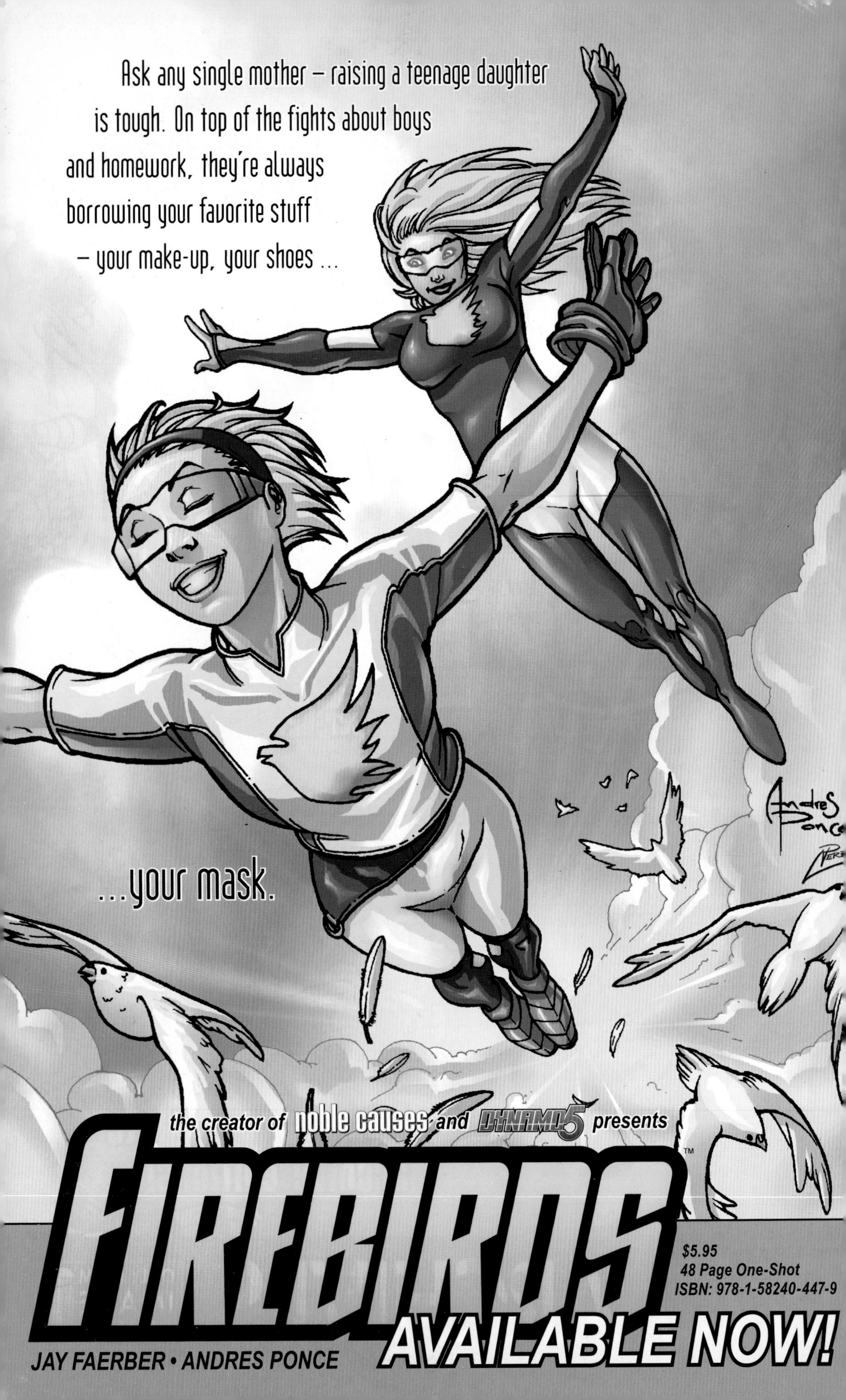

Ask any single mother – raising a teenage daughter is tough. On top of the fights about boys and homework, they're always borrowing your favorite stuff – your make-up, your shoes ...
...your mask.
the creator of noble causes and DYNAMO5 presents
FIREBIRDS™
$5.95
48 Page One-Shot
ISBN: 978-1-58240-447-9
AVAILABLE NOW!
JAY FAERBER • ANDRES PONCE